PostgreSQL 9 High Availability Cookbook

Over 100 recipes to design and implement a highly available server with the advanced features of PostgreSQL

Shaun M. Thomas

BIRMINGHAM - MUMBAI

PostgreSQL 9 High Availability Cookbook

First published: July 2014

Production reference: 1100714

Published by Packt Publishing Ltd.
Livery Place
35 Livery Street
Birmingham B3 2PB, UK.

ISBN 978-1-84951-696-9

www.packtpub.com

Cover image by Pratyush (tysoncinematics@gmail.com)

Credits

Author
Shaun M. Thomas

Reviewers
Hans-Jürgen Schönig
Sheldon E. Strauch
Vasilis Ventirozos
Tomas Vondra

Acquisition Editors
Anthony Albuquerque
Harsha Bharwani

Content Development Editor
Sriram Neelakantan

Technical Editor
Tanvi Bhatt

Copy Editors
Janbal Dharmaraj
Sayanee Mukherjee
Karuna Narayanan

Project Coordinator
Kartik Vedam

Proofreaders
Maria Gould
Ameesha Green
Paul Hindle

Indexers
Hemangini Bari
Tejal Soni
Priya Subramani

Graphics
Sheetal Aute
Disha Haria
Abhinash Sahu

Production Coordinator
Melwyn D'sa

Cover Work
Melwyn D'sa

About the Author

Shaun M. Thomas has been working with PostgreSQL since late 2000. He is a frequent contributor to the PostgreSQL Performance and General mailing lists, assisting other DBAs with the knowledge he's gained over the years. In 2011 and 2012, he gave presentations at the Postgres Open conference on topics such as handling extreme throughput, high availability, server redundancy, and failover techniques. Most recently, he has contributed the Shard Manager extension and the walctl WAL management suite.

Currently, he serves as the database architect at OptionsHouse, an online options brokerage with a PostgreSQL cluster that handles almost 2 billion queries per day. Many of the techniques used in this book were developed specifically for this extreme environment.

He believes that PostgreSQL has a stupendous future ahead, and he can't wait to see the advancements subsequent versions will bring.

I'd like to thank my wife, Jennifer, for putting up with the weeks of long nights and for providing the encouragement I needed to get it all done. This book is my thank you letter to the PostgreSQL community, which helped me out of jams more times than I can count. I'd also like to thank OptionsHouse for putting me in charge of the busiest database I'd ever seen, forcing me to learn enough to keep it all running smoothly.

About the Reviewers

Hans-Jürgen Schönig is the founder and CEO of Cybertec Schönig & Schönig GmbH (`www.postgresql-support.de`), a company that focuses on PostgreSQL support, training, and consulting, as well as on scalable PostgreSQL solutions.

He has 15 years of experience in the field of PostgreSQL and has written several books that deal with PostgreSQL in the past couple of years.

Sheldon E. Strauch is a 20 year veteran of software consulting at companies such as IBM, Sears, Ernst & Young, and Kraft Foods. He has a Bachelor's degree in Business Administration and leverages his technical skills to improve business self-awareness. His interests include data gathering, management, and mining; maps and mapping; business intelligence; and application of data analysis for continuous improvement. He is currently focused on the development of end-to-end data management and mining at Enova International, a financial services company located in Chicago. In his spare time, he enjoys the performing arts, particularly music, and traveling with his wife Marilyn.

Vasilis Ventirozos has been working with databases for more than a decade on mission critical applications for companies in both the telecom and lottery industries. While he has worked with a number of database technologies, he considers PostgreSQL his database of choice. He currently works at OmniTI, a full-stack IT services company focused on highly scalable web infrastructure, providing PostgreSQL-related consulting and management.

Tomas Vondra has been working with PostgreSQL since 2003; although he's been working with various other databases since then (both open source and commercial), he instantly fell in love with PostgreSQL and the wonderful community built around it.

He is currently working at GoodData, a company that operates a BI cloud platform built on PostgreSQL, as a "performance specialist" and is mainly responsible for tracking and improving performance. In his free time, he's usually writing PostgreSQL extensions and patches or hacking something else related to PostgreSQL.

www.PacktPub.com

Support files, eBooks, discount offers, and more

You might want to visit www.PacktPub.com for support files and downloads related to your book.

Did you know that Packt offers eBook versions of every book published, with PDF and ePub files available? You can upgrade to the eBook version at www.PacktPub.com and as a print book customer, you are entitled to a discount on the eBook copy. Get in touch with us at service@packtpub.com for more details.

At www.PacktPub.com, you can also read a collection of free technical articles, sign up for a range of free newsletters and receive exclusive discounts and offers on Packt books and eBooks.

http://PacktLib.PacktPub.com

Do you need instant solutions to your IT questions? PacktLib is Packt's online digital book library. Here, you can access, read and search across Packt's entire library of books.

Why Subscribe?

- Fully searchable across every book published by Packt
- Copy and paste, print and bookmark content
- On demand and accessible via web browser

Free Access for Packt account holders

If you have an account with Packt at www.PacktPub.com, you can use this to access PacktLib today and view nine entirely free books. Simply use your login credentials for immediate access.

Table of Contents

Preface

Welcome to *PostgreSQL 9 High Availability Cookbook*! As a database, PostgreSQL is beginning to take its place in the world of high transaction rates and very large data installations. With this comes an increasing demand for PostgreSQL to act as a critical piece of infrastructure. System outages in these environments can be spectacularly costly and demand a higher caliber of management and tooling.

It is the job of a DBA to ensure that the database is always available for application demands and clients' needs. Yet, this is extremely difficult to accomplish without the necessary skills and experience with a common operating system and PostgreSQL tools. Installing, configuring, and optimizing a PostgreSQL cluster is a tiny fraction of the process. We also need to know how to find and recognize problems, manage a swarm of logical and physical replicas, and scale to increasing demands, all while preventing or mitigating system outages.

This book is something the author wishes existed 10 years ago. Back then, there were no recipes to follow to build a fault-tolerant PostgreSQL cluster; we had to improvise. It is our aim to prevent other DBAs from experiencing the kind of frustration borne from reinventing the wheel. We've done all the hard work, taken notes, outlined everything we've ever learned about keeping PostgreSQL available and written it all down in here.

We hope you find this book useful and relevant; it is the product of years of trial, error, testing, and a large amount of input from the PostgreSQL community.

What this book covers

Chapter 1, Hardware Planning, sets the tone by covering the part that the appropriate hardware selection plays in a successful PostgreSQL cluster of any size.

Chapter 2, Handling and Avoiding Downtime, provides safe settings and defaults for a stable cluster and explains the basic techniques for responding to mishaps.

Chapter 3, Pooling Resources, presents PgBouncer and pgpool, two tools geared toward controlling PostgreSQL connections. Together, these can provide an abstraction layer to reduce the effect of outages and increase system performance.

Chapter 4, Troubleshooting, introduces a battery of common Unix and Linux tools and resources that can collect valuable diagnostic information. It also includes a couple of PostgreSQL views that can assist in finding database problems.

Chapter 5, Monitoring, further increases availability by adding Nagios, check_mk, collectd, and Graphite to watch active PostgreSQL clusters. This chapter helps us stay informed, and find potential problems before they happen.

Chapter 6, Replication, discusses several PostgreSQL replication scenarios and techniques for more durable data. This includes logical replication tools such as Slony, Bucardo, and Londiste.

Chapter 7, Replication Management Tools, brings WAL management to the forefront. It talks about integrating Barman, OmniPITR, repmgr, or walctl into PostgreSQL to further prevent data loss and control complicated multiserver clusters.

Chapter 8, Advanced Stack, explains how to use LVM, DRBD, and XFS to build a solid foundation and keep data on two servers simultaneously to prevent costly outages.

Chapter 9, Cluster Control, incorporates Pacemaker into the advanced stack. Fully automate PostgreSQL server migrations in case of impending maintenance or hardware failure.

Chapter 10, Data Distribution, shows how PostgreSQL features such as foreign data wrappers and materialized views can produce a scalable cluster. Included with this chapter is a simple data-sharding API technique to reduce dependency on a single PostgreSQL server.

What you need for this book

This book is written for Unix systems with a focus on Linux in particular. Such servers have become increasingly popular to host databases for companies both large and small. As such, we highly recommend that you have a virtual machine or development system running a recent copy of Debian, Ubuntu, Red Hat Enterprise Linux, or a variant such as CentOS or Scientific Linux.

You will also need a copy of PostgreSQL. If your chosen Linux distribution isn't keeping the included PostgreSQL packages sufficiently up to date, the PostgreSQL website maintains binaries for most popular distributions. You can find these at `http://www.postgresql.org/download/`.

Users of Red Hat Enterprise Linux and its variants should refer to the following URL to add the official PostgreSQL YUM repository to important database systems: `http://yum.postgresql.org/repopackages.php`.

Users of Debian, Ubuntu, Mint, and other related Linux systems should refer to the PostgreSQL APT wiki page at the following URL instead: `https://wiki.postgresql.org/wiki/Apt`.

Be sure to include any "contrib" packages in your installation. They include helpful utilities and database extensions we will use in some recipes.

Users of BSD should still be able to follow along with these recipes. Some commands may require slight alterations to run properly on BSD, so be sure to understand the intent before executing them. Otherwise, all commands have been confirmed to work on BASH and recent GNU tools.

Who this book is for

This book is written for PostgreSQL DBAs who want an extremely fault-tolerant database cluster. While PostgreSQL is suitable for enterprise environments, there are a lot of tertiary details even a skilled DBA might not know. We're here to fill in those gaps.

There is a lot of material here for all levels of DBA. The primary assumption is that you are comfortable with a Unix command line and maintain at least some regular exposure to PostgreSQL as a DBA or system administrator.

If you've ever experienced a database outage, restored from a backup, or spent hours trying to repair a malfunctioning cluster, we have material that covers all these scenarios. This book holds the key to managing a robust PostgreSQL cluster environment and should be of use to anyone in charge of a critical piece of database infrastructure.

Sections

This book contains the following sections:

Getting ready

This section tells us what to expect in the recipe, and describes how to set up any software or any preliminary settings needed for the recipe.

How to do it...

This section characterizes the steps to be followed for "cooking" the recipe.

How it works...

This section usually consists of a brief and detailed explanation of what happened in the previous section.

There's more...

It consists of additional information about the recipe in order to make the reader more anxious about the recipe.

See also

This section may contain references to the recipe.

Conventions

In this book, you will find a number of styles of text that distinguish between different kinds of information. Here are some examples of these styles and an explanation of their meaning.

Code words in text, database table names, folder names, filenames, file extensions, pathnames, dummy URLs, user input, and Twitter handles are shown as follows: "The final query is a bit more complicated since it uses a `CASE` statement."

A block of code is set as follows:

```
SELECT name, setting
 FROM pg_settings
WHERE context = 'postmaster';
```

Any command-line input or output is written as follows:

```
sudo apt-get install postgresql-9.3-pgfincore
```

New terms and **important words** are shown in bold. Words that you see on the screen, in menus or dialog boxes for example, appear in the text like this: "Click on the **Dashboard** link on the top menu bar."

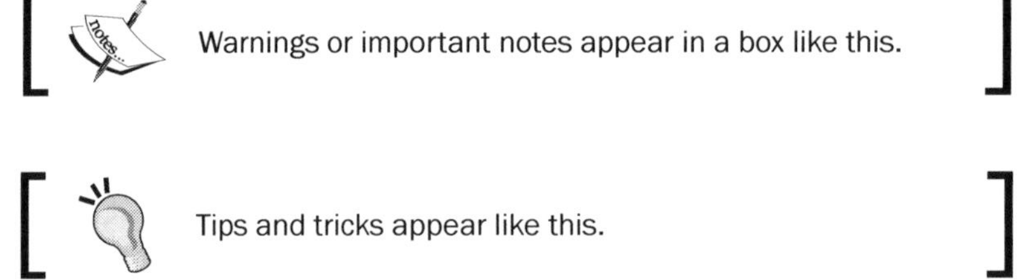

Warnings or important notes appear in a box like this.
Tips and tricks appear like this.

Reader feedback

Feedback from our readers is always welcome. Let us know what you think about this book—what you liked or may have disliked. Reader feedback is important for us to develop titles that you really get the most out of.

To send us general feedback, simply send an e-mail to `feedback@packtpub.com`, and mention the book title via the subject of your message.

If there is a topic that you have expertise in and you are interested in either writing or contributing to a book, see our author guide on www.packtpub.com/authors.

Customer support

Now that you are the proud owner of a Packt book, we have a number of things to help you to get the most from your purchase.

Downloading the example code

You can download the example code files for all Packt books you have purchased from your account at http://www.packtpub.com. If you purchased this book elsewhere, you can visit http://www.packtpub.com/support and register to have the files e-mailed directly to you.

Errata

Although we have taken every care to ensure the accuracy of our content, mistakes do happen. If you find a mistake in one of our books—maybe a mistake in the text or the code—we would be grateful if you would report this to us. By doing so, you can save other readers from frustration and help us improve subsequent versions of this book. If you find any errata, please report them by visiting http://www.packtpub.com/submit-errata, selecting your book, clicking on the **errata submission form** link, and entering the details of your errata. Once your errata are verified, your submission will be accepted and the errata will be uploaded on our website, or added to any list of existing errata, under the Errata section of that title. Any existing errata can be viewed by selecting your title from http://www.packtpub.com/support.

Piracy

Piracy of copyright material on the Internet is an ongoing problem across all media. At Packt, we take the protection of our copyright and licenses very seriously. If you come across any illegal copies of our works, in any form, on the Internet, please provide us with the location address or website name immediately so that we can pursue a remedy.

Please contact us at copyright@packtpub.com with a link to the suspected pirated material.

We appreciate your help in protecting our authors, and our ability to bring you valuable content.

Questions

You can contact us at questions@packtpub.com if you are having a problem with any aspect of the book, and we will do our best to address it.

1
Hardware Planning

In this chapter, we will learn about selection and provisioning of hardware necessary to build a highly available PostgreSQL database. We will cover the following recipes in this chapter:

- Planning for redundancy
- Having enough IOPS
- Sizing storage
- Investing in a RAID
- Picking a processor
- Making the most of memory
- Exploring nimble networking
- Managing motherboards
- Selecting a chassis
- Saddling up to a SAN
- Tallying up
- Protecting your eggs

Introduction

What does high availability mean? In the context of what we're trying to build, it means we want our database to start and remain online for as long as possible. A critical component of this is the hardware that hosts the database itself. No matter how perfect a machine and its parts may be, failure or unexpected behavior along any element can result in an outage.

So how do we avoid these unwanted outages? Expect them. We must start by assuming hardware can and will fail, and at the worst possible moment. If we start with that in mind, it becomes much easier to make decisions regarding the composition of each server we are building.

Make no mistake! Much of this planning will rely on worksheets, caveats, and compromise. Some of our choices will have several expensive options, and we will have to weigh the benefits offered against our total cost outlay. We want to build something stable, which is not always easy. Depending on the size of our company, our purchasing power, and available hosting choices, we may be in for a rather complicated path to that goal.

This chapter will attempt to paint a complete picture of a highly available environment in such a way that you can pick and choose the best solution without making too many detrimental compromises. Of course, we'll offer advice to what we believe is the best overall solution, but you don't always have to take our word for it.

For the purposes of this chapter, we will not cover cloud computing or other elastic allocation options. Many of the concepts we introduce can be adapted to those solutions, yet many are implementation-specific. If you want to use a cloud vendor such as Amazon or Rackspace, you will need to obtain manuals and appropriate materials for applying what you learn here.

Planning for redundancy

Redundancy means having a spare. A spare for what? Everything. Every single part, from motherboard to chassis, power supply to network cable, disk space to throughput, should have at least one piece of excess equipment or capacity available for immediate use. Let's go through as many of these as we can imagine, before we do anything that might depend on something we bought.

Getting ready

Fire up your favorite spreadsheet program; we'll be using it to keep track of all the parts that go into the server, and any capacity concerns. If you don't have one, Open Office and Libre Office are good free alternatives for building these spreadsheets. Subsequent sections will help determine most of the row contents.

How to do it...

We simply need to produce a hardware spreadsheet to track our purchase needs. We can do that with the following steps:

1. Create a new spreadsheet for parts and details.
2. Create a heading row with the following columns:
    - Type
    - Capacity
    - Supplier
    - Price
    - Count
    - Total cost
3. Create a new row for each type of the following components:
    - Chassis
    - CPU
    - Hard Drive (3.5")
    - Hard Drive (2.5")
    - Hard Drive (SSD)
    - Motherboard
    - Network Card
    - Power Supply
    - RAID Controller
    - RAM
    - SAN
4. In the `Chassis` row, under the `Total cost` column, enter the following formula: `=D2*E2`
5. Copy and paste the formula into the `Total Cost` column for all the rows we created. The end result should look something like the following screenshot:

	A	B	C	D	E	F
1	Type	Capacity	Supplier	Price	Count	Total Cost
2	Chassis					0
3	CPU					0

How it works...

What we've done is prepare a spreadsheet that we can fill in with information collected from the rest of this chapter. We will have very long discussions regarding each part of the server we want to build, so we need a place to collect each decision we make along the way.

The heading column can include any other details you wish to retain about each part, but for the sake of simplicity, we are stuck to the bare minimum. This also goes for the parts we chose for each column. Depending on the vendor you select to supply your server, many of these decisions will already be made. It's still a good idea to include each component in case you need an emergency replacement.

The `Total Cost` column exists for one purpose: to itemize the cost of each part, multiplied by how many we will need to complete the server.

> To make sure we account for the redundancy element of the spreadsheet, we strongly suggest inflating the number you use for the `Count` column, which will also increase the price automatically. This helps so we automatically include extra capacity in case something fails. If you would rather track this separately, add a `Spare Count` column to the spreadsheet instead.

We'll have discussions later as to failure rates of different types of hardware, which will influence how many excess components to allocate. Don't worry about that for now.

There's more...

It's also a very good idea to include a summary for all of our `Total Cost` columns, so we get an aggregate cost estimate for the whole server. To do that with our spreadsheet example, keep in mind that the `Total Cost` column is listed as column **F**.

To add a `Sum Total` column to your spreadsheet on row **15**, column **F**, enter the formula `=SUM(F2:F12)`. If you've added more columns, substitute for column **F** whichever column now represents the `Total Cost`. Likewise, if you have more than 13 rows of different parts, use a different row to represent your summary price than row **15**.

See also

There are a lot of spreadsheet options available. Many corporations supply a copy of Microsoft Excel. However, if this is not the case, there are many alternatives as follows:

- **Google Docs**: `http://docs.google.com/`
- **Open Office**: `http://www.openoffice.org/`
- **Libre Office**: `http://www.libreoffice.org/`

All of these options are free to use and popular enough that support and documentation are readily available.

Having enough IOPS

IOPS stands for **Input/Output Operations Per Second**. Essentially, this describes how many operations a device can perform per second before it should be considered saturated. If a device is saturated, further requests must wait until the device has a spare bandwidth. A server overwhelmed with requests can amount to seconds, minutes, or even hours of delayed results.

Depending on application timeout settings and user patience, a device with low IOPS appears as a bottleneck that reduces both system responsiveness and the perception of quality. A database with insufficient IOPS to service queries in a timely manner is unavailable for all intents and purposes. It doesn't matter if PostgreSQL is still available and serving results in this scenario, as its availability has already suffered. We are trying to build a highly available database, and to do so, we need to build a server with enough performance to survive daily operation. In addition, we must overprovision for unexpected surges in popularity, and account for future storage and throughput needs based on monthly increases in storage utilization.

Getting ready

This process is more of a thought experiment. We will present some very rough estimates of IO performance for many different disk types. For each, we should increment entries in our hardware spreadsheet based on perceived need.

The main things we will need for this process are numbers. During development, applications commonly have a goal, expected client count, table count, estimated growth rates, and so on. Even if we have to guess for many of these, they will all contribute to our IOPS requirements. Have these numbers ready, even if they're simply guesses.

> If the application already exists on a development or stage environment, try to get the development or QA team to run operational tests. This is a great opportunity to gather statistics before choosing potential production hardware.

How to do it...

We need to figure out how many operations per second we can expect. We can estimate this by using the following steps:

1. Collect the amount of simultaneous database connections. Start with the expected user count, and divide by 50.

2. Obtain the average number of queries per page. If this is unavailable, use ten.
3. Count the amount of tables used in those queries. If this is unavailable, use three.
4. Multiply these numbers together, then double it. Then multiply the total by eight.
5. Increment the `Count` column in our hardware spreadsheet for one or more of the following, and round up:
    - For 3.5" hard drives, divide by 500
    - For 2.5" hard drives, divide by 350
    - For SSD hard drives, divide by 25000, then add two
6. Add 10 percent to any count greater than 0 and then round up.

How it works...

Wow, that's a lot of work! There's a reason for everything, of course.

In the initial three steps, we're trying to figure out how many operations might touch an object on disk. For every user that's actively loading a page, for every query in that page, and for every table in that query, that's a potential disk read or write.

We double that number to account for the fact we're estimating all of this. It's a common engineering trick to double or triple calculations to absorb unexpected capacity, variance in materials, and so on. We can use that same technique here.

Why did we suggest dividing the user count by 50 to get the connection total? Since we do not know the average query runtime, we assume 20 ms for each query. For every query that's executing, a connection is in use. Assuming full utilization, up to 50 queries can be active per second. If you have a production system that can provide a better query runtime average, we suggest using that value instead.

However, why do we then multiply by eight? In a worst (or best) case scenario, it's not uncommon for an application to double the amount of users or requests on a yearly basis. Doubled usage means doubled hardware needs. If requirements double in one year, we would need a server three times more powerful (*1 + 2*) than the original estimates. Another doubling would mean a server seven times better (*1 + 2 + 4*). CPUs, RAM, and storage are generally available as powers of two. Since it's fairly difficult to obtain storage seven times faster than what we already have, we multiply the total by eight.

That gives a total IOPS value roughly necessary for our database to immediately serve every request for the next three years, straight from the disk device. Several companies buy servers every three or four years as a balance between cost and capacity, so these estimates are based on that assumption.

In the next step, we get a rough estimate to the amount of disks necessary to serve the necessary IOPS. Our numbers in these steps are based on hard drive performance. A 15,000 RPM hard drive can serve under ideal conditions, 500 operations per second. Likewise, a 10,000 RPM can provide roughly 350 operations per second. Current SSDs as of this writing commonly reach 100,000 IOPS. However, because they are so fast, we need far fewer of them, and thus risk is not as evenly distributed. We artificially increase the amount of these drives because, again, we are erring toward availability.

Finally, we add a few extra devices for spares that will go in a closet somewhere, just in case one or more drives fail. This also insulates us from the rare event that hardware is discontinued or otherwise difficult to obtain.

There's more...

Figuring out the number of IOPS we need and the devices involved is only part of the story.

A working example

Sometimes these large lists of calculations make more sense if we see them in practice. So let's make the assumption that 2,000 users will use our application each second. This is how that would look:

- 2000 / 50 = 40
- Default queries per page = 10
- Default tables per query = 3
- 40 * 10 * 3 * 2 = 2400
- 2400 * 8 = 19200
- 19200 IOPS in drives:
    - 3.5" drives: 19200 / 500 = 38.4 ~ 39
    - 2.5" drives: 19200 / 350 = 54.9 ~ 55
    - SSDs: 2 + (19200 / 25000) = 2.8 ~ 3
- Add 10 percent.
- 3.5" drives: 39 + 3.9 = 42.9 ~ 43
    - 2.5" drives: 55 + 5.5 = 60.5 ~ 61
    - SSDs: 3 + 0.3 = 3.3 ~ 4

We are not taking space into account either, which would also increase our SSD count. We will be discussing capacity soon.

Making concessions

Our calculations always assume worst case scenarios. This is both expensive and in many cases, overzealous. We ignore RAM caching of disk blocks, we don't account for application frontend caches, and the PostgreSQL shared buffers are also not included.

Why? Crashes are always a concern. If a database crashes, buffers are forfeit. If the application frontend cache gets emptied or has problems, reads will be served directly from the database. Until caches are rebuilt, query results can be multiple orders of magnitude slower than normal for minutes or hours. We will discuss methods of circumventing these effects, but these IOPS numbers give us a baseline.

The number of necessary IOPS, and hence disk requirements, are subject to risk evaluation and cost benefit analysis. Deciding between 100 percent coverage and an acceptable fraction is a careful balancing act. Feel free to reduce these numbers; just consider the cost of an outage as part of the total. If a delay is considered standard operating procedures, fractions up to 50 percent are relatively low risk. If possible, try to run tests for an ultimate decision before purchase.

Sizing storage

Capacity planning for a database server involves a lot of variables. We must account for table count, user activity, compliance storage requirements, indexes, object bloat, maintenance, archival, and more. We may even have to consider application features that do not exist. New functionality often brings new tables, new storage standards, and archival needs. Planning done now may have little relevance to future usage.

So how do we produce functional estimates for disk space, with so many uncertain or fluctuating elements? Primarily, we want to avoid a scenario where we do not have enough space. Running out of disk space results in ignored queries at best, and a completely frozen and difficult to repair database at worst. Neither are ingredients of a highly available environment.

So we have a lower bound in this case, enough to avoid catastrophe though it's in our best interest to allocate more than the bare minimum.

Getting ready

Since there are a lot of variables that contribute to the volume of storage we want, we need information about each of them. Gather as many data points as possible regarding things such as: largest expected tables and indexes, row counts per day, indexes per table, desired excess, and anything else imaginable. We'll use all of it.

[This is much easier if we already have a database, and are now trying to ensure it is highly available. Even if the database is only in development or staging environments at this moment, a few activity simulations at expected user counts should provide a basis for many of our numbers. No matter the case, revisit estimates as concrete details become available.]

How to do it...

We can collect some of the information we want from PostgreSQL if we have a running instance already. If not, we can use baseline numbers. Follow these steps if you already have a PostgreSQL database available:

1. Submit this query to get the amount of space used by all databases:

```
SELECT pg_size_pretty(sum(pg_database_size(oid))::BIGINT)
  FROM pg_database;
```

2. Wait one week.
3. Perform the preceding query again.
4. Subtract the first reading from the second.

[**Downloading the example code**

You can download the example code files for all Packt books you have purchased from your account at `http://www.packtpub.com`. If you purchased this book elsewhere, you can visit `http://www.packtpub.com/support` and register to have the files e-mailed directly to you.]

If we don't have an existing install and are working with a project that has yet to start development, we can substitute a few guesses instead. Without a running PostgreSQL instance, use the following assumptions:

- Our databases have a total size of 100 GB
- After one week, our install grew by 1.5 GB

Next, we can calculate our growth needs for the next three years. Perform the following steps:

1. Multiply the change in install size by four.
2. Apply the following formula, where x is the most recent size of the databases, and y is the value from the previous step: $x * (1 + y/x)^{36}$.
3. Multiply the previous result by two.

How it works...

In the end, this is the magic of compounding interest. If we have an existing database installed, it can tell us not only how much space it currently consumes, but also how quickly it's currently growing. If not, we can start with a medium size and substitute a growth assumption that will cause the cumulative total to double in size every year. Remember, we begin by working with worst case scenarios, and modify the numbers afterwards.

> What if we don't need compounding interest because our expected growth is linear? It's always easier to start with too much space than to add more later. If you know your table count will rarely change, users will not increase in number, or data streams are relatively consistent, feel free to drop the compounded interest formula. Otherwise, we suggest using it anyway.

The PostgreSQL query we used takes advantage of the system catalog and known statistics regarding the database contents. The `pg_database_size` function always returns the number of bytes a database uses, so we must use the `pg_size_pretty` function to make it more human readable.

Once we know the size of the database instance and its growth rate, we can apply a simple compounding interest function to estimate the volume at any point in the future. This not only accounts for the current growth rate, but incorporates additional accumulation caused by increases in clients, table counts, and other unspecified sources. It's extremely aggressive, since we take the weekly growth rate, translate that to a monthly rate, and apply the compounding monthly instead of yearly.

And then we use a standard engineering tactic and double the estimate, just in case. Using the provided values—that of a 100 GB database that grows at 1.5 GB per week—we would have an 815 GB database install in three years. With a system that large, we should allocate at least 1630 GB. If we simply added the 1.5 GB weekly growth rate for three years, the final tally would only be 334 GB, and we could get by with 668 GB.

There's more...

Don't let our formulas define your only path. Let's explore how they apply in a real world situation, and how we can modify them to better fit our systems.

Real-world example

There are quite a few very large databases using PostgreSQL. Whether or not they have thousands of tables and indexes, billions of rows, or handle billions of queries per day, statistics help us plan for the future. Let's apply the previous steps to an example database that actually exists:

- The database is currently 875 GB
- The database was 865 GB last week
- The database grows by 10 GB per week
- Thus, the database grows by 40 GB every four weeks
- Using the formula we discussed in the step two of this recipe, the number become this: *875 * (1 + 40/875)^36 = 4374 GB*
- Doubled, this is 8748 GB

Keep in mind that this estimation technique may grossly exaggerate the necessary space. If we take the existing 40 GB monthly growth rate, the database would only be 2315 GB in three years. Of course, 2.3 TB is still a very large database, it's just half as large as our estimate.

Adjusting the numbers

We already mentioned that the growth curve used here is extremely aggressive. We can't risk ever running out of space in a production database and still consider ourselves highly available. However, there is probably a safe position between the current growth rate of the database, and the compounded estimate, especially since we are doubling the allocation anyway.

In the preceding real-world example, the database is likely to have a size between 2315 GB and 4374 GB. If we split the difference, that's 3345 GB. Further more, we don't necessarily have to double that number if we're comfortable having a disk device that's 70 percent full three years from now instead of 50 percent. With that in mind, we would probably be safe with 5 TB of space instead of 9 TB. That's a vast saving if we're willing to make those assumptions.

Incorporate the spreadsheet

At the beginning of this chapter, we created a hardware cost spreadsheet to estimate the total cost of a highly available server. If we were following the chapter, our spreadsheet already accounts for the minimum number of devices necessary to provide the IOPS we want.

Suppose we needed 15,000 IOPS, and decided to use 2.5-inch drives. That would require over 40 drives. Even at only 300 GB each, that's 12 TB of total available space. Yet the case for SSDs is the opposite. For our previous example, we would need at least five 1 GB SSD drives, or one very large PCIe SSD to provide 5 TB of space for the adjusted sample.

Whichever solution we finally choose, we can take the advice from every section so far. At this point, the spreadsheet should have a device count that should satisfy most, if not all, of our space and IOPS requirements.

Investing in a RAID

RAID stands for **Redundant Array of Independent (or Inexpensive) Disks**, and often requires a separate controller card for management. The primary purpose of a RAID is to combine several physical devices into a single logical unit for the sake of redundancy and performance.

This is especially relevant to our interests. Carnegie Mellon University published a study in 2007 on hard drive failure rates. They found that hard drives fail at about 3 percent per year. Further more, they found that drive type and interface contributed little to disk longevity, and that hard drives do not reflect a tendency to fail early as was commonly accepted. These findings were largely corroborated by a parallel study released the same year by Google.

What does this mean? For our purposes in building a highly available server, it means hard drives should be looked at with great disdain. Larger databases will depend on tens or hundreds of hard drives in order to represent several terabytes of data. With a 3 percent failure rate per year, a 100-drive array would lose roughly nine devices after three years.

This is the primary reason that all of our calculations regarding disk devices automatically assume a 10 percent excess inventory allotment. If a drive fails, we need an immediate replacement. Vendors are not always capable of delivering a new drive quickly enough. Having a spare on hand, ideally at the hosting facility or in the server itself, helps ensure continuous uptime.

So how does RAID figure into this scenario? If we hosted our database on several bare hard drives, knowing that around 10 percent of these drives will fail in three years, outages would be inevitable. What we want is an abstraction layer, one that can present any amount of hard drives as a single whole, keeping reserves for drive errors, handling checksums for integrity, and mirroring for redundancy.

RAID provides all of that in several convenient configurations. Good controller cards often include copious amounts of cache and other management capabilities. Instead of manually assigning dozens of drives, split them into several usable array allocations that reflect much lower operational risk.

Knowing all of this, databases have special needs when it comes to RAID and the performance characteristics associated with each RAID type. Now we will explore the selection criteria for our database, and how to simplify the process.

Getting ready

That was a long introduction, wasn't it? Well, we also strongly suggest taking a look at the *Having enough IOPS* and *Sizing storage* recipes before continuing. Make sure the hardware spreadsheet has a drive count for the type of drives going into the server we're designing. If we're using PCIe instead of standard SSD drives, this section can be skipped.

How to do it...

Only a few RAID levels matter in a database context. Perform these steps to decide which one is right for this server:

- If this is an **OLTP** (**Online Transaction Processing**) database primarily for handling very high speed queries, use RAID level 1+0
- If this is a non-critical development or staging system, use RAID level 5
- If this is a non-critical **OLAP** (**Online Analytic Processing**) reporting system, use RAID level 5
- If this is a critical OLAP reporting system, use RAID level 6
- If this is a long-term storage OLAP warehouse, use RAID level 6

How it works...

We made a lot of snap decisions here. There are quite a few RAID levels we simply ignored, so there should be some discussion regarding the reasoning we used.

Let's begin with RAID level 0. Level 0 stripes data across all disks at once. It's certainly convenient, but a single drive failure will lose all stored information in the array. What about RAID level 1? Level 1 acts as a full mirror of all data stored. For every set of drives, a second set of drives has an exact copy. If a drive fails in one set, the second set is still available. However, if that set also experiences any failure, all data is lost.

When we talk about RAID 1+0, we actually combine the mirroring capability of RAID 1 with the striping of RAID 0. How? Take a look at the following diagram for six disks:

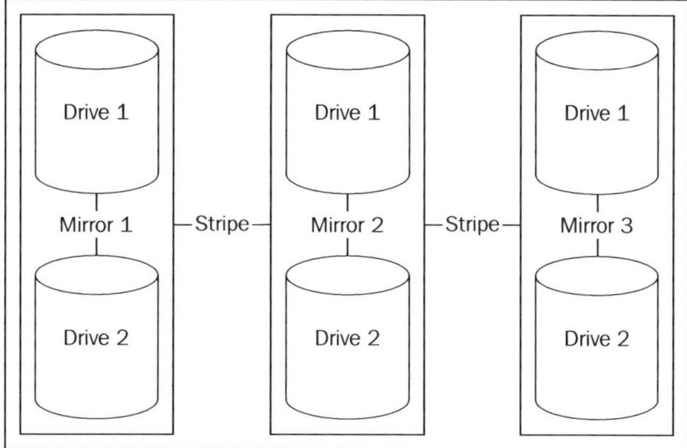

In this RAID 1+0, we have three sets, each consisting of two disks. Each of the two disks mirror each other, and the data is striped across all three sets. We could lose a disk from each set and still have all of our data. We only have a problem if we lose two disks from the same set, since they mirror each other. Overall, this is the most robust RAID level available, and the most commonly used for OLTP systems.

RAID level 5 and 6 take a different approach. Again, let's look at six drives and see a very simplified view of how RAID 5 would operate in that situation:

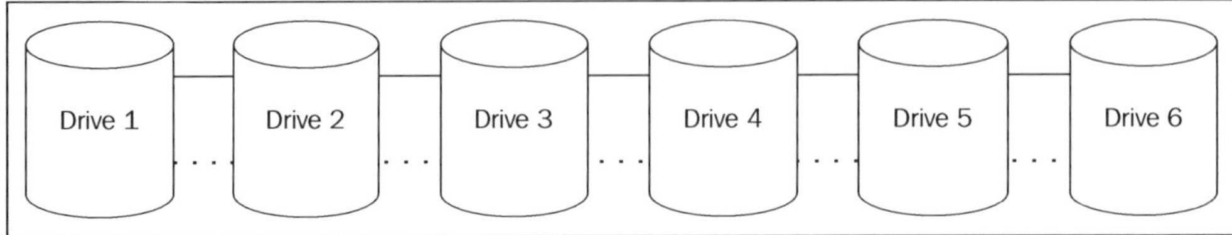

The solid line shows that the data is spread across all six drives. The dotted line is the parity information. If a drive fails and the block can't be read directly from the necessary location, a RAID 5 will use the remaining parity information from all drives to reconstruct the missing data. The only real difference between a RAID 5 and a RAID 6 is that a RAID 6 contains a second parity line, so up to two drives can fail before the array begins operating in a degraded manner.

Using a RAID 5 or 6 offers more protection than a RAID 0, with less cost than a RAID 1+0, which requires double the amount of desired space. We selected these for non-critical OLAP systems because they usually need space over performance, and are not as sensitive to immediate availability pressures as an OLTP system.

There's more...

We mentioned controller cards earlier, and noted that they also offer on-board cache. RAID has been around for a long time, and though disks are getting much larger, they haven't experienced an equivalent increase in speed. In scenarios that use RAID 5 or 6, writes can also be slowed since each write must be committed to several devices simultaneously in the form of parity.

To combat this, RAID controllers allow configuration of the cache itself, to buffer writes in favor of reads, or vice versa. Don't be afraid to adjust this and run tests to determine the best cache mix. If everything else fails, start with a 100 percent for writes, as they are the most in need of caching. Keep a close eye on write performance, and give it priority. Generally, the OS cache does a better job of caching reads, and has much more memory available to do so.

See also

- Disk failures in the real world: `http://www.cs.cmu.edu/~bianca/fast07.pdf`
- Failure Trends in a Large Disk Drive Population: `http://research.google.com/pubs/pub32774.html`
- RAID: `http://en.wikipedia.org/wiki/RAID`

Picking a processor

In selecting a CPU for our server, we have a lot to consider. At the time of this writing, the current trend among processors in every space—including mobile—is toward multiple cores per chip. CPU manufacturers have found that providing a large number of smaller processing units spreads workload horizontally for better overall scalability.

As users of PostgreSQL, this benefits us tremendously. PostgreSQL is based on processes instead of threads. This means each connected client is assigned to a process that can use a CPU core when available. The host operating system can perform such allocations without any input from the database software. Motherboards have limited space, so we need more cores on the same limited real estate, which means more simultaneously active database clients.

Once again, our discussion veers toward capacity planning for a three or four year cycle. Limited processing capability leads to slow or delayed queries, or a database that is incapable of adequately handling increasing amounts of simultaneous users. Yet simply choosing the fastest CPU with the most cores and filling the motherboard can be a staggering waste of resources. So how, then, do we know what to buy?

That's what we're here to figure out.

Getting ready

Luckily, there are only really two manufacturers that produce commodity server-class CPUs. Further more, each vendor has a line of CPU designed specifically for server use. AMD and Intel both provide a good similar price to performance curves, but that's where the comparison ends.

At the time of this writing, the Intel Xeon CPUs benchmark significantly higher than equivalently priced AMD Opterons. This is true for both mid-range and high-end processors. Before going through this recipe, it would be a good idea to visit AnandTech, Tom's Hardware, Intel, and AMD, just to get a basic idea of the landscape. There are a lot of benchmarks that compare various models of CPUs, so don't take our word for it.

Because of this current performance disparity, we'll focus exclusively on Intel processors for now. This situation has changed in the past, and may do so again in the future.

How to do it...

We can collect some of the information we want from the database if we have one already. If we already have a PostgreSQL database available, we can execute a query to start our calculations. This works best if used at the most active time of day.

Execute this query as a superuser to get the count of simultaneous active users if you have PostgreSQL 9.2 or higher:

```
SELECT count(1) FROM pg_stat_activity
WHERE state = 'active';
```

Use this query if you have an older version:

```
SELECT count(1) FROM pg_stat_activity
WHERE current_query NOT LIKE '<IDLE>%';
```

If we don't have a PostgreSQL server, we need to make an educated guess. Use these steps to approximate:

1. Work with the application developers to obtain a count of expected clients active per second.
2. Divide the previous number by 50.

Once we have some idea of how many queries will be active simultaneously, we need to figure out the processor count. Follow these steps:

1. If we already know how many disks will store our data, use this number. In the case of an SSD base, use 0.
2. Subtract the previous number from our count of active users.
3. Divide the previous result by two.
4. Apply the following formula, where *x* is the value from the previous step: *x * (1.4)^3*.

How it works...

Before we can even begin to decide on a processor count, we need a baseline. With a working PostgreSQL server to base our numbers on, we can just use the amount of existing users during a busy period. Without that, we need to guess. This guess can actually be pretty close, depending on how the application was targeted. If the intent is to service 1000 users per second, we should start there since that's the same assumption the company is using to buy application and web servers.

After that, we are applying a commonly accepted formula used by PostgreSQL administrators for a very long time. The ideal number of active connections is equal to twice the amount of available processor cores, plus the amount of disk spindles. Amusingly, the disk spindles increase the ideal number of connections because they contribute seek times, which forces the processor to wait for information. While a processor is waiting for input for one connection, the operating system may decide to lend the processor to another until the data is retrieved.

So, we apply that accepted formula in reverse. First, we subtract the number of spindles, and then divide by two to obtain how many CPUs we should have for our expected workload.

Afterward, we assume a 40 percent increase in active clients on a yearly basis, and increase the CPU core count accordingly for three years. Note that this is a very aggressive growth rate. If we have historical growth data available, or the company is expecting a different value, we should use that instead.

When purchasing CPUs, no matter how cores are distributed, the final total should be equal or greater than the number we calculated. If it isn't, the application may require more aggressive caching than expected, or we may need to horizontally scale the database. We're not ready to introduce that yet, but keep it in mind for later.

There's more...

The processor count is only part of the story. Intel CPUs have a few added elements we need to consider.

Hyperthreading

Newer generations of Intel processors often provide a feature called **hyperthreading**, which splits each physical processor core into two virtual cores. Historically, this was not well received, as benchmarks often illustrated performance degradation when the feature was enabled.

Since the introduction of Nehalem-based architecture in 2008, this is no longer the case. While doubling the processor count does not result in a doubling of throughput, we've run several tests that show up to 40 percent improvement over using physical cores alone. This may not be universal, but it does apply to PostgreSQL performance tests. What this means is that the commonly accepted formula for determining ideal connection count requires modification.

Current advice is to only multiply the physical core count by two. Assuming a 40 percent increase by enabling hyperthreading, the new formula becomes: *2 * 1.4 * CPUs + spindles*. With that in mind, if we wanted to serve 1000 connections per second, and used SSDs to host our data, our minimum CPU count would be: *1000 / 50 / 1.4*, or 14. Half of that is seven, but no CPU has seven physical cores, so we would need at least eight. If we used the physical cores alone for our calculation, we would need 10.

Turbo Boost

Recent Intel processors also have something called **Turbo Boost**. Some vendor motherboards disable this by default. Make sure to go through BIOS settings before performing acceptability tests, as turbo mode can provide up to 25 percent better performance in isolated cases.

This is possible because the maximum speed of the core itself is increased when resources are available. A 2.6 GHz core might operate temporarily at 3.0 GHz. For queries that are dependent on nested loops or other CPU-intensive operations, this can drastically reduce query execution times.

Power usage

Intel family chips often have low voltage versions of their high performance offerings. While these processors require up to 30 percent less electricity, they also run up to 25 percent slower. Low power name designations are not always consistent, so when choosing a processor, make sure to compare specifications of all similarly named chips.

Beware of accidentally choosing a low power chip meant for a high performance database. However, these chips may be ideal for warehouse or reporting database use, since those systems are not meant for high throughput or vast amounts of simultaneous users. They often cost less than their high-performance counterparts, making them perfect for systems expecting low utilization.

See also

- Intel Xeon CPUs: `http://en.wikipedia.org/wiki/Xeon`
- AMD Opteron CPUs: `http://en.wikipedia.org/wiki/Opteron`
- AnandTech: `http://www.anandtech.com/`
- Tom's Hardware: `http://www.tomshardware.com/`

Making the most of memory

The primary focus when selecting memory for a highly available system is stability. It's no accident that most, if not all, server-class RAM is of the error-correcting variety. There are a few other things to consider, which may not appear obvious at first glance.

Due to the multi-core nature of our CPUs, the amount of addressable memory may depend on the core count. In addition, speed, latency, and parity are all considerations. We also must consider the number of channels reported by each CPU; failing to match this with an equal count of memory sticks will drastically reduce performance.

Let's make our server fast and stable by considering our memory options.

Getting ready

Some of the decisions we will make depend on the capabilities of the CPU. Make sure to read through the *Picking a processor* recipe before continuing. If we have a PostgreSQL database available, there's also a query that can prepare us for selecting the most advantageous count of memory modules. It's also a very good idea to complete the *Sizing storage* recipe to get a better idea for choosing an amount of memory.

How to do it...

We can collect some of the information we want from PostgreSQL if we have an install already. Follow these steps if there's an existing database install that we can use:

1. Execute the following query to obtain the size of all databases in the instance:

```
SELECT pg_size_pretty(sum(pg_database_size(oid))::BIGINT)
  FROM pg_database;
```

2. Multiply the result by eight.

If we don't have an existing database, we should use a size estimate of the database install after three years. Refer to the *Sizing storage* recipe to obtain this estimate. Then, perform the following steps:

1. Divide the current or estimated database storage size by ten to obtain the minimum amount of memory.
2. Multiply our ideal CPU chip count by four to get the memory module count.
3. Divide the minimum memory amount by the module count to get the minimum module size.
4. Round up to the nearest available memory module size.

How it works...

The important part of this recipe is starting with a viable estimate of the database size. Since a lack of RAM won't cause the database to crash or operate improperly, we can use looser guidelines to obtain this number. Hence, three years down the road, an existing database install could be eight times larger than its current size.

Why do we then divide that number by ten? Our goal here is to maximize the benefit of the OS-level cache, which will consume a majority of our RAM. This estimate gives us a value that is ten times smaller than the space our database consumes. At this scale, data that is frequently fetched from disk is likely to be served from memory instead. The alternative is read latency due to insufficient memory for disk caching.

Most current CPUs are quad-channel, and thus operate best when the number of modules per processor is a multiple of four. Since we should have determined how many processor cores would be ideal for our system in the *Picking a processor* recipe, we automatically know the most efficient memory module count. Why do we multiply by four, regardless of how many memory channels the CPU has? Adding more memory modules is not wasted on chips with fewer channels, and provides a possible upgrade path.

Dividing the memory amount by the module count gives our minimum module size. RAM comes in many dimensions, and our calculation is not likely to match any of the available dimensions for purchase, so we need to round up. Why not round down? The operating system will utilize all available RAM to cache and buffer important data. Unless the greater amount is extremely expensive in comparison, any excess memory will not be wasted.

There's more...

We didn't focus on memory speed, timings, or latency here. Timing and latency can affect performance, but our primary focus is stability. We're always free to order faster or better memory as our budget allows.

Memory speed, on the other hand, is a more visible factor. Every memory speed works with a multiplier to match the highest compatible motherboard bus speed. This directly controls how quickly the CPU can utilize available RAM. Before buying memory, research the stated clock speed and try to match it with one of the faster settings compatible with both the CPU and motherboard.

For example, DDR3-1600 is twice as fast as DDR3-800 since it operates at 200 MHz, as opposed to 100 MHz. Database benchmarks would be vastly different between these two memory speeds, even with the same CPU. Fast memory means PostgreSQL can make more immediate use of cached data, and produce results more quickly.

Exploring nimble networking

The network card enables the database server to exchange data with the outside world. This includes far more than web servers, spreadsheets, loading jobs, application servers, and other data consumers. The database server is part of a large continuum of activity, much of which will center around maintenance, management, and even filesystem availability.

Little of this other traffic involves PostgreSQL directly. Much happens in the background regardless of the database and its current workload. Yet even one mishandled network packet across an otherwise normal driver can render the entire server invisible to the outside world, or in extreme cases, even lead to a system panic and subsequent shutdown. On a busy database server, network cards can handle several terabytes of traffic on a daily basis; the margin of error for such a critical piece of hardware is exceptionally slim.

What's more, network bandwidth can easily be saturated by an aggressive backup strategy, which is something critical to a highly available database. For PostgreSQL systems utilizing streaming replication or WAL archival, that traffic contributes quite a bit of bandwidth to the overall picture. If our backups are delayed, or replicas sit idle waiting for network packets, our exposure to risk is high indeed.

That's not to say everything is doom and gloom! With the right network setup and accompanying hardware, there should be more than enough room for any and all traffic our database server needs. Let's explore all the copious options for connecting our database to the outside world, and making sure it stays there.

Getting ready

This is one of those times it pays to do research. At the time of this writing, the current high-speed network standards include 1 Gb/s, 10 Gb/s, 40 Gb/s, and even 100 Gb/s Ethernet. However, 40 Gb/s network cards are still extremely rare, and 100 Gb/s is generally reserved for fiber-based switches and data center use.

This means we will be covering 1 Gb/s and 10 Gb/s interfaces. While we will do our best to outline all important aspects of these technologies to simplify the process, we strongly encourage using the Internet to validate current availability and performance characteristics.

How to do it...

Let's begin with a few basic calculations. Look at these following numbers that represent an estimate of interface speed after accounting for overhead:

- *1000 Mb/s * B/10 b = 100 MB/s*
- *10,000 Mb/s * B/10 b = 1,000 MB/s*

Next, consider how many ways this will be distributed. If we have an existing PostgreSQL setup, follow these steps:

1. Execute the following query to determine the number of existing replicas:

   ```
   SELECT count(1)+1 AS streams
     FROM pg_stat_replication;
   ```

2. Multiply streams by 160 for maximum MB/s needed by replication streams.

3. Execute the following queries together in a psql connection during a busy time of day on a production database:

```
SELECT SUM(pg_stat_get_db_tuples_fetched(oid)) AS count1
  FROM pg_database;
SELECT pg_sleep(1);
SELECT SUM(pg_stat_get_db_tuples_fetched(oid)) AS count2
  FROM pg_database;
```

4. Subtract the results of `count1` from `count2` for the number of rows fetched from the database per second.
5. Divide the number of rows per second by 10,000 for MB/s used by PostgreSQL connections.
6. Add MB/s for streams to MB/s for connections.

Without an existing database, follow these steps for some basic bandwidth numbers:

1. Multiply the desired number of PostgreSQL replicas by 160 for the maximum MB/s needed by replication streams.
2. Assume one WAL stream for an off-site disaster recovery database copy.
3. Start with at least one live hot streaming standby copy.
4. Include any additional database mirrors.
5. Estimate the active client count as discussed in *Picking a Processor*.
6. Multiply the active client count estimate by 5 for MB/s used by PostgreSQL connections.
7. Add MB/s for streams to MB/s for connections.

No matter which checklist we follow, we should double the final tally.

How it works...

If we have an existing database, there is a wealth of statistical information at our fingertips. The first query we ran gave us a slightly inflated count of copies of our database. For each copy, data must be transferred from the database to another server. This data is based on PostgreSQL WAL output, and these files are 16 MB each. A busy server can produce more than ten of these per second, so we multiply the count of streams by 160 to produce an aggressive amount of network overhead used by database replicas. As usual, this may be overzealous; it's always best to observe an actual system to measure maximum WAL segments generated during heavy write loads.

In PostgreSQL 9.2 and higher, database replicas can stream from other database replicas. This means network traffic can be distributed better among streaming clients, reducing network bandwidth pressure on production systems. PostgreSQL 9.2 also allows direct backup of streaming replicas. This means one or two replicas may be the most the production database ever needs to supply with WAL traffic.

For the next set of numbers, we need to know how much data database connections commonly retrieve. PostgreSQL tracks the number of table rows fetched, but it's a cumulative total. By waiting until a busy time of day and asking the database how many rows have been fetched before and after a one-second wait, we know how many rows are fetched per second.

However, we still don't know how many bytes these rows consume. A good estimate of this is 100 bytes per row. Then we only have to multiply the number of rows by 100 to find the amount of bandwidth we would need. So why do we divide by 10,000? What's 10,000 multiplied by 100? One million. On dividing by 10,000, we produce the number of megabytes per second those tuple fetches probably used.

If an average of 100 bytes per row isn't good enough, we can connect to one of our primary databases and ask what the average is. Use this query:

```
SELECT sum(pg_relation_size(oid)) / sum(reltuples)
  FROM pg_class;
```

By adding the amount of streaming traffic to the amount of connection traffic, we have a good, if slightly inflated, idea of how much bandwidth the server needs.

Without a working database to go by, we need to use a few guesses instead. Luckily, the number of streams for a reliable database infrastructure starts at two: one for a live standby, and one for an off-site archive. Each additional desired mirror should increase this total. Again, we multiply by 160 to obtain the maximum megabytes per second that all these streams are likely to require.

The amount of bandwidth client connections use is slightly harder to estimate. However, if we worked through previous chapter sections, we have a CPU estimate, which also tells us the maximum number of database clients the server can reliably support. If we take that value and multiply by five, that provides a rough value in megabytes per second as well.

Again, we just add those two totals together, and we know the minimum speed of our network.

Finally, we multiply the final tally by two, to account for any unknown maintenance, backup, and filesystem synchronization overhead.

There's more...

Besides producing an estimate through some simple calculations, we also want to make note of a few other networking details.

A networking example

This may be easier to visualize with a real example. Let's start with a very active database that has one streaming replica, and one off-site archive. Further more, connected clients regularly fetch five-million rows per second. Now, let's go through our steps:

1. *2 * 160 = 320 MB/s*
2. *5,000,000 / 10,000 = 50 MB/s*
3. *320 + 50 = 370 MB/s*
4. *370 * 2 = 740 MB/s*

That's a very high value! A 1 Gb/s interface can only supply 100 MB/s at most, so we would need eight of those to produce the necessary bandwidth. Yet a 10 Gb/s interface can supply 1000 MB/s, so it can easily handle 740 MB/s, and have room to spare. Would we rather have eight network cables coming out of our server, or one?

Remember redundancy

One of the first things this chapter suggested was to consider extra inventory. What we haven't really covered yet involves online backups. Most server-class motherboards include not just one, but two on-board network modules. Each module commonly provides four Ethernet interfaces.

Usually each interface is considered separate, and two interfaces from each module are connected to two switches in the data center. This allows server administrators to seamlessly perform maintenance on either switch without disrupting our network traffic. Further more, if a switch or network module fails, there's always a backup available.

In our working example, we would need eight 1 Gb/s interfaces to avoid experiencing network congestion. However, we've already used four of our eight available interfaces simply to satisfy basic server hosting requirements. That doesn't leave enough available capacity, and as a consequence, this server would experience a network bottleneck.

This would not be the case with a 10 Gb/s interface. Each of the interfaces connected to redundant switches can carry the entire network requirements of the server.

Save the research

We suggested doing research on 1 Gb/s and 10 Gb/s network cards. Well, don't do too much. It's very likely the infrastructure department already has a standard server profile for high-bandwidth systems. This is primarily due to the fact 10 Gb/s is a very complicated standard compared to 1 Gb/s or lower. There are several different cable types available along with complimentary network modules, one or more of which are probably already deployed in the data center.

Just make sure that the infrastructure knows to allocate high-bandwidth resources if our calculations call for it.

See also

- To read more about how 10-gigabit Ethernet works, please visit the following URL: `http://en.wikipedia.org/wiki/10-gigabit_Ethernet`

Managing motherboards

We have been working up to this for quite some time. None of our storage, memory, CPU, or network matters if we have nothing to plug all of it into.

This could have been a long section dedicated to properly weighing the pros and cons of selecting a motherboard manufacturer for maximum stability. It turns out most server vendors have already done all the hard work in that regard. In fact, few vendors even disclose many details about the motherboard in their servers outside of model documentation. We can't really read hundreds of pages of documentation about every potential server we would like to consider, so what is the alternative?

No matter where we decide to purchase our server, vendors will not sell—or even present—incompatible choices. If we approached this chapter as intended, we already have a long list of parts, counts, and necessary details to exclude potential offerings very quickly. These choices will often come in the form of drop-down lists for every component the motherboard and chassis will accept.

The chassis will come later. For now, let's focus on CPU, RAM, RAID, and network compatibility.

Keep in mind that motherboards and the requisite case are almost exclusively a package deal. This means we can't keep an extra motherboard available in case of failure, unlike other swappable elements. This breaks our redundancy rule, but there are ways of circumventing that problem.

Getting ready

This is one of the times when the hardware spreadsheet will show its true usefulness. So, as long as we have been keeping track of our counts through each section, this segment of server selection will be much simpler. By this point, our spreadsheet should look something like this:

	A	B	C	D	E
1	**Type**	**Capacity**	**Supplier**	**Price**	**Count**
2	CPU	10-core			3
3	Network Card	10GbE			3
4	RAID Controller	1GB, RAID 10			3
5	RAM	16GB			10

We don't care about the total cost for each part yet. It might be a good idea to create a separate tab or copy of the spreadsheet for each vendor we want to consider. This way, we can comparison shop. Also remember that the counts are inflated by at least one replacement in case of failure. So we want to look for two 10-core CPUs, eight 16 GB memory modules, and so on.

How to do it...

Now it's time to do some research. Follow these steps:

1. Make a list of desired server vendors. This list may even be available from the infrastructure department, if our company has one.
2. For each vendor, check their available 1U and 2U products.
3. For each 1U or 2U server, remove from consideration any that can't fulfill minimum CPU requirements.
4. Repeat for RAM.
5. Repeat for RAID controller cards.
6. Repeat for network interface cards.
7. Fill in actual selections where appropriate to obtain unit prices.
8. Make corrections to the spreadsheet.

How it works...

While this is straightforward, it requires a lot of time. The amount of server variants available, even from a single vendor, can be staggering. This is one of the reasons we only consider 1U and 2U servers. The other is that 4U servers and larger are often designed for much different use patterns related to vertical scaling, incorporating more CPUs, hard drives, even multiple concurrent motherboards.

For our purposes, that is simply too powerful. When purchasing servers with the explicit intention to obtain multiple, redundant, and compatible examples, this becomes more difficult as the cost and complexity of the servers increase.

Although we have reduced our sample size, there is still more work to do. When considering the compatible CPUs, if we want ten-core chips, and the motherboard only supports up to eight-core chips, we can remove that from consideration. This also applies to available memory slots and sizes. Yet there's an unwritten element to RAM: maximum amount. If the motherboard only supports up to 384 GB, and our earlier calculations show we may eventually want 512 GB, we can immediately cross it off our list.

Since RAID and network cards must be plugged directly into the motherboard or an expansion daughter card, it's the amount of these available slots that directly concerns us. We need at least two for both cards that should drastically reduce the size of our list, especially in the case of 1U servers.

While doing this compatibility verification, it is difficult to ignore prices listed next to each choice, or the total price changing with each selection. We might as well take advantage of that and fill in the rest of the spreadsheet, and make a copy for each vendor or configuration. Some overall choices are likely to be better complete matches, or offer better future expandability, or better price points, so tracking all of this is beneficial.

There's more...

RAID controllers and network interfaces are somewhat special cases. Some servers, in order to reduce size, integrate these directly into the motherboard. This is especially true when it comes to network modules. If at all possible, try to resist integrated components.

If these fail, the entire server will require replacement. This makes it much more difficult and expensive to fulfill our redundancy requirement. Server-class motherboards without integrated network interfaces are rare, but we can use these as our backup path if their minimum speed matches what we've configured.

For instance, if we want a 10 GbE card, and the motherboard has integrated a 10 GbE module, we can reduce the amount of excess cards on our spreadsheet by one. It's very likely the integrated version is of lower quality, but it can suffice until the bad card is replaced.

Redundancy doesn't have to be expensive.

See also

Here is a list of well-known server vendors we could consider while completing this section:

- **Penguin Computing**: `www.penguincomputing.com`
- **Dell**: `www.dell.com`
- **HP**: `www.hp.com`

Selecting a chassis

To round out our hardware selection phase, it's time to decide just what kind of case to order from our server vendor. This is the final protective element that hosts the motherboard, drives, and power supplies necessary to keep everything running. And like always, we place heavy emphasis on redundancy.

For the purposes of this section, we will concentrate primarily on 1U and 2U rack-mounted servers. Why not 4U or larger? Our goal is to obtain at least two of everything, with similar or matching specifications in every possible scenario. The idea is to scale horizontally, in order to more easily replace a failed component or server. As the size of the chassis increases, its cost, complexity, and resource consumption also rise. In this delicate balancing act, it's safer to err toward two smaller systems with respectable capabilities than one giant server that's twice as powerful.

Getting ready

Since the server chassis and motherboard are generally a package deal, it's a good idea to refer to the *Managing motherboards* recipe. We will be using a very similar process to choose a server case. This time, we will focus on adequate room for hard drives and redundant power supplies.

How to do it...

Now it's time to do some more research. Follow these steps:

1. Refer to the final list of servers from our motherboard selection.
2. For our ideal count of active (not replacement) hard drives, remove any choice that doesn't have enough drive slots. Use this list if it's not immediately obvious:
   - Maximum 2.5" drives in a 2U server is 24
   - Maximum 3.5" drives in a 2U server is 8
   - Maximum 2.5" drives in a 1U server is 8
   - Maximum 3.5" drives in a 1U server is 4
3. Remove from consideration any chassis that does not support dual power supplies. This should happen rarely in server-class systems.
4. As the list dwindles, give higher priority to cases with more fans or lower average operating temperatures.

How it works...

This time, our job was much easier than considering motherboard constraints. This time, drives determine most of our decision.

Hot-swappable hard drives are slightly larger than their standard brethren, due to the swap enclosure. Yet cases exist than can hold up to 24 hot-swap drives across the front when stacked vertically. If we need that many storage devices, we save space by taking advantage of cases that can accommodate them. We also need to remember to reserve two drives for the operating system in a RAID-1, separate from our PostgreSQL storage. We can't diagnose problems on a server that can't boot.

Some cases reserve mounts inside, or at the rear, for operating-system drives. They are harder to replace, but make more room for storage dedicated to PostgreSQL. Here, operating system drives are treated as operating overhead without sacrificing case functionality.

If we need more drives than are available in any configuration, we should consider **Direct Attached Storage** (**DAS**), **Network Attached Storage** (**NAS**), or **Storage Area Network** (**SAN**). Some vendors supply drive extension cages specifically to provide more hot-swap bays for specific server models. While we want to conserve space when possible, these are relatively inexpensive and much smaller than a NAS or SAN if we haven't progressed to requiring such a device.

Regarding the dual power supplies, this is not negotiable. Many data centers provide two power rails per server rack. The intent is to provide two separate sources of power to the server in case the server's power supply fails, or power is cut to one of the sources. Sometimes these power sources even have separate generators. We're not the only ones interested in redundancy; data centers want to avoid outages too.

The last, more optional element involves investigating the case itself. Many server cases have several fans inside and along the rear, and as a consequence, are very loud. This won't matter when the server is in the data center, but the number of fans and the shape of the airflow will directly affect the server temperature. Higher temperatures decrease system stability. It's not uncommon for vendors to list maximum operating temperatures of each case, so try to gravitate toward the cooler ones if all else is equal.

There's more...

We use the word *vendor* frequently, and there's a reason for that. Short of outright accusing bare cases and motherboards of being faulty, they are simply not stable enough for our use. There are some great cases available that in many ways exceed the capabilities provided by established server providers.

We don't suggest the smaller vendors for a few reasons. Larger companies often have replacement policies for each server component, including the case and motherboard. Building a system ourselves may provide more satisfaction, but vendors presumably spend time testing for compatibility and failure conditions. They produce manuals hundreds of pages long detailing viable parts, configurations, and failure conditions of the entire unit.

However, one could just as easily argue that redundant servers increase failure tolerance, as there's always an available backup. Bare cases and motherboards are usually cheaper, and user-serviceable besides. That is a completely valid path, and if risk assessment suggests it's viable, give it a try. The advice we give is by no means set in stone.

Saddling up to a SAN

SAN stands for Storage Area Network. Working in the industry, you may have encountered NAS as well. How exactly is that different, and how is it relevant to us?

It's subtle, but important. While both introduce networked storage, only a SAN grants direct block-level access, as if the allocation were raw, unformatted disk space. NAS systems operate one level higher, providing a fully formatted file system such as NFS or CIFS. This means our PostgreSQL database does not have direct control over the filesystem; locks, flushes, allocation, and read cache management are all controlled by a remote server.

When building a highly available server, raw I/O and synchronization messages are very important, and NFS is more for sharing storage than extending the storage capabilities of a server. So what must we consider when deciding on how to best utilize a SAN, and when should we do this instead of using a cheaper solution such as direct attached storage?

We won't be discussing how to evaluate a SAN, which vendors produce the best hardware, or even basic configuration strategies. There are several entire books dedicated to SAN management and evaluation that are far beyond the scope of our overview. For building a highly available PostgreSQL architecture, all we need to consider is the when and why, not the how.

Getting ready

Because we're going to cover both SAN performance and storage allocation, we recommend referring to the *Having enough IOPS* and *Sizing storage* recipes. Just like physical disks, we need to know how much space we need, and roughly how fast it should be to fulfill our transaction and query requirements.

Do we need a SAN? We can ask ourselves a few questions:

- Do our IOPS or storage requirements demand more than 20 hard drives?
- Will the size of our database reach or exceed 3TB within the next three years?
- Would the risk to the company be too high if we ever ran out of space?
- Is there already a SAN available for testing?

If we answer yes to any of these, a SAN might be in our best interests. In that case, we can determine if it would fulfill our needs.

How to do it...

Follow these steps if possible:

1. Request a LUN from the infrastructure department with the necessary IOPS and storage requirements.
2. If a SAN isn't available, many SAN vendors will provide testing equipment to encourage purchase. Try to obtain one of these.
3. Have the infrastructure department format the allocation and attach it to a testing server. Keep note of the path to the storage.
4. Create a basic PostgreSQL testing database with the following command-line operations as the `postgres` user:

   ```
   createdb pgbench
   pgbench -i -s 4000 pgbench
   ```

5. Drop the system caches as a user capable of performing root-level commands, as follows:

   ```
   echo 3 | sudo tee /proc/sys/vm/drop_caches
   ```

6. Test the storage read IOPS with one final command as the `postgres` user:

   ```
   pgbench -S -c 24 -T 60 pgbench
   ```

How it works...

The first part of our process is to decide whether or not we actually need a SAN at all. If the database will remain relatively small, capable of residing easily on local hard drives for several years, we don't need a SAN just yet.

While it might seem arbitrary, setting 3 TB as a cutoff for local storage comes with a few justifications. First, consider the local drives. Even if they were capable of saturating a 6 Gbps disk controller, 3 TB would require over an hour to transfer to another local storage device. If that weren't a bottleneck, there is still the network. With a 10 Gbps NIC and assuming no overhead, that's 40 minutes of transfer at full speed.

That directly affects speed of backups, synchronization, emergency data restores, and any number of other critical operations. Some RAID cards also require special configuration when handling over 4 TB of storage, out of which 3 TB is uncomfortably close if we ever need an extension. SAN devices can perform local storage snapshots for nearly instant data copies intended for other servers. If the other server also uses the same SAN, there's no transfer overhead.

And lastly, while RAID devices can be extended when online, there is a limit imposed by how many local disks are available to our server, either directly in the chassis, or from direct attached storage extensions. If there's ever any risk we can reach that maximum, SAN devices do not have any of these inherent limitations, which we can use to our advantage.

If a SAN is ever available for testing, we're still not done. Depending on the speed of configuration of the SAN or the storage allocation itself, performance may not be sufficient, so we should test the claims made by the SAN manufacturer before committing all of our storage to it.

A very easy way to do this is with a basic `pgbench` test. The `pgbench` command is provided by the PostgreSQL software, and can test various aspects of a server. For our uses, we want to focus on the disk storage. We start by creating a new `pgbench` database with `createdb`, so the `pgbench` command has somewhere to store its test data. The `-i` option to `pgbench` tells it to initialize new test data, and the `-s` option describes the scale of test data we want. A scale of 4000 creates a database of roughly 60 GB. Feel free to adjust this scale to be larger than the amount of available RAM, which guarantees that the server cannot cache all of the test data and taint our performance results by inflating the numbers.

After initializing a new test database, there is a Linux command that can instruct the server to drop all available cached data. This means none of our test data is in memory before we start the benchmark. Again, we don't want to inflate our results, otherwise the SAN looks more capable than it really is.

The test itself comes from pgbench again, which is instructed to only read the test data with the `-S` option. Further more, we tell the benchmark to launch 24 clients with the `-c` parameter, and to run the test for a full minute with the `-T` option. While we used 24 clients here, consider any amount up to three times the number of available processor cores.

This process should reveal how capable the SAN is, and if our production database will be safe and have good performance while relying on remote storage.

There's more...

Notice how we never ask for a specific number of disks when requesting a SAN allocation. Modern SAN equipment operates on an implied service level agreement based on installed components. In effect, if we need 6,000 IOPS and 10 TB of space, the SAN will combine disks, cache, and even SSDs if necessary, to match those numbers as closely as possible.

This not only reduces the amount of risky micromanagement we perform as DBAs, but acts as an abstraction layer between storage and server. In this case, storage can be modified any number of ways, enhanced, adjusted, or copied, without affecting the database installation itself.

The main problem we encounter when using a SAN instead of several servers configured with local storage, is that the SAN becomes a single point of failure. This is something to keep in mind as our journey to high availability progresses.

See also

Here is a list of several SAN vendors, from well known companies, to companies with great potential:

- **EMC**: `www.emc.com`
- **NetApp**: `www.netapp.com`
- **Whiptail**: `www.whiptail.com`
- **VCE**: `www.vce.com`

Tallying up

Now it's time to get serious. For several pages, we have discussed all the components that go into a stable server, and have strongly suggested obtaining multiple spares for each. Well, that applies to the server itself. Not only does this mean having a spare idle server in case of a catastrophic failure, but it means having an online server as well.

Determining how many excess servers we should have isn't quite that simple, but it's fairly close. This is where the project starts to get expensive, but high availability is never cheap; the company itself might depend on it.

Getting ready

For this, we want to consider the overall state of the application architecture. The database doesn't exist in a vacuum. Work with the system and application teams to get an idea of the other servers that depend on the database.

How to do it...

This won't be a very long list. In any case, follow these steps:

1. For every critical OLTP system, allocate one online replica.
2. For each two non-cached application or web servers, consider one online replica.
3. For each ten cached application or web servers, consider one online replica.
4. For every stage or QA database server analog, allocate one spare server.

How it works...

OLTP systems, by their very nature, produce a very high transactional volume. Any disruption to this volume is extremely visible and costly. A primary goal with running a highly available service such as a database, is to minimize downtime. So for any database instance that is a critical component, there should be a copy of the server configured in such a manner that near-immediate promotion to production status is possible.

Any server that needs direct access to the database, whether it be a queue system, application server, or web frontend, is sensitive to database overload. One way of diffusing this risk is to set up one database copy for every two to four directly-connected servers. These copies are only usable for reads and not writes, but a properly designed application can accommodate this limitation. Not only does this reduce contention on the database instance that must handle data writes, it all but eliminates the likelihood of one misbehaving query from taking down the entire constellation of client-visible services.

When a sophisticated cache is involved, the risk to the frontend is greatly reduced. Properly designed, a failed read from the database can default to a cached copy until reads can be re-established. This means we can subsist on fewer database replicas. If the application does not provide that kind of cache, our job as database advocate becomes one of working with appropriate technical leads until such a cache is established.

The extra QA resource may seem excessive at first, but it has a very important role. While the testing teams may never touch the spare server, we can use it in their stead. We can never safely configure a production system for online failover without first testing that configuration on two similarly equipped systems. To do otherwise risks failure of the automatic activation of alternate production servers, which is a de facto outage. Database migrations, upgrades, resynchronization, backup restores, all of these can be tested in the QA environment before they are needed for production use. Without a second server, none of this would be possible.

There's more...

We have brought this up as a tip before, but this deserves special attention. PostgreSQL 9.2 and above now has the capability to stream replicated data from one database standby to another. Even with 10 GbE network cards, there is a limit to the amount of data our master server can or should transmit before its role is put at risk.

While there is still a limit to the number of replicas, we can maintain with this new functionality, overall traffic—and therefore risk—is mitigated. If our database is stuck on a version before 9.2, we may never realize these new benefits. At the time of this writing, PostgreSQL 9.3 is the latest release, and 9.4 is well underway. A crafty DBA can encourage the company to adopt a forward stance regarding upgrades by providing an upgrade proposal, procedural checklist, and deployment integration tests.

Now that `pg_upgrade` is a standard part of PostgreSQL, producing a robust upgrade plan and associated compatibility tests is much easier than in the past. By pushing for upgrades early, we can use new features such as cascading replication, and with PostgreSQL, that can heavily influence our resulting architecture. Consider this when choosing your hardware.

Protecting your eggs

Did we suggest that having several servers was serious? We lied. The place where our servers live, the data center, also has several redundancies in place. Extra network lines, separate power sources, multiple generators, air conditioning and ventilation, everything a server can require.

Yet, some have joked that a common backhoe is the natural enemy of the Internet. There is more truth to that statement than its apparent lack of gravitas might suggest. Data centers are geographically insecure. Inclement weather, natural disasters, disrupted backbones, power outages, and of course, accidentally damaged trunk lines (from an errant backhoe?), and simple human-error can all remove a data center from the grid. When a data center vanishes from the Internet, our servers become collateral damage.

However, we've done everything right! We have duplicates of everything, multiple parts, cables, even whole servers. What can we possibly do about the data center?

Well, it's complicated...

Getting ready

For this section, we will need a list of every database server in our proposed architecture, and the desired role for each.

How to do it...

This won't be a very long list. In any case, follow these steps:

1. For every critical OLTP operating pair, allocate at least one standby.
2. For every two online standby replicas, consider at least one standby.
3. For every other database instance, allocate one standby.

How it works...

This type of scenario is known as **Disaster Recovery**. In order to truly diffuse a data center outage, we need backups of every major database server, and even minor servers. The reasoning is simple: we don't know how long we have to operate at reduced capacity. At that point, even non-critical reporting services still need analogs, otherwise business decisions that depend on activity analysis may not be possible.

We only really need half the amount of database servers, as most disaster recovery scenarios are severe enough for raised alertness, reduced refresh times, manually extended queue timeouts, and more. Not only is this less expensive than having a copy of every server as the primary data center, but it also encourages closer monitoring until it can be restored. Larger companies can opt for complete parity between data centers, but this is not a requirement.

As DBAs, our scenario often resembles this:

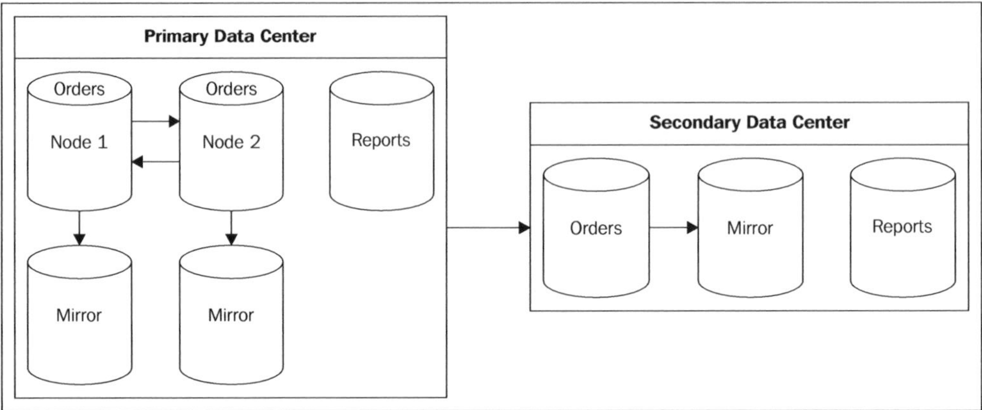

Notice that we didn't make any reservations for QA or development database servers. In the case of a disaster, the primary concern is ensuring the continued availability of the application platform. Further development or testing is likely on hold for the duration of the outage in any case.

There's more...

We cannot stress the importance of this section strongly enough. Some may consider an entire extra data center as optional due to the cost. It is not. Others may think a total of three servers for every primary system is too much maintenance overhead. Again, it is not. The price of a few servers must be weighed against the future of the company itself; it is the cost of admission into the world of high availability.

By the time we begin utilizing failover nodes, or any replicas in a separate data center, the damage has already been done. In the absence of these resources, a database crash can result in hours or even days of unavailability depending on the size of our database, exponentially compounding the effects of the original problem.

With this in mind, all critical production systems the author designs always have a minimum of four nodes: two mirrored production systems, and two mirrored disaster recovery analogs. This ensures even the disaster recovery system is online with one node while the other node is experiencing maintenance. Outages are unexpected, and we must always be prepared for them.

2
Handling and Avoiding Downtime

In this chapter, we will learn how we should react when outages inevitably occur and how to prepare ourselves for them. We will cover the following recipes in this chapter:

- Determining acceptable losses
- Configuration – getting it right the first time
- Configuration – managing scary settings
- Identifying important tables
- Defusing cache poisoning
- Exploring the magic of virtual IPs
- Terminating rogue connections
- Reducing contention with concurrent indexes
- Managing system migrations
- Managing software upgrades
- Mitigating the impact of hardware failure
- Applying bonus kernel tweaks

Introduction

Every piece of software has bugs. All hardware eventually fails or becomes obsolete. No environment is perfect. As a consequence, even a perfectly healthy database will require downtime periodically. How do we reconcile this need with client expectations, which imply that data is always available, no matter the circumstances?

As users ourselves, we know the frustration associated with attempting to use an application or website that isn't responding. Maybe the only impediment is a message indicating maintenance. No matter the cause, we have to remember to come back later and hope everything is working normally by then. Even with our knowledge about the complexity of software and databases, it is sometimes difficult to ignore an error message that prevents us from managing a bank account or making an online purchase.

Every day, users will be less understanding. Business owners and investors who may be losing millions in potential sales and liabilities while a system is unavailable are even less understanding. Yet, there are several tools available that decrease the likelihood of outages and others that help guarantee we're agile enough to handle them when outages—despite our best efforts—occur anyway.

As is often the case with high availability architecture, the trick is planning ahead.

Determining acceptable losses

We know that the PostgreSQL database will be offline at some point in the future. Maybe we need an upgrade to remove a critical security vulnerability or address a potential data corruption issue. Perhaps a RAM module is producing errors and needs immediate replacement. Maybe the primary data center was struck by lightning.

No matter the reason, we need to make decisions quickly. A helpful way is to ensure that the decision-making process is basing the answers on what the user expects for various levels of liability and on the context of the user. The QA department will not require the same response level as 10,000 shoppers who can't make a holiday purchase during a critical sale.

System outage and response escalation expectations are generally codified in a **Service Level Agreement** (**SLA**). How long should the maintenance last? How often should planned outages occur? When should users be informed and to what extent? Who is included in the set of potential database users? All of these things, and more, should be defined before a production system is released. Otherwise, we risk alienating clients with unexpected and arbitrary downtime or outages that persist for hours.

Clients who have their trust broken may leave and never return. So, let's teach them when to expect short amounts of unavailability and set their minds at ease with prompt contact and status management.

Getting ready

Much of our work depends on knowing how much downtime the business is willing to tolerate and who uses the database and when. We also need to know how long the application can obscure a PostgreSQL outage through caches, queues, and connection management. Try to get a complete picture of the database's role before continuing.

How to do it...

Try to answer all of these questions:

- Who uses the database? For each type of user, answer these questions:
    - When does this user access the database?
    - What is the maximum query timeout they will tolerate?
    - Will the user lose money during an outage?
    - Is the user likely to return later?
    - Should this user be included in maintenance notifications?
    - Should this user be included in emergency notifications?
- Can we get the user to agree to or even sign the SLA?
- What uptime percentage is expected? 99 percent? 99.9 percent? 99.99 percent? More?
- What are the company's official business hours?
- When should notifications be sent?
- How long can the platform operate without the database?
- How long should regular maintenance windows be?
- How often can maintenance occur?
- Which weekdays can we consider for maintenance?
- What is an emergency?
- What situations require the activation of disaster recovery nodes?
- Can we get a lawyer to write all of these into a contract?

How it works...

That is a lot of questions, and the list probably isn't even complete. It is, however, a very good start. Notice how we want to know who (or what) is using the database on a regular basis. This is not the same as a user who connects to the database. In this context, we want to know the type of user. Is it the business, another department, a critical application component, or even just a regular website user? Each of these will have different expectations, reactions, usage times, and impact.

The next question we need to answer is how uptime is defined. One frequently quoted value is the number of nines, referring to a percentage approaching 100 percent. Three nines for example, would be 99.9 percent of a year, which is almost nine hours. Four nines is only about 50 minutes. Keep in mind that the SLA can be written to include or exclude planned maintenance, depending on the audience. Unplanned outages definitely count, and remember that this is the total cumulative time for the entire year.

The next important aspect is the latest time a business is officially available. Maintenance should begin after this time and no sooner. Critical PostgreSQL nodes should not be taken offline if more than 5 percent of active users are utilizing the platform and database. It is not uncommon for regular maintenance windows to appear very late at night. Disaster recovery systems, standby nodes, and stage or development copies are all excellent candidates for updates following official business hours. We still want these systems available for developers and QA staff or in case of an unexpected production-level outage, so it pays to be a little more cautious.

The rest are a mix of important questions that need answers, the last of which implies the involvement of a lawyer. If possible, have the SLA in a contract form for all applicable clients and users. A signed agreement acts as a barrier to litigation and liability and sets very definite boundaries to user expectations early in the process.

Configuration – getting it right the first time

An important aspect of setting up a highly available database is starting with a stable configuration that will not require a lot of future modifications. Even settings that can be changed during database operation can drastically alter its performance profile and behavior. Other settings may require a full database restart, which can lead to a short outage, depending on how resilient the frontend application is.

We want to avoid introducing instability into our PostgreSQL database from the very beginning. To that end, we are going to explore common (and perhaps, uncommon) configuration options to use in a highly available installation.

Getting ready

The PostgreSQL documentation describes all of the settings we will be discussing. We recommend that you visit the `PostgreSQL.org` website and read the documentation regarding server configuration. There's probably too much to absorb before continuing with this section, but we recommend that you familiarize yourself with the settings presented here.

We will approach each setting in the order commonly encountered in a recent `postgresql.conf` file generated in a new database.

How to do it...

Find these settings in the `postgresql.conf` file for the desired PostgreSQL instance and perform the following steps:

1. Set `max_connections` to three times the number of processor cores on the server. Include virtual (hyperthreading) cores. Set `shared_buffers` to `4GB` for servers with up to 64 GB of RAM. Use `8GB` for systems with more than 64 GB of RAM.

2. Set `work_mem` to `8MB` for servers with up to 32 GB of RAM, `16MB` for servers with up 64 GB of RAM, and `32MB` for systems with more than 64 GB of RAM. If `max_connections` is greater than 400, divide this by two.
3. Set `maintenance_work_mem` to `1GB`.
4. Set `wal_level` to `hot_standby`.
5. Set `checkpoint_segments` to (system memory in MB / 20 / 16).
6. Set `checkpoint_completion_target` to `0.8`.
7. Set `archive_mode` to `on`.
8. Set `archive_command` to `/bin/true`.
9. Set `max_wal_senders` to 5.
10. Set `wal_keep_segments` to (3 * `checkpoint_segments`).
11. Set `random_page_cost` to `2.0` if you are using RAID or SAN; `1.0` for SSD-based storage.
12. Set `effective_cache_size` to half of the available system RAM.
13. Set `log_min_duration_statement` to `1000`.
14. Set `log_checkpoints` to `on`.

How it works...

The commonly accepted formula for estimating `max_connections` is to take the number of processor cores, multiply them by two, and add disk spindles. With the relatively recent improvement of virtual cores, contributing factors such as SSD or other high-performance storage, and so on, we have a bit more freedom than we had earlier. In addition, even if we were to follow this estimation method, allowing a few extra connections can prevent highly visible connection rejections. A slightly lower performance is a small price to pay for availability.

The advice for `shared_buffers` is very different from the accepted practice of simply setting it to a quarter of the available RAM. We must consider buffer flushing and the synchronization time. In the case of a forced checkpoint, an amount of RAM equal to `shared_buffers` could be flushed to disk. This kind of write storm can easily cripple even high-end hardware. Highly available hardware often has far more RAM that could easily be flushed to a disk in an emergency. As such, we don't recommend that you use more than 8 GB until this situation improves substantially.

The `work_mem` setting is the amount of memory used by several temporary operations, including data sorts. Thus, a single query can consume multiple instances of this amount simultaneously. A good estimate is to assume that each connection will use up to four instances at a time. Setting this too high can lead to over-committed memory and cause the kernel to start killing processes until RAM is available. This can lead to PostgreSQL shutdown or a server crash, depending on what processes are stopped. Systems with very high connection counts (over 400) have increased risk for such a cascade, so we reduce `work_mem` in these cases.

The `maintenance_work_mem` setting is similar to the `work_mem` setting in that there can be multiple instances. However, this is reserved for background workers and maintenance such as *vacuum*, *analyze*, or *create index* activities. Starving these kinds of Memory operations can drastically increase the disk I/O, which can detrimentally affect query performance. For the cost of a few GBs of RAM, we get a more stable server.

The only reason we set `wal_level` to `hot_standby` is because in a highly available environment, we should have at least one online streaming standby. Other recipes will detail how we set these up, but this is the starting point.

The number of `checkpoint_segments` is not a simple thing to set. The calculation we used assumes up to 5 percent of system memory, which could be in transit as checkpoint data, and each segment is 16 MB in size. This time, we are trying to avoid forced checkpoints, because we ran out of segments during data acquisition.

We also want to reduce disk contention when possible, so we increase `checkpoint_completion_target` to `0.8`. We don't want to overwhelm the disk subsystem, and this setting will cause PostgreSQL to spread writes over 80 percent of the time specified by `checkpoint_timeout`. By default, `checkpoint_timeout` is set to 5 minutes, which should suffice until we start working with larger batches of data or a busy OLTP system.

Next, we enable `archive_mode` by setting it to `on`. This setting can only be changed by restarting PostgreSQL, which we want to avoid. It's very likely that we will be using WAL archival in some respect, even if we don't yet know which method to use at this point. This means we also need to set `archive_command` to a command that always succeeds, or PostgreSQL will fill our logs with complaints that it couldn't archive old WAL files. Using `/bin/true` as a placeholder, we can change it when we choose an archival method.

We increase `max_wal_senders` because it's needed for certain synchronization and backup methods. Five is a good starting point, and we can always decrease it later; we definitely need more than zero. Additionally, `wal_keep_segments` is set to a relatively high number. In this case, we keep it up to three multiples of `checkpoint_segments` worth, in case a streaming standby falls behind.

If this count of segments is exhausted while the standby is behind, it can never catch up until the remaining WAL segments are provided some other way or the standby is re-imaged. We'll discuss this more when it's time to talk about WAL archival. This uses more disk space, so multiply the total number of these segments by 16 MB to estimate total disk usage.

The cost of reading a random disk block, as opposed to reading it sequentially, directly affects how the query planner decides to execute a query. By decreasing `random_page_cost`, we tell PostgreSQL that our storage's random read performance is very fast. A highly available server should have equally capable storage, so we lower this to something more reasonable. In the case of SSD or PCIe-based storage, there is effectively no difference between a random or sequential read, so the setting should reflect this.

The last setting that modifies server behavior is `effective_cache_size`, which tells the query planner how much RAM is probably being used by the OS to cache data. Generally, this makes PostgreSQL prefer indexes, because it's likely that the indexed data is in memory. As most Unix systems are fairly aggressive when caching, at least half of the available RAM on a dedicated database server will be full of cached data.

Finally, we want better logging. We increase the logging of slow queries by setting `log_min_duration_statement` to `1000`. This is in milliseconds, so any query that runs for over one second will be logged. This helps us find slow queries without flooding the logs with thousands or even millions of entries by logging everything. Similarly, we want `log_checkpoints` enabled, because it provides extremely beneficial information on checkpoints. We can see how long they took, how frequently they ran, and also how much disk-sync time they required. We need to know if checkpoints start taking too long or occur too frequently so that some values can be adjusted. This setting really should be enabled in all PostgreSQL servers.

There's more...

Many, if not most of these settings, show up frequently in the PostgreSQL mailing lists. As a result, we used many of the prescribed values or formulas. However, several of these settings show up very often; a tool is available to estimate them by analyzing the server hardware and by taking parameter hints. The `pgtune` program is a contributed utility for automatically estimating many system-dependent server settings.

We urge caution if you are relying primarily on this utility. It is extremely liberal when estimating `work_mem` and `shared_buffers` and doesn't seem to modify `checkpoint_segments` at all. Still, we feel that the values it produces are much better than the defaults for larger servers, so feel free to experiment.

See also

There are many more configuration settings we haven't included. We recommend that you browse the PostgreSQL documentation to learn more. In addition, we've included a link to the `pgtune` utility, which may be useful in optimizing your `postgresql.conf` file:

- **PostgreSQL Server Configuration**: `http://www.postgresql.org/docs/9.3/static/runtime-config.html`
- **pgtune**: `https://github.com/gregs1104/pgtune`

Configuration – managing scary settings

When it comes to highly available database servers and configuration, a very important aspect is whether or not a changed setting requires a database restart before taking effect. While it is true that many of these are important enough and they should be set correctly before starting the server, our requirements evolve sometimes.

If or when this happens, there is no alternative but to restart the PostgreSQL service. There are, of course, steps we can take to avoid this fate. Perhaps, an existing server didn't need the WAL output to be compatible with hot standby servers. Maybe, we need to move the logfile, enable WAL archival, or increase the amount of connections.

These are all scenarios that require us to restart PostgreSQL. We can avoid this by identifying these settings early and paying special attention to them.

Getting ready

PostgreSQL has a lot of useful views for DBAs to get information about the database and its current state. For this section, we will concentrate on the `pg_settings` view, which supplies a wealth of data regarding the current server settings, defaults, and usage context. We recommend that you peruse the PostgreSQL documentation for this view.

How to do it...

Follow these steps to learn more about PostgreSQL settings:

1. Execute the following query to obtain a list of settings that require a server restart and their current value:

```
SELECT name, setting
 FROM pg_settings
WHERE context = 'postmaster';
```

2. Execute this query for a list of only those settings that are not changed from the default and require restart:

```
SELECT name, setting, boot_val
FROM pg_settings
 WHERE context = 'postmaster'
   AND boot_val = setting;
```

3. Execute the following query for a list of all settings and a translation of how the setting is managed:

```
SELECT name,
       CASE context
       WHEN 'postmaster' THEN 'REQUIRES RESTART'
       WHEN 'sighup' THEN 'Reload Config'
       WHEN 'backend' THEN 'Reload Config'
       WHEN 'superuser' THEN 'Reload Config / Superuser'
  WHEN 'user' THEN 'Reload Config / User SET'
       END AS when_changed
  FROM pg_settings
 WHERE context != 'internal'
 ORDER BY when_changed;
```

How it works...

The first query, and the simplest one, merely identifies the name and value for each setting that can only be modified by restarting PostgreSQL. In relation to all the available settings, this list is relatively short. However, there are a few notable settings that could affect us.

We already mentioned `wal_level`, `shared_buffers`, `max_connections`, and `max_wal_senders` in another recipe. However, this list also includes parameters related to SSL and WAL archival. We will eventually discuss WAL archival separately, so that leaves SSL. When setting up a secure PostgreSQL server that encrypts connection traffic, we require a host SSL certificate. If this certificate is ever compromised, we need to regenerate it. Unfortunately, we can't simply tell PostgreSQL to re-read the existing certificate; if we overwrite it, the entire database must be restarted.

The second query only shows the settings that we have not already changed but would require server restart. This list is potentially more interesting and concise, as we are presumably seeking further parameters to modify. Of course, the opposite can also be argued; we have only modified the settings we care about.

The final query is a bit more complicated as it uses a `CASE` statement, yet it also simplifies the contents of the view. First, consider the `WHERE` clause, which purges internal settings. We don't care about these specifically because they can only be set when compiling PostgreSQL itself. While such an action may be necessary to apply an emergency patch from the PostgreSQL developers, we cannot modify several of these parameters without rebuilding the entire contents of every affected database. These settings are for experts only, and these experts rarely even consider changing them.

Within `SELECT`, we fetch the setting name as well as how it is modified. Note that all settings that require a server reload to take effect are found in `postgresql.conf`. Subsequent changes applied at the session level can also be overridden using `SET` syntax, so we included that as well.

There's more...

Of course, the `pg_settings` view can provide more than just an insight into the parameters that require a server restart.

Distinct settings

A common request on the PostgreSQL mailing lists is for users to provide a list of settings they've changed. This helps everyone diagnose where a problem could originate or give us an idea of a database's usage pattern. Now that we know about this view, we can easily provide that data with the following query:

```
SELECT name, setting
  FROM pg_settings
 WHERE boot_val IS DISTINCT FROM setting;
```

The `IS DISTINCT FROM` clause isn't as well known as it should be. It can be easy to forget that `!=` or `<>` evaluates to `NULL` when either side of the equation is `NULL`. Thus, if the default `boot_val` value is `NULL`, we would fail to obtain the entire list of modified settings.

The `IS DISTINCT FROM` clause considers `NULL` as a distinct value instead of an unknown one, permitting direct comparisons.

More information

The `pg_settings` view also provides the `short_desc` and `extra_desc` columns. We can use these as shortcuts to remember why we might have changed a setting, without pulling up the PostgreSQL documentation.

See also

- The `pg_settings` view has a lot more information than what we have presented here. Check the documentation at `http://www.postgresql.org/docs/9.3/static/view-pg-settings.html` for more details.

Identifying important tables

Another aspect of maintaining a highly available database is to know all important information about the contents of the database itself. In this case, we aim to focus on tables and indexes that receive the most activity. If any problems that might require maintenance or a restart arise, the most active portions are the likely origin.

What is activity? Inserts, updates, deletes, and selects are a good start. PostgreSQL collects statistics on all of this information, making it easy to collect and track. It also tracks how often indexes or tables are scanned and how many rows were affected by each. In addition, we can find out how much disk space any object consumes, and given the help of a couple contributed tools, we can also find out how much of this space is currently reusable.

Data like this tells us which tables and indexes are the most active, which objects have the highest row turnover, and which objects require a high disk I/O. Armed with these statistics, we can properly distribute tables to high performance tablespaces, direct extra maintenance toward particularly active tables, or remove inefficient indexes.

All of these operations increase the stability, responsiveness, and throughput of a PostgreSQL database. First, however, we need to isolate our targets.

Getting ready

Many of these techniques rely on functions and views described in greater detail within the PostgreSQL documentation. In particular, we use a few system administration functions such as `pg_relation_size` and `pg_total_relation_size` and system views such as `pg_class`, `pg_index`, `pg_stat_user_tables`, and `pg_stat_user_indexes`. We also make use of a contributed module named `pgstattuple`.

We strongly recommend that you get familiar with these functions and views in the PostgreSQL documentation before continuing. After we are finished, we hope to convey just how useful these views are and encourage further exploration. When you are building a highly available database, there is rarely such a thing as too much information about the database.

How to do it...

Follow these steps to learn a little about the database:

1. Use this query to get a list of the top 20 largest tables in the current database:

```
SELECT oid::REGCLASS::TEXT AS table_name,

       pg_size_pretty(
         pg_total_relation_size(oid)
       ) AS total_size

  FROM pg_class

 WHERE relkind = 'r'

   AND relpages > 0

 ORDER BY pg_total_relation_size(oid) DESC

 LIMIT 20;
```

2. Use this query to get a list of the top 20 largest indexes in the current database and their parent tables:

```
SELECT indexrelid::REGCLASS::TEXT AS index_name,

       indrelid::REGCLASS::TEXT AS table_name,

       pg_size_pretty(
         pg_relation_size(indexrelid)
       ) AS total_size

  FROM pg_index

 ORDER BY pg_relation_size(indexrelid) DESC

 LIMIT 20;
```

3. Use this query to find the top 20 most active tables by determining the ones that receive the most inserts, updates, or deletes:

```
SELECT relid::REGCLASS AS table_name,

       n_tup_ins AS inserts,

       n_tup_upd + n_tup_hot_upd AS updates,

       n_tup_del AS deletes

  FROM pg_stat_user_tables

 ORDER BY (n_tup_ins + n_tup_upd +
           n_tup_hot_upd + n_tup_del) DESC

 LIMIT 20;
```

4. Use this variant to obtain top tables with fetch activity by checking index and table scans:

```
SELECT relid::REGCLASS AS table_name,
       coalesce(seq_scan, 0) AS sequential_scans,
       coalesce(idx_scan, 0) AS index_scans,
       coalesce(seq_tup_read, 0) AS table_matches,
       coalesce(idx_tup_fetch, 0) AS index_matches
  FROM pg_stat_user_tables
 ORDER BY (coalesce(seq_scan, 0) +
          coalesce(idx_scan, 0)) DESC,
       (coalesce(seq_tup_read, 0) +
       coalesce(idx_tup_fetch, 0)) DESC
 LIMIT 20;
```

5. Use this query for the top 20 indexes with read activity in the current database:

```
SELECT indexrelid::REGCLASS AS index_name,
       coalesce(idx_scan, 0) AS index_scans,
       coalesce(idx_tup_read, 0) AS rows_read,
       coalesce(idx_tup_fetch, 0) AS rows_fetched
  FROM pg_stat_user_indexes
 ORDER BY (coalesce(idx_scan, 0) +
          coalesce(idx_tup_read, 0)) DESC
 LIMIT 20;
```

How it works...

Each of these queries offers a distinct piece of information about the database. Simply executing them in a vacuum offers very little insight. We have to look at the results of each to learn anything. In addition, all of the system catalog views only return statistics for the current database we're connected to.

If the PostgreSQL instance has dozens of databases and we're only connected to one, the statistics will only apply to that particular database. To obtain stats on every database in the instance, we would need to connect to each one and collect the information separately.

The first query returns the 20 largest tables in the database, including associated indexes and the **The Oversize Attribute Storage Technique** (**TOAST**) data. This way, if a table has a large amount of excessively long row data or several indexes, we still get its true size in relation to all other tables. We will likely make use of the `pg_size_pretty` function several times through this book. When given a size in bytes, it converts it to a more convenient and readable notation such as megabytes or gigabytes.

The next query returns the 20 largest indexes in the database. While it is very likely that these will be associated with the largest tables, this won't necessarily be the case. Indeed, large composite indexes, functional indexes, or bloated indexes will also be listed here. Indexes (which are not primary keys) that show up in this list are good candidates for optimization, either by substituting them with partial indexes or replacing them with a more efficient version.

After size, we move on to table activity. The third query returns the 20 most active tables based on writes. In many cases, this will immediately identify tables with high turnover that will frequently invoke `autovacuum` or `autoanalyze` and may require manual adjustment. Often, user session tables appear here due to inefficient storage of web session data; identification provides ammunition for process revision. Overly active tables are bottlenecks and should be minimized if possible.

Then, we may wish to know table select information. The fourth query is somewhat crude, but the intent is to return 20 tables that are most often read by user sessions. Again, it will likely identify tables with extremely inflated read activity in comparison to the database average. These cases can often be reduced by better frontend data caches, and identifying them is the first step down this path.

Finally, we can see the top 20 indexes using read activity. This can further isolate potential indexes that should be monitored. If we invert the sorting of this query, we can also identify indexes that are not producing many matches at all and are simply wasting space.

There's more...

Though we've already obtained a wealth of information from PostgreSQL, it still has a few tricks up its sleeve.

Reset stats

Running these queries multiple times in a row, it's hard to ignore the fact that the numbers increase, and there's no associated timestamp. Several statistics-tracking systems will track the differences between readings and display this as the rate, but if we're doing this by hand, we need another way to zero out statistics for ease of analysis. Use this function to reset all activity statistics to zero:

```
SELECT pg_stat_reset();
```

Of course, we suggest that you capture this data before resetting it.

Use pgstattuple

The `pgstattuple` contributed extension is also useful for analysis, but it produces a deep scan of single objects identified through other means. It's best to use the extension to get storage-related data regarding indexes or tables matched with the preceding queries.
To use it, it must first be installed by a superuser account. It can also only be utilized by a superuser account.

To install the extension, execute this SQL query:

```
CREATE EXTENSION pgstattuple;
```

To use it, select from it as if it were a normal table or view. The only difference is that we use it as a function with the name of the table we want to analyze. For example, to obtain storage statistics on the `pg_class` table, we could execute this:

```
SELECT * FROM pgstattuple('pg_class');
```

Of particular interest is the `free_percent` column. If this is very high, the table mostly has empty space and could benefit from `CLUSTER` or `VACUUM FULL`. In addition, we should tell developers if this table becomes bloated frequently, as it is possible that they can modify the application to use it more efficiently.

If this isn't possible, we can also set `autovacuum` to be more aggressive for each specific table if necessary.

See also

The tools discussed in this section have a lot of documentation and examples. Please refer to these sites for more information:

- **System Administration Functions**: `http://www.postgresql.org/docs/9.3/static/functions-admin.html`
- **The Statistics Collector**: `http://www.postgresql.org/docs/9.3/static/monitoring-stats.html`
- **pgstattuple**: `http://www.postgresql.org/docs/9.3/static/pgstattuple.html`
- **pgAgent**: `http://www.pgadmin.org/docs/1.18/pgagent.html`

Defusing cache poisoning

Not every DBA has experienced disk cache poisoning. Those who have recognize it as a bane to any critical OLTP system and a source of constant stress in a highly available environment.

When the operating system fetches disk blocks into memory, it also applies arbitrary aging, promotion, and purging heuristics. Several of these can invalidate cached data in the presence of an originating process change such as a database crash or restart. Any memory stored by PostgreSQL in shared memory is also purged upon database shutdown.

Perhaps the worst thing a DBA can do following a database crash or a restart is to immediately make the database available to applications and users. Unless storage is based on SSD or a very capable SAN, random read performance will drop by two or three orders of magnitude as data is being supplied by slow disks instead of by memory. As a result, all subsequent queries will greatly over-saturate the available disk bandwidth. This delays query results and slows down the cache rebuild, potentially multiplying query execution times for several hours.

In a highly available system, we cannot ignore this kind of risk. Saturated disk bandwidth means random reads are spread very thin. We need to figure out how to reinstate the disk cache and possibly, the PostgreSQL shared buffers before declaring that the database is usable. Otherwise, the claim turns out to be false. Queries can often become so slow that applications will ignore results and return errors to users.

Getting ready

We recommend that you check the PostgreSQL documentation for system administration functions and views maintained by the statistics collector. We will be using the `pg_relation_filepath` function and the `pg_stat_user_tables` view.

We will also make use of a contributed utility named `pgFincore`. This utility is not included with standard PostgreSQL but is often packaged for popular Linux distributions. To install it on an Ubuntu server along with the PostgreSQL server, use this command:

```
sudo apt-get install postgresql-9.3-pgfincore
```

Afterwards, activate it in the database with this query:

```
CREATE EXTENSION pgfincore;
```

How to do it...

First, follow these steps to create a static table that stores the top 20 active tables and indexes:

1. Execute the following query as a superuser and ignore any errors:

   ```
   DROP TABLE IF EXISTS active_snap;
   ```

2. Next, recreate the snapshot table by running this query as a superuser:

   ```
   CREATE TABLE active_snap AS
   (SELECT t.relid AS objrelid,
           s.setting || '/' ||
           pg_relation_filepath(t.relid) AS file_path
      FROM pg_stat_user_tables t, pg_settings s
     WHERE s.name = 'data_directory'
     ORDER BY coalesce(idx_scan, 0) DESC
     LIMIT 20)
   UNION
   (SELECT t.indexrelid AS objrelid,
           s.setting || '/' ||
           pg_relation_filepath(t.indexrelid) AS file_path
      FROM pg_stat_user_indexes t, pg_settings s
     WHERE s.name = 'data_directory'
     ORDER BY coalesce(idx_scan, 0) DESC
     LIMIT 20);
   ```

To restore the disk cache to the operating system easily, follow these steps:

1. As a superuser in the database connected with psql, execute the following query in the critical OLTP database before shutting down the database:

   ```
   COPY active_snap (file_path) TO '/tmp/frequent_tables.txt';
   ```

2. Shut down PostgreSQL.
3. Perform maintenance, updates, or recovery.
4. Execute these commands from the command-line:

   ```
   for x in $(tac /tmp/frequent_tables.txt); do
       for y in $x*; do
           dd if=$y of=/dev/null bs=8192
           dd if=$y of=/dev/null bs=8192
       done
   done
   ```

5. Restart PostgreSQL.

If we're not comfortable with Unix commands, this pure SQL method will work as well. Follow these steps instead:

1. Shut down PostgreSQL.
2. Perform maintenance, updates, or recovery.
3. Restart the database.
4. As a superuser in the database, execute the following SQL query in the critical OLTP database:

```
UPDATE pg_database
   SET datallowconn = FALSE
 WHERE datname != 'template1';
```

5. Next, execute the entire contents of this SQL block:

```
DO $$
DECLARE
    obj_oid oid;
BEGIN
    FOR obj_oid IN SELECT objrelid FROM active_snap
    LOOP
        PERFORM pgfadvise_willneed(obj_oid::regclass);
    END LOOP;
END;
$$ LANGUAGE plpgsql;
```

6. Finally, execute the following query to re-enable connections:

```
UPDATE pg_database SET datallowconn = TRUE;
```

How it works...

The first part of this recipe has two steps. We could perform this work at any time, so the table may have existed from our previous work. Therefore, the first step is to drop the `active_snap` table. None of the steps following this one remove this table, because in the case of a crash, we want its contents as a starting point for restoring the cache contents.

After dropping the `active_snap` table, we recreate it with the top 20 tables and top 20 indexes that are sorted by how often they're used in selects. This is only a close approximation based on the collected database statistics, but it's better than leaving the data entirely uncached.

Though it is not available at the time of writing this book, PostgreSQL 9.4 introduces the `pg_prewarm` extension. It can load database objects into the operating system cache or PostgreSQL shared buffers.

After creating the list of the most accessed tables and indexes, we have one of two paths. In the first and simplest one, we merely preserve the `file_path` contents of the `active_snap` table, as this tells us exactly where the files are located. After preserving the table, we can do anything we want, including restarting the database server.

After we're done with maintenance or crash recovery, we can actually restore the file cache before starting the PostgreSQL service. To do this, we use an imposing block of shell scripting. While it looks complex, it's actually just two loops to get a full list of every file that has a name similar to the ones we identified. As PostgreSQL objects exist in 1 GB chunks, there can be several of these that we may have to find. Then, we use the `dd` utility to read the file into memory, twice. We do it twice because the first time, it loads the data into memory, and the second time, it encourages marking of the blocks as frequently used so that the OS is less likely to purge them.

Afterward, we can start PostgreSQL and enjoy a database that is much less likely to have problems retrieving frequently used data. If we don't have command-line access to the system where PostgreSQL runs, this process is a little more complicated but still manageable.

In the second scenario, we actually stop the database first. Any of our cache recovery must come after the database is restarted. Until that time, we're free to perform any activity necessary to get the server or database contents in order. After we start the database, the *fun* begins.

We need to reject user connections while we load the database cache. The easiest way to do this without complicated scripts is to simply reject all connections that don't target the `template1` database. It's extremely unlikely that applications or users will use this, as it generally contains nothing and they have no permissions within it. For our use, it allows us to reconnect and re-enable connections from `template1` if we get disconnected for some reason.

Then, we can use the contents of our previously initialized `active_snap` table to tell the `pgFincore` module to load all of those tables and indexes into memory. After this is complete, we re-enable database connections and our work is finished.

Our `active_snap` table is pretty handy, but it depends on the existence of statistical data that might not be available in the case of a system crash. Be wary of using this approach if statistical information is not trustworthy or is missing.

See also

The tools discussed in this section have a lot of documentation and examples. Please refer to these sites for more information:

- **System Administration Functions**: `http://www.postgresql.org/docs/9.3/static/functions-admin.html`
- **The Statistics Collector**: `http://www.postgresql.org/docs/9.3/static/monitoring-stats.html`
- **pgFincore**: `https://github.com/klando/pgfincore`

Exploring the magic of virtual IPs

As we're running a highly available database, we have at least one standby copy available at all times, right? Of course we do. However, after promoting a standby copy to act as a primary, we need to redirect traffic to the new server. How can we do this easily?

One common method is to use a database connection pool. The pool acts as a connection proxy and simply needs each known node to be registered so that it can redirect connections to the proper primary database server. We will eventually discuss this approach, but there's actually a simpler tool available to us that requires no additional software.

Another method is to change DNS to redirect network connections to the new server. The beauty of this technique is that it masquerades the entire access path to the server so that services other than PostgreSQL can access the new server as well. Unfortunately, subdomains are tied to a single IP address. As DBAs, we probably don't have access to most of the network hardware; that means relying on an external infrastructure department.

Instead, we can tie the subdomain to an IP address that isn't associated with any particular server. Then, it's simply a matter of changing the server that claims it owns that IP address. Luckily, this is something we can control directly.

Getting ready

To perform this process, we need both the `ifconfig` and the `arping` commands. The `arping` command may not be present by default, so install it before continuing. If you are on a Debian or Ubuntu system, issue this command:

```
sudo apt-get install arping
```

How to do it...

For these steps, assume `eth0` is the primary interface and `127.0.0.10` is the IP we are trying to claim. Follow these steps to move or create a virtual IP:

1. First, connect to the PostgreSQL node that had the IP address earlier. This is often the primary server.
2. Release the IP address with the following command:

   ```
   sudo ifconfig eth0:pgvip down
   ```

3. Ping the desired IP address with this command:

   ```
   ping -c 3 127.0.0.10
   ```

4. If the preceding command reaches any PostgreSQL server, restart from the beginning with this system instead.
5. Next, connect to the new server that should own the IP address.
6. Claim the IP address with the following command:

   ```
   sudo ifconfig eth0:pgvip 127.0.0.10
   ```

7. Tell the network about the location of the new IP address with this command:

   ```
   sudo arping -c 3 -A -I eth0 127.0.0.10
   ```

How it works...

If we haven't created a virtual IP yet, we can skip the first three steps. Otherwise, in order to use an IP address, it must be available. Setting up an IP address on multiple servers can wreak havoc on network traffic routing.

It's important to never operate while two PostgreSQL servers claim the same IP address.

Next, we ping the desired address to ensure there are no replies. This should prove that our IP address is free for use. It should end with something like this:

```
--- 127.0.0.10 ping statistics ---
3 packets transmitted, 0 received, +3 errors, 100% packet loss,
  time 2015ms
```

We want to see 100 percent packet loss. This means that the IP address is currently unclaimed. If this results in an active server, we need to repeat the command that we used to shut down the existing virtual IPs there as well.

Provided the address is available, we simply connect to the desired server and use `ifconfig` to create a new virtual IP. We named the virtual IP `pgvip`, and attached it to the `eth0` interface, and used `127.0.0.10` as the target address to claim.

After this step, the IP address is only visible on the local server, so we need to tell the upstream switches and routers that the IP is in use. The `arping` command does precisely this when passed the `-A` parameter. We use the `-c` setting to send three gratuitous broadcasts to help ensure that at least one was accepted. Like `ifconfig`, we need to tell `arping` to use `eth0` with the `-I` parameter; otherwise, traffic may be misrouted.

There's more...

This is really only a demonstration of virtual IP functionality. In the case of a server reboot, network assignments created through `ifconfig` will disappear. For our purposes, this is actually the desired result. If a PostgreSQL server tried claiming a virtual IP address upon reboot and we had already assigned it to a different system, traffic could go to either system and result in severe consequences. Would either database handle the requests? Would the misrouted network packets cause invalid data or some other result? We don't know; network routing can affect any level of the communication process. The end result is that the database is unusable in this state.

That said, the process of maintaining virtual IP addresses is easily automated. Later in this book, we will discuss at least one tool that automatically assigns the virtual IP to the current primary PostgreSQL server. Until then, this is still a very powerful tool to add to our arsenal.

Terminating rogue connections

There comes a time in every DBA's life when they must disconnect a PostgreSQL client from the server; for us, that time is now. There are varying degrees of escalation available for this purpose, and several system catalog views to provide viable targets. Why would we want to forcefully cancel a query or disconnect a user?

To prevent utter havoc, should a user forget an important clause, a query could require several hours to complete. During this time, it is consuming an entire CPU and saturating the storage bandwidth while doing so. A buggy application could start a transaction and stop responding, leaving an idle transaction potentially holding locks and causing a wait backlog.

There are many reasons to evict a connection, and most of them revolve around maintaining a regular flow of queries. If we're unable to maintain low latency and high throughput, our work in building a highly available environment is wasted.

Getting ready

Luckily, PostgreSQL provides most of the tools we need. However, there is a more advanced command-line utility named `tcpkill` that we may need to use later. If it's not already installed, we recommend that you do so before continuing. Debian or Ubuntu-based systems can use this command as a root-capable user:

```
sudo apt-get install dsniff
```

How to do it...

The full escalation path starts very subtly to avoid major disruptive action. Try to follow these steps carefully, assuming `eth0` is the network interface that PostgreSQL is using:

1. Connect to the database as a superuser and execute the following query for PostgreSQL 9.2 and higher versions:

   ```
   SELECT pid, client_port, state,
          now() - query_start AS duration, query
     FROM pg_stat_activity
    WHERE now() - query_start > INTERVAL '2 seconds'
      AND state != 'idle'
    ORDER BY duration DESC;
   ```

2. Use this query for 9.1 and lower versions:

   ```
   SELECT procpid AS pid, client_port,
          now() - query_start AS duration, current_query
     FROM pg_stat_activity
    WHERE now() - query_start > INTERVAL '2 seconds'
      AND current_query != '<IDLE>'
    ORDER BY duration DESC;
   ```

3. Starting from the top, carefully examine the queries in this list. Make note of `pid` for any query that should be disconnected.
4. Stop the currently executing query for the selected pids with the following query:

   ```
   SELECT pg_cancel_backend(pid);
   ```

5. Execute the first query again and check the results for the targeted `pid`.
6. If the query is still running or the state has switched to **idle in transaction**, execute the following query:

   ```
   SELECT pg_terminate_backend(pid);
   ```

7. Execute the first query again and check the results for the targeted `pid`.
8. If the query is still running, disconnect from the database and connect to the server as a root-capable user.

9. Run the following command to terminate the client's network connection, using the contents of the `client_port` column:

   ```
   sudo tcpkill -i eth0 -9 port client_port
   ```

10. Wait until the output from `tcpkill` resembles several identical lines.

How it works...

We begin the process by getting a list of every process ID, duration, and query currently running for longer than 2 seconds. Though 2 seconds is arbitrary; it helps filter out short and fast queries that we aren't interested in. If we examine the queries listed in these results, we may decide that one or more need to be canceled or disconnected. The results should resemble this output:

```
 pid  | client_port |        state        |    duration     | query
------+-------------+---------------------+-----------------+--------
 1835 |       41604 | idle in transaction | 00:00:08.017202 | begin;
(1 row)
```

If this is the case, the `pid` column conveys important information necessary to target the client connection. We begin by invoking `pg_cancel_backend` in an attempt to terminate the currently running query. Often, this is enough to clear locks or stop a query from consuming excessive resources. It's important to rerun the status query to ensure that the command successfully stopped the client's activity.

If the target connection is still active, we need to escalate to the next step: disconnect the client from the database. For this, we use `pg_terminate_backend` instead. This is roughly equivalent to using an operating system utility to terminate the client process, but it is something we can do directly from PostgreSQL. Again, we check for success using the status query, just in case.

In very rare cases, `pg_terminate_backend` can fail, and the client connection will remain unscathed. How is this possible? Networks, despite their apparent maturity, are notoriously unreliable. Misrouted packets, retransmissions, blocked sockets, timeouts, stalls, and more issues wait to disrupt the communication line between PostgreSQL and a connected client.

Sometimes the network socket is in such a state that PostgreSQL was interrupted while writing output. In this case, PostgreSQL is waiting for the client to acknowledge receipt of the data, or for the operating system to mark the network connection as broken. If this never happens, PostgreSQL will wait patiently forever until the client properly handles the terminate command.

This isn't ideal for us if the process is locking necessary tables or rows. If we can't get PostgreSQL to terminate the client, we need to use another approach. The `tcpkill` command gives us the ability to interrupt a network connection directly; this causes the operating system to close the network socket. When this happens, the PostgreSQL client exits automatically.

All we need to do is run `tcpkill` with the `-i` parameter to tell it about the network interface the database is using, the port to focus on, and how aggressive to be. We know the port from the `client_port` column of our status query, and specifying `-9` tells `tcpkill` to block all incoming and outgoing packets so that there's no ambiguity regarding our intent.

The output from a `tcpkill` command should look like this towards the end:

```
127.0.0.10:5432 > 127.0.0.1:37601: R 315492496:315490496(0) win 0
127.0.0.10:5432 > 127.0.0.1:37601: R 315492538:315490538(0) win 0
127.0.0.10:5432 > 127.0.0.1:37601: R 315492622:315490622(0) win 0
```

It's important to not be impatient. Sometimes, it can take a minute or two before the connection finally dies.

There's more...

If a connected application encounters a bug and goes haywire, it might be convenient to disconnect several clients simultaneously. PostgreSQL lets us run query results through functions, so we could kill all connections that were idle in the transaction for at least 2 minutes by running this query as a superuser:

```
SELECT pg_terminate_backend(pid)
  FROM pg_stat_activity
 WHERE now() - query_start > INTERVAL '2 minutes'
   AND state = 'idle in transaction';
```

The `pg_stat_activity` view offers a lot of characteristics to differentiate target queries. We could terminate only connections from a specific IP address or those that connected to the database over a week ago. There is a lot of opportunity here to maintain a highly available system through direct intervention.

Reducing contention with concurrent indexes

When administering a PostgreSQL installation, we will eventually need to create new tables and indexes. In the case of new indexes, the table is locked in *shared exclusive access* mode for the duration of the creation process, blocking any insert, update, or delete activity. This both prevents inconsistencies, and allows the database to modify the table structure to reflect the new index.

Unfortunately, this process is fundamentally incompatible with maintaining a highly available server. While building the index, PostgreSQL needs to examine every valid table row, which means loading it from the disk into memory. For large or active tables, this can cause excessive strain on the system. Other database activities will reduce available disk bandwidth, and the required lock will block all modifications of data in that table. Combined, this can lead to a table being locked for a very long time.

Beginning with PostgreSQL 8.2, indexes can be created concurrently with other activities. This means PostgreSQL constructs the index in the background and only requests an exclusive lock that is long enough to attach it to the table. Early after its introduction, some DBAs felt reluctant to use it and have not changed their evaluation of its safety as it matured.

This may seem trivial as the feature has been around for a very long time, but not enough new administrators know about this functionality. Using it properly and knowing the caveats can avert several DBA headaches.

Getting ready

We just need to find an index to create. For the purposes of this discussion, we may also want to create a small `pgbench` database for demonstration purposes. Execute the following commands as the `postgres` user to build a sufficient sample:

```
createdb pgbench
pgbench -i -s 200 pgbench
```

How to do it...

Follow these steps to test concurrent index creation:

1. Connect to the `pgbench` database and execute the following command as a superuser or the `postgres` user:

   ```
   CREATE INDEX CONCURRENTLY idx_account_bid

       ON pgbench_accounts (bid);
   ```

2. In another connection, attempt to execute the following insert before the preceding command completes:

```
INSERT INTO pgbench_accounts

VALUES (50000000, 100, 15000, 'testing');
```

How it works...

By adding the `CONCURRENTLY` modifier, PostgreSQL will begin the process of building an index. While it does this, it also tracks the incoming insert, update, and delete activities to include them in the new index.

In the connection where we invoked the `CREATE INDEX` statement, we will not see a prompt again until PostgreSQL finishes building the index. So, how can we tell it apart from any regular index creation? One of the reasons we built an example was to prove that concurrency is present. The `INSERT` statement in the second connection should succeed before the index is complete. The process is the same for a production PostgreSQL instance. Any incoming writes to a table undergoing a concurrent index creation will complete normally until the final lock is necessary.

There's more...

While concurrent indexes are very useful, they have some very important elements we need to consider.

No transactions

As of PostgreSQL 9.3, concurrent index creation cannot take place inside a transaction. Why not? Remember that the process needs to look inside all the incoming transactions that could modify the table being indexed. PostgreSQL normally never allows what most experienced DBAs know as *dirty* reads of uncommitted data. As a consequence, concurrent indexes must be built outside of a transaction by internal database mechanisms.

One at a time

As concurrent index creation is not transaction safe, PostgreSQL will only build one at a time. Some enterprising DBAs have circumvented this limitation by building a queue system to send concurrent index-creation requests until the queue is empty. More advanced PostgreSQL installations may want to consider a similar system to utilize concurrent indexes extensively.

Danger with OLTP use

Concurrent indexes are not a panacea; they still follow rules for lock acquisition. Specifically, PostgreSQL cannot acquire a lock to attach the index so long as any earlier transactions are still running. While it waits for the lock, any new transactions that need to modify the table contents will also wait. This feedback loop of waits can quickly consume all available client connections on a busy OLTP system.

It's best to avoid this situation by following the normal index-creation protocol on OLTP systems: only create indexes when the volume is low. We can also massively reduce the risk by avoiding long-running transactions that could potentially block the final lock request. OLTP systems should have few of these in any case.

See also

PostgreSQL has an excellent manual page discussing indexes and concurrency. Please refer to this page for more information:

- `http://www.postgresql.org/docs/9.3/static/sql-createindex.html`

Managing system migrations

As DBAs, it is likely that we will eventually preside over a server replacement. Whether this is to avoid failed hardware or due to system upgrades, our job is to move PostgreSQL from one system to the next.

It is not simple to perform a server migration while simultaneously maintaining maximum availability. One of the easiest methods is limited to users of shared storage such as a SAN. Such storage can be reassigned to another server easily. Without a SAN or other means of shared storage, we need to utilize another method.

Luckily, PostgreSQL added streaming database replication in Version 9.1. With this, we can make a copy on the new server and switch to it when we're ready.

Getting ready

For this demonstration, we will need another server or virtual machine to receive a copy of our database. Have one ready to follow along. We will also be using a PostgreSQL tool named `pg_basebackup`. Check the PostgreSQL documentation regarding this utility for more information.

If the donor server is configured as described in the *Configuration – getting it right the first time* recipe, modify its `pg_hba.conf` file and add the following line:

```
host    replication    rep_user    0/0    md5
```

Then, create a user to control replication with this SQL query issued as a superuser:

```
CREATE USER rep_user WITH PASSWORD 'rep_test' REPLICATION;
```

Then, reload the server to activate the configuration line. If you are attempting this in a real production system, use a better password and replace `0/0` with the actual IP address of the new server.

How to do it...

Assuming `192.168.1.10` is our donor server, follow these steps to create a copy:

1. Connect to the new server as the `postgres` user.
2. Issue the following command to copy data from the donor system:

   ```
   pg_basebackup -U rep_user -h 192.168.1.10 -D /path/to/database
   ```

3. Create a file named `recovery.conf` in `/path/to/database` with the following contents:

   ```
   standby_mode = 'on'
   primary_conninfo = 'host=192.168.1.10 port=5432 user=rep_user'
   ```

4. Create a file named `.pgpass` in the home directory of the `postgres` user with the following line:

   ```
   *:5432:replication:rep_user:rep_test
   ```

5. Set the correct permissions for the `.pgpass` file with this command:

   ```
   chmod 0600 ~postgres/.pgpass
   ```

6. Start the new server using the following command:

   ```
   pg_ctl -D /path/to/database start
   ```

7. Inform application owners to stop their applications or bring available services up with a maintenance message.
8. Issue the following command on the donor server to write any pending data to the database:

   ```
   CHECKPOINT;
   ```

9. Connect to PostgreSQL on the donor server and issue the following query to check replication status:

   ```
   SELECT sent_location, replay_location
     FROM pg_stat_replication
    WHERE usename = 'rep_user';
   ```

10. Periodically, repeat the preceding query until `sent_location` and `replay_location` match.
11. Issue a command on the primary server to stop the database. This command should work on most systems:

    ```
    pg_ctl -D /path/to/database stop -m fast
    ```

12. Issue this command on the new server:

    ```
    pg_ctl -D /path/to/database promote
    ```

13. Inform application owners to start their applications or bring available services up normally configured to use the new database server address.

How it works...

We start the somewhat long journey on the new server by invoking the `pg_basebackup` command. When PostgreSQL introduced streaming replication, they also made it possible for a regular utility to obtain copies of database files through the client protocol. To create a copy of every file in the donor system, we specify its address with the `-h` parameter. Using the `-U` parameter, we can tell `pg_basebackup` to use the `rep_user` user we created specifically to manage database replication.

When PostgreSQL detects the presence of a `recovery.conf` file, it begins to recover as if it crashed. The value we used for the `primary_conninfo` setting will cause the replica to connect to the primary server. Once established, the replica will consume changes from the primary database server until it is synchronized. After starting the database, any activity that occurs in the primary system will also eventually be replayed in the copy.

As we created the replication user with a password, we need an automatic method to convey the password from the replica to the primary. PostgreSQL clients often seek `.pgpass` files to obtain credentials automatically; used in this context, the new server acts as a client.

Once we start the new server, everything should be ready, so we need all sources of new data in the database to stop temporarily. Once this has happened, we issue `CHECKPOINT` to flush the activity to disk. Afterward, we monitor the status of the replication stream until it is fully synchronized with the donor.

After the synchronization is verified with our replication lag query, we stop the source PostgreSQL database; its job is complete. All that remains is to promote the new database to full production status and tell various departments and application owners that the database is available at the new location. Before replication, this was a much more involved process.

There's more...

We can use what we learned in the *Exploring the magic of virtual IPs* recipe to make this even simpler for end users. Until near the end, the process is the same. However, if applications and users were using the virtual address instead of the actual server IP for the old database, they can continue to use the virtual location after the migration.

Simply detach the virtual IP from the old database server, and attach it on the new one before informing the users that the migration is complete. As an added benefit, we can use the virtual IP address as a form of security. Until we create it, users will be unable to locate the database. We can take advantage of this and perform database checks before going fully online.

Once we have created the virtual IP address, any applications that were using the database before we started the migration will need to reconnect. Yet, even this necessity can be removed; we will discuss this in a future chapter.

See also

System migrations are extremely complicated. This section only touches on a small number of concepts. Please refer to these PostgreSQL documentation links for a deeper exploration of the material we covered:

- **The pg_basebackup Utility**: `http://www.postgresql.org/docs/9.3/static/app-pgbasebackup.html`
- **Log-Shipping Standby Servers**: `http://www.postgresql.org/docs/9.3/static/warm-standby.html`
- **Hot Standby**: `http://www.postgresql.org/docs/9.3/static/hot-standby.html`

Managing software upgrades

Software in the server space is normally fairly stable. However, elements such as security updates and bug fixes must be applied. Highly available servers can't be stopped often, but without important upgrades, they could crash or experience a breach, which would be far more serious.

Then how do we ensure that updates can be applied safely while maintaining consistent availability? Once again, this often comes down to preparation. We prepare by having duplicate online data copies and by abstracting access paths. With architecture like this in place, we can switch to a backup server while upgrading the primary; thus, the database never actually goes offline.

We'll explore this scenario here, especially as it will be a very common one.

Getting ready

For this section, we need at least one extra server with PostgreSQL installed. This server should be running a copy of our database. We can follow the *Managing system migrations* recipe to build a copy if we don't already have one available. We will also use ideas introduced in the *Exploring the magic of virtual IPs* recipe. Reviewing these recipes now might be a good idea.

How to do it...

For this scenario, assume that we have two servers with the addresses `192.168.1.10` and `192.168.1.20`, where `192.168.1.10` is currently the primary server. In addition, we have a virtual IP address of `192.168.1.30` on the `eth0:pgvip` Ethernet device. To upgrade the PostgreSQL software on both nodes, follow these steps:

1. Stop the database copy on `192.168.1.20` as the `postgres` user using this command:

   ```
   pg_ctl -D /path/to/database stop -m fast
   ```

2. Perform any necessary software upgrades. For example, to upgrade a Debian or Ubuntu server to the latest PostgreSQL 9.3, use the following command as a root-capable user on `192.168.1.20`:

   ```
   sudo apt-get install postgresql-9.3
   ```

3. Start the database copy on `192.168.1.20` as the `postgres` user:

   ```
   pg_ctl -D /path/to/database start
   ```

4. As a root-capable user on `192.168.1.10`, stop the virtual IP address with the following command:

   ```
   sudo ifconfig eth0:pgvip down
   ```

5. As a database superuser, issue a checkpoint to the database on `192.168.1.10`:

   ```
   CHECKPOINT;
   ```

6. Connect to PostgreSQL on `192.168.1.10` and issue the following query to check replication status:

   ```
   SELECT sent_location, replay_location
     FROM pg_stat_replication
    WHERE usename = 'rep_user';
   ```

7. Periodically, repeat the preceding query until `sent_location` and `replay_location` match.
8. As `postgres`, stop the PostgreSQL service on `192.168.1.10` with this command:

   ```
   pg_ctl -D /path/to/database stop -m fast
   ```

9. As postgres, promote the PostgreSQL replica on 192.168.1.20 with this command:

   ```
   pg_ctl -D /path/to/database promote
   ```

10. As a root-capable user on 192.168.1.20, start the virtual IP address with the following command:

    ```
    sudo ifconfig eth0:pgvip 192.168.1.30 up
    ```

11. If necessary, inform the developers and support staff to restart the application's database connection pools.

12. Repeat any necessary software upgrades on 192.168.1.10 as already performed on 192.168.1.20.

13. Erase the existing database on 192.168.1.10 as the postgres user this way:

    ```
    rm -Rf /path/to/database
    ```

14. Use pg_basebackup on 192.168.1.10 to make a copy of the upgraded database on 192.168.1.20:

    ```
    pg_basebackup -U rep_user -h 192.168.1.20 -D /path/to/database
    ```

15. Create a file named recovery.conf in /path/to/database with the following contents:

    ```
    standby_mode = 'on'
    primary_conninfo = 'host=192.168.1.20 port=5432
      user=rep_user'
    ```

16. Start the newly created copy as the postgres user on 192.168.1.10 using the following command:

    ```
    pg_ctl -D /path/to/database start
    ```

How it works...

This entire process is very long, but we hope to illustrate that it is actually very straightforward. The first step is to upgrade the mirror copy of the database under the assumption that it is not actively utilized by applications or users. The role of the secondary node in this case is to act as an emergency backup for the primary database node. As it's not being used, we are able to stop the database, perform any updates necessary, and start it and allow it to synchronize again.

Afterwards, we isolate the primary database node by disabling the virtual IP address. This allows the streaming replica to replay the last few active transactions so that it's fully synchronized before we make it the new primary database. We accomplish this by issuing CHECKPOINT and watching the replication status until it matches on both systems. When the replication status matches, we can stop the primary PostgreSQL server; its role in the process is complete.

As software upgrades may take some time to complete or require a server restart, we need to immediately make the secondary node available as the primary database. We start by promoting the replica to become the new primary by sending the `promote` command to `pg_ctl`. Once the database is writable, we reinstate the `192.168.1.30` virtual IP address so that applications and users can reconnect safely.

This process of node switching is fairly quick, provided we already have a replica ready to take over. With the replica acting as a primary, the next step is to perform any upgrades necessary, just as we did on the secondary node. After the upgrades are finished, we cannot simply restart the primary database again, as the replica has been acting as a primary database for a period of time.

This means that we need to rebuild the primary database as a new replica. This makes both nodes ready for the next upgrade and maintains the two-node relationship. We start this process by erasing the old contents of the database and then use `pg_basebackup` to copy the current primary database. Then, we create a new `recovery.conf` file and direct it to act as a new replica. Once the replica is started, we have the same configuration as we had earlier, but now, the roles are reversed; `192.168.1.20` is the primary, and `192.168.1.10` is the replica.

There's more...

Astute readers may have noticed that using `pg_basebackup` to copy the entire database following a minor upgrade is somewhat wasteful. We agree! In the later recipes, we will make use of `rsync` or PostgreSQL-specific software to perform these tasks instead. This recipe was already pretty long, and setting up `rsync` properly for this operation would have added quite a bit more time. The point is to show you the switching process; feel free to substitute better methods you know for synchronizing data.

See also

- In addition to `rsync`, a newer utility named `pg_rewind` can make resetting replicas much easier. It is beyond the scope of this chapter, so we recommend that you read more about it at `https://github.com/vmware/pg_rewind`.

Mitigating the impact of hardware failure

Software can have bugs, and PostgreSQL is no exception. Bugs in the database software rarely, if ever, lead directly to data corruption. Hardware can fail too, but hardware problems are not always so straightforward.

Disk, CPU, or memory failures don't always cause the server to crash. In fact, these failures can persist for weeks or even months before their detection by a monitoring infrastructure. Disk failures are generally abstracted away by RAID or SAN devices, and these arrays are designed to readily handle online rebuilds. Other types of failures are more subtle.

CPU or memory problems can manifest in several different ways. In order for PostgreSQL to function, the data from disk must be read into memory to be processed by the CPU. During any of these transition states, a bad CPU or RAM module can inject an invalid checksum or data value inconsistent with the rest of the database. However, PostgreSQL generally assumes that the database is consistent and that transaction logs have been faithfully recorded and applied.

When running a dual-node database, where one node is always connected and synchronized with the other, a failure like this can corrupt data on both nodes nearly simultaneously. When both nodes contain invalid data, our promise of providing a highly available system is impossible. We have no backup to switch to or no alternate node to host the database while we repair the problem. Data corruption can require intricate investigative and mitigation efforts, which are much harder to complete while the database is online.

The only reasonable way to prevent this type of scenario is by exercising extreme caution and with some extra preparation work.

Getting ready

We need to cover a few different scenarios here. One of the things we want to do is transfer files from one server to another. A popular way to do this is with the `rsync` command. On Debian or Ubuntu systems, we can install it as a root-capable user this way:

```
sudo apt-get install rsync
```

We also need it properly configured in order to use it. Create a file named `/etc/rsyncd.conf` and fill it with this content:

```
[archive]
    path = /db/wal_archive
    comment = Archived Transaction Logs
    uid = postgres
    gid = postgres
    read only = true
```

We're now ready to protect our data from hardware problems.

How to do it...

The first thing we need to do is secure the WAL stream. Follow these steps to build a semipermanent copy of archived WAL data in the /db/wal_archive directory:

1. On the primary node, modify the postgresql.conf file to include the following setting:

   ```
   archive_command = 'cp -an %p > /db/wal_archive/%f'
   ```

2. Create the /db/wal_archive directory as a root-capable user using the following commands:

   ```
   sudo mkdir -p -m 0700 /db/wal_archive
   sudo chown -R postgres /db/wal_archive
   ```

3. Reload the PostgreSQL service using the following command:

   ```
   pg_ctl -D /path/to/database reload
   ```

4. As a root-capable user, create a script named del_archives in the /etc/cron.daily directory and fill it with this content as a single line:

   ```
   find /db/wal_archive -name '0000*' -type f -mtime +2 -
   delete
   ```

5. Make sure that the script is executable using the following command:

   ```
   chmod a+x /etc/cron.daily/del_archives
   ```

Next, we should set up a copy on a remote location. In this case, let's assume that the database is at 192.168.1.10 and we have another server set up specifically for WAL storage at 192.168.1.100. Impose an hour's delay by following these steps:

1. On 192.168.1.100, create a /db/wal_archive directory as a root-capable user with these commands:

   ```
   sudo mkdir -p -m 0700 /db/wal_archive
   sudo chown -R postgres /db/wal_archive
   ```

2. Ensure that the server at 192.168.1.100 has the rsync.conf file we discussed earlier.
3. As a root-capable user on 192.168.1.10, create a script named sync_archives in the /etc/cron.d directory with this content:

   ```
   * * * * * postgres find /db/wal_archive -name '0000*' \
                 -type f -mmin +60 | \
                 xargs -I{} rsync {} 192.168.1.100::archive
   ```

How it works...

To ensure that WAL data is available for recovery or emergency restore, we need to secure it on a tertiary location away from the primary or secondary server. We start this by telling PostgreSQL to store the old WAL files instead of deleting them. The `cp` command we used to copy the files will not overwrite the existing archives due to the `-n` setting. This prevents accidentally corrupting the existing transaction logs.

Then, we need to create the directory where the files will reside. The `mkdir` command does this, and the `chown` command ensures that the PostgreSQL server can write to that directory. Once the directory is in place, we need to reload the server because we changed `archive_command`.

Once a WAL file is no longer needed by PostgreSQL, it's stored in our `/db/wal_archive` directory until it gets deleted. This is why we create the `del_archives` script. We only really need two or three days worth of live WAL files. This allows us to send very old files to tape, and newer files are available for **Point In Time Recovery** (**PITR**) or restore. Once we make the script executable with the `chattr` command, we will not have to worry about accidentally filling the disks with WAL files.

The final steps might be the most important of all. We create a directory on a *completely different server* rather than on any of our existing database nodes. Once this directory is there, we create an automated `rsync` job on the database master that will run every minute and copy all WAL files older than 1 hour to the new storage area. Why only an hour? Current versions of PostgreSQL don't have the ability to delay the replay stream, so if we encounter a hardware problem, corrupt data will immediately synchronize to our spare server. This gives us up to an hour for monitors, maintenance, and logs to discover the problem before the corrupted WAL files pollute the tertiary storage server.

We could use PITR instead at this point. However, an imposed 1 hour delay allows us to have live access to databases that obtain their WAL files from the tertiary server. Otherwise, we would have to restore from backup and apply WAL files to reach our desired point in time.

There's more...

In securing the WAL stream, there are a few other options available to us.

Copy WAL files more easily

If we have a version of PostgreSQL of 9.2 or above, there is a new command that, much like `pg_basebackup`, utilizes the replication mechanism for a new purpose. Assuming PostgreSQL is configured as described in the *Configuration – getting it right the first time* recipe, there should be five available replication streams. As we're smart and have a dual-node cluster, we are already using at least one to create a copy of the database.

The next step would be to have a copy of the WAL files alone, as they are critical to PITR, which helps isolate the database. Instead of using rsync to copy these between nodes, we can simply pull them directly from the primary node. With 192.168.1.30 as the virtual database IP address and rep_user as the name of the replication user, we could use the following command to obtain WAL data:

```
pg_receivexlog -h 192.168.1.30 -U rep_user -D /db/wal_archive
```

This command acts like a service. This means it will only copy from the replication stream while it is actually running. To use pg_receivexlog effectively, it needs to be started as a background service and should be restarted if the virtual IP is moved or the server it's running on is ever restarted.

Add compression

PostgreSQL WAL files are very compressible. As such, we can save quite a bit of space while storing them for long periods of time. Since PostgreSQL archive_command can be anything we wish, we can incorporate compression right into the process. For example, we could use this postgresql.conf setting instead:

```
archive_command = 'gzip -qc %p > /db/wal_archive/%f'
```

Now, whenever PostgreSQL moves a WAL file into the archive, it also compresses it.

Secondary delay

We have already discussed maintenance in the previous sections. What we never covered was self-imposed archival delay. If we're performing maintenance or the primary node crashes, it is a very good idea to either delete the /etc/cron.d/sync_archive script or comment out the rsync command itself until the maintenance is complete. This hour-long barrier helps avoid propagating corrupt data, but there's no reason to take excess risks.

Some environments have another pair of servers in a different data center that acts as disaster recovery. If this is our setup, any running server on the disaster-recovery side should be stopped while we modify or rebuild the primary or secondary servers. The reasoning is the same: if there is a problem with the maintenance, we have an untainted copy of everything.

Feel free to re-enable all the synchronization after verifying that crash recovery or maintenance hasn't introduced invalid data.

See also

- As we introduced the pg_receivexlog utility, we would be remiss if we didn't include its helpful documentation as well. Follow this link for more information: http://www.postgresql.org/docs/9.3/static/app-pgreceivexlog.html.

Applying bonus kernel tweaks

Most operating system kernels are optimized for generalized use. While this does not preclude operation as a server, we have to change a few settings to fully utilize our available hardware. This isn't simply a series of configuration modifications meant to increase performance but critical kernel-related tweaks meant to prevent outages.

Though, while we're on the subject, there's no reason to not include purely performance-enhancing changes. Getting the most out of our hardware prevents unnecessary operating strain on existing resources. A server running too close to its limits cannot be considered highly available; an unexpected increase in demand can render a server unusable under the right circumstances.

Getting ready

While the following settings are based on Linux servers, some of the concepts are universal. We'll try to provide enough information to illustrate this. However, keep that in mind for this recipe. Otherwise, look for a directory named `/etc/sysctl.d`. Any system with this directory can be easily configured by adding a file that contains extra settings here. Otherwise, we need to find a file named `/etc/sysctl.conf`, which servers a similar purpose but requires direct modification.

The settings we are going to change include the following:

```
kernel.sched_migration_cost = 5000000
kernel.sched_autogroup_enabled = 0
vm.dirty_background_ratio = 1
vm.dirty_ratio = 5
vm.zone_reclaim_mode = 0
vm.swappiness = 0
```

How to do it...

If there's a `/etc/sysctl.d` directory, follow these steps to activate:

1. Create a file named `30-postgresql.conf` in the `/etc/sysctl.d` directory with the settings we mentioned earlier.
2. Execute this command as a root-capable user to activate:

   ```
   sudo sysctl -p /etc/sysctl.d/30-postgresql.conf
   ```

Otherwise, follow these steps:

1. Place the settings in `/etc/sysctl.conf`.
2. Execute this command as a root-capable user to activate:

   ```
   sudo sysctl -p
   ```

How it works...

In this case, it's all about the settings. Each of our two illustrated steps simply ensures that the settings are in a location where they become permanent parts of the server. Any future reboot will automatically apply these newly selected values instead of the defaults. The `sysctl` command activates them immediately, so we don't need to reboot to modify system behavior.

The `sched_migration_cost` setting is the total time the scheduler will consider a migrated process *cache hot* and, thus, less likely to be remigrated. By default, this is 0.5 ms (500000 ns). As the size of the process table increases, the complexity inherited by the process scheduler eventually results in high CPU overhead, merely to assign processors to PostgreSQL tasks.

Depending on the count of database clients, we have observed overhead as high as 70 percent, greatly reducing database performance. Our suggested setting of 5 ms gives PostgreSQL enough time to process one or more queries before the task is eligible for migration and prevents the CPU task scheduler from being overworked.

The `sched_autogroup_enabled` setting causes the operating system to group tasks by origin to improve perceived responsiveness. On server systems, large daemons such as PostgreSQL are launched from the same system task. As they're all in the same large group, they can be effectively choked out of CPU cycles in favor of less important tasks. The default setting is `1` (enabled) on some platforms. By setting this to `0` (disabled), PostgreSQL query performance can be improved by up to 30 percent on databases with hundreds of user connections.

We modify `zone_reclaim_mode` to completely disable its operation by setting it to `0`. According to the Linux kernel documentation, it may be beneficial to switch off zone reclaim when memory should be used for caching files from disk. Without this, the kernel aggressively balances memory between zones, causing excess overhead and reducing available memory for caching disk data.

The `dirty_background_ratio` setting is a percentage, which we've set to `1`. This is the amount of memory that can be marked as modified before the operating system begins writing data to disk in the background. It is closely tied to `dirty_ratio`, which is the percentage of memory where the operating system blocks all other write activities and aggressively writes dirty memory until everything has been flushed. This kind of occurrence effectively stops all database activity until the flush is complete.

By setting the background ratio to such a low value, the constant background writes make it much less likely that we will reach that trigger point. A highly available server can not afford long unplanned periods of stopped query handling. The constant writing actually slightly reduces performance, which is a risk we have to weigh against the stability of the server.

Lastly, we set `swappiness` to `0`; this disables memory swapping. When Linux runs low on memory, it normally starts moving *idle* processes to disk to free up RAM. We don't want to risk any of our PostgreSQL clients getting this treatment, so we tell Linux to only swap if there is no other option. This is common to dedicated servers such as a critical PostgreSQL system.

There's more...

Some kernel settings have different names with different versions. For instance, `sched_migration_cost` is renamed `sched_migration_cost_ns` in the newer kernel releases. In addition, `dirty_background_bytes` and `dirty_bytes` have been added to newer systems due to the amount of memory available on new servers.

Imagine a server with 512 GB of RAM. In such a case, up to 5 GB of memory could be dirty before the operating system writes anything to disk. In the event of an emergency flush, the disk subsystem may not be capable of handling such a large amount. The new settings allow us to use the same logic as before, but with bytes instead of percentages. In systems with more than 64 GB of RAM, these settings should be used instead of `dirty_ratio` and `dirty_background_ratio`.

A good place to start for setting `dirty_background_bytes` is up to double the size of the RAID or disk controller cache. This ensures that there is never more memory waiting to be written than the controller can handle. Similarly, we can set `dirty_bytes` to eight to ten times the size of the controller cache. This prevents long flushing delays if the background writer ever falls behind.

As always, your mileage may vary. Some PostgreSQL servers may experience slightly faster writes with larger amounts of dirty memory buffers. However, the goal of this book is to reduce the overall risk, even if that's at the cost of some performance. Long periods of database timeouts due to an overwhelmed disk subsystem do not fit this model.

3
Pooling Resources

In this chapter, we will learn to combine and abstract connectivity to isolate and protect the database. We will cover the following recipes in this chapter:

- Determining connection costs and limits
- Installing PgBouncer
- Configuring PgBouncer safely
- Connecting to PgBouncer
- Listing PgBouncer server connections
- Listing PgBouncer client connections
- Evaluating PgBouncer pool health
- Installing pgpool
- Configuring pgpool for master/slave mode
- Testing a write query on pgpool
- Swapping active nodes with pgpool
- Combining the power of pgBouncer and pgpool

Introduction

Abstraction can protect a database from even the busiest platform. At the time of writing this book, applications and web services often involve hundreds of servers. If we follow a simple and naïve development cycle where applications have direct access to the database, each of these servers may require dozens of connections per program, even with a small server pool that can result in hundreds or thousands of direct connections to the database. Is this what we want? Consider the scenario illustrated in the following diagram:

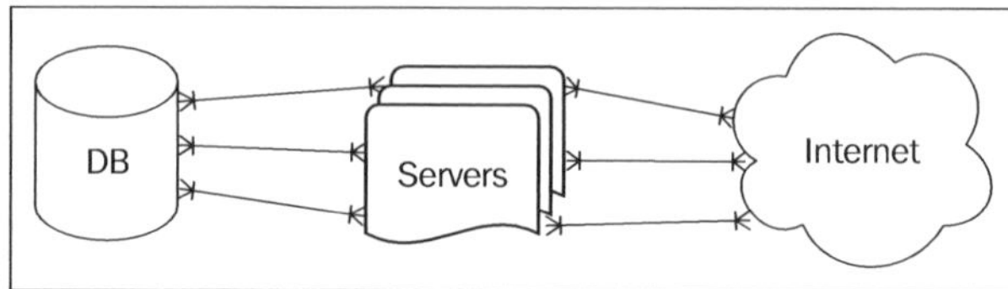

We need a way to avoid overwhelming the database with the needs of too many clients. As we suggested in the previous chapter, a PostgreSQL server experiences its best performance when the amount of active connections is less than three times the available CPU count. With a thousand incoming client connections, we will need hundreds of CPU cores to satisfy the formula.

Every incoming connection requires resources such as memory for query calculations and results, file-handle and port allocations for network traffic, process management, and so on. In addition, each connection is another process the OS has to schedule for CPU time. Very large servers are extremely capable, but resources are not infinite. Even if the database can handle thousands of connections, performance will suffer for each in excess of design capacity. We need to change the map to something slightly different, as seen here:

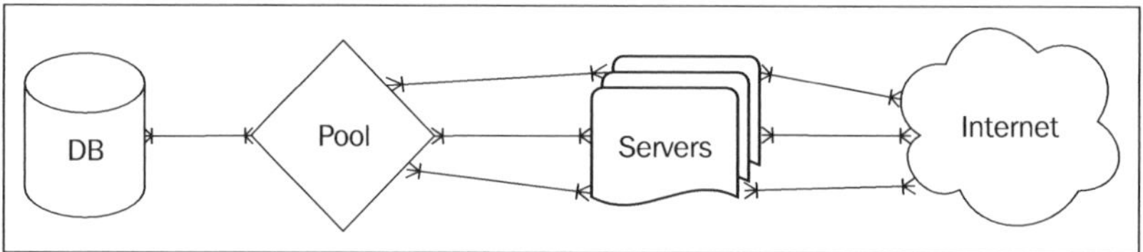

By inserting a connection pool in front of the database, hundreds of PostgreSQL server processes are reduced to dozens. A database pool works by recycling database connections as soon as the client completes its current transaction or when its database work is complete. Instead of hundreds of mostly idle database connections, we maintain a specific set of highly active connections.

Two popular tools for PostgreSQL that provide pooling capability are `pgBouncer` and `pgpool`. In this chapter, we will explore how to use these services properly and reduce overhead and database availability.

Determining connection costs and limits

Excessive database connections are not without risk. The level of risk we incur and what exactly qualifies as excessive are important to determine early. The company and our customers will find it extremely inconvenient if normal database activity exhausted system memory, caused timeouts due to increased context-switching, or overwhelmed the kernel with an overly large process table.

To maintain a highly available server, we must know the full impact of every single connection in terms of required memory and CPU resources. Servicing several disparate applications from various external servers is difficult, so we must provide availability while simultaneously avoiding resource exhaustion. If we properly assess the ideal balance between connection count and performance early on, we can avoid costly emergencies.

Irrespective of whether we helped specify the hardware that will host our PostgreSQL installation, it's still our job to figure out how many clients it can comfortably support. Since this chapter is primarily focused on database pools, we can use this opportunity to choose a practical pool size as well.

Getting ready

We will make a few rough calculations in this section. If possible, obtain data regarding the amount of CPU cores, available RAM, and the number of disk spindles in the storage pool.

Linux systems have a live filesystem that tracks most of this information. To obtain the number of CPUs, simply execute this at the command line, and add one to the highest value since indexing starts at zero:

```
grep ^processor /proc/cpuinfo
```

For the amount of RAM in kilobytes, use this command:

```
grep MemTotal /proc/meminfo
```

Finding the amount of disk spindles can vary greatly between RAID and SAN implementations, so we suggest you obtain the number from the infrastructure department.

How to do it...

Start by calculating the number of connections that the RAM can accommodate by following these steps:

1. Begin the estimate with 8 MB used per connection.
2. Add four times the value of the `work_mem` PostgreSQL configuration setting in megabytes, for a per-client total.

3. Obtain the amount of RAM in megabytes.
4. Divide half of the RAM size by the per-client MB total.

Next, calculate the number of connections the CPU and disk resources can support by following these steps:

1. Obtain the CPU count in cores, including virtual if present.
2. Double the CPU core count.
3. Add the number of disk spindles.

Use the lower of the two values as the final ideal connection count.

How it works...

To know how much RAM a connection may use, we start with a baseline of eight megabytes. This accounts for library overhead, likelihood of using temporary table space, and other various allocations necessary for a session to function. To that, we add four times the `work_mem` setting used by the server to sort and query calculations.

Why four? Large and complex queries will use more, while short and simple queries will use less, so we start with something in the middle. It's actually possible that this multiplier is somewhat pessimistic, so it trends toward assuming higher memory use. That's fine, since overestimating in this case is safer than running out of memory in the presence of several simultaneous complex queries.

With this total, we can see how many connections will use half of the available RAM. We only use half of the system RAM here, since the database itself needs memory. In addition, queries are much faster when tables are available in the operating system page cache. If too much RAM is reserved for client use, query performance can suffer considerably.

In the next set of calculations, we start with the CPU total and double this amount. The more disk spindles available, the less time each CPU spends waiting for results. By adding the number of disks, we get an approximation of how many connections our CPUs can actually support without excessive idling.

By taking the lower of these two calculations, we account for whatever bottleneck will constrain system performance the most. This is our ideal connection count, and it works as a first approximation for the size of any connection pool we create.

There's more...

For an example of this in action, consider a system with 32 GB of RAM, eight CPU cores, and eight disk spindles. We used 8 MB for our `work_mem` setting, so this means we may need up to 40 MB per database connection. 16 GB of RAM can then safely support about 409 connections, assuming memory is our only resource limit.

Otherwise, our eight CPUs and eight disks can support up to 24 connections. This is quite a discrepancy! However, 24 is the safer of the two limits to prevent latency. If we find that a certain amount of latency is not overly disruptive, we can increase the connection count, but not higher than 400, otherwise we risk actually exhausting the available RAM.

> Please keep in mind that the focus of this book is high availability at nearly all costs, and as such, our formulas are extremely pessimistic. We encourage experimentation with these values; you may find a better balance than what we suggest here.

Installing PgBouncer

The first pooling resource we will explore is named **PgBouncer**. This is a very popular connection pool written by Skype developers in 2007. The project has been maintained by various developers in subsequent years, but its role of lowering the cost of connecting to PostgreSQL has never changed.

PgBouncer allows PostgreSQL to interact with orders of magnitude of clients than is otherwise possible because its connection overhead is much lower. Instead of huge libraries, accounting for temporary tables, query results, and other expensive resources, it essentially just tracks each client connection in a queue. Then, based on configuration settings, it creates several PostgreSQL connections and assigns them to the connections on a first-come, first-served basis.

This means hundreds, or even thousands of database clients, can theoretically share a single PostgreSQL connection. Of course, we will never suggest implementing a ratio that absurd without testing, yet the possibility presents several new opportunities for better resource allocation.

The first step to get this exciting new functionality is installation of the software. PgBouncer is popular enough for most Linux systems to package it along with other PostgreSQL tools, so we will cover some of the most popular distributions. For the sake of completeness, we also intend to cover pure source installs, which means we can utilize the latest release regardless of the distribution.

Getting ready

Obtain a copy of the latest PgBouncer source code to complete the installation. At the time of writing this book, the latest version is 1.5.4, released on November 28, 2012.

In order to compile the source code properly, we need the PostgreSQL development libraries in addition to the normally installed system binaries. For example, to build on a Debian- or Ubuntu-based system, we will need to install libraries by executing this at the command line:

```
sudo apt-get install postgresql-server-dev-9.3
```

We also need the `libevent` development libraries. Install these from the distribution package repository on a Debian- or Ubuntu-based system with this command:

```
sudo apt-get install libevent-dev
```

Then, we simply need a root-capable user to install PgBouncer as a system-wide service.

How to do it...

To install in a Debian- or Ubuntu-based system, execute this command:

```
sudo apt-get install pgbouncer
```

To install in a CentOS, Fedora, or other RHEL-based system, execute this command:

```
sudo yum install pgbouncer
```

Otherwise, follow these steps to complete a full source-based installation:

1. Use these commands to extract the PgBouncer source and enter the source directory:

   ```
   tar -xzf pgbouncer-1.5.4.tar.gz
   cd pgbouncer-1.5.4/
   ```

2. Next, build and install the actual software with these commands:

   ```
   ./configure --prefix=/usr
   make
   sudo make install
   ```

3. Create a location where PgBouncer can maintain activity logs with these commands:

   ```
   sudo mkdir /var/log/pgbouncer
   sudo chown postgres /var/log/pgbouncer
   ```

4. Create a directory where PgBouncer can keep its service lock file with these commands:

   ```
   sudo mkdir /var/run/pgbouncer
   sudo chown postgres /var/run/pgbouncer
   ```

5. Create a configuration directory and fill it with a sample configuration file with these commands:

   ```
   sudo mkdir /etc/pgbouncer
   sudo cp etc/pgbouncer.ini /etc/pgbouncer
   sudo chown -R postgres /etc/pgbouncer
   ```

6. Copy the `init/pgbouncer` initialization script from this chapter's provided source code into the `/etc/init.d` directory on the server.

7. Change the copied initialization script to make it executable with this command:

```
sudo chmod a+x /etc/init.d/pgbouncer
```

8. Finally, add the service to system startup and shutdown.
   - For Debian or Ubuntu systems, use this command: `sudo update-rc.d pgbouncer defaults`
   - For CentOS, Fedora, or RHEL systems, use this command: `sudo chkconfig --add pgbouncer`

How it works...

As we said before, it's very likely that a system with the vendor-supplied PostgreSQL packages provides packages for PgBouncer. These versions are likely to install to the expected directories; they include initialization scripts and basic working configuration files.

In case we want or need to install PgBouncer ourselves, the process is a bit more involved. Assuming that we downloaded a version from the PgBouncer project page, we start the process by extracting the source from the archive, and then enter the resulting directory to perform the necessary installation steps.

The first of these steps is to compile the source into binaries and libraries. PostgreSQL supplies a tool named `pg_config` that lists all of the flags and configuration settings used when it was compiled. In order to pass these to the `configure` script for PgBouncer, we invoke it for these options, and execute them as one single operation. Afterwards, regular `make` and `make install` commands as a root-capable user, distribute the software to all expected locations within the operating system so that they match the PostgreSQL installation.

When we launch PgBouncer, it will try to log connection and service activity to `/var/log/pgbouncer`, so we need to create the location and ensure it's writable by the `postgres` user. Similarly, PgBouncer keeps track of its process ID by saving information in `/var/run/pgbouncer`. Again, this location should exist and be writable by the `postgres` user.

The PgBouncer source code provides a fairly rudimentary initialization script to start and stop the service, but it only works properly in Debian or derivatives such as Ubuntu or Mint. Also, it doesn't account for location flags defined by the source `configure` script, so it will require quite a bit of manual modification to be functional.

Thus, we wrote a generic initialization script that should work on any Linux distribution. This script is included as code accompanying this chapter, so feel free to use it instead of attempting to locate or build one from scratch. If we move it into the `/etc/init.d` directory and mark it as executable, standard operating system tools will be able to manage PgBouncer.

Finally, we add PgBouncer to the list of other services that start or stop when the server is shut down or booted up. This ensures the service is always available, and we don't have to remember to start or stop it ourselves. Depending on our Linux distribution, the command that registers the script will vary, so we supplied two very common samples.

There's more...

Why did we provide a separate initialization script instead of simply modifying the one within the source distribution? It turns out that only three changes are required for it to work on a Debian-based system. However, as we said before, this ignores operating systems based on Red Hat, SUSE, Slackware, and several others. We wish the authors of this tool were more inclusive.

Fortunately, the initialization script we supplied should support most major Linux distributions. Further, it is fully **Linux Standard Base** (**LSB**) compliant. Some major high-availability tools assume service control scripts and exit with specific codes under various conditions. When we start discussing the more powerful techniques for automated failover and server control, we will be ready.

See also

- The PgBouncer site contains version downloads, documentation, and much more. Feel free to visit the site to learn more about the project at `http://pgfoundry.org/projects/pgbouncer`.

Configuring PgBouncer safely

Once PgBouncer is installed, we need to configure it to honor our ideal pool size calculations. The settings included with the supplied configuration file are for demonstration purposes only and are unlikely to match our requirements. This situation is easy to rectify, but it requires a bit of research on our part.

Getting ready

The PgBouncer settings are explained in detail in the example configuration file. However, we suggest making full use of the service documentation while following this recipe. We will endeavor to explain important parameters, but there's more available than we cover here.

When we installed PgBouncer, we ensured the configuration directory was writable by the `postgres` system user, which is the same user that owns the PostgreSQL service. For the sake of simplicity, we suggest using either this user or a root-capable user that can modify files on its behalf.

We also need the calculated pool size from the *Determining connection costs and limits* recipe, so keep it handy.

How to do it...

Presuming that our calculated pool size was 25, with a memory-imposed maximum of 350, follow these steps to properly configure PgBouncer:

1. Execute this query as the `postgres` user while connected to any database within PostgreSQL:

   ```
   COPY (
       SELECT '"' || rolname || '" "' ||
                     coalesce(rolpassword, '') || '"'
         FROM pg_authid
   )
   TO '/etc/pgbouncer/userlist.txt';
   ```

2. Open the `/etc/pgbouncer/pgbouncer.ini` file as the `postgres` system user.
3. Under the section labeled `[databases]`, create the following entry:

   ```
   postgres = host=localhost
   ```

4. Under the section labeled `[pgbouncer]`, find the `listen_addr` entry and change it to the following:

   ```
   listen_addr = *
   ```

5. Under the section labeled `[pgbouncer]`, find the `auth_type` entry and change it to the following:

   ```
   auth_type = md5
   ```

6. Under the section labeled `[pgbouncer]`, find the `admin_users` entry and change it to the following:

   ```
   admin_users = postgres
   ```

7. Under the section labeled `[pgbouncer]`, find the `max_client_conn` entry and change it to the following:

   ```
   max_client_conn = 1000
   ```

8. Under the section labeled `[pgbouncer]`, find the `default_pool_size` entry and change it to the following:

   ```
   default_pool_size = 25
   ```

9. Under the section labeled `[pgbouncer]`, find the `reserve_pool_size` entry and change it to the following:

   ```
   reserve_pool_size = 5
   ```

10. Start the PgBouncer service by executing the following at the command line as a root-capable user:

```
sudo service pgbouncer start
```

How it works...

The first thing we do is create an authentication file that PgBouncer can use. As a third-party daemon, it does not have direct access to PostgreSQL authentication. Yet, it still must authenticate users before assigning pool resources. Unfortunately, this means we need to create a copy of the current users and their encrypted passwords that PgBouncer can use. This file should be regenerated any time new users are created or passwords are changed.

The next thing we do is alter the `pgbouncer.ini` file where configuration settings are stored. The first section that concerns us is the `[databases]` section, which keeps track of every database that PgBouncer has mapped. This can be a one-to-one association or an alias that changes various connection parameters such as port, host, or username. Feel free to experiment.

All the subsequent settings are to change the operation of PgBouncer. By changing `listen_addr`, PgBouncer will monitor all IP addresses assigned to this server. If we make use of virtual IPs, this is especially important. Later, we ensure that the `auth_type` is set to `md5` so that all the encrypted passwords we exported are actually used. We set `admin_users` to `postgres` because PgBouncer has an administration console that we can use to control pooling behavior. For now, setting it to the database `superuser` is a good start.

The `max_client_conn` setting does not restrict PostgreSQL clients, but it restricts PgBouncer clients. This is mainly to prevent clients from waiting too long before being assigned a connection. If throughput is generally good, feel free to increase this.

The `default_pool_size` and `reserve_pool_size` settings are actually per-user and per-database. Thus, even if we only have one primary database in our instance, every user can have 25 connections before PgBouncer puts them in the wait queue. If the number of PostgreSQL connections gets too high and starts affecting query throughput, we may need to reduce these settings. It may be best to reserve the pool for applications that need it, so we have better control of PostgreSQL connections that it might create.

Once the settings are saved, we start PgBouncer. When we do that, it will watch port `6432` on the same server where the database is running, assuming that we installed it there.

There's more...

Now that PgBouncer is running, there are a couple things that require further explanation.

What about pool_mode?

Perceptive readers probably noticed the `pool_mode` configuration setting both in the documentation and in the example file. The possible options for this setting can basically be summarized this way:

- **Session**: A PostgreSQL setting is assigned to a client until the client disconnects. This is considered the safest method, but greedy applications can monopolize limited connections by never freeing them. This is the default, and we didn't change it in our instructions.
- **Transaction**: Connections are assigned to clients until they complete a single transaction. Once the transaction is either committed or aborted, the connection re-enters the pool and is assigned to another client. This is a good setting to use for applications that insist on holding persistent database connections as it still enables connection cycling within the pool. Unfortunately, some applications that use cursors expect them to persist between transactions for fetching purposes. Since the connection is reset between every transaction, these cursors are also deallocated and the application will not function normally.
- **Statement**: After every single SQL statement completes, the connection re-enters the pool for reassignment to another client. There are few, if any, valid situations where this setting should be used. Only servers that never make use of features such as transactions, cursors, or prepared queries should use this value. Most PostgreSQL systems can avoid it completely.

Problems with prepared statements

Database applications and object relation mappers that uses prepared queries will have a problem if we enable transaction-level pooling. Once a statement is prepared for execution, it can be reused until it is deallocated. By default, we know that connections are reset between sessions, so these prepared statements are lost. We can fix this by changing `server_reset_query` in `/etc/pgbouncer/pgbouncer.ini` to the following:

```
server_reset_query =
```

By setting a blank value, objects allocated between transactions can persist. However, this also means that the application should check for a prepared statement before creating it. Since the connections are recycled, the application may be assigned a connection where prepared statements are not in their expected states. This is a lot of extra work on the application side, so we generally don't suggest using transaction mode while prepared statements or cursors are present.

See also

Although our suggestions on proper configuration will get things working, there are more options available. We suggest reading the following documentation to learn more about PgBouncer:

- **PgBouncer Config File**: `http://pgbouncer.projects.pgfoundry.org/doc/config.html`.
- **PgBouncer FAQ**: `http://pgbouncer.projects.pgfoundry.org/doc/faq.html`.

Connecting to PgBouncer

Once PgBouncer is installed, configured, and operational, we still need to utilize it. How do we connect to PgBouncer instead of PostgreSQL?

Getting ready

Make sure PgBouncer is configured and running. Take a look at the *Configuring PgBouncer safely* recipe. Then, execute this at the command line to check for the service:

```
pgrep -lf pgbouncer
```

We should see a line similar to this:

```
21281 /usr/bin/pgbouncer -d /etc/pgbouncer/pgbouncer.ini
```

If this is not the case, we need help beyond the scope of this book. Feel free to check the PgBouncer mailing list for assistance. The community is willing to help too, so let them.

How to do it...

If our PostgreSQL server is on `192.168.56.30`, we can connect to PgBouncer by using port `6432`. With `psql`, we can connect to the `postgres` database through PgBouncer with this command:

```
psql -p 6432 -h 192.168.56.30 postgres
```

With PgAdmin, we will just change the connection settings to resemble this:

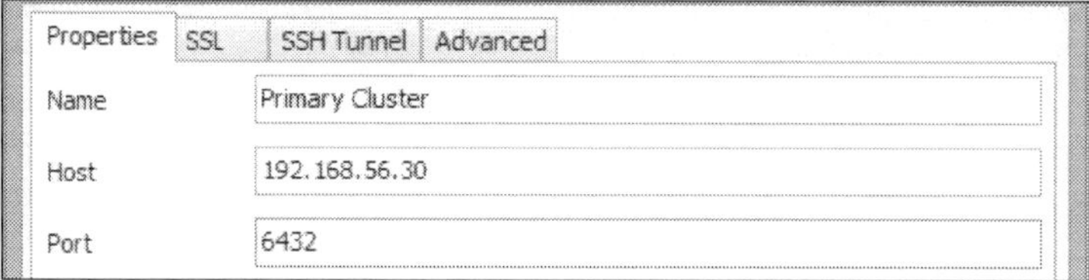

How it works...

PgBouncer works like a simulated PostgreSQL server. Thus, any standard PostgreSQL client or driver should be fully compatible. The only difference is that the default port is `6432` instead of `5432`. Effectively, this makes PgBouncer a connection proxy, and it can be treated as such.

See also

- After we connect to PgBouncer, we may want community assistance with common problems. We suggest the PgBouncer mailing list, which is active with community members willing to offer assistance; check `http://lists.pgfoundry.org/mailman/listinfo/pgbouncer-general`.

Listing PgBouncer server connections

PgBouncer provides an administration console to view pool status or control the service. For now, we will focus on viewing the list of server connections that PgBouncer maintains. These connections are held for distribution to database clients as necessary, and they can tell us much more about the health of the pool. Let's explore the PgBouncer console a bit.

Getting ready

We need to know how to connect to PgBouncer instead of PostgreSQL, so check the *Connecting to PgBouncer* recipe for a refresher. In this section, we will use something known as a pseudo-database. When in use, PgBouncer reserves the database name `pgbouncer` for its own internal purposes to access its administration console. This database does not actually exist, but it will still connect from the perspective of our PostgreSQL client.

In the highly unlikely event that the `pgbouncer` database actually exists within your PostgreSQL installation, we recommend renaming it to avoid confusion.

How to do it...

Follow these steps to get the status of PgBouncer connections to PostgreSQL:

1. Connect to the `pgbouncer` database on port `6432` of the PostgreSQL server as the `postgres` user.
2. Issue the following query:

   ```
   SHOW SERVERS;
   ```

How it works...

By connecting to the `pgbouncer` database name on port `6432`, we connect to PgBouncer using a simulated database that doesn't actually exist. This name tells PgBouncer that we want the administration console. If we configured PgBouncer according to the *Configuring PgBouncer safely* recipe, the `postgres` user is the only database user allowed to use the console.

The author wishes that this information was also available as a view so that we could fetch only interesting fields, but the PgBouncer syntax is easier to type. By sending `SHOW SERVERS` as a query, PgBouncer responds with a list of every connection to PostgreSQL it is using to fulfill client requests. Fields of particular interest include the following:

- `user`: This column lists the users that are currently connected to the database. If we used advanced settings, this could differ from the user that connected to PgBouncer.
- `database`: This shows the database that the connection is attached to. A PostgreSQL server can host many databases, so this is very helpful information. Again, advanced settings can change this from the database name used to create the connection to PgBouncer.
- `state`: This column answers the question: is the connection active, used, or idle? Connections are marked as active when they are assigned to a client. Connections marked as used have handled at least one query, but haven't been checked for validity. Used connections are still idle and available, they merely haven't been verified by PgBouncer. The idle status means the connection is verified as available, and it hasn't been used recently. On active servers, PgBouncer connections will almost never be marked as idle.
- `connect_time`: It displays the exact time PgBouncer created the connection to PostgreSQL. We can use this to determine connection freshness. If most of these are recent, it means that the connections are probably opening and closing too frequently. Connections to PostgreSQL are relatively expensive to allocate, and connection pools are partially meant to reduce this cost. We may need to consider changing some of the PgBouncer connection timeout settings based on the contents of this field.
- `request_time`: This column provides the last time the listed connection handled query activity. On busy servers, this should always be a very recent timestamp. Otherwise, we are potentially wasting server resources by maintaining unnecessary idle connections. In this case, we need to examine the pool size settings and consider reducing them. Alternatively, there may be a problem with the marked PostgreSQL connection, or the assigned client can be frozen. This indicates that we need to check the database health, or ask the development or support departments to investigate applications for normal operation.

Feel free to browse the PgBouncer documentation for other available fields.

There's more...

We like referring readers to external resources on occasion. Unfortunately, the PgBouncer documentation is incomplete in important ways. Our explanation of the **state** field is a good example of this. The interpretation we used for that field came from a post in the mailing list by one of the authors. Keep this in mind when seeking assistance not covered by this book. Mailing lists can fill a huge void left by spartan documents meant to cover bare necessities.

See also

We know that we've listed these documentation links before, but we're still working with complicated configuration settings and usage. We've listed them here again for convenience:

- **PgBouncer Usage**: `http://pgbouncer.projects.pgfoundry.org/doc/usage.html`.
- **PgBouncer General Mailing List**: `http://lists.pgfoundry.org/mailman/listinfo/pgbouncer-general`.

Listing PgBouncer client connections

In addition to PostgreSQL server connection status, PgBouncer's administration console can provide details regarding clients within its queue. Maintaining a healthy and active PgBouncer queue is the key to high throughput over limited resources. In this case, we artificially limited the amount of server connections available to clients, which means that there is potential for stubborn or broken clients to prevent connection turnover.

This, of course, will effectively remove the connections from the pool, creating a bottleneck that could lead to choking transaction throughput. Let's explore the PgBouncer console a bit more to learn what it knows about the database clients attempting to communicate with PostgreSQL.

Getting ready

In this section, we will continue our previous exploration into the PgBouncer console. Check the *Listing PgBouncer client connections* recipe for a refresher. Remember to use the `pgbouncer` database name to enter the administration console.

How to do it...

Follow these steps to get the status of PgBouncer clients:

1. Connect to the `pgbouncer` database on port `6432` of the PostgreSQL server as the `postgres` user.
2. Issue the following query:

   ```
   SHOW CLIENTS;
   ```

How it works...

As before, we connect to the `pgbouncer` database name on port `6432` to use the administration console. By sending `SHOW CLIENTS` as a query, PgBouncer responds with a list of every client using or waiting for a PostgreSQL connection. Fields of particular interest include the following:

- `user`: This displays the user that is currently connected to the database. If we used advanced settings, this could differ from the user that is connected to PgBouncer.
- `database`: This column indicates the database that the client is attached to. A PostgreSQL server can host many databases, so this is very helpful information. Again, advanced settings can change this from the database name used to create the connection to PgBouncer.
- `state`: This column shows whether the connection is active, used, waiting, or idle. Clients are marked as active when they are currently using a connection. If the client is queued prior to a connection becoming available, they are marked as waiting. The used and idle status assignments do not seem to actually be valid for the client state, so don't worry about them.
- `connect_time`: This provides the exact time PgBouncer created the connection to PostgreSQL. Although we specifically ask about the client status, this element is associated with the connection to PostgreSQL. Since connections are recycled, they can be hours or even days old. In determining health, we actually want slightly older connections in this list, as that suggests low connection turnover, and connection turnover can be expensive.
- `request_time`: This lists the last time the listed client transmitted query activity. On busy servers, this should always be a very recent timestamp. Otherwise, we are potentially wasting server resources by maintaining unnecessary idle connections. In this case, we need to examine the pool size settings and consider reducing them. Alternatively, there may be a problem with the marked PostgreSQL connection, or the assigned client could be frozen. This will indicate that we need to investigate the database health, poll the development, or support departments to check applications for normal operation.

Feel free to browse the PgBouncer documentation for other available fields.

There's more...

If this recipe looked familiar, that's because the important fields are exactly the same as those in the *Listing PgBouncer server connections* recipe. Though their interpretation is slightly different, and the list itself is probably more dynamic due to active client states, it's effectively the same data.

The primary difference is the waiting state that we discussed, which doesn't exist when listing server connections. If there are too many clients waiting for too long, it can be a sign of a potential issue. Perhaps the connection pool is too small, resulting in insufficient connection assignments. Maybe a client has gone haywire and is opening hundreds of connections and never closing them, which could lock up all the available connections in the pool.

Whatever the case is, we look for regular state transitions between waiting and active. It is unfortunate that there is no field that details the connection assignment time. With this datum, we can readily discover the clients that are unfairly monopolizing database resources.

See also

We know that we've listed these documentation links before, but we're still working with complicated configuration settings and usage. We've listed them again for convenience:

- **PgBouncer Usage**: `http://pgbouncer.projects.pgfoundry.org/doc/usage.html`
- **PgBouncer General Mailing List**: `http://lists.pgfoundry.org/mailman/listinfo/pgbouncer-general`

Evaluating PgBouncer pool health

Though PgBouncer provides similar information regarding both server and client database connections, the status and health of each pool are also available. If we didn't already clarify, PgBouncer pools are separated by username, database name, and the server's hostname. Thus, each PostgreSQL server may have as many connection pools as there are different databases a user might access via PgBouncer.

PgBouncer supplies somewhat detailed information when seeking server or client status. However, these are not database views, so we can't summarize or aggregate the output to make it more usable. When running a highly available database server, we need to monitor aggregate values, if possible, to watch for potential patterns of misconfiguration or abuse.

Unfortunately, since PgBouncer acts as a proxy, we can't rely on the `pg_stat_activity` system view for summaries. This means PgBouncer and its administrative console are the main sources of debugging and status information. Thankfully, there is quite a lot of useful information. Let's explore.

Getting ready

As before, we continue to use the PgBouncer administration console, so we recommend following the *Listing PgBouncer client connections* recipe before continuing here. Remember to use the `pgbouncer` database name to enter the administration console.

How to do it...

Follow these steps to get the status of PgBouncer clients:

1. Connect to the `pgbouncer` database on port `6432` of the PostgreSQL server as the `postgres` user.
2. Issue the following query for pool status:

    ```
    SHOW POOLS;
    ```

3. Issue the following query for pool statistics:

    ```
    SHOW STATS;
    ```

How it works...

Connecting to the `pgbouncer` database name on port `6432` connects us to PgBouncer using a simulated database that doesn't actually exist. This name tells PgBouncer that we want the administration console. If we configured PgBouncer according to the *Configuring PgBouncer safely* recipe, the `postgres` user is the only database user allowed to use the console.

By sending `SHOW POOLS` as a query, PgBouncer responds with a row for every PostgreSQL database to which it is acting as a proxy. Each column is a summary for various client and server metrics, mainly related to activity or status. Here is a detailed summary of the columns:

- `cl_active`: This column shows the number of clients that are currently assigned a server connection. This number should not exceed the value we get by adding `default_pool_size` and `reserve_pool_size` from the `pgbouncer.ini` configuration file. If the total is regularly below the maximum, we may consider reducing the pool size.
- `cl_waiting`: It denotes the number of clients waiting for a server connection. Since this is a snapshot of the current activity, the number can fluctuate drastically between checks. However, if it regularly remains above zero, and the `maxwait` column is increasing, the pools are probably too small.

- `sv_active`: This column details how many PostgreSQL server connections are assigned to the PgBouncer clients. These clients are not necessarily active, just associated with the connection. The `cl_active` and `sv_active` columns should always be equal.
- `sv_idle`: This column provides a count of PostgreSQL server connections that are not in use at all. PgBouncer marks connections as *idle* after it sends a reset query to clear out the allocated objects and settings. Thus, not only is the connection idle but it's also immediately ready for assignment. If there are several of these, it's because PgBouncer doesn't need them; think about reducing the pool size.
- `sv_used`: This indicates the count of *dirty* PostgreSQL server connections. These connections are actually idle, but they have not yet been reset by PgBouncer for reuse. This means we need to add `sv_used` to `sv_idle` to get the real count of idle connections for this database and user combination. As with `sv_idle`, a large amount of used connections indicate reducing pool size limits.
- `maxwait`: This column outlines the maximum number of seconds a client has waited for a connection. Combined with the `cl_waiting` cumulative total, we can infer either an excess or shortage of throughput based on the connection availability. This statistic is constantly updated, so if no clients are waiting, it will show zero. This kind of live feedback allows us to adjust our pool sizes to ideal levels.

By sending `SHOW STATS` as a query, PgBouncer responds with a row for every PostgreSQL database to which it is acting as a proxy. Each column is a summary of various network and time metrics. Here is a detailed summary of these columns:

- `total_requests`: This column represents the total number of transactions that PgBouncer has directed through the pool. The documentation suggests that the SQL requests are summarized here, but this is probably a miscommunication. Tests clearly show that only queries outside of transactions, or transactions themselves, increase the counter. As transactions are more expensive than simple queries, they can represent a larger ratio of excess work.
- `total_received`: This column tracks the total amount of data in bytes sent to PgBouncer through the network for this database and user combination. In order to have a healthy pool, we need to illustrate high throughput. Thus, we must also examine the next column.
- `total_sent`: This column tracks the total amount of data in bytes sent from PgBouncer to the clients accessing the database. The ratio of this value to `total_received` can indicate that PgBouncer is handling too many large queries, which reduces pool connection throughput. It's also possible that a misconfigured batch job is improperly accessing the database via PgBouncer.
- `total_query_time`: This is the amount of time in microseconds that PgBouncer has spent communicating with a client in this pool. This can be a particularly difficult column to read because it's cumulative, based on all clients accessing PostgreSQL connections. For now, we suggest ignoring it.

- `avg_req`: This column shows the average number of requests per second since the last stat update. As with `total_requests`, this is the amount of transactions, not queries, handled by PgBouncer.
- `avg_recv`: This column details the average number of bytes sent to PgBouncer by each client since the last stat update. In low activity pools, this may reset to zero between samples.
- `avg_sent`: This column indicates the average amount of bytes that PgBouncer has sent to each client since the last stat update. In low activity pools, this may reset to zero between samples. Along with `avg_recv`, we can again obtain a ratio of sent bandwidth versus received to look for potential excessive query output.
- `avg_query`: This column provides the average query duration in microseconds for all connections in this pool. This is a much more useful metric than `total_query_time` as it actually tells us the average throughput of the pool. If the average query time is 50 ms, for example, we can expect each PostgreSQL connection to handle 20 clients per second. This is valuable data to properly size the connection pools.

Feel free to browse the PgBouncer documentation for other available fields.

There's more...

We've mentioned adjusting pool size several times in this recipe. Since pgpool acts as a single proxy for several database and user combinations, we can actually override the default in cases where pools require more direct management. For instance, if we change our entry in `/etc/pgbouncer.ini` for the `postgres` database to `postgres = host=localhost pool_size=5`, no user connecting to the postgres database can use more than five connections, even if the default is 50 per pool. Keep this in mind when analyzing the pools, clients, servers, and other statistics that PgBouncer collects on our behalf. We will most likely need several adjustments before reaching an ideal state that won't overwhelm the PostgreSQL server, yet adequately supplies client requirements.

See also

We know we've listed these documentation links before, but we're still working with complicated configuration settings and usage. We've listed them again for convenience:

- **PgBouncer Usage**: `http://pgbouncer.projects.pgfoundry.org/doc/usage.html`.
- **PgBouncer General Mailing List**: `http://lists.pgfoundry.org/mailman/listinfo/pgbouncer-general`.

Installing pgpool

The next pooling resource we will explore is named **pgpool-II**, but we'll refer to it simply as **pgpool**. This is another popular connection proxy, but it predates PgBouncer by almost a year, having been available since late 2006. The scope of pgpool is also much larger, providing functionality such as query-based replication, connection pooling, load balancing, parallel-query, and more.

Perhaps surprisingly, we won't discuss most of these features in this book. Interesting as they may be, these advanced features don't directly apply to building a highly available PostgreSQL cluster. Of course, we always encourage experimentation.

One feature pgpool exposes, which is directly relevant to this book, is *server* pooling. What does this mean? If we have two PostgreSQL servers, we can make use of a virtual IP address so that clients need not modify configuration files when we switch the primary database server. However, in order to move the IP address between servers, it must first be removed from one server and recreated on the other. This disconnects all active clients and causes a small disruption in availability.

However, pgpool can pool servers so that the active primary server is hidden from database clients. We can promote the secondary within pgpool, and it will handle failover internally. From the application or client's perspective, the database was never offline.

The first step to gain this ability is installation. The pgpool proxy is so popular that many Linux systems package it along with other PostgreSQL tools, so we will cover some of the more popular distributions. For completeness, we also intend to cover pure source installs since that means we can utilize the latest release, regardless of distribution.

Getting ready

For the sake of completeness, obtain a copy of the latest pgpool source code. At the time of writing this book, the latest version is 3.3.2, released on November 29, 2013.

In order to properly compile the source code, we need PostgreSQL development libraries in addition to the normally installed system binaries. For example, to build properly on a Debian- or Ubuntu-based system, we need to install libraries by executing this at the command line:

```
sudo apt-get install postgresql-server-dev-9.3
```

Later, we simply need a root-capable user to install PgBouncer as a system-wide service.

How to do it...

To install in a Debian- or Ubuntu-based system, execute this command:

```
sudo apt-get install pgpool2
```

To install in a CentOS, Fedora, or other RHEL-based systems, execute this command:

```
sudo yum install pgpool-II-93
```

Otherwise, follow these steps to complete a full source-based installation:

1. Use these commands to extract the pgpool source and enter the source directory:
   ```
   tar -xzf pgpool-II-3.3.2.tar.gz
   cd pgpool-II-3.3.2
   ```
2. Next, build and install the actual software with these commands:
   ```
   ./configure --prefix=/usr --sysconfdir=/etc/pgpool/
   make
   sudo make install
   ```
3. Create a location where pgpool can maintain activity logs with these commands:
   ```
   sudo mkdir /var/log/pgpool
   sudo chown postgres /var/log/pgpool
   ```
4. Create a directory where pgpool can keep its service lock file with these commands:
   ```
   sudo mkdir /var/run/pgpool
   sudo chown postgres /var/run/pgpool
   ```
5. Copy the `init/pgpool` initialization script from this chapter's provided source code into the `/etc/init.d` directory on the server.
6. Change the copied initialization script to make it executable with this command:
   ```
   sudo chmod a+x /etc/init.d/pgpool
   ```
7. Finally, add the service to system startup and shutdown:
   - For Debian or Ubuntu systems, use this command: `sudo update-rc.d pgpool defaults`
   - For CentOS, Fedora, or RHEL systems, use this command: `sudo chkconfig --add pgpool`

How it works...

It's very likely that any system with vendor-supplied PostgreSQL packages also provides packages for pgpool. These versions are likely to install to expected directories, including initialization scripts and basic working configuration files. This is definitely not the case with the source distribution.

If, for any reason, we would rather install the source package, we have a lot of work ahead. Assuming that we downloaded a version from the pgpool project page, we start the process by extracting the source from the archive, and then enter the resulting directory to perform the necessary installation steps.

The first of these steps is to compile the source into binaries and libraries. The pgpool `configure` script is fairly standard, so we can change the location of the configuration files with the `sysconfdir` flag. For the purposes of these instructions, we do not need to alter any other installation or compilation settings.

> To get a list of all the parameters recognized by the pgpool build process, issue this command while in the source directory:
>
> **`./configure -help`**
>
> This applies to most software that use configure scripts.

Later, regular `make` and `make install` commands as a root-capable user, distributes the software to all expected locations within the operating system so that they match the PostgreSQL installation.

When we launch pgpool, it will try to log connection and service activity to `/var/log/pgpool`, so we need to create that location and ensure it's writable by the `postgres` user. Similarly, pgpool keeps track of its process ID by saving information in `/var/run/pgpool`. Again, this location should exist and be writable by `postgres`.

The pgpool source code provides a fairly robust initialization script to start and stop the service, but it only works properly in Red Hat derivatives such as Fedora, CentOS, or Scientific Linux. Also, it doesn't account for the location flags defined by the source `configure` script, so it would require quite a bit of manual modification to be functional.

Thus, we wrote a generic initialization script that should work on any Linux distribution. This script is included in the code accompanying this chapter, so feel free to use it instead of attempting to locate or build one from scratch. If we move it into the `/etc/init.d` directory and mark it as executable, standard operating system tools will be able to manage pgpool.

Finally, we add the service to the list of other services that start or stop when the server is shut down or booted up. This ensures pgpool is always available, and we don't have to remember to start or stop it ourselves. Depending on our Linux distribution, the command that registers the script will vary, so we supplied two very common samples.

There's more...

As with PgBouncer, we provided a very similar initialization script for pgpool. While the pgpool-supplied script is very capable, it does not account for operating systems based on Debian, SUSE, Slackware, and several others. While distributions often supply their own control scripts, anyone compiling from source is simply out of luck.

Thankfully, the initialization script that we supplied should support most major Linux distributions. As usual, it is fully LSB compliant as well. We suggest using our script if at all possible as it is specifically designed to facilitate other recipes in this book. Feel free to examine its contents to see how and why we can make such a bold claim.

See also

- The pgpool website is currently written as a large informative wiki. This makes finding downloads a little more difficult than usual. We've listed the proper download location so that you can easily obtain the software at `http://pgpool.net/mediawiki/index.php/Downloads`.

Configuring pgpool for master/slave mode

When creating a highly available PostgreSQL server, one important element to consider is server load. One database server, no matter how powerful its hardware may be, cannot scale infinitely. Regardless of any frontend application-side caching, the database should be able to weather cache failures or unexpected demand.

We can offset much of this risk by leveraging database replicas. Each replica is available for read-only use, and applications are welcome to use them instead of the primary server. Unfortunately, as the amount of replicas increase, the application must track the connection settings for each, and it may even need to know which is currently configured as the primary server.

Server additions, configuration changes, and deep knowledge of the database architecture complicate the application layer and may result in connection management problems. However, we've installed pgpool specifically to avoid mangling the application in order to fit database needs.

The pgpool service provides load balancing through a mechanism designated **master/slave mode**. Due to the design of PostgreSQL, pgpool always knows which server is the primary server, and which servers can only accept read-only queries. This abstraction layer allows applications to connect to pgpool and relinquish traffic management to its capable design.

Getting ready

In order to properly demonstrate pgpool's master/slave mode, we suggest installing PostgreSQL on two servers or virtual machines as a test. Then, configure one as the primary and the second as a streaming replica. *Chapter 6, Replication*, specifically details how to create and maintain PostgreSQL replicas.

Then, install pgpool on the primary server according to the *Installing pgpool* recipe. We also need the calculated pool size from the *Determining connection costs and limits* recipe, so keep it handy.

How to do it...

For these instructions, assume we have two servers. The primary server is located at `192.168.56.10` and the replicated server is at `192.168.56.20`. Our PostgreSQL data is located in the `/db/pgdata` directory. In addition, our calculated pool size is 25, with a memory-imposed maximum of 350. Follow these steps to properly configure pgpool for master/slave mode:

1. Bootstrap the configuration file with some basic defaults by executing the following commands as a root-capable user:

   ```
   cd /etc/pgpool/
   cp pgpool.conf.sample-stream pgpool.conf
   ```

2. As a root-capable user, open the `/etc/pgpool/pgpool.conf` file for modifications.
3. Change the `listen_addresses` setting to read as follows:

   ```
   listen_addresses = '*'
   ```

4. Search for `backend_` in the configuration file. Erase all of the entries and replace them with the following text:

   ```
   # Host number 1 (primary)
   backend_hostname0 = '192.168.56.10'
   backend_weight0 = 1
   backend_data_directory0 = '/db/pgdata'
   backend_flag0 = 'DISALLOW_TO_FAILOVER'

   # Host number 2 (replica)
   backend_hostname1 = '192.168.56.20'
   backend_weight1 = 1
   backend_data_directory1 = '/db/pgdata'
   backend_flag1 = 'DISALLOW_TO_FAILOVER'
   ```

5. Change the `num_init_children` setting to read as follows:

   ```
   num_init_children = 25
   ```

6. Change the `max_pool` setting to read as follows:

   ```
   max_pool = 10
   ```

7. Find the `replication_mode` setting as follows, and make sure it reads:

   ```
   replication_mode = off
   ```

8. Find the `load_balance_mode` setting as follows, and make sure it reads:

   ```
   load_balance_mode = on
   ```

9. Find the `master_slave_mode` setting as follows, and make sure it reads:

   ```
   master_slave_mode = on
   ```

10. Find the `master_slave_sub_mode` setting as follows, and make sure it reads:

    ```
    master_slave_sub_mode = 'stream'
    ```

11. Find the `parallel_mode` setting as follows, and make sure it reads:

    ```
    parallel_mode = off
    ```

12. Start the pgpool service by executing the following at the command line as a root-capable user:

    ```
    sudo service pgpool start
    ```

How it works...

The first thing we do is copy the `pgpool.conf.sample-stream` file to act as our default configuration settings. This file has already been customized to contain several of the settings we need for pgpool to operate in master/slave mode. Later, we open it to make a few modifications and double-check to ensure that all the necessary settings are correct.

The first setting we change is the `listen_addresses` value. The default value of `localhost` will only allow connections that originate from the server where pgpool is installed. Since pgpool is supposed to act as a connection proxy, this severely limits its functionality. The setting we used will allow it to listen on all network interfaces available to the server.

The next thing we do is create two entries for PostgreSQL server hosts. This allows pgpool to connect to both the primary database and the replica. There are two settings that may be non-obvious in their intent.

The first is `backend_weight`, which allows us to customize the ranking of each database server. Higher ranks mean a greater ratio of database traffic from pgpool. With this, more powerful servers will handle more client connections, or we can reduce query pressure on an overwhelmed server.

The next is `backend_flag`, which currently has only two possible values. The default value of `ALLOW_TO_FAILOVER` tells pgpool that the listed server is part of the automated failover system. Properly configuring the failover system is beyond the scope of this recipe, so we disable that for now by using the value `DISALLOW_TO_FAILOVER`.

Next, we need to limit the potential size of the connection pool. We start the process by setting `num_init_children` to `25` to reflect our calculated ideal pool size. Next, we limit the number of pools by setting `max_pools` to `10`. This means there could be up to `250` PostgreSQL connections to each server, lower than our maximum of `350`.

Finally, we ensure that `replication_mode` and `parallel_mode` are disabled, while `load_balance_mode` and `master_slave_mode` are enabled. Replication mode is what pgpool uses to keep servers in sync when there is no other replication mechanism available. It will just interfere with our setup. Parallel mode requires the replication mode, so we can't use that either.

When pgpool is using load balancing, it honors `backend_weight` for each server. By connecting to pgpool, database clients can potentially access one of several PostgreSQL databases. Once a client is assigned to a server, it will never deviate until it disconnects. This prevents excessive connection management by pgpool and avoids race conditions based on replication pace of each PostgreSQL server.

When using master/slave mode with a database replica, we must set `master_slave_sub_mode` to `stream`. This tells pgpool to use regular PostgreSQL replication status functions to differentiate primary PostgreSQL servers from replicas. With this knowledge, pgpool can directly write queries to the primary node, while replicas absorb read-only activity.

Once the settings are saved, we start pgpool. Once we do that, it will watch port `9999` on the same server where the primary database is running, assuming that we installed it there.

There's more...

Perceptive readers may notice that this is very different from how PgBouncer manages pools. Each pool is still defined by the user login and database name, but `max_pools` is actually a hard limit. Once ten users and database combinations are allocated due to incoming connections, there can be no more. Further more, each pool can only have a maximum of `num_init_children` clients.

Unlike PgBouncer, pgpool does not queue excess connections beyond this maximum. If we start noticing application problems due to insufficient connections, we may need to increase `num_init_children`. Despite the name, pgpool is more of a server abstraction layer than a database pool.

See also

The pgpool software is *extremely* complicated due to its extensive feature-set. We strongly recommend perusing its manual and the following indicated tutorial:

- **Pgpool Manual**: `http://www.pgpool.net/docs/latest/pgpool-en.html`.
- **pgpool-II Tutorial** (**watchdog in master-slave mode**): `http://www.pgpool.net/pgpool-web/contrib_docs/watchdog_master_slave/en.html`.

Testing a write query on pgpool

The load-balancing mode in pgpool presumably distributes connections according to server weight. Then, master/slave mode defines which servers are read-only as opposed to writable.

But can we depend on this behavior? We should at least verify these claims before using such a configuration in a production environment. Our uptime depends upon it.

Getting ready

Make sure pgpool is installed and configured according to the *Installing pgpool* and *Configuring pgpool for master/slave mode* recipes. We will follow these two recipes by testing a pool setup with write activity, so we need a fully functional pgpool environment.

To simplify this recipe, perform all the tests as the `postgres` system user. To facilitate this, we may need to set all the `pg_hba.conf` authentication types to `trust`, though we strongly suggest user and password combinations instead.

If our primary PostgreSQL server is on `192.168.56.10`, we can connect to pgpool by using port `9999`. With `psql`, we can connect to the `postgres` database through pgpool with this command:

```
psql -p 9999 -h 192.168.56.10 postgres
```

How to do it...

Follow these steps to test as the `postgres` database user. Feel free to substitute where appropriate:

1. Connect to the primary database and create a test table with the following SQL:

   ```
   CREATE TABLE foo (bar INTEGER);
   ```

2. Connect to pgpool and issue a query that will write to the test table with the following SQL:

   ```
   INSERT INTO foo SELECT generate_series(1, 100);
   ```

3. Execute the following bash snippet at the command line to test the `INSERT` redirection:

   ```
   for x in {1..10}; do
     psql -h 192.168.56.10 -p 9999
          -U postgres -d postgres \
          -c "INSERT INTO foo SELECT generate_series(1, 100)"
   done
   ```

4. Execute the following bash snippet at the command line to test the `DELETE` redirection:

   ```
   for x in {1..100}; do
     psql -h 192.168.56.10 -p 9999 \
          -U postgres -d postgres \
          -c "DELETE FROM foo WHERE bar=$x"
   done
   ```

How it works...

In order to successfully test the capabilities of pgpool, we will try a couple of different scenarios that cause PostgreSQL to write to the database. If we tried to write to the replica instead of the primary server, we will get an error like this:

```
ERROR:  cannot execute INSERT in a read-only transaction
```

Our first step is to create a table where we can try to insert data. We connect directly to the primary server for this step so that we know the table exists and that pgpool didn't get a chance to taint our results. The test table has only one column, so we can populate it with the `generate_series` PostgreSQL function.

The first test we attempt is with a single connection to pgpool that we create manually. Since the server weight is equal for both the primary and replica servers, we have a 50 percent chance of being assigned to the read-only replica server. This test should succeed, but there's still a 50 percent chance that it was just a coincidence.

Therefore, our second test runs the same `INSERT` statement ten times in a loop. Each psql line is a separate connection attempt, so each should carry a 50 percent chance of being directed to the read-only server. Yet, all of these tests will also succeed.

Finally, we run one final loop that will delete all the rows we inserted, and this time the loop will invoke 100 times. Again, all of these are separate connection attempts, and all of them will execute without an error.

There's more...

There is one caveat to this functionality. It is not uncommon for databases to perform the write activity within a function body. For example:

```
CREATE FUNCTION test_insert()
RETURNS VOID AS
$$
  INSERT INTO foo SELECT generate_series(1, 100);
$$ LANGUAGE SQL;
```

By creating this function, we obfuscate the `INSERT` statement enough that `pgpool` won't recognize it. This means that pgpool will improperly send the query to a read-only server and produce an error. We can avoid this by using the `black_function_list` configuration setting. For example, if we add our new function to this setting, it resembles this:

```
black_function_list = 'currval,lastval,nextval,setval,test_insert'
```

Now, pgpool will understand that queries which include a call to `test_insert` should only execute on the primary node. This configuration setting also honors regular expressions, so it's a very good idea to follow a naming scheme when building functions that may alter database contents.

Swapping active nodes with pgpool

With pgpool installed, we have an abstraction layer above PostgreSQL, which hides the active node from the client. This allows us to change the primary node so that we can perform maintenance, and yet we never have to actually stop the database.

This kind of design will work best when pgpool is not installed on one of the PostgreSQL servers, but it has its own dedicated hardware or virtual machine. This allows us full control over each PostgreSQL server, including the ability to reboot for kernel upgrades, without potentially disrupting pgpool.

Let's discuss the elements involved in switching the primary server with a replica so that we can have high availability in addition to regular maintenance.

Getting ready

Make sure pgpool is installed and configured according to the *Installing pgpool* and *Configuring pgpool for master/slave mode* recipes. We will need two nodes so that we can promote one and demote the other.

Next, we will ready the operating system so that pgpool can invoke remote commands. If we have two PostgreSQL servers at `192.168.56.10` and `192.168.56.20`, we should execute these commands as the `postgres` system user on each, as shown:

```
ssh-keygen
ssh-copy-id 192.168.56.10
ssh-copy-id 192.168.56.20
```

The `ssh-keygen` command will prompt for a key password. This can make SSH keys more secure, but it also makes them extremely difficult to use within an automated context. For this and future SSH keys, use a blank password.

We will also use scripts located in the `pgpool_scripts` directory of the code for this chapter. Have these scripts available before continuing.

How to do it...

Assuming our database is located at `/db/pgdata`, follow all of these steps to enable and configure automatic and forced pgpool primary server migration:

1. Copy the scripts from the `pgpool_scripts` directory of this book to the PostgreSQL cluster data directory.
2. Execute this command as a root-level user to make them executable:

   ```
   chmod a+x /db/pgdata/pgpool_*
   ```

3. Execute the following at the command line as a root-capable user:

   ```
   sudo sed -i "s/'DISALLOW/'ALLOW/" /etc/pgpool/pgpool.conf
   ```

4. Execute these commands as a root-capable user to enable pgpool control operations, where `pass` is a password defined for pgpool administration:

   ```
   mv /etc/pgpool/pcp.conf.sample /etc/pgpool/pcp.conf
   echo postgres:$(pg_md5 pass) >> /etc/pgpool/pcp.conf
   ```

5. Edit the `/etc/pgpool/pgpool.conf` file and make the following changes:

   ```
   failover_command = '%D/pgpool_failover %d %P %h %H %D %R'
   recovery_1st_stage_command = 'pgpool_recovery'
   ```

6. Execute this command as a root-capable user to restart pgpool:

   ```
   sudo service pgpool restart
   ```

7. Detach the primary node from pgpool with this command, where `pass` is the password we created in step four:

   ```
   pcp_detach_node 10 192.168.56.10 9898 postgres pass 0
   ```

8. Perform some fake maintenance as the `postgres` user on the primary node with this command:

   ```
   pg_ctl -D /db/pgdata status
   ```

9. Reattach the primary node as a replica with these commands, again using `pass` as the pgpool control password:

   ```
   pcp_recovery_node 10 192.168.56.10 9898 postgres pass 0
   pcp_attach_node 10 192.168.56.10 9898 postgres pass 0
   ```

How it works...

pgpool depends on external helper scripts to perform remote operations on the servers it proxies. The pgpool source includes a few examples, but they use antiquated commands and may not work on our system. The scripts included in this book should work on most major Linux distributions. Thus, we move them into the PostgreSQL data directory and mark them as executable. They must reside here for pgpool to invoke them.

Next, we enable failover on all nodes by changing nodes marked `DISALLOW_TO_FAILOVER` to `ALLOW_TO_FAILOVER` with a quick command-line operation. Without this change, pgpool will not perform any migrations, regardless of how many nodes have crashed or how many times we request one.

Next, pgpool won't let us use the control commands until we create a user and password. This is not the same as any PostgreSQL user or operating system users. We use `postgres` to simplify, but any username will work. We encrypt the password with `pg_md5`, so pgpool will check against the encrypted value it expects.

Then, we need to tell pgpool that we defined scripts for failover and recovery operations. We do that by setting `failover_command` and `recovery_1st_stage_command` properly in `pgpool.conf`. Perceptive readers may note that we didn't change any settings to include the `pgpool_remote_start` script. This is because pgpool specifically seeks it by name. Don't forget to install it with the others. After we restart pgpool, all of our changes are incorporated, and failover should work as expected.

By calling the `pcp_detach_node` command on the primary server at port `9898`, pgpool removes the indicated node from the active list of available servers. If the server is the primary node, it automatically promotes the replica to act as the new primary. Our version of the failover script also shuts down the primary PostgreSQL server to prevent unpooled connections from making changes that won't be caught by the newly promoted server.

At this point, we can do anything to the PostgreSQL server, including upgrade of the PostgreSQL software to the latest bugfix for our current version. Later, we use `pcp_recovery_node` to tell pgpool that it should refresh node zero with a copy of the node currently serving as the primary server. If the command succeeds, we can reattach it to the pool by invoking `pcp_attach_node`.

There's more...

If pgpool doesn't seem to call our scripts, we may need to install the `pgpool_recovery` extension. Assuming that we still have the pgpool source available, follow these steps as a root-capable user to install the pgpool PostgreSQL extension library:

```
cd pgpool-II-3.3.2/sql/
make
sudo make install
```

Then, connect to the `template1` PostgreSQL database and install the `pgpool_recovery` extension with the following SQL query:

```
CREATE EXTENSION pgpool_recovery;
```

See also

- The steps in this recipe are particularly sensitive. If you require clarification not covered by this recipe, you can find the pgpool manual at `http://www.pgpool.net/docs/latest/pgpool-en.html`.

Combining the power of PgBouncer and pgpool

While pgpool works well as an abstraction layer above PostgreSQL, its handling of excess client connection attempts is less than ideal. If the maximum number of clients per pool was twenty, for instance, any connections over twenty with the same login credentials and target database will simply wait indefinitely. Further, there is no concept of transaction-level connection reuse.

PgBouncer can allow prospective client connections to number in the thousands and still maintain high throughput. We can also tell it to reuse connections after any client completes a transaction so that clients do not have to disconnect between operations. Yet, it cannot balance connections across multiple PostgreSQL servers, and it certainly has no concept of primary server or replica. In this respect, it really is a bouncer, holding users at the door with minimal knowledge of what's inside the building.

Until there's a product that combines the best elements of these two services, we can do so manually. This way, we get the best of both utilities, while still maintaining high availability and isolation of the PostgreSQL cluster from the outside world.

Getting ready

Install pgpool according to the instructions in the *Installing pgpool* recipe. Then, install pgbouncer according to the instructions in the *Installing PgBouncer* recipe. Then, configure both as described in the *Configuring pgpool for master/slave mode* and *Configuring PgBouncer safely* recipes.

With that done, we simply need to change a few configuration settings to gain full integration.

How to do it...

Assuming PgBouncer and pgpool are installed on the same node as the primary server at `192.168.56.10`, we can combine PgBouncer and pgpool with one change. Follow these steps:

1. Open the `/etc/pgbouncer/pgbouncer.ini` configuration file, and add the following line under the `[databases]` section:

   ```
   * = host=192.168.56.10 port=9999
   ```

2. Then, reload PgBouncer with the following command:

   ```
   sudo service pgbouncer reload
   ```

How it works...

We did much of the really hard work in all the previous installation and configuration instructions. By adding a single line in the `pgbouncer.ini` configuration file and reloading Pgbouncer, every connection to PgBouncer will automatically pass through pgpool as well.

We now have automatic server load balancing and robust connection pooling.

There's more...

When adding final touches to the configuration files, pay close attention to `default_pool_size` in `pgbouncer.ini` and `num_init_children` in `pgpool.conf`. Since pgpool doesn't like having more connections than `num_init_children`, no PgBouncer pool should exceed this number of connections. Thus, the value of `default_pool_size` added to `reserve_pool_size` should always be equal to or less than `num_init_children` in PgBouncer.

4 Troubleshooting

In this chapter, we will learn several techniques to track sources of poor performance or stop potential outages before they occur. We will cover the following recipes in this chapter:

- Performing triage
- Installing common statistics packages
- Evaluating the current disk performance with iostat
- Tracking I/O-heavy processes with iotop
- Viewing past performance with sar
- Correlating performance with dstat
- Interpreting /proc/meminfo
- Examining /proc/net/bonding/bond0
- Checking the pg_stat_activity view
- Checking the pg_stat_statements view
- Debugging with strace
- Logging checkpoints properly

Introduction

A DBA managing a highly available database server is charged with a huge responsibility. The amount of integration, speed of operations, and urgency behind resolving performance degradation can be extremely stressful. Some personalities thrive under this kind of pressure, while others will find it impossible to concentrate and will become paralyzed in fear.

We're not going to claim that every DBA in this position is a battle-weary veteran, typing furiously to save the day while disaster looms. This kind of scenario only exists in movies and often leads to compounding the original problem. In reality, a DBA's job includes many more calculated reactions even when managing a transaction-heavy database with frightfully low tolerance for downtime. The best tip we can give and the whole reason behind this book is to have an expansive bag of tricks.

For the purposes of this chapter, our bag is full of common Linux utilities useful for troubleshooting. With them, we approach system malfunctions like scientists. Given the behavior of the database or the underlying operating system, it is our job to produce a hypothesis for the cause. The tools serve as our instruments, ready to measure and sample, to either prove or disprove until we successfully isolate and address the problem.

With enough practice, we can begin to expect certain output, given PostgreSQL's behavior. Like a good mechanic who can diagnose an engine by its sound, we will hear the subtle tone of distress deep in the database cluster and have an answer. The first step towards this goal is to learn the tools.

Performing triage

When things go wrong or begin to look strange to an experienced eye, it is time to investigate. But where do we start?

Is the RAID running in parity mode, thereby drastically reducing the I/O throughput? Is the upstream switch saturated, robbing the database of bandwidth? Are we out of memory and swapping to disk or are we causing memory reclamation threads to terminate processes? Has the operating system task scheduler gotten overloaded and spiraled into oblivion?

Maybe! We've seen all of these scenarios and many more. We can't fix a problem that we are unable to locate. Any time that we spend analyzing an unlikely path is ultimately wasted, and it only increases downtime. We must take an inventory of the known symptoms and extrapolate this evidence into one or more avenues of investigation.

Anything less is simply guesswork.

Getting ready

We do not need a spreadsheet for this. A computer with a network connection should be enough to quickly rule out several possibilities. Enough practice will render this process second nature and some checks unnecessary.

How to do it...

When deciding how to analyze a possible system problem, consider the items in this checklist:

- Can `ping` reach the PostgreSQL server?
- Is it possible to use `ssh` to enter the server?
- Do simple commands such as `echo` immediately return a command prompt?
- Does `uptime` show the following:
  - A system load higher than the number of available CPUs
  - Whether the server has rebooted recently
- Can `psql` connect to PostgreSQL locally?
- Does the `free` command show the following:
  - Any swap space used?
  - Less free memory than used memory after accounting for cache?
- Does the `df` command indicate that the database storage is:
  - Present and accounted for?
  - Used below 95 percent?

How it works...

With the exclusion of `psql`, all of the commands we use in this checklist are present on almost every Unix system. They do nothing more than provide a very general idea of the system's health.

If we can ping a server, that doesn't mean it is running. The network service is one of the first things that the operating system starts and one of the last things it stops. The server can be stuck somewhere in its boot process or equally frozen in a shutdown. It does indicate, however, that something is available for further checks.

The next thing we try is to `ssh` to the server. If this command hangs indefinitely or returns with any kind of error, the server is effectively unusable. At this point, we would request the infrastructure or server administration departments to attempt to log in through the local console. Unfortunately, a failed `ssh` attempt often means that the server requires a manual reboot and further analysis. If we have a replication server, now would be a good time to use it until we have a diagnosis.

The next thing we will check is shell responsiveness. Commands such as `echo`, `ls`, or `cat` are frequently used and should return control immediately after completing. If there is a significant delay, it's also likely that we experienced a long delay after logging in to the server. This is usually caused by an overloaded CPU, but extremely high I/O can also result in intermittent lag.

We can check the CPU tangentially using the `uptime` command. Its output looks like this:

```
08:53:57 up 9 days, 4:07, 12 users, load average: 9.38, 8.01, 6.53
```

This particular system has been up for 9 days, indicating that it hasn't rebooted recently. If it had, this would be a sign that the system kernel might be at fault, since it can result in unexpected system crashes and reboots. The last three numbers indicate how stressed the CPU is at an average of 1, 5, and 15 minutes. If this server has only four CPUs, it is currently overloaded, and we should consider upgrading it.

If we use `psql` while we are logged in to the server locally, we don't have to contend with network overhead. If the server isn't running, we'll see output like this:

```
psql: could not connect to server: No such file or directory
      Is the server running locally and accepting
      connections on Unix domain socket "/tmp/.s.PGSQL.5432"?
```

Output like this would demand investigation, starting with the PostgreSQL logs. If we can connect, there are system views that we can analyze, which we will explain in the subsequent sections.

The `free` command is very inexpensive, and its output tells us a lot. For example:

```
              total     used      free   shared   buffers    cached
Mem:           2002     1559       443        0       153      1258
-/+ buffers/cache:       147      1855
Swap:          2043        0      2043
```

Invoked with the `-m` parameter, the `free` output is listed in megabytes. We can see that this system has 2 GB of RAM, and only 147 MB is used after we account for disk cache and buffers. We can also see that we are not using swap space. If the used column shows that more than 50 percent of the system memory is allocated or any swap is active, we don't have enough memory.

Finally, we use `df` to detail how much space we are using on our disks. Provided we know the source of the database storage, we can immediately see how much space is used. For example, this output suggests a problem:

```
Filesystem           Size  Used Avail Use% Mounted on
/dev/sda1             40G  5.6G 34.2G  14% /
/dev/sdc1              2T  1.9T   50M  97% /db
```

Invoked with the `-h` setting, the `df` output becomes *human readable* instead of a very large number of kilobytes. We can instantly see that our database mount is nearly full, and the amount of available space is so low that the database might actually be in danger.

There's more...

These types of *at a glance* commands are our first means of defense. We need quick methods, which do not require complex interpretation, to assess the server. Given that a problem exists, one or more of these tests should show abnormal results right away. If not, more advanced techniques are necessary. We will endeavor to describe as many of these as possible.

Installing common statistics packages

There are several common data-gathering tools, and each of them has its own place. Several are already installed for extremely basic information, but for the purposes of this chapter, we need more depth.

For instance, we may want to know the exact distribution of CPU resources, aggregate views of memory paging volume, or disk I/O utilization. For more in-depth needs, we could analyze specific processes for storage interaction or resource locks. If we weren't watching at the exact time a problem occurred, we might want a historical record of various server performance metrics.

In order to have all these capabilities, we must first install the requisite tools. We might find it quite shocking that these tools are not installed by default, considering their role in server administration.

Packages installed in this section will be referenced in all the subsequent sections, so please, don't skip this section!

Getting ready

Red Hat-based systems such as Fedora, RHEL, CentOS, and Scientific Linux have a prerequisite package that is not part of the included distribution repositories. To install one of our statistic tools, we need to add the **RepoForge** library. Red Hat systems can do this by obtaining the most recent RepoForge package for their OS version and architecture at `http://repoforge.org/use/`.

Once the package is downloaded, it can be installed with this command as a root-level user:

```
sudo rpm -ivh rpmforge-release-*.rpm
```

How to do it...

Debian, Mint, or Ubuntu users can install the tools by executing this command as a root-level user:

```
sudo apt-get install dstat iotop sysstat
```

Red Hat, Fedora, CentOS, and Scientific Linux users can install the tools by executing this command as a root-level user:

```
sudo yum install dstat iotop sysstat
```

How it works...

Red-Hat-based systems do require a bit of preparation. However, Debian-based distributions have all the necessary elements from the beginning. Once the software sources are accounted for, the only command we need installs all three statistics and monitoring tools simultaneously.

See also

As Red-Hat-based systems require extra work, we've listed two links that provide more information on installing RepoForge on these systems:

- **RepoForge**: `http://repoforge.org/`
- **CentOS—installing RPMforge**: `http://wiki.centos.org/AdditionalResources/Repositories/RPMForge`

Evaluating the current disk performance with iostat

Due to the disparity in speed between storage and RAM, one of the first signs of distress that a DBA will observe is directly related to disk utilization. A badly written query, an unexpected batch-loading process, a forced checkpoint, overwhelmed write caches—the number of things that can ruin disk performance is vast.

The first step in tracking down the culprit(s) is to visualize the activity. The `iostat` utility is fairly coarse in that it does not operate at the process level. However, it does output storage activity by device and includes columns such as reads or writes per second, the size of the request queue, and how busy it is compared to its maximum throughput.

This allows us to see the devices that are actually slow, busy, or overworked. Furthermore, we can combine this information with other methods of analysis to find the activity's source. For now, let's explore the tool itself.

Getting ready

As `iostat` is part of the `sysstat` package, we should ensure that the statistics-gathering elements are enabled. Debian, Mint, and Ubuntu users should modify the `/etc/default/sysstat` file and make sure that the `ENABLED` variable resembles this line:

```
ENABLED="true"
```

Red Hat, Fedora, CentOS, and Scientific Linux users should make sure that the `SADC_OPTIONS` variable in `/etc/sysconfig/sysstat` is set to the following:

```
SADC_OPTIONS="-d"
```

Once these changes are complete, restart the `sysstat` service with this command as a root-level user:

```
sudo service sysstat restart
```

How to do it...

Leverage some sample `iostat` output by following these steps:

1. Obtain the statistics of the disk activity every second, with this command:

   ```
   iostat -d 1
   ```

2. Show 10 seconds of disk activity in megabytes per second with this command:

   ```
   iostat -dm 1 10
   ```

3. Show extended disk activity in megabytes per second for the `sda` device with this command:

   ```
   iostat -dmx sda 1
   ```

How it works...

The `iostat` utility has a rather unique method of interpreting command-line arguments. If no recognized disks are part of the command, it simply shows information about all of them. After devices, it checks for timing statistics. To get a second-by-second status, we specify 1 second as the final argument. By providing the `-d` argument, we remove CPU utilization from the report.

The default output rate of `iostat` is in kilobytes per second. Current hardware is often so fast that these results can be almost too high to easily compare, so we set the `-m` parameter in the second command to change the output to megabytes per second. We also take advantage of the fact that the last two parameters are related to timing. The first parameter specifies the interval, and the second is the number of samples. So, the second command takes 10 samples at the rate of one per second.

The last command adds two more elements. First, we place a disk device (`sda`) before the timing interval. We can list as many devices as we want, and `iostat` will restrict the output to not include any other devices. This is especially helpful in servers that can have dozens of disk devices, thus making it hard to isolate potential performance issues. Then, we include the `-x` argument, which lists extended statistics.

Without extended statistics, the output is not very useful. For example, watching the `sda` device for 1 second will normally look like this:

```
Device:       tps    kB_read/s    kB_wrtn/s    kB_read    kB_wrtn
sda        806.59      3147.25      4742.86       5728       8632
```

The last two columns only list the cumulative activity for the sampling interval. This is of limited use. However, the first three columns display the number of **transactions per second** (**tps**) and how much data was either read from or written to that device per second. Depending on the hardware we purchased, we might actually know its limits regarding these measurements, so we have a basic idea of how busy it might be.

If we enable extended statistics with the `-x` argument, we gain several extra fields, including the following:

- `r/s`: This column lists the number of reads per second from the device. This was previously aggregated into the `tps` field.
- `w/s`: This column shows the number of writes per second to the device. This was previously aggregated into the `tps` field.
- `avgqu-sz`: This column describes the amount of requests in the disk's queue. If this gets very large, the disk will have trouble keeping up with requests.
- `await`: This column outlines the average time a request spends waiting in the queue and being serviced, in milliseconds. An overloaded disk will often have a very high value in this column as it is unable to keep up with requests.
- `r_await`: This column details the average time read requests spend waiting in the queue and being serviced, in milliseconds. This helps isolate whether or not the read activity is overloading the disk.
- `w_await`: This column depicts the average time write requests spend waiting in the queue and being serviced, in milliseconds. This helps isolate whether or not the write activity is overloading the disk.
- `%util`: This column represents the percentage of time the device was busy servicing I/O requests. This is actually a function of the queue size and the average time waiting in the queue. It is also one of, if not the most important, metrics. If this is at or near 100 percent for long periods of time, we need to start analyzing the sources of I/O requests and think about upgrading our storage.

There's more...

Our examples of iostat always include the -d argument to only show disk information. By default, it shows both CPU and disk measurements. The CPU data looks like this:

```
avg-cpu:  %user   %nice %system %iowait  %steal   %idle
           9.38    0.00   16.67   11.46    0.00   62.50
```

This can be useful for analysis as well, though there are several other tools that also provide this data. If we use the -c parameter instead of -d, we will see only the CPU statistics, and no information about disk devices will be included in the output.

See also

- Always examine the manual for the tools that we use in these recipes. In this case, the manual for iostat is available by executing this command:

  ```
  man iostat
  ```

Tracking I/O-heavy processes with iotop

Many DBAs and system administrators are familiar with the top command, which displays the processes that use the most CPU or RAM. However, this does not help us find the processes that cause high amounts of system I/O.

Fortunately, there is a command, much like top, that is designed specifically for displaying the processes that make storage requests. The iotop utility displays a continuously updated list of the processes and any I/O they are handling. Provided that the server is dedicated to PostgreSQL, we can use this information to almost instantly identify one or more database backends that make disk requests.

Just like top, processes are only sorted to the head of the list as long as their I/O continues to limit its long-term usefulness. Let's learn more about iotop and see if we can benefit from its functionality.

Getting ready

The iotop command can only be executed by root-level users, as it uses some kernel resources available only to superusers. Be ready with the sudo command!

How to do it...

Follow these steps to obtain a sample output from the `iotop` command:

1. Enter interactive mode with this command (exit by pressing *q*):

   ```
   sudo iotop
   ```

2. Obtain batch output for 10 seconds with this command:

   ```
   sudo iotop -b -n 10
   ```

3. Restrict batch output to only active processes, include a timestamp, and suppress the headers with this command:

   ```
   sudo iotop -bot -qqq
   ```

How it works...

While it may be somewhat inconvenient to need superuser access to invoke `iotop`, we're willing to make that sacrifice in this case. Our first command simply starts `iotop` like we would use `top` interactively. We can sort the output into different columns with the arrow keys, reverse the sort order by pressing the *r* key, and quit by pressing *q*. Of the columns presented here, we may be interested in the following:

- `TID`: This column provides the **PID** of the process that makes I/O requests. This can be used to investigate or terminate the program.
- `DISK READ`: This column illustrates the number of bytes read per second by the listed process.
- `DISK WRITE`: This column details the number of bytes written per second by the listed process.
- `IO`: This column shows the percentage of time that the listed process spent issuing I/O requests.
- `COMMAND`: This column depicts the name of the process that handles I/O. If this is a master process, it might include command-line switches as well.

While this kind of use is informative for live troubleshooting, it's less applicable for historical applications. Thus, for the second command, we add the `-b` argument to put `iotop` in batch mode. This means that all the output is simply printed to the screen, which we can redirect to a file if desired. In addition, we used the `-n` parameter to only obtain 10 readings—one for each second—for later analysis.

Readers working along by trying these examples might notice that the amount of output in batch mode is overwhelming. By default, `iotop` lists every process it can see, whether or not it is actually utilizing disk resources. We can stop this behavior with the `-o` parameter, so only active processes are included in any output. By adding the `-t` argument, we also gain a timestamp that we can use to correlate disk activity across data-gathering techniques.

The -q argument acts to suppress excessive iotop output. By specifying it once, iotop only includes the column labels at the top of the output. If you specify it twice, it will never include the column labels. If you specify it a third time, it will also remove the summary data that iotop normally prints after every iteration. This type of output is ideal for importing into reporting tools or even analyzing by hand by searching for interesting time periods.

There's more...

While the iotop data is not actually part of the statistics gathered automatically by the sysstat package, we can log the data for posterity anyway. Follow these steps as a root-level user to log the iostat data:

1. Create a file named iotop at /etc/cron.d/ and fill it with this line:

   ```
   * * * * * root iotop -boat -qqq -d 5 -n 2 >> /var/log/iotop
   ```

2. Reload the configuration files of the cron service with this command:

   ```
   sudo service cron reload
   ```

By adding the -a parameter, iotop will log the cumulative total of the I/O used between the readings, instead of the I/O per second. We use the -d argument to add a 5 second delay between two readings, as specified by the -n parameter. Together, this means that we get a 5 second sample logged to /var/log/iotop every minute.

See also

- Always examine the manual for the tools that we use in these recipes. In this case, the manual for iotop is available by executing this command:

  ```
  man iotop
  ```

Viewing past performance with sar

While there are many tools to view or analyze the current server performance and behavior, how do we examine historical activity? Most Linux systems rotate logfiles in /var/log for varying periods of time. Unfortunately, these are programs and system logs, not performance measurements.

When we installed the sysstat package in a previous recipe, we gained the use of the sar utility. Some argue that sar is the Swiss Army knife of metric collection. A simple invocation can display past data regarding memory, CPUs, IRQs, disk devices, networks, or even TTYs.

When administering a highly available server, there are a few things as helpful as performance trends. Let's examine them.

Getting ready

As `sar` and `iostat` are both part of the `sysstat` package, we recommend that you review the *Evaluating the current disk performance with iostat* recipe before continuing.

How to do it...

Collect some sample `sar` data by following these steps:

1. Display the default `sar` output with the following command:

   ```
   sar
   ```

2. Show the disk device status every 5 seconds with this command:

   ```
   sar -d 5
   ```

3. View memory usage between 4:00 A.M. and 6:00 A.M. today with this command:

   ```
   sar -r -s 04:00:00 -e 06:00:00
   ```

Examine the I/O statistics for any existing past dates by following these steps:

1. Find the appropriate `sysstat` log directory:
   - Red Hat, Fedora, CentOS, and Scientific Linux should use the `/var/log/sa` directory
   - Debian, Mint, and Ubuntu users should use the `/var/log/sysstat` directory
2. List the contents of that directory and choose a file. Files are simply binary formats containing `sar` data for each retained date. Files are prefixed with `sa`. Thus, `sa23` is the `sar` data for the 23rd of the month.
3. Execute the following command to view past I/O statistics for the 3rd of the month:

   ```
   sar -f /var/log/sysstat/sa03 -b
   ```

How it works...

By default, `sar` operates in CPU mode. Simply using the command as named, we will receive CPU activity samples for every 10 minutes of the current day. Once `sar` produces this output, it exits. If we want the current data, we must invoke it much like we did with `iostat`.

In our second example, we've chosen to emulate the `iostat` output by providing a summary of disk activity every 5 seconds until we cancel the command. The `-d` argument tells `sar` to display the disk statistics. Just like `iostat`, `sar` accepts two optional parameters for interval and count. As we didn't specify a count, `sar` will print disk performance every 5 seconds.

The third example is where we finally begin leveraging the real power of `sar`. If we had examined our PostgreSQL log and noticed a large amount of idle queries between 4:00 A.M. and 6:00 A.M., we would need a method to obtain data for that time period. Well, `sar` has one argument (`-s`) to specify the start time of a data extract and another (`-e`) to set the end time. These parameters must be written in `HH:MM:SS` format, or `sar` will ignore them with an error. We also elected to use the `-r` argument to display memory usage data, just to illustrate another metric that `sar` can expose.

Our final example depends entirely on what Linux distribution we're using. Unfortunately, each stores its collected `sar` data in different areas within `/var/log`. With that said, the directory assigned to `sysstat` for data storage keeps a default of 7 days worth of historical information for analysis.

Everyday, this data is collected in a file prefixed with `sa` and suffixed with the current month's day. On weeks that span 2 months, the count simply restarts with 01. Once again, we use a different output mode for `sar` and display the I/O activity.

There's more...

Seven days may not be enough for some administrators. To increase this amount, modify `/etc/sysconfig/sysstat` or `/etc/sysstat/sysstat` and change the `HISTORY` setting to the desired amount of days to retain data. For example, to keep 3 weeks of records, we could use this:

```
HISTORY=30
```

See also

- Always examine the manual for the tools that we use in these recipes. In this case, the manual for `sar` is available by executing this command:

  `man sar`

This is especially true for `sar`, as it has so many different operating modes and display formats.

Correlating performance with dstat

Eventually, we will want to view multiple types of system activity simultaneously. While `sar` has many operating modes, its output is linear. Without a tool to interpret its exhaustive data, we are left with a lot of manual analysis of several `sar` invocations. While `iostat` and `iotop` are wonderful tools, they are rather limited in scope by comparison.

So, let us introduce `dstat`. While `dstat` can't access historical data like `sar`, it can display output from several different operation modes side by side. It also includes color coding to easily distinguish units. It's a very pretty command-line tool and summarizes several different metrics at a glance.

For servers that are of particular importance, we actually keep a terminal window that displays the `dstat` results open so that we get an early warning when numbers begin to look bad.

Getting ready

Unlike the `sysstat` package, `dstat` is ready to use immediately after being installed.

How to do it...

The output from `dstat` is very colorful. Obtain a few samples with these steps:

1. Display default information with this command:

   ```
   dstat
   ```

2. Display only system load and network activity with this command:

   ```
   dstat -n -l
   ```

3. Display CPU usage, I/O, and disk utilization averaged over 5 second intervals with this command:

   ```
   dstat -c -r --disk-util 5
   ```

4. For the next 10 seconds, display the time, memory usage, interrupts and context switches, disk activity from only the `sda` device, and the process using the most I/O. In addition, capture the results to a `csv` file, all with this command:

   ```
   dstat -tmyd -D sda --top-io --output /tmp/stats.csv 1 10
   ```

How it works...

We hope it's obvious by now that the number of combinations available for the `dstat` output is effectively infinite. By default, the `dstat` output resembles this:

```
----total-cpu-usage---- -dsk/total- -net/total- ---paging-- ---system--
usr sys idl wai hiq siq| read  writ| recv  send|  in   out | int   csw
  4   2  91   2       1|  92   341 |           |           | 150  1011
  8  15      72       5|2328  1112 |  32   815 |           | 844  1865
  9  15   1  68       7|2696  1232 |  34   879 |           | 896  2020
  7  14   2  69       7|2344  1184 |  30   929 |           | 814  1950
  7  19      67       7|2464  1264 |  32  1009 |           | 847  2057
  7  16   3  68       6|3480  1456 |  37  1151 |           | 958  2410
```

The default output from `dstat` enables CPU, disk, network, memory paging, and system modules. In this particular example, we can see that the `wai` column is extremely high, suggesting that the server is currently I/O bound.

Another interesting thing about `dstat` is that it really only displays the exact modules we request. For the second example, the output becomes this:

```
-net/total- ---load-avg---
 recv  send| 1m   5m  15m 
           |0.31 0.14 0.15
  36   962 |0.53 0.18 0.17
  34   884 |0.53 0.18 0.17
  36   954 |0.53 0.18 0.17
  31   906 |0.53 0.18 0.17
  40  1092 |0.53 0.18 0.17
```

In this second example, we've only enabled the network (`-n`) and system load (`-l`) modules, thus extremely reducing the output width. Yet, at the same time, this sparse format makes it very easy to combine several different metrics without absurdly wide terminal windows.

The third sample begins using `dstat` plugins. By activating the `--disk-util` argument, `dstat` will show the utilization percentage for all active storage devices. This is in addition to the CPU stats (`-c`) and I/O (`-r`) that we already activated.

By adding the last parameter (`5`), we again take advantage of a common trend for system view utilities. The last two optional parameters are for sample interval and count. In the case of `dstat`, any number printed while the interval is greater than one is actually the average of all the metrics collected during that time period. So, for our third example, these numbers are all 5 second cumulative averages. For posterity, the output looks like this:

```
----total-cpu-usage---- --io/total- sda-
usr sys idl wai hiq siq| read  writ|util
  3   2  92   2       1|6.77  31.8 |5.96
  3  14   2  77       4| 174   176 |97.5
  3  14   2  77       3| 152   179 |96.8
  2  15   6  73       3| 137   184 |97.5
  3  17   3  74       4| 132   199 |98.2
```

This may be difficult to see, but the last line in this output is not bold like the rest. This means that this particular line had not yet reached the requested interval of 5 seconds. It's not an important detail, but it shows just how much attention the `dstat` developers paid to convey information visually. We easily see a high percentage of CPU waits, and the `sda` device is utilized over 90 percent by the read and write activity. It looks like a visual presentation works pretty well.

For our fourth and final example, we try to include as many separate types of data as possible. At the beginning, we enable the `-t`, `-m`, `-y`, and `-d` switches. This adds timestamp, memory performance, interrupts and context switches, and device activity to the `dstat` output. We also take advantage of the `-D` parameter to limit disk statistics to the `sda` device. Default disk statistics are inclusive, but now, we can actually restrict the output to interesting devices.

Next, we add `--top-io` to list the process that's using the most I/O while `dstat` runs. Earlier, we needed `iotop` to get that data. Of course, `iotop` provides more depth and lists more than one culprit, but for quick identification, it's hard to beat `dstat`. Then, we use the `--output` parameter to send the `csv` output to `/tmp/stats.csv` so that we can potentially use a spreadsheet program to analyze or graph the data we gathered.

Finally, we take advantage of both the interval and count parameters so that we capture only 10 seconds of statistics. For all of that work, we're rewarded with this output:

```
----system---- ------memory-usage----- ---system-- --dsk/sda-- ----most-expensive----
     time     | used  buff  cach  free| int   csw | read  writ|     i/o process
26-01 17:56:57|82.6  1856   138  1780 | 113   662 | 101   241 |bash          1663   749
26-01 17:56:58|82.5  1856   143  1775 |1085  1477 |3136  1520 |pgbench         16    16
26-01 17:56:59|82.5  1856   148  1771 |1054  1389 |2512  1480 |pgbench         18    18
26-01 17:57:00|82.5  1864   152  1767 | 893  1153 |2096  1400 |pgbench         14    14
26-01 17:57:01|82.5  1872   154  1765 | 574   783 |1152   760 |pgbench         11    11
26-01 17:57:02|82.5  1872   159  1759 |1203  1597 |3096  1688 |pgbench         20    20
```

Oh! It looks like all of the I/O and load we saw earlier was due to a `pgbench` test. How embarrassing!

See also

- Always examine the manual for the tools that we use in these recipes. In this case, the manual for `dstat` is available by executing this command:

  `man dstat`

Interpreting /proc/meminfo

Administrators familiar with the Linux `/proc` filesystem know that it a valuable source for both device status and performance information. The `meminfo` entry in this directory will always provide copious data regarding the status, contents, and state of the memory in our server.

We care about this as DBAs because file cache and write buffering can drastically affect disk I/O. We are not especially interested in analyzing PostgreSQL's memory usage itself. At the time of writing this book, current recommendations suggest that PostgreSQL's performance doesn't really improve after shared buffers reach 8 GB. However, for client connections, inode caches, and dirty page flushing, it's more than relevant.

On a modern Linux kernel, there are over 40 different lines of information in `/proc/meminfo`. Much of this data is not exceptionally useful to a DBA, so this recipe will focus on important fields only.

Getting ready

We will be using the `watch` and `grep` commands in this recipe. It will be a good idea to experiment with them and, perhaps, skim the `man` pages before continuing.

How to do it...

Follow these steps to capture an interesting memory status from `/proc/meminfo`:

1. Obtain basic memory states with the following command:

   ```
   grep -A3 MemTotal /proc/meminfo
   ```

2. Execute this command to extract dirty memory buffers and pending writes:

   ```
   grep -A1 Dirty /proc/meminfo
   ```

3. View the state of various memory caches with the following command:

   ```
   grep -A1 Active /proc/meminfo
   ```

4. Show swap usage with the following command:

   ```
   grep Swap /proc/meminfo
   ```

How it works...

The first command we execute is nothing but a basic summary of the current memory state. For a test system with 2 GB of RAM running PostgreSQL, it would resemble this:

```
MemTotal:         2050908 kB
MemFree:           840088 kB
Buffers:             9288 kB
Cached:           1102228 kB
```

This output is similar to what we would learn using the `free` command. The `MemTotal` row should speak for itself, as it is the total size of the memory in the system. The `MemFree` row is the total amount of completely unallocated system memory, including buffers or cache. The `Buffers` row in this context is mostly related to internal kernel bookkeeping, so we can ignore it. If we examine the value reported by the `Cached` row, we can see that over 1 GB of data is cached in memory.

The second command outlines dirty memory. Dirty memory, in this case, is the memory that is modified and awaiting synchronization to disk. On the same 2 GB test system, a long `pgbench` test might produce results like this:

```
Dirty:                29184 kB
Writeback:               40 kB
```

As we've said, the `Dirty` row details how much memory is waiting to be written to disk. On systems with very large amounts of RAM, this value can indicate that too much RAM is dirty. The consequences of this can include long query execution times or system stalls if the underlying storage is unable to quickly absorb that many disk writes. In practice, this should rarely be larger than the size of the disk controller's write cache.

However, what about the `Writeback` row? This field details how much of the dirty memory is currently being written to disk. When storage is overwhelmed, the amount reflected here will rise, as the write-back buffer fills with more write requests. This is a definite sign that the system has encountered far more writes than it was designed to handle. In this essence, each of these fields is a warning sign that the application must be modified to reduce write workload or the database needs faster storage with a bigger write cache.

With our next command, we examine the contents of the cache itself. Still using our 2 GB test system, the cache looks like this:

```
Active:             1105760 kB
Inactive:             32764 kB
Active(anon):        207696 kB
Inactive(anon):        9340 kB
Active(file):        898064 kB
Inactive(file):       23424 kB
```

We won't get into too much detail regarding how the kernel actually works, but we will note that all the fields named `Inactive` are something of a misnomer. Any time something is loaded into cache, it first gets included in the `Inactive` list. Based on the subsequent amount and timing of requests for this data, it might be promoted into the `Active` set. Once it is in that list, various aging algorithms might eventually return it to the inactive list. Inactive cache data is always a candidate for replacement by more important data.

In the context of PostgreSQL, we need to pay attention to the `Active(file)` entry. This is the amount of disk pages in cache. Disk reads are expensive, and as databases process data from disk, this is very important to us. We want as many disk pages as possible to be in the `Active(file)` list, but this doesn't mean we discount `Inactive(file)`. Remember, inactive cache is still in memory and eligible for database use; it simply hasn't been promoted to the active list. Thus, we want the total amount of file cache to be as high as possible, reflecting the prioritization of disk reads for database processing.

We include `Active(anon)` and `Inactive(anon)` for one reason: database clients. Temporary data allocated to database clients is often assigned to anonymous cache. This is good for the client program, but with enough of these, we lose valuable memory from use as disk cache. One remedy for this is to buy more memory, but another more scalable solution is to utilize database connection pooling. This book includes a chapter specifically dedicated to optimizing the connection count, as this helps preserve memory for data caching.

The last extract we obtain from `/proc/meminfo` is related to swap usage and looks like this:

```
SwapCached:              0 kB
SwapTotal:         2093052 kB
SwapFree:          2093052 kB
```

Again, we can get this kind of data using the `free` command as well. We mainly include it here in case any readers want to search for all of these fields with a single command for monitoring purposes.

There's more...

The `watch` utility will execute any command and its arguments until it is canceled with *Ctrl* + *C*. Instead of using those `grep` statements every time we want to see interesting fields in the `/proc/meminfo` file, we can simply use `watch`. For example, to observe the state of dirty buffers waiting to be committed to disk, we can use the following command:

```
watch -n 5 grep -A1 Dirty /proc/meminfo
```

See also

The Linux kernel documentation is somewhat verbose. Nonetheless, more technically apt readers can find much more information regarding `/proc/meminfo` at `https://www.kernel.org/doc/Documentation/filesystems/proc.txt`.

Examining /proc/net/bonding/bond0

Highly available databases often come in pairs for redundancy purposes. These servers can have any number of procedures to keep the data synchronized, and this book suggests direct connections when possible. Direct connections between servers ensure fast communication between redundant servers, and it resembles the following network design:

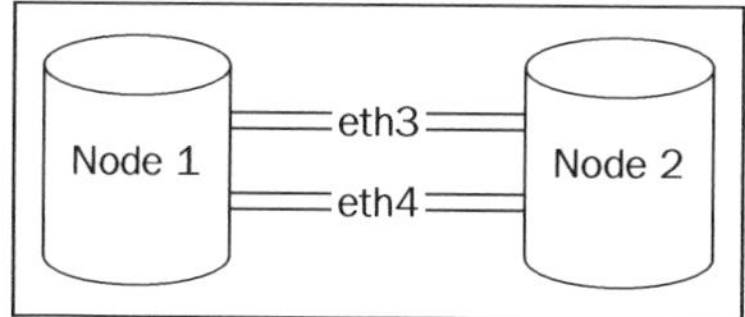

In some cases, it can be advantageous to connect the database servers to a general network fabric. Depending on the interaction of the upstream network devices, this can significantly increase the network packet's **round-trip-time** (**RTT**). This is usually fine for PostgreSQL replication, but OLTP systems may be more sensitive. Block-level replication systems, such as DRBD, which operate beneath the filesystem, fare even worse.

Each of our database servers should be equipped with at least two independent network interfaces. In order to prevent downtime, these interfaces must be linked with a bond. Network bonds act as an abstract layer that can route traffic over either interface, and like many kernel-level services, bond status can be checked via the Linux `/proc` filesystem.

The health and current communication channel of the server network bond is surprisingly relevant to throughput. In order to rule out potential delays caused by upstream network hardware, we need to understand how the bond is operating.

Getting ready

As we are going to examine the network bond on two paired PostgreSQL servers, connect to each before continuing. We don't need any special permissions or attributes for this recipe.

How to do it...

In order to check the status of the network bond, follow these steps:

1. Determine the current bonding method by executing this command:

   ```
   grep Mode /proc/net/bonding/bond0
   ```

2. Check the currently active interface with this command:

   ```
   grep Active /proc/net/bonding/bond0
   ```

How it works...

Surprised that it's so simple? Don't be. Much like `/proc/meminfo` and `/proc/cpuinfo`, the difficulty is not in obtaining the information we need, but in interpreting it. The first thing that concerns us is the bond mode. There are several modes, but only one is relevant to us for a dual-failover configuration. The mode should reflect some kind of an `active-backup` status; otherwise, it's combining the interfaces for bandwidth and throughput purposes. The line we want looks like this:

```
Bonding Mode: fault-tolerance (active-backup)
```

Next, we check the currently active interface. If the system was configured so that the network bond is in `active-backup` mode, only one is active at any one time. The other serves act as a backup in case the network connection or the interface itself fails. In an ideal situation, similar interfaces on both servers—`eth3`, for instance—are attached to the same switch. If not, we should talk to our network and server administrators to correct the setup.

We suggest that you use the same interface name on both the servers for one simple reason: it's difficult to diagnose network routes on bonded interfaces. For best throughput and RTT, our network should look like this:

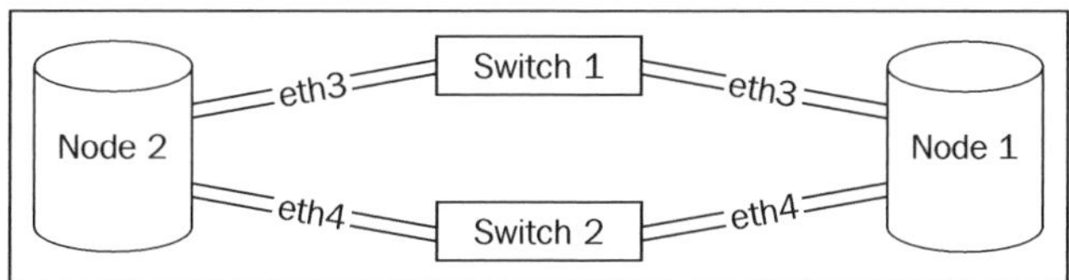

We hope it's clear from the diagram that this architecture introduces a possible source of network lag. As the servers cannot transfer data to each other directly, at least one extra switch that increases the RTT is involved. As our servers hopefully have two network interfaces, each server is communicating with the same two switches. However, if each server is currently working through a different switch, this actually adds at least two more jumps, as the switches must communicate with an upstream router. If we follow the dotted path, that unfortunate situation looks like this:

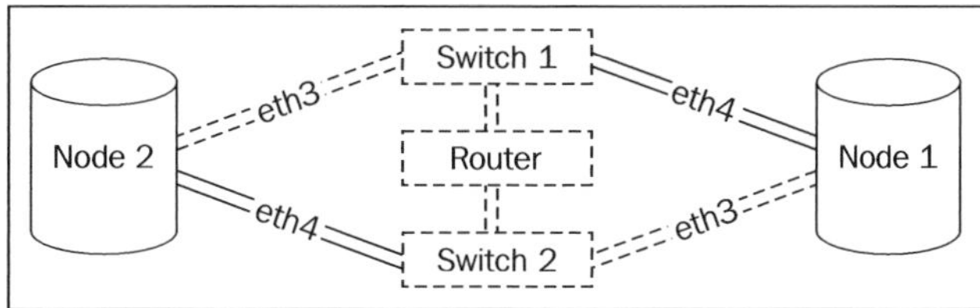

We've seen this increase `ping` time from 0.03 ms to 0.3 ms. This may not seem like much, but when the network RTT is 10 times slower, replication and monitoring can suffer significantly. This is one of the few obscure troubleshooting techniques that can elude even experienced network administrators. Armed with this, we should be able to diagnose replication and idle-wait problems using nothing more than `grep`.

See also

- By their nature, networks are standardized to encourage intercommunication. As a result of this, link aggregation (bonding) is available on Wikipedia as a standard term. If you want to learn more about how it works, please visit the longer explanation on Wikipedia at `http://en.wikipedia.org/wiki/Link_aggregation`.

Checking the pg_stat_activity view

Another source of valuable troubleshooting information is PostgreSQL itself. There are numerous views, tables, and functions dedicated to tracking and reporting various statistics and operating statuses for each hosted database. Principal among these is the `pg_stat_activity` view.

This view tells us what every database client is doing, where it is connected from, which user account it is operating under, and other important values. When administering a highly available database, we must either have an iron control over what executes in the database or the ability to quickly and easily assess its execution state. Besides using this data to track suspicious activity, we can also cancel long-running queries or Cartesian Products, or simply examine the connection turnover.

We probably use this view into the database more than any other, and it forms the backbone of several monitoring utilities as well. Let's explore just why this system catalog is so indispensable.

Getting ready

While any user can view the contents of the `pg_stat_activity` view, only a superuser can freely examine the contents of every column. To avoid security exploits, regular users cannot view the current query activity, any connection information, or fields related to query time or status.

To get the most out of this view safely, we want to grant elevated privileges to specific users dedicated to monitoring and status checks. In order to do this, we must first connect to the database as a superuser (such as the `postgres` user) for the duration of this recipe.

How to do it...

Perform the following steps to prepare `pg_stat_activity` for generalized use:

1. Execute this SQL statement as a database superuser to create a function:

   ```
   CREATE OR REPLACE FUNCTION pg_stat_activity()
   RETURNS SETOF pg_stat_activity AS $$
       SELECT * FROM pg_stat_activity;
   $$ LANGUAGE sql SECURITY DEFINER;
   ```

2. Execute this SQL statement to secure the function we created:

   ```
   REVOKE ALL ON FUNCTION pg_stat_activity() FROM PUBLIC;
   ```

3. Create a user dedicated to monitoring with this SQL statement:

   ```
   CREATE USER db_mon WITH PASSWORD 'somepass';
   ```

4. Grant the monitoring user the ability to use our function with this SQL statement:

```
GRANT EXECUTE ON FUNCTION pg_stat_activity() TO db_mon;
```

Now, connect to PostgreSQL as the `db_mon` user and examine the contents of `pg_stat_activity` by executing this SQL query:

```
SELECT * FROM pg_stat_activity();
```

How it works...

The `pg_stat_activity` view is a wealth of information for a database administrator. However, it is all but useless for monitoring due to the security measures that encumber it. However, these fields are obfuscated specifically to prevent system compromises and data leaks. So, our entire goal is to prevent abusing the view while still loosening the security.

The first step we take is to create a function that is capable of returning a set of rows similar to the `pg_stat_activity` view itself. The `SETOF` modifier tells PostgreSQL that our function does exactly that. It's no coincidence that the body of our function is merely a `SELECT` statement on the `pg_stat_activity` view.

Why did we use a function to abstract the view? After all, it seems excessive to create a whole function for such a simple statement. The answer is in the `SECURITY DEFINER` function modifier that we added; it allows the function to execute as the user that created it. Thus, if we create the function as the `postgres` user, it runs as if the `postgres` user invoked it. As the `postgres` user is a superuser, the function can see all of the hidden columns, no matter who runs the function.

By default, all new functions are available to all users. However, this function executes as a superuser, and we don't want just anyone to execute it and see what everyone else is doing. So, we revoke all permissions from the `PUBLIC` context. At this point, only a superuser can call our function.

As we want to be able to monitor database status values, we create a user for this very purpose. We named our user `db_mon`, but any user name works just as well. As long as it has a secure password or is only used locally, our security exposure is minimal. Then, we grant `EXECUTE` privileges on the `pg_stat_activity` function, and our work is complete. The `db_mon` user can now view all user queries. We can also grant `EXECUTE` to other DBAs or support staff who may need it.

What data is available? Important fields include, but are not limited to, the following:

- `pid` or `procpid`: In versions of PostgreSQL 9.2 and above, this field is named `pid`; all older versions use `procpid`. This tells us that the process ID assigned to the backend server process by the operating system is extremely valuable for debugging or connection-management purposes.
- `username`: This displays the name of the user who owns this connection.

- `backend_start`: This provides the date and time when the connection was established.
- `xact_start`: This tracks the date and time when the current transaction started, if any.
- `query_start`: This reports the date and time of the last query submitted.
- `waiting`: This tells us whether or not the connection is currently blocked by something and will show either `t` for true or `f` for false.
- `state`: In versions of PostgreSQL 9.2 and above, this column reports the current state of the connection. States marked as `active` are executing a query; the `idle` ones are not. If a connection is marked `idle in a transaction`, look carefully at the `query_start` and `xact_start` fields for excessive delays. If a connection was in a transaction and encountered an error, it will report `idle in the transaction (aborted)`; applications should catch errors and either roll back the transaction or disconnect, so `idle` aborted transactions are a possible source of trouble. Unfortunately, this field does not exist in older versions, so a certain context is lost during investigation.
- `query`: In versions of PostgreSQL 9.1 and above, this column contains most or all of the last known query this connection executed. This field does not exist in older versions.
- `current_query`: In versions of PostgreSQL 9.1 and below, this column contains most or the entire last known query that this connection executed. In newer versions, this field was split into the `state` and `query` fields to provide better insight into the connection activity during transactions.

There's more...

Mind the version! PostgreSQL versions below 9.2 do not have the `state` or `query` fields and supply only the `current_query` column. While it might be tempting to use `query` and `current_query` interchangeably, older PostgreSQL versions are strictly at a disadvantage.

In PostgreSQL 9.1 and below, queries are only reflected in the `pg_stat_activity` view while they are actually executing. As soon as the query finishes, the `current_query` column will be empty or report `idle in transaction` if the query was part of a transaction. This means we lose a lot of operating context unless we just happened to be logging every database query.

On very high-volume OLTP systems, recording every query is not feasible. We've personally administered databases that handle over 1 billion queries per day, at a rate of 60,000 per second. Even with a conservative query length of 50 characters, we would produce over 50 GB of logs every day.

Troubleshooting stuck, idle, or otherwise faulty connections is much easier in the newer versions of PostgreSQL. If at all possible, upgrade to 9.2 or above.

See also

- PostgreSQL has extremely informative documentation regarding how it collects and maintains statistics. The `pg_stat_activity` view is described in more depth there, so take a look at `http://www.postgresql.org/docs/9.3/static/monitoring-stats.html`.

Checking the pg_stat_statements view

We mentioned in another recipe that logging every query on a highly available database that handles high volumes of query traffic is undesirable. DBAs often solve this problem by only logging slow queries by setting `log_min_duration_statement` to a reasonable number of milliseconds in `postgresql.conf`. Later, only queries that cross this threshold are logged, along with binding parameters if the query was a prepared statement.

We strongly encourage this practice, as it is invaluable for catching outlying queries that could benefit from optimization. Unfortunately, faster queries are still invisible to us. Worse, queries that execute often probably have their data sources cached in memory, so it's unlikely that they contribute to I/O. The database could be executing an inefficient or redundant query thousands of times per second, and besides an elevated server load, we would never know.

This situation is not conducive to long-term viability of a highly available database. Phantom queries like this don't simply gorge on valuable CPU resources; they can multiply unseen until the combined load requires more expensive hardware or the database buckles under the stress.

However, PostgreSQL can see everything, and now, so can we, with `pg_stat_statements`.

Getting ready

Activating and using this extension requires us to modify the `postgresql.conf` configuration file and restart PostgreSQL. As usual, we need to ensure that we have access to a PostgreSQL superuser and a user capable of restarting the service, such as the `postgres` or `root` system users.

How to do it...

Begin by installing the `pg_stat_statements` module. Follow these steps:

1. Modify the `shared_preload_libraries` line in `postgresql.conf` to include the module:

   ```
   shared_preload_libraries = 'pg_stat_statements'
   ```

2. If you are using PostgreSQL 9.1 or older, add this line to `postgresql.conf`:

   ```
   custom_variable_classes = 'pg_stat_statements'
   ```

3. Restart PostgreSQL with a command similar to this:

   ```
   pg_ctl -D /db/pgdata restart
   ```

4. Log in to PostgreSQL as a superuser into any database that should have access to `pg_stat_statements` and execute the following SQL statement:

   ```
   CREATE EXTENSION pg_stat_statements;
   ```

Perform the following steps to prepare `pg_stat_statements` for generalized use:

1. Execute this SQL statement as a database superuser to create a function:

   ```
   CREATE OR REPLACE FUNCTION pg_stat_statements()
   RETURNS SETOF pg_stat_statements AS $$
       SELECT * FROM pg_stat_statements;
   $$ LANGUAGE sql SECURITY DEFINER;
   ```

2. Execute this SQL statement to secure the function we created:

   ```
   REVOKE ALL ON FUNCTION pg_stat_statements() FROM PUBLIC;
   ```

3. Create a user dedicated to monitoring with this SQL statement:

   ```
   CREATE USER db_mon WITH PASSWORD 'somepass';
   ```

4. Grant the monitoring user the ability to use our function with this SQL statement:

   ```
   GRANT EXECUTE ON FUNCTION pg_stat_statements() TO db_mon;
   ```

Now, connect to PostgreSQL as the `db_mon` user, and examine the contents of `pg_stat_statements` by executing this SQL statement:

```
SELECT * FROM pg_stat_statements();
```

How it works...

In our opinion, the first set of instructions should not be required. The `pg_stat_statements` module is so valuable that we feel everyone can benefit from its contents. In any case, the first thing we must do is add `pg_stat_statements` to the `shared_preload_libraries` configuration setting. Several PostgreSQL modules are only available after being added this way.

The next step is only necessary if we are running a version older than PostgreSQL 9.2. The `custom_variable_classes` setting allows us to further configure the `pg_stat_statements` module later. Current versions of PostgreSQL will handle this for us.

As the `pg_stat_statements` module depends on activating an external library, we must restart PostgreSQL for it to take effect. Once the module is loaded, there are necessary functions that access the module; we must also install these functions in any database where we want `pg_stat_statements` to be available. By executing the `CREATE EXTENSION` statement, we register these functions with the current database.

The next set of instructions focuses on making the `pg_stat_statements` module usable to nonsuperusers and mirrors the process we used in the *Checking the pg_stat_activity view* recipe. We begin by creating a function that runs as the user who defined it. As we created the function as a superuser, this means regular users can use it to examine the contents of `pg_stat_statements`.

To prevent any user from executing this elevated privilege function, we revoke all access from the `public` context. Then, if we don't already have a user set aside for monitoring database activity, we create one and then grant it access to execute `pg_stat_statements()`, because this is one of its acknowledged roles.

Newer versions of PostgreSQL add more fields to this view, seemingly with every release. Many of the new fields focus on the I/O related to disk timing and blocks being dirtied, so they are intended for more advanced usage. However, the columns we can count on include the following:

- `query`: This column displays up to 1024 characters of the query being tracked
- `calls`: This column contains the total number of times the SQL has been executed
- `total_time`: This column provides the total time spent processing the query, in milliseconds
- `rows`: This column lists the total number of rows ever returned by the query

This is actually enough to perform quite a bit of investigation. We can divide `total_time` by `calls` to obtain the average execution speed. Perhaps, we want to know the total ratio of *insert* statements to *select* statements. Simply sorting the data by the `calls` column can reveal outliers that execute far more often than most queries. We used these ourselves to find a query that represented more than 50 percent of all the calls in the database. Our developers were very happy to cache the results of this query for us.

There's more...

Of course, this extremely useful view has a few extra features that we want to explain.

Reset the stats

Statistics stored in the `pg_stat_statements` view accumulate until they are forcefully reset. If we don't want to monitor value deltas between checks, we can simply reset the status of the module and cause it to erase the data it has collected. To do that, execute this SQL statement as a superuser:

```
SELECT pg_stat_statements_reset();
```

Catch more queries

By default, the `pg_stat_statements` module only tracks the first 1,000 queries it encounters during database operation. Normally, this is enough, especially in versions of PostgreSQL above 9.1. Newer versions provide better aggregation, because they remove SQL variables and constants from the query before including them in the view. However, older versions or databases that experience a high variance in query construction may want to increase this number. To do that, add this line to the `postgresql.conf` file:

```
pg_stat_statements.max = 10000
```

Then, we have to restart PostgreSQL again. Once this is finished, the `pg_stat_statements` module will track 10,000 queries instead of 1,000. Feel free to experiment with other values.

See also

- We feel strongly that the `pg_stat_statements` view is indispensable, but we can only convey a tiny amount in a usage recipe. For an in-depth explanation of its contents and usage, please check the documentation at: `http://www.postgresql.org/docs/9.3/static/pgstatstatements.html`.

Debugging with strace

Sometimes, the only way to truly observe a server process is by using the kernel itself. This kind of data is invaluable for troubleshooting or research into PostgreSQL activity.

The Linux `strace` utility provides detailed system trace data for any process or service running on the server. For use with PostgreSQL, this utility means we can target the database itself or any of the background processes it uses for maintenance.

Perhaps, more importantly, we can debug or examine any client connection. Is the network connection permanently hung? Is the client sending thousands of simple SQL requests instead of bulk-handling the results of a single large query? The `strace` command output is both intricate and verbose. Let's use `strace` to inspect our server and see what we can discover.

Getting ready

There are certain limitations to using `strace`. Because of its high-level access to process information, only root-level users are allowed to examine an application's activity. Make sure to have this capability before continuing.

As we want activity we can depend on, open a connection to PostgreSQL for us to locate later. We will be using this connection to generate debug output.

How to do it...

Follow these steps to examine the PostgreSQL processes in various ways:

1. In our PostgreSQL connection, execute the following query to find the process ID of the server backend assigned to us:

   ```
   SELECT pg_backend_pid() AS pid;
   ```

2. As our root-capable user, attach `strace` to the preceding `pid` (4200, for example) with this command:

   ```
   sudo strace -p 4200
   ```

3. In our PostgreSQL connection, execute the following query to generate some activity:

   ```
   SELECT 1;
   ```

4. In the terminal where `strace` is running, press *Ctrl* + *C* to disconnect.
5. Attach `strace` again, but collect the statistics with the following command:

   ```
   strace -c -S calls -p 4200
   ```

6. Now, execute the following query to generate some complex activity:

   ```
   SELECT * FROM information_schema.columns;
   ```

7. In the terminal where `strace` is running, press *Ctrl* + *C* to disconnect.
8. Attach `strace` a final time, but limit the output with the following command:

   ```
   strace -e recvfrom -p 4200
   ```

9. Execute the following query to generate a simple activity:

   ```
   SELECT 1;
   ```

How it works...

We can connect to any process with `strace`, but for demonstrative purposes, we elect to control the environment by watching a connection we directly control. The `pg_backend_pid` function returns the process ID of the backend process that serves our client, which then lets us monitor its activity on the server.

With the `pid` of the backend, we can monitor it with the `-p` parameter to `strace`, which watches the listed process ID. As we don't want too much output, we elect to execute a very simple query that does not touch the tables, functions, or views. Our output should resemble this:

```
Process 4200 attached - interrupt to quit
recvfrom(11, "Q\0\0\0\16SELECT 1;\0", 8192, 0, NULL, NULL) = 15
sendto(11, "T\0\0\0!\0\1?colu
mn?\0\0\0\0\0\0\0\0\0\0\27\0\4\377\377\377\377"...,
66, 0, NULL, 0) = 66
```

Once we press *Ctrl* + *C*, `strace` exits, and we can try a different combination of parameters. For example, the `-c` setting disables the normal output in favor of summarizing the kernel calls. If we use the `-S` parameter to change the `sort` column, we can focus on repeated calls. As counts will be boring with only a few columns, we've suggested a query that will touch on several database objects. Once we exit from the second `strace` command, the output looks like this:

```
% time     seconds  usecs/call     calls    errors syscall
------ ----------- ----------- --------- --------- ----------------
100.00    0.000003           0      1603           lseek
  0.00    0.000000           0        60           sendto
  0.00    0.000000           0        12           brk
  0.00    0.000000           0         1           recvfrom
------ ----------- ----------- --------- --------- ----------------
100.00    0.000003                  1676           total
```

Finally, we would like to introduce the `-e` parameter, which limits the `strace` output to the calls listed. In our case, we chose `recvfrom`, which is a network-related call that the backend uses to await requests. When in this mode, `strace` will only print `recvfrom` calls and nothing else.

The `-e` setting also provides several shortcuts. If the first keyword is `trace`, instead of a recognized call, we can specify a type of call to watch. For example, this revision of our last `strace` command would watch all network-related activities:

```
strace -e trace=network -p 4200
```

There's more...

Output from strace can be somewhat esoteric, especially as it limits the content length by default to increase readability. If we want to really capture a lot of data with extreme verbosity that will help a human make a diagnosis, we need to increase the string length. For strace, the parameter for that is -s. If we wanted to greatly extend the length of the string output, we can do that with this command:

```
strace -p 4200 -s 2000
```

Then, if we execute the following query:

```
SELECT 'This is a very long query to view.';
```

We would see this output:

```
recvfrom(11, "Q\0\0\0001select 'This is a very long query to
view.';\0", 8192, 0, NULL, NULL) = 50
```

Instead of this:

```
recvfrom(11, "Q\0\0\0001select 'This is a very long"..., 8192, 0,
NULL, NULL) = 50
```

This is all that is required to monitor PostgreSQL, as even simple queries and data are truncated with default settings.

See also

- Always examine the manual for the tools that we use in these recipes. In this case, the manual for strace is available by executing this command:

  ```
  man strace
  ```

Logging checkpoints properly

Checkpoints are an integral part of a PostgreSQL server. Table data is not modified during query execution until modified rows, index pages, and other structures are committed to the **Write Ahead Log** (**WAL**). WAL files are also known as checkpoint segments. When the count of these segments reaches checkpoint_segments—or the time since the last checkpoint exceeds checkpoint_timeout—the data files are modified to reflect the changes.

This decoupled writing ensures database integrity at the cost of doubling the necessary disk writes. This is the main reason why experienced PostgreSQL DBAs interested in performance move the WAL location to a separate storage device. However, even moving the WAL files to another device may not sufficiently reduce write pressure. Database activity is variable in nature, and checkpoints only happen every few minutes or after a threshold of data modifications.

As PostgreSQL tries to avoid overwhelming the operating system, writes necessary to satisfy a checkpoint are spread evenly over the checkpoint interval. Unfortunately, the operating system may choose to buffer these writes unevenly, resulting in unexpected write spikes. A busy database might have saturated disk bandwidth already, thus tying up any resources necessary for writing data modifications.

The way we combat this is by logging all checkpoints and analyzing the output of our log for checkpoint activity. We may need to leverage tablespaces, storage improvements, or application revisions to really address resource collisions like this, so it's in our best interest to be proactive.

Getting ready

You need to know where to find PostgreSQL logs. We usually suggest a few specific modifications to the `postgresql.conf` file for logging, including the following:

```
log_directory = 'pg_log'
log_checkpoints = on
```

This means logs will be found within our PostgreSQL data directory, in a subdirectory named `pg_log`. Some distributions use `/var/log/postgresql` instead. Regardless, find where the logs are kept. To ensure access, examine these as the `postgres` user, who should either own the logs directly or have the necessary read access.

How to do it...

Assuming our logs are located at `/db/pgdata/pg_log`, follow these steps to examine the checkpoint activity:

1. Execute this command to find the most recent logfile:

   ```
   ls -lt /db/pgdata/pg_log/postgres*.log | head -n 1
   ```

2. If the latest log is named `postgresql-2014-02-02.log`, view all the checkpoints in this log with the following command:

   ```
   grep checkpoint /db/pgdata/pg_log/postgresql-2014-02-02.log
   ```

3. Execute the following command to obtain the five longest disk syncs:

```
grep 'checkpoint complete:' \
    /db/pgdata/pg_log/postgresql-2014-02-02.log \
    | sed 's/.* sync=/sync=/; s/total=.*; //;' \
    | sort -n | tail -n 5
```

How it works...

We need to first find the most recent logfile. The `ls` command's `-t` parameter will sort the data by the last modified time, which the `head` command limits to one line of results. Distributions that provide PostgreSQL may adhere to a log-rotation scheme instead. In these cases, the latest logfile will reside in `/var/log/postgresql` and always have the same name. Older logs will have a number appended until the retention period passes.

No matter how we locate the most recent logfile, we use two relatively simple commands to examine its contents. These logfiles can be extremely useful; however, for now, we will focus on the checkpoint activity. Of those two commands, the first simply isolates all the checkpoint data in the order it occurred. One complete checkpoint will resemble these lines:

```
2014-02-02 19:54:02 CST LOG:  checkpoint starting: time

2014-02-02 20:00:36 CST LOG:  checkpoint complete: wrote 129631
buffers (24.7%); 0 transaction log file(s) added, 0 removed, 2
recycled; write=392.875 s, sync=1.789 s, total=394.667 s; sync
files=203, longest=1.004 s, average=0.008 s
```

This data is helpful in determining the time period of the checkpoint. Combined with other troubleshooting tools such as `sar`, we can correlate the checkpoint with disk activity. In the case of this example, we wrote 24.7 percent of a 4 GB buffer as well, which is quite a bit of data. However, these writes are spread over more than 6 minutes, reducing contention.

As useful as the raw log lines are, we can apply a few filters and sorting to expose the disk synchronization time. Our last command makes use of `grep` to isolate the checkpoints, `sed` to remove excess data, `sort` to focus on the longest syncs, and `tail` to restrict the output to the top five. Of these, the `sed` command is the most complex. However, it merely removes all the content before the first `sync` field and removes the `total` field, leaving only the data related to disk synchronization. Then, our top five most expensive checkpoints look like this:

```
sync=0.891 s, sync files=87, longest=0.470 s, average=0.010 s
sync=1.203 s, sync files=129, longest=0.302 s, average=0.009 s
sync=1.789 s, sync files=203, longest=1.004 s, average=0.008 s
sync=2.004 s, sync files=187, longest=1.031 s, average=0.010 s
sync=5.083 s, sync files=104, longest=3.076 s, average=0.048 s
```

The first four could be improved, but the last example is clearly much larger than we would normally expect or desire. Relatively few files were synchronized, yet the longest sync of over 3 seconds would likely adversely affect query performance. Disk synchronization times exhibited here indicate a high level of contention. If we were to execute `sar` for the time periods indicated by the longest checkpoint, we would most likely see 100 percent disk utilization.

If this utilization is primarily data reads, we may be able to ignore it if the checkpoint time occurred outside of operational hours. In such cases, the cause is probably related to maintenance or voluminous batch jobs. Otherwise, we should expand our investigation to track the source of the disk activity until all the checkpoints are below a desirable threshold.

There's more...

Some checkpoint data is stored in a PostgreSQL view named `pg_stat_bgwriter`. This is more of a summary view of the checkpoint activity, but it is available to any user who can execute SQL statements in the database. Within this view, there are three fields related to this recipe that directly concern us:

- `checkpoints_timed`: This column provides the number of checkpoints that occur based on a schedule. These are normal checkpoints and indicate regular operation.
- `checkpoints_req`: This column stores the number of checkpoints that PostgreSQL has forced to occur in order to keep up with write activity. If there are too many of these, database performance can be extremely reduced and disk contention can have other adverse affects.
- `checkpoint_sync_time`: This column describes the total amount of time that the checkpoint system has spent in sync status, in milliseconds. This is basically a sum of all of the `sync` columns for all the checkpoints since the statistics were last reset. This is a good value to graph if you are monitoring the database, as a sudden spike in the elapsed sync time can indicate trouble.

See also

The WAL is integral to how PostgreSQL operates. We strongly recommend that you learn as much about its functionality as possible. The PostgreSQL documentation provides a great deal of depth in its explanation of how the WAL really works. Please make use of these links:

- **WAL Configuration**: `http://www.postgresql.org/docs/9.3/static/wal-configuration.html`
- **Write Ahead Log**: `http://www.postgresql.org/docs/9.3/static/runtime-config-wal.html`
- **The Statistics Collector**: `http://www.postgresql.org/docs/9.3/static/monitoring-stats.html`

5
Monitoring

In this chapter, we will learn how to effectively monitor PostgreSQL's server status and database performance. Primarily, we will focus on using Nagios, `check_mk`, `check_postgres`, collectd, and Graphite; all of these tools excel at system monitoring. We will cover the following recipes in this chapter:

- Figuring out what to monitor
- Installing and configuring Nagios
- Configuring Nagios to monitor a database host
- Enhancing Nagios with check_mk
- Getting to know check_postgres
- Installing and configuring collectd
- Adding a custom PostgreSQL monitor to collectd
- Installing and configuring Graphite
- Adding collectd data to Graphite
- Building a graph in Graphite
- Customizing a Graphite graph
- Creating a Graphite dashboard

Introduction

One aspect of PostgreSQL administration, which is unfortunately ignored too frequently, is system monitoring. Provisioning, constructing, and maintaining a high availability cluster is difficult by itself, without the extra complications inherent in setting up yet more infrastructure.

Larger companies with an established **Network Operations Center** (**NOC**) probably have extremely mature incidence response and escalation procedures in place. Others may rely on a few basic monitors and alerts or ad hoc scripts set to trigger on certain thresholds. If we aren't part of the first group, we certainly can't include ourselves in the second and consider our cluster protected. When availability is important for business continuity, we should take the time to ensure that its activity is continuously reported, graphed, and summarized.

In this chapter, we will focus on what we should monitor, how often we should check system status, and how to present the data for easy consumption. When the database goes down, we need to know immediately. When the storage is higher than our projected limits, we need to plan accordingly. When database behavior is unexpected or abnormal, we should have a baseline for comparison. There are several tools available to do all of these things, and we're going to examine a stack of complementary services to automate everything.

There's no need to build any of our own tools. System monitoring is a very mature field; we'd be wasting our time and needlessly putting our database architecture at risk. Let's protect our investment properly with professional tools vetted by hundreds or thousands of equally concerned and attentive DBAs.

Figuring out what to monitor

Modern servers have a lot of active hardware and software that can stop working at any time. A failure can start with the operating system, storage, database, network connectivity, heat, or a number of other sources.

So, which elements do we rank highest to ensure system availability? Which hardware needs the closest monitoring? What kind of tests should we use to ensure that the software is operating as expected?

When dedicating monitoring resources to check hardware and software, we must answer several questions to distribute effort efficiently. Every test takes time, uses network resources, and must save its results to a status file. If our system checks are too frequent or numerous, we could end up overwhelming our monitor server. Failing to prioritize the alerting criteria can actually be more dangerous; if we become too accustomed to ignoring irrelevant alerts, legitimate system issues can propagate unchecked.

Thus, the first step in building a monitoring infrastructure is to decide what it will monitor and why.

Getting ready

We're going to be building a spreadsheet. This spreadsheet will rank all of our hardware and software so that we know which systems deserve the most focus. Have a spreadsheet program available before starting.

How to do it...

Follow these steps to rank the priority and frequency of monitoring hardware and software:

1. Create a spreadsheet with six columns labeled `Monitor`, `Importance`, `Frequency`, `Warning Level`, `Critical Level`, and `Action`.
2. Under the `Monitor` column, list every piece of hardware and software on the server.
3. Under the `Importance` column, rank every monitor at one of these three levels: `minor`, `major`, or `critical`.
4. Under the `Frequency` column, choose a monitoring interval. We suggest that you use one of these choices: 10 seconds, 30 seconds, 1 minute, 1 hour, 12 hours, or 1 day.
5. Under the `Warning Level` column, choose a threshold where the status of this resource should be considered a warning and might require further examination.
6. Under the `Critical Level` column, choose a threshold where the status of this resource should be considered critical and in need of immediate attention.
7. Under the `Action` column, pick an appropriate action that the monitor should take when a check triggers an alert. We suggest one of these choices: `ignore`, `email support`, `email DBAs`, and `panic`.

How it works...

The spreadsheet we're making requires only six columns to fit this recipe. Feel free to include any other relevant information when making your own spreadsheet. In fact, we suggest that you retain this document in source control for reference purposes and revisions. Its mere existence can prove beneficial as a necessary compliance document.

When we say to list every piece of hardware or software under the `Monitor` column, we expect a few to be forgotten. Part of this step is a mental filter; if we can't think of the resource, it probably isn't important enough to watch. There are limits to this, and we strongly suggest that you have at least two other objectives for people to verify that the list is complete.

For `Importance` and `Frequency`, we're really deciding how active this resource is and its likelihood to fail or require intervention. For example, consider a disk space monitor. Usable disk space is a major concern, but it's not likely to grow quickly. We can safely check disk space every hour or even every day and remain completely covered.

The `Warning Level` and `Critical Level` columns are essential to route the triggered alerts. A level of *warning* means a resource may need someone to double-check its status or acknowledge a problem for later review. If a resource reaches a *critical* status, every person interested in the server should be alerted immediately.

Finally, the monitoring software needs to know what action to take if an alert is triggered. If we ever choose *ignore*, we should simply disable that particular alert entirely. On the other hand, the support staff can usually solve simple resource problems or forward the alert to a DBA. At other times, we want the DBA to know immediately due to the importance or complexity of the hardware or software being monitored. As a last resort, the alert can merely panic and alert everyone in every contact list in the hope that at least one person is available to address the issue.

In the end, the first few lines of our spreadsheet may look something like this:

	A	B	C	D	E	F
1	**Monitor**	**Importance**	**Frequency**	**Warning Level**	**Critical Level**	**Action**
2	Disk Space of /db	major	1 hour	1.5TB	2TB	email support
3	PostgreSQL online	critical	10 seconds	N/A	no	email DBAs
4	Server Ping	critical	10 seconds	100ms	500ms	email support
5	OS User Count	minor	1 minute	10	20	ignore
6	/db Mount	critical	10 seconds	N/A	missing	panic

There's more...

If we have access to a collaborative spreadsheet tool such as Google Docs or an internal Wiki, we should maintain this information there. Not only does this act as a central resource, but it ensures that all monitors have a logical reason to exist and have a predetermined escalation path. When problems arise, any time spent on deciding what to do or who to inform only serves to increase the overall amount of risk.

In the rare instance that management or business interests question our system monitoring policies, we have an immediate answer. As DBAs, we want our company to know that the database is in good hands, and a strict monitoring policy helps accomplish this.

Installing and configuring Nagios

Nagios is a well-known monitoring tool. We won't make any claims that it is the best or most suited tool for watching a highly available PostgreSQL installation. However, the community is large, the functionality is extensive and established, and interoperability with other tools and libraries is high.

As an unfortunate consequence, the amount of installation prerequisites is rather lengthy. To get Nagios working properly, we need an HTTP server, Perl, and a mail daemon. Some plugins require PHP, while others need MySQL, SNMP, or any number of esoteric utilities and acronyms. There might be DBAs who also have strong skills as webmasters, but we can't depend on that. Getting Nagios installed with all of its foundation services is very complex, so we don't recommend that you do so.

Due to its history, the likelihood that Nagios is available on major Linux distributions is very high. Installing Nagios through the distribution will handle most, if not all, configuration and interoperability concerns. While an installation of this type only has minimal settings enabled and only monitors the monitoring server itself, it's a step in the right direction.

This recipe will focus on using distribution packaging tools such as `yum` or `apt-get` to install and configure a basic Nagios setup.

Getting ready

Red-Hat-based systems such as Fedora, RHEL, CentOS, and Scientific Linux have a prerequisite package that is not part of the included distribution repositories. To install Nagios, we need to add the **Extra Packages for Enterprise Linux** (**EPEL**) library. Red Hat systems can do this by obtaining the most recent EPEL package for their OS versions and architectures from `http://download.fedoraproject.org/pub/epel`.

Look for the package file that begins with **epel-release** and download it to the monitoring server. Once the package is downloaded, it can be installed with this command as a root-level user:

```
sudo rpm -ivh epel-release-*.rpm
```

How to do it...

Follow these steps to install and configure Nagios on a Debian, Mint, or Ubuntu monitoring server:

1. Execute these commands as a root-level user to install Nagios and useful plugins:

   ```
   sudo apt-get install nagios3 nagios-plugins-extra
   Sudo apt-get install nagios-nrpe-plugin
   ```

2. When prompted, enter a password for the `nagiosadmin` user.

Follow these steps to install Nagios on a Red Hat, Fedora, CentOS, and Scientific Linux monitoring server:

1. Open the `/etc/selinux/config` file and change the `SELINUX` parameter to match the following:

   ```
   SELINUX=permissive
   ```

2. Execute the following command as a root-level user:

   ```
   sudo setenforce 0
   ```

3. Execute this command as a root-level user to install Nagios:

```
sudo yum install nagios nagios-plugins-all
```

4. Set the `nagiosadmin` password by executing this command as a root-level user:

```
htpasswd -c /etc/nagios/passwd nagiosadmin
```

5. Execute these commands as a root-level user to start Nagios on system boot:

```
sudo chkconfig nagios on
sudo chkconfig httpd on
```

6. Execute these commands as a root-level user to start Nagios:

```
sudo service httpd start
sudo service nagios start
```

How it works...

Red Hat-based distributions focus primarily on system stability and lack many third-party utilities and daemons. Luckily, this is not a concern for us, as groups exist to rectify this situation. One such group maintains EPEL, which we can exploit to simplify the process of installing Nagios.

Debian-based servers, for better or worse, are not so strict. Though they are often just as stable, the package repository is much more extensive. Thus, we can install Nagios with one invocation of `apt-get`. When installing the `nagios3` package, all the necessary prerequisites are retrieved and installed as well. The process even prompts us for a password for the `nagiosadmin` user, which we use to access the web-based administration console.

Installing the `nagios` package on Red-Hat-based systems is somewhat more complicated. RHEL servers, especially, will often enable **SELinux** by default for the sake of security. We choose to set SELinux in permissive mode so that it warns us of potential security problems but still allows basic functionality. Nagios makes use of external servers, which SELinux would otherwise block. Using the `setenforce` utility, we also manually switch to permissive mode without rebooting the server. Due to our modification of `/etc/selinux/config`, future server reboots will leave SELinux in permissive mode.

With SELinux out of our way, we can install Nagios with `yum`, which should resolve and install any prerequisites for us. Unlike the Debian-based install, it will not automatically prompt us for a password for the `nagiosadmin` user. Thus, we must use the `htpasswd` utility to create one. To do so, we use the `-c` parameter to set the location of the password file we want to modify. Then we set the second parameter to `nagiosadmin`, as that's the name of the user for whom we are creating a password.

Next, we need to configure Nagios to start when the server starts. On Red-Hat-based systems, the `chkconfig` utility handles this for us. Finally, we can leverage the service utility to actually start Nagios.

There's more...

We know that Nagios is running by accessing its HTTP location. By default, provided we know the name or IP address of the monitor server, we can access Nagios via a web browser. Assuming that `192.168.56.20` is the IP of the server we're using to monitor PostgreSQL, the web interface would exist at `http://192.168.56.20/nagios`.

The Debian-based install will be at `http://192.168.56.20/nagios3`.

Our default Nagios dashboard should resemble this:

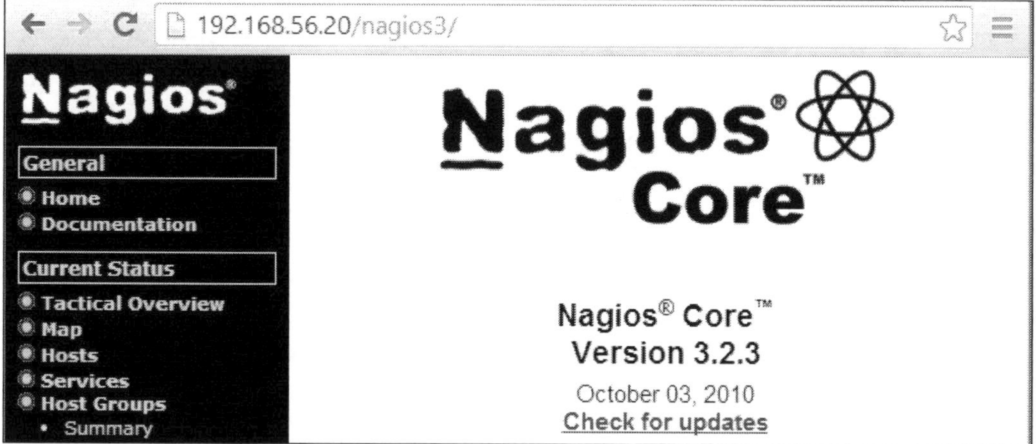

See also

As we mentioned earlier, installing Nagios is not easy due to all the other resources it depends on. Please refer to the following links to learn more about installing and configuring Nagios. We've also included a link to a comparison of various monitoring tools in case you want to try one of the Nagios alternatives:

- **Nagios Quickstart Installation Guides**: `http://nagios.sourceforge.net/docs/3_0/quickstart.html`
- **Nagios Core Documentation**: `http://nagios.sourceforge.net/docs/nagioscore/3/en/toc.html`
- **Comparison of network monitoring systems**: `http://en.wikipedia.org/wiki/Comparison_of_network_monitoring_systems`

Configuring Nagios to monitor a database host

Once Nagios is installed, it will automatically configure a few basic monitors directed toward its own server. If we click on the **Hosts** link in the web administration site, we are presented with this:

Host Status Details For All Host Groups

Host ↑↓	Status ↑↓	Last Check ↑↓	Duration ↑↓	Status Information
localhost	UP	2014-02-09 16:41:34	0d 2h 3m 50s	PING OK - Packet loss = 0%, RTA = 0.05 ms

The local server is all that we are currently watching. This is useful to verify that Nagios is working as intended, but we need to monitor one or more database servers as well. In this recipe, we will learn how to watch external servers. By the end, we should see at least one more server listed by Nagios.

Getting ready

Initially, Nagios can only monitor remote servers by checking exposed services such as HTTP, FTP, or PostgreSQL. To check items such as CPU, RAM, or disk space, we need to rely on **Nagios Remote Plugin Executor** (**NRPE**) to forward system information to the monitoring server upon request. This means that NRPE must be installed on any server we want to monitor, including our PostgreSQL servers.

To install this on Debian-based servers, use the following command:

```
sudo apt-get install nagios-nrpe-server
```

Red Hat derivatives will need to use this command:

```
sudo yum install nrpe
```

Next, open `/etc/nagios/nrpe.cfg` and change the `allowed_hosts` setting to include the IP address or hostname of the monitor server. If `192.168.56.5` is the monitor server, it should look like this:

```
allowed_hosts=192.168.56.5
```

How to do it...

Follow these steps on the monitoring system to watch the `192.168.56.10` server, which is the first node of our PostgreSQL cluster:

1. Find the configuration directory for Nagios:
   - Debian-based servers should use this path: `/etc/nagios3/conf.d`
   - Red-Hat-based servers should use this path: `/etc/nagios/objects`
2. As a root-level user, create a file named `db_conf.cfg` in the preceding path.
3. In the `db_conf.cfg` file, define a `hostgroup` entry by adding this text:

   ```
   define hostgroup {
       hostgroup_name  pg-servers
       alias           PostgreSQL Servers
   }
   ```

4. In the `db_conf.cfg` file, define a `host` entry by adding this text:

   ```
   define host {
       use           generic-host
       host_name     pg-1
       alias         PostgreSQL Node 1
       address       192.168.56.10
       hostgroups    pg-servers
   }
   ```

5. In the `db_conf.cfg` file, define a `service` entry by adding this text:

   ```
   define service {
       use                    generic-service
       hostgroup_name         pg-servers
       service_description    Current Load
       check_command          check_nrpe_1arg!check_load
   }
   ```

6. Red-Hat-based systems should modify `commands.cfg` in `/etc/nagios/objects/` to include the following code:

   ```
   define command {
    command_name check_nrpe_1arg
    command_line $USER1$/check_nrpe -H $HOSTADDRESS$ -c $ARG1$
   }
   ```

7. Reload the Nagios configuration files:
   - Debian-based servers should use this command: `sudo service nagios3 reload`
   - Red-Hat-based servers should use this command: `sudo service nagios reload`

How it works...

This recipe has a lot of moving parts, but it merely looks more complicated than it really is. We begin by locating the directory where supplementary configuration files are stored. Once this is located, we can create an entry to watch our PostgreSQL servers. To do this, we create a file named `db_conf.cfg`.

> You don't have to use `db_conf.cfg`. Nagios should recognize any file that ends with a `.cfg` extension. If you'd rather separate hosts, host groups, and services, feel free to do so.

The order of the elements that we are creating does not matter; Nagios has a very advanced parser that checks configuration entries all at once. Knowing this, we feel it's logical to begin with the PostgreSQL `hostgroup` so that we have a way of grouping all of our database servers together. Once this is defined, we can create dozens or hundreds of PostgreSQL servers and apply the same checks to all of them.

The second entry we create in our `db_conf.cfg` file tells Nagios that this is a host it should monitor. Unless told otherwise, Nagios will ping this server to ensure that it's online, and this will be the only check until we configure more.

The meaning of the `use` line is probably not obvious. Nagios has several requirements to define a configuration entry. Instead of copying the same settings over and over again, we can create a template and then use it later. In this case, Nagios comes preconfigured with several basic templates, and we're making use of one for our newly created hosts.

The next entry we create in `db_conf.cfg` is a service we want to check. In this case, we are going to take advantage of NRPE to obtain the current system load. By setting `hostgroup-name` to `pg-servers`, Nagios will check the system load on all PostgreSQL servers; there's no need to create a service entry for each host.

The `check-command` is probably somewhat opaque as well. Every service requires a command to execute. Commands are defined like other Nagios objects and must be named for reference. The `check_nrpe_1arg` command is defined elsewhere, and we're using it here. Nagios separates commands from their parameters with an exclamation point. Therefore, in this example, we're invoking NRPE to check the system load on the remote server.

Red-Hat-based systems don't have a Nagios command named `check_nrpe_1arg`, so we create this one manually on those servers. With the newly defined command block, Nagios will use NRPE whenever the services invoke `check_nrpe_1arg`.

Finally, we tell Nagios to reload its configuration files. This causes Nagios to reread all configuration files, including the one we created. If everything goes well, clicking on **Host Groups** in the web interface should produce this summary:

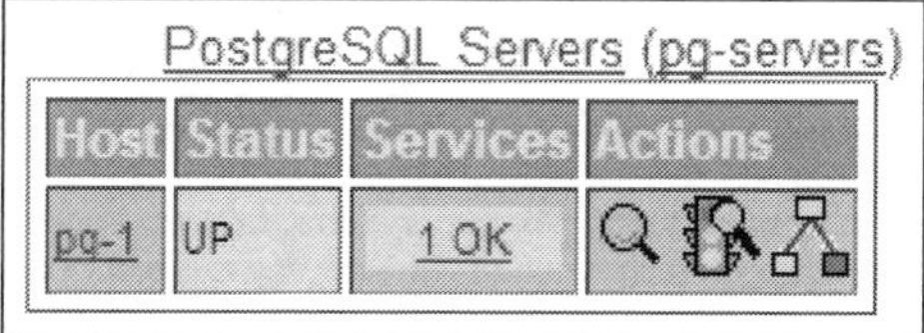

There's more...

Wait a minute! We never added a check for PostgreSQL itself! As we can't allow PostgreSQL to remain unmonitored, create a user on our PostgreSQL server with the following command:

```
CREATE USER nagios;
```

Then, make an entry in the `pg_hba.conf` file to allow trusted checks from the monitoring server with this line:

```
host     template1    nagios     192.168.56.5/32    trust
```

Then, reload the PostgreSQL configuration with this command :

```
pg_ctl -D $PGDATA reload
```

Next, add a service entry to our `db_conf.cfg` file like this:

```
define service {
        use                     generic-service
        hostgroup_name          pg-servers
        service_description     PostgreSQL Status
        check_command           check_pgsql
}
```

After reloading our Nagios configuration files, click on the **Services** link in the web interface. It should now list two monitored services for the `pg-1` server as seen here:

Host	Service	Status	Last Check
pg-1	Current Load	OK	2014-02-09 18:58:32
	PostgreSQL Status	OK	2014-02-09 18:59:06

See also

- Nagios configuration objects are fairly complicated. To use them properly, we strongly suggest that you browse the Nagios object manual located at `http://nagios.sourceforge.net/docs/3_0/objectdefinitions.html`.

Enhancing Nagios with check_mk

While Nagios is well established in the system administration community, it retains a few shortcomings due to its long legacy. This is not to suggest that Nagios is a bad platform! However, we can make it better for our own uses and for other administrators that help us monitor our database clusters.

`check_mk` is a popular extension to Nagios that provides a better interface, more built-in monitors, and—for those interested—a GUI management system. This management GUI is actually one of the main things we will cover in this recipe, as it has some idiosyncrasies of its own. However, once we're done presenting the basics, we encourage you to experiment with some of its more powerful features.

Getting ready

To complete this recipe, we will need a configured Nagios installation. Please follow the steps in the *Installing and configuring Nagios* recipe. However, either skip the *Configuring Nagios to monitor a database host* recipe or follow these two steps:

1. Delete the `db_conf.cfg` file that we created for our database host.
2. Reload the `nagios` service.

How to do it...

For the purposes of this recipe, our database has a local hostname of `pg-1`, and the monitor server is named `monitor-server`. Follow these steps to use `check_mk` to create and configure the host and service monitors for our PostgreSQL server:

1. Install `check_mk` according to the comprehensive instructions at `https://mathias-kettner.com/checkmk_manual_install.html`.
2. Navigate to the monitor server in a web browser to the `check_mk` URL: `http://monitor-server/check_mk`
3. Enter `nagiosadmin` as the username and the password created during the installation of Nagios in the *Installing and configuring Nagios* recipe.
4. Click on **Hosts** in the **WATO – Configuration** segment of the left sidebar.
5. Click on the **Create new folder** icon.
6. Name the folder `PostgreSQL Servers`, and click on **Save & Finish**.
7. Click on the **PostgreSQL Servers** folder.
8. Click on the **Create new host** icon.
9. Set the **Hostname** to `pg-1`, the **Alias** to `PostgreSQL Node 1`, and click on **Save & Finish**.

10. Click on the highlighted **inventory** link in the information box above the list of hosts.
11. Click on **Activate missing** above the list of hosts.
12. Click on the orange icon that says there are **2 Changes**.
13. Click on the **Activate Changes!** icon.
14. Wait for 5 minutes; then, click on **All services** in the **Views** segment of the left sidebar.

How it works...

While we could have included instructions on installing `check_mk`, they are actually very long and would have required several pages of explanation. The official `check_mk` site does an admirable job presenting the installation process, so why duplicate it? The abundant documentation is a great reason to use `check_mk`.

Once we log in, we see a very large and somewhat imposing interface. However, for now, we are only interested in the left sidebar. What we're looking for is the **web administration tool** (**WATO**) section, as seen here:

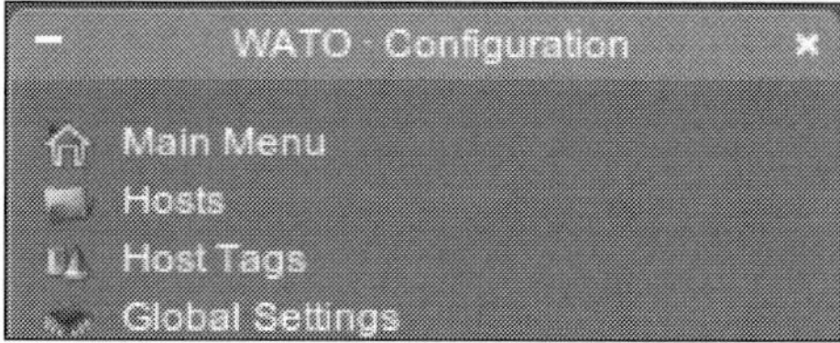

The interface is actually very friendly to new users. Once we click on **Hosts**, we can either create a new host right away or create a folder first. We recommend that you always group the servers in specific folders to make bulk actions easier. Thus, we click on this enticing icon:

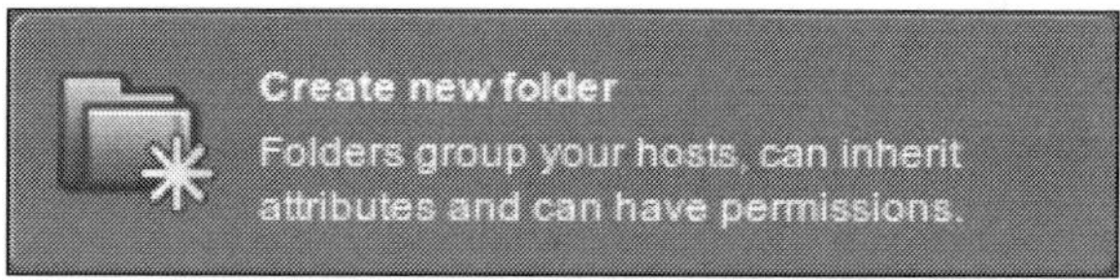

After we name and save the folder, we can enter the folder and create the new host. After creating the host and saving its configuration, we are presented with this notice:

Now you should do an inventory in order to auto-configure all services

When check_mk inventories a server, it attempts to automatically detect the services and resources it can monitor. Nagios definitely can't do this! Once we activate all of the changes we made, we need to wait for a minute or two for check_mk to add the new checks and collect the status of each. Once some time has elapsed, we can click on **All services** to see our newly monitored PostgreSQL server:

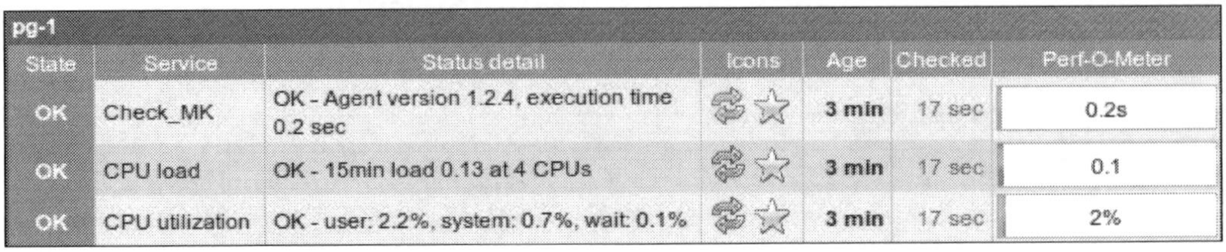

pg-1

State	Service	Status detail	Icons	Age	Checked	Perf-O-Meter
OK	Check_MK	OK - Agent version 1.2.4, execution time 0.2 sec		**3 min**	17 sec	0.2s
OK	CPU load	OK - 15min load 0.13 at 4 CPUs		**3 min**	17 sec	0.1
OK	CPU utilization	OK - user: 2.2%, system: 0.7%, wait: 0.1%		**3 min**	17 sec	2%

On our particular test server, check_mk found over 20 services it knew how to monitor. We don't have to select all of them, of course, but adding the same services to Nagios would have been much more difficult.

There's more...

check_mk doesn't just provide a handy web interface, but it actually has a very advanced command-line utility. For instance, if we stopped the recipe after creating the folder and server and then activated the changes, we could have performed the server inventory with these two commands:

```
cmk -I pg-1
cmk -O
```

The first command checks the pg-1 server for new services. The second saves the services it found and reloads Nagios so that it can see them as well. The command-line tool makes a great companion to the web interface when handling several server clusters.

See also

We really like the check_mk documentation. It's comprehensive, verbose, and full of examples. Check some of the following links for more information:

- **Quick Manual Installation Guide**: https://mathias-kettner.com/checkmk_turbostart.html
- **Calling check_mk**: https://mathias-kettner.com/checkmk_calling.html
- **Catalog of check plugins**: https://mathias-kettner.com/checkmk_check_catalogue.html

Getting to know check_postgres

Our friends at Bucardo created a useful, general purpose PostgreSQL checking utility. The `check_postgres` tool currently has an inventory of more than 50 checks to monitor PostgreSQL servers.

While this is an exceptionally useful tool, integrating it into our overall stack is necessary to fully take advantage of its capabilities. This recipe will cover the basic usage and integration with Nagios for easy PostgreSQL monitoring of large database clusters.

Getting ready

Though some Linux distributions package the `check_postgres` utility for easy installation, the versions that are included are usually very old. We recommend that you obtain a copy of the latest `check_postgres` source code. At the time of writing this book, the latest version is 2.21.0, released on September 24, 2013. Obtain the latest copy of the `check_postgres` source code from `http://bucardo.org/wiki/Check_postgres`.

As we want to use Nagios to execute the `check_postgres`, please follow the steps in the *Configuring Nagios to monitor a database host* recipe to produce a working installation with a basic database host configuration. We will be making further modifications to the `db_conf.cfg` file introduced there.

How to do it...

Install `check_postgres` by following these steps:

1. Use these commands to extract the `check_postgres` source and enter the source directory:

   ```
   tar -xzf check_postgres-2.21.0.tar.gz
   cd check_postgres-2.21.0/
   ```

2. Next, build and install the actual software with these commands:

   ```
   perl Makefile.PL
   make
   sudo make install
   ```

As the `postgres` user on a PostgreSQL server, try using these commands to obtain database information:

1. Check the state of the database size with this command:

   ```
   check_postgres.pl --action=database_size -w 100MB -c 200MB
   ```

2. Create a large table by executing this SQL as the `postgres` user in the `postgres` database:

```
CREATE TABLE bigtable AS
SELECT generate_series(1,1000000) AS vals;
```

3. Cause a critical alert by executing this command:

```
check_postgres.pl --action=table_size -w 10MB -c 20MB
```

Integrate `check_postgres.pl` into Nagios by following these steps:

1. Create a `command` section in the `db_conf.cfg` file with this content:

```
define command {
  command_name  check_pg
  command_line  /usr/local/bin/check_postgres.pl -H $HOSTADDRESS$
--action $ARG1$ -w $ARG2$ -c $ARG3$
}
```

2. Create a `service` section in the `db_conf.cfg` file that looks like this:

```
define service {
  use                  generic-service
  hostgroup_name       pg-servers
  service_description  PostgreSQL Database Size
  check_command        check_pg!database_size!100MB!200MB
}
```

3. Reload the Nagios configuration files:

   - Debian-based servers should use this command: `sudo service nagios3 reload`
   - Red-Hat-based servers should use this command: `sudo service nagios reload`

How it works...

This recipe comes in three parts because we're doing three distinctly different things. Installing `check_postgres` itself is actually very easy. The entirety of the utility is contained within a single file, so we can simply move `check_postgres.pl` to a suitable location in our `PATH` environment setting. However, we suggest that you use the standard installation process as we did.

While executing `sudo make install`, look for this line near the end:

```
Installing /usr/local/bin/check_postgres.pl
```

This will indicate where the `check_postgres.pl` script is located. Ours was installed in `/usr/local/bin`, but yours may be elsewhere.

Next, we try a couple of basic commands to ensure that check_postgres works. The first command makes use of the database_size action and alerts us if our database is larger than the warning (-w) or critical (-c) thresholds that we set. The table_size action performs a similar task but applies the thresholds to every table in the database. By default, check_postgres connects to the postgres database, so we placed a large table there to trigger a critical alert. The output is very large as it lists every table, but it should begin like this:

```
POSTGRES_TABLE_SIZE CRITICAL: DB "postgres" (host:192.168.56.10)
largest table is "public.bigtable": 35 MB
```

As we have verified that the check works, we want Nagios to invoke it instead. This removes the need to create ad hoc invocations and allows us to search for large tables on all the database servers that Nagios is monitoring.

We will start the process by adding a command to Nagios in the db_conf.cfg file we created for our single test server. Remember where check_postgres.pl was installed, because we need to specify the full path to the script, just in case it's not part of the standard PATH environment. We will set the first argument to set the action we want to perform and reserve the second and third for the warning and critical levels respectively. By making our check_pg command so generic, we can use it for every action that check_postgres supports. Otherwise, we would have needed a separate command section for each check.

Then, we will add a service check. We will need to add one of these for each check_postgres action that we want to enact. In our example, we only enabled the database_size check and applied the same thresholds that we used when manually invoking the script. By reloading the Nagios configuration files, it will incorporate the new PostgreSQL database size check and apply it to any server that we have in the pg-servers group.

There's more...

Though the documentation explains all the actions available for check_postgres, it may be inconvenient to refer to it regularly. Though the check_postgres.pl script accepts the usual --help parameter, it has a notable ability as well. If we specify the --man parameter instead, check_postgres will actually display the entire manual. This is similar to investigating the check_postgres man page like this:

```
man check_postgres
```

Sometimes, man pages don't get installed properly or are not available for one reason or another. The --man parameter should always work on any system that also contains the perl documentation package.

See also

As check_postgres is developed by Bucardo, their site contains various resources related to its operation. We recommend these links for more information:

- **The check_postgres Wiki**: http://bucardo.org/wiki/Check_postgres
- **The check_postgres Documentation**: http://bucardo.org/check_postgres/check_postgres.pl.html

Installing and configuring collectd

When monitoring multiple clusters of servers, we need a data collection method that's both scalable and configurable. The **collectd** daemon is a scalable statistics-gathering service, perfect for large clusters as it operates on a client-server model. A common collectd cluster may look like this, with collectd running on every server:

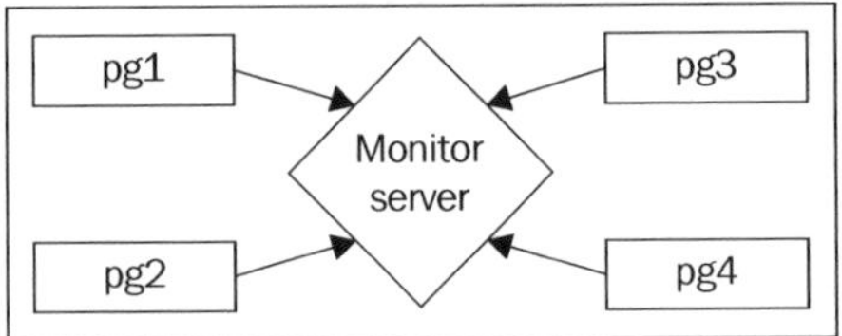

We can direct the statistics of several PostgreSQL servers to a central aggregate server. This server may process the data directly or forward it to a graph system for easy visualization. To gain this type of functionality, we need to spend some time installing and configuring collectd.

Getting ready

For the sake of completeness, obtain a copy of the latest collectd source code. At the time of writing this book, the latest version is 5.4.1, released on January 26, 2014. Obtain the latest copy of the collectd source code from http://collectd.org/download.shtml.

In order for collectd to interface with PostgreSQL, we need PostgreSQL development libraries in addition to the normally installed system binaries. For example, to build properly on a Debian-based system, we would also need to install libraries by executing this on the command line:

```
sudo apt-get install postgresql-server-dev-9.3
```

Red-Hat-based systems can sometimes lag behind, so we suggest that you obtain the postgresql93-libs package from http://yum.postgresql.org/rpmchart.php.

Later, we simply need a root-capable user to install collectd as a system-wide service.

Some companies have policies that disallow development tools from being installed on production hardware. If this is the case in your company, it may be necessary to use a staging or development server for these steps. Once the binaries are available, they should be deployed to the production system following the standard deployment protocol. This applies to all the recipes that call for development libraries.

How to do it...

Assume that we have a monitor server named `mon1` and a PostgreSQL server named `pg1`. Follow these steps on both servers unless notified otherwise:

1. Use these commands to extract the collectd source and enter the source directory:

   ```
   tar -xzf collectd-5.4.1.tar.gz
   cd collectd-5.4.1/
   ```

2. Next, build and install the actual software with these commands:

   ```
   ./configure --sysconfdir=/etc/collectd
   make
   sudo make install
   ```

3. Copy the `init/collectd` initialization script from the source code provided with this chapter, into the `/etc/init.d` directory on the server.
4. Change the copied initialization script to make it executable with this command:

   ```
   sudo chmod a+x /etc/init.d/collectd
   ```

5. In the `/etc/collectd` directory, create a file named `collectd.conf` with the following contents:

   ```
   PIDFile      "/var/run/collectd.pid"

   LoadPlugin   load
   LoadPlugin   syslog

   Include      "/etc/collectd/network.conf"
   Include      "/etc/collectd/local.conf"
   ```

6. On the `mon1` server only, create a file named `network.conf` in the `/etc/collectd` directory with the following contents:

   ```
   LoadPlugin network
   <Plugin network>
     Listen "*" "25826"
   </Plugin>
   ```

7. On the `pg1` server only, create a file named `network.conf` in the `/etc/collectd` directory with the following contents:

   ```
   LoadPlugin network
   <Plugin network>
     Server "192.168.56.10" "25826"
   </Plugin>
   ```

8. On the `mon1` server only, create a file named `local.conf` in the `/etc/collectd` directory with the following contents:

   ```
   LoadPlugin csv
   <Plugin csv>
          DataDir "/tmp/collectd"
   </Plugin>
   ```

9. Then, add the service to the system startup and shutdown process:
   - For Debian or Ubuntu systems, use this command: `sudo update-rc.d collectd defaults`
   - For CentOS, Fedora, or RHEL systems, use this command: `sudo chkconfig --add collectd`

10. Finally, start the collectd service on both servers:

    ```
    sudo service collectd start
    ```

How it works...

Our initial steps focus mainly on extracting and building the collectd source. We pass one parameter to the `configure` script to set the configuration file's location and leave the rest at their defaults.

By default, collectd installs in the `/opt/collectd` directory. If you are unhappy with this arrangement, we suggest that you change the `--prefix` and `--exec-prefix` parameters when executing the `configure` script.

Our next steps involve copying the provided initialization script into the server's `/etc/init.d` directory to start and stop collectd. While there are several contributed scripts and configurations in the `contrib` directory of the collectd source code, ours will work with almost any Linux distribution.

Once collectd is installed, we need to configure it. The provided configuration file is a good example, but we need something simpler. The `collectd.conf` file we created is enough to ensure that collectd starts and operates as expected. We included two other configuration files as well so that we can share multiple configuration files on several servers.

The first of these is `network.conf`. This file should contain network-related collectd settings. In our particular example, the monitor server is configured to `Listen`, while our PostgreSQL server sends data to a collectd `Server`.

For the sake of demonstration, we configured the monitor server to store collected data to the `/tmp/collectd` directory in CSV format. We don't recommend this configuration in a production environment, but it's safe to use for now. After adding collectd to the list of services on this server and starting it, both servers should be linked. How can we prove this?

On the monitoring server, we should see a file named after the current date in the `/tmp/collectd/pg1/load/` directory. The file should contain one or more lines like this:

```
1392592062.376,0.000000,0.010000,0.050000
```

In this case, the `load` plugin we declared in the `collectd.conf` file provides data on system load. Using commas as separators, the first column is the Unix time in seconds, followed by an average of 1, 5, and 15 minutes. In the preceding example, the server is essentially idle.

The file in `/tmp/collectd/pg1/load/` may not appear immediately. collectd uses buffers and cache to avoid excessive traffic and output. Be patient and check every minute or two until it appears.

See also

As collectd works on a client-server model and has several collection plugins available, it also has a lot of documentation. Please use these links for more information:

- **The collectd Documentation**: `http://collectd.org/documentation.shtml`
- **The collectd Manpage**: `http://collectd.org/documentation/manpages/collectd.conf.5.shtml`

Adding a custom PostgreSQL monitor to collectd

The primary reason we chose to install collectd stems from its ability to monitor arbitrary data points. Due to the existence of a PostgreSQL plugin for collectd, we can actually collect data from the database itself. Monitoring PostgreSQL becomes as easy as writing a query!

We'll include a few sample queries we developed for monitoring PostgreSQL servers. Feel free to develop your own as we explain how to leverage the PostgreSQL collectd module.

Getting ready

As the collectd PostgreSQL module needs to log in to a database within the cluster to gather its statistics, we should create a user specifically for this purpose. Execute this SQL query with an appropriate password:

```
CREATE USER perf_mon WITH PASSWORD 'testpw';
```

In addition, follow the instructions in the *Installing and configuring collectd* recipe so that there is a fully functional collectd client and server.

How to do it...

To create a collectd custom PostgreSQL query, simply follow these steps on a server running both collectd and PostgreSQL:

1. Create a file named `local.conf` in the `/etc/collectd` directory with these contents:

```
LoadPlugin postgresql

<Plugin postgresql>
  <Query tps>
    Statement "SELECT datname, \
                      xact_commit + xact_rollback AS tps \
                 FROM pg_catalog.pg_stat_database;"

    <Result>
      Type derive
      InstancePrefix "TPS"
      InstancesFrom "datname"
      ValuesFrom "tps"
    </Result>
  </Query>

  <Database postgres>
    Host "localhost"
    User "perf_user"
    Password "testpw"
    Instance "Production"

    Query tps
  </Database>
</Plugin>
```

2. Reload the collectd configuration files with this command:

   ```
   sudo service collectd reload
   ```

3. Wait for 2 to 5 minutes.
4. Check the contents of the files in the `/tmp/collectd/pg1/postgresql-Production/` directory on the monitor server.

How it works...

This recipe is almost entirely based on the PostgreSQL collectd plugin. The large block of code that we inserted into the `local.conf` file will configure that module with a single query that it will execute and transmit to the monitor server. The monitor system will automatically accept these results and integrate them into any data that it's already storing.

The `<Query>` block deserves some explanation. Every custom query that we define must have a name. In this case, **TPS** stands for **Transactions Per Second**, and it is a common database metric. The first thing we add is the statement being executed. The statement we included gathers basic data from the `pg_stat_database` table for every database in this particular PostgreSQL instance.

However, it is within the `<Result>` section that we truly make use of the query. In collectd, data is classified by the type of information it represents. For our purposes, these types are **gauge** and **derive**. Gauges represent values that are valid only at the time of observation. For example, most cars have a gauge to display their current speed. Derived values, on the other hand, are the difference in value between two subsequent readings. Transaction counters in the `pg_stat_database` statistics table are cumulative; thus, we must use the `derive` type when declaring results to collectd.

The `InstancePrefix` setting simply helps us distinguish query results when sending them to collectd. It will associate this prefix with all the results and will help us find the data when it's time to view it. The `InstancesFrom` setting has a similar purpose. By giving a column name (`datname` here), each row is labeled with the value in that column. For example, a database named `pgbench` would be given an instance name of `pgbench`.

The `ValuesFrom` setting also needs a column name to gather data. We took the contents of the `xact_commit` and `xact_rollback` columns, added them together, and named the result `tps`. Combined with the `InstancesFrom` setting, each database now has an associated transaction count.

The PostgreSQL collectd module allows us to create as many `<Query>` sections as we desire. But we need to execute the queries somewhere. By creating a `<Database>` section, we provide connection information to the module so that it can execute specified queries and gather the results. The name we give the `<Database>` block both defines which database name collectd should use when connecting, and what label it should use for tracking purposes.

Within the `<Database>` section, we can specify an `Instance` name, but we prefer to think of it as an environment designator. Why is this? If we have multiple environments, such as development, stage, testing, reporting, production, and so on, each one may have the same database name. By giving the instance itself a name, we can tell all the statistics apart from one another.

At the end of the `<Database>` section, we tell collectd which `<Query>` sections it should apply to that particular database. This means we can have multiple database sections, where some of our custom queries apply to specific instances.

Once we reload the configuration files, collectd will activate the PostgreSQL module and begin checking each database for the transaction count. If we wait for this information to reach the monitor server, it should eventually appear in the `/tmp/collectd/pg2/postgresql-Production` directory. Using these settings, this directory should contain one file for each database that it's tracking. For example, the contents of this directory on our test server looks like this:

```
drwxr-xr-x 2 root root 4096 Feb 16 17:42 ./
drwxr-xr-x 4 root root 4096 Feb 16 17:42 ../
-rw-r--r-- 1 root root 6149 Feb 16 18:42 derive-TPS-pgbench-2014-02-16
-rw-r--r-- 1 root root 6871 Feb 16 18:42 derive-TPS-postgres-2014-02-16
-rw-r--r-- 1 root root 6149 Feb 16 18:42 derive-TPS-template0-2014-02-16
-rw-r--r-- 1 root root 6132 Feb 16 18:42 derive-TPS-template1-2014-02-16
```

This makes use of every keyword we defined: the instance prefix, database name, type of graph, and database instance. collectd takes every precaution to separate data for manual consumption or for graphing purposes.

There's more...

We know that CSV data is not very exciting. collectd is primarily a transmission and aggregation system with plugin capabilities. This makes it very good at collecting performance data and sending that data to other presentation systems, but its own output is minimal to nonexistent. This is by design and keeps collectd efficient when handling data from hundreds of servers.

However, don't fret! This chapter has several sections devoted to viewing collectd data.

See also

We found some information pertaining to collectd data types as well as the PostgreSQL module for collectd. We suggest that you use these links for more insight:

- **Data source**: `https://collectd.org/wiki/index.php/Data_source`
- **PostgreSQL Plugin**: `https://collectd.org/wiki/index.php/Plugin:PostgreSQL`

Installing and configuring Graphite

When viewing the collected data and statistics regarding our highly available database, we can simply settle for the raw numbers. They tell a story and include precise measurements necessary for making decisions regarding architecture and incidence response. However, many would argue that this is much easier with graphs and charts, as they enable the identification of trends.

There are a lot of graphing libraries and tools, but relatively few of them are tailored to the needs of an agile monitoring team. The makers of **Graphite** helped fill this role, and they did so with an extremely versatile tool. Graphite makes visualizing the collected system statistics easy. Unfortunately, due to the number of its installation requirements, administrators might skip it in favor of something easier to use.

We don't want this to happen to our readers! Follow along, and we'll help you take advantage of one of the most powerful system visualization suites available.

Getting ready

Red-Hat-based systems will need to add the EPEL library. The most recent EPEL packages are available for several Red-Hat-based distributions at `http://download.fedoraproject.org/pub/epel`.

Look for the package file that begins with `epel-release` and download it to the monitoring server. Once the package is downloaded, install it with this command as a root-level user:

```
sudo rpm -ivh epel-release-*.rpm
```

Once `epel` has been installed, install the `python-pip`, `django`, and `cairo` packages and their requirements with this command:

```
sudo yum install python-pip django cairo
```

Debian-based systems should have an easier time due to the larger standard repositories. Execute these commands to install equivalent packages:

```
sudo apt-get install python-django python-django-tagging
sudo apt-get install python-pip python-cairo
```

Some build requirements include Python development libraries. These will depend on the Linux distribution in use but will likely be called `python-dev`, `python26-devel`, or some variant. Find and install the latest version available in the package repository before continuing.

How to do it...

Follow these steps to install, configure, and start Graphite on the dedicated monitoring server:

1. Install the web-based visualization frontend with this command:

   ```
   sudo pip install graphite-web
   ```

2. Install the data-caching daemon with this command:

   ```
   sudo pip install carbon Twisted=11.1
   ```

3. Install the data storage engine with this command:

   ```
   sudo pip install whisper
   ```

4. Create a file named `local_settings.py` in the `/opt/graphite/webapp/graphite/` directory with these contents:

   ```
   SECRET_KEY = 'Put some unique text here.'
   ```

5. Initialize the Graphite management database with this command:

   ```
   sudo python /opt/graphite/webapp/graphite/manage.py syncdb
   ```

6. Copy two of the default storage configuration files with these commands:

   ```
   cd /opt/graphite/conf
   sudo mv carbon.conf.example carbon.conf
   sudo mv storage-schemas.conf.example storage-schemas.conf
   ```

7. Start the carbon daemon with the following command:

   ```
   sudo /opt/graphite/bin/carbon-cache.py start
   ```

8. Start the Graphite website with the following commands:

   ```
   cd /opt/graphite/bin
   sudo su -c "./run-graphite-devel-server.py \
           /opt/graphite &> /var/log/graphite.log &"
   ```

How it works...

Once the prerequisites are installed, we need to install all of the pieces Graphite needs in order to function. These modules include Graphite-web for web-based graph construction, `carbon` for aggregating inputs, and `whisper` to store raw graph data. In the case of `carbon`, we must also specify which version of the twisted module to use, as `carbon` is currently incompatible with newer versions.

The next step isn't strictly necessary, but each Graphite installation maintains a unique secret series of characters. We recommend that you generate one and save it in the `SECRET_KEY` variable of the `local_settings.py` file. When it is time to secure the Graphite installation, having a secret key will make it easier.

As we have changed no other configuration settings, initializing the Graphite management database will create a sqlite database file in the `/opt/graphite/storage` directory. This file will store Graphite users, saved graphs and dashboards, and other elements specific to Graphite. We could have installed this in a PostgreSQL database as well. If the amount of Graphite users increases significantly, we recommend that you reinstall the management database into a PostgreSQL database to avoid usage contention. Until then, SQLite should suffice.

Next, there are two configuration files that `carbon` uses to control its cache and aggregation abilities as well as the output storage format. When we copy the example configuration files for `carbon.conf` and `storage-schemas.conf`, `carbon` will save data with the `whisper` module that we installed earlier. Furthermore, `whisper` will aggregate and store data according to the contents of `storage-schemas.conf`.

Finally, we start the `carbon` daemon and Graphite itself. Starting `carbon` is fairly easy due to the manner in which its management script was written. However, Graphite is meant to be displayed through a web server such as Apache or Nginx. As we're skipping the process of integrating Graphite with a web server, we have the option of starting Graphite with a Python-based development web server instead. The command we invoke sets up this Python development web server and directs it to serve Graphite pages. We recommend that you use a more formal installation process on an actual monitoring server.

If everything was successful, we should be able to see Graphite. The default port is `8080`, so if we direct a web browser to the monitoring server on that port, we should see this:

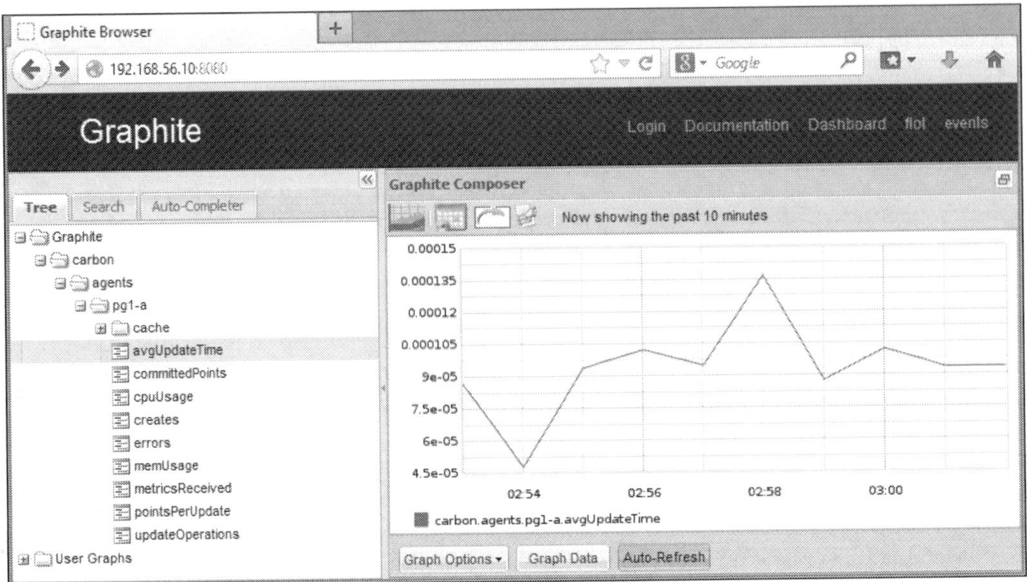

We selected a basic data point that `carbon` tracks for itself, and set the graph time range for 10 minutes. Currently the data available to Graphite is very minimal, but we hope to fix that soon.

See also

Graphite has rather extensive documentation as does the pip utility that we used to install most of its components. We suggest that you read further on these topics if possible, as our installation and configuration examples were extremely minimalistic. Use the following links for more information:

- **Graphite wiki**: `http://graphite.wikidot.com/`
- **Updated Graphite Documentation**: `http://graphite.readthedocs.org/en/latest/`
- **Python Package Index | pip**: `https://pypi.python.org/pypi/pip`

Adding collectd data to Graphite

Graphite has a good interface and a lot of graph options but no real data. collectd gathers a lot of data but has no real interface. Luckily, we can combine the two, thanks to a collectd module named `write_graphite`.

In order to feed the collectd data into Graphite, we simply need to modify two configuration files on the monitoring server and restart collectd. After we do this, we can enable more collectd modules, add more PostgreSQL queries, and so on. All the collectd data will be transmitted to Graphite until we break the connection.

This is powerful functionality, as we will demonstrate.

Getting ready

In this recipe, we will be using both collectd and Graphite. Please follow the instructions in the *Installing and configuring collectd* and *Installing and configuring Graphite* recipes before continuing.

How to do it...

To send the collectd data to Graphite, follow these steps only on the server monitoring our PostgreSQL nodes:

1. Add the following section to the *top* of the `storage-schemas.conf` file in the `/opt/graphite/conf` directory:

   ```
   [collectd]
   pattern = ^collectd\.
   retentions = 10s:1d,1m:7d,5m:30d,10m:90d,1h:1y
   ```

2. Restart the `carbon` daemon with the following commands:

   ```
   sudo /opt/graphite/bin/carbon-cache.py stop
   sudo /opt/graphite/bin/carbon-cache.py start
   ```

3. Replace the contents of the `local.conf` file in `/etc/collectd` with the following contents:

   ```
   LoadPlugin write_graphite

   <Plugin write_graphite>
     <Node "mon1">
       LogSendErrors true
       Prefix "collectd."
       StoreRates true
       SeparateInstances true
     </Node>
   </Plugin>
   ```

4. Restart the collectd daemon with the following command:

   ```
   sudo service collectd restart
   ```

How it works...

The first thing we need to do is prepare `carbon` and `whisper` for the data that will be arriving from collectd. By default, `whisper` will apply storage settings in the order they appear in the `storage-schemas.conf` file and has an existing default at the end. Thus, we must place our settings at the top of the file to ensure they're properly applied.

After naming the storage schema `[collectd]`, we specify a pattern for carbon to recognize the collectd data. Any incoming data that fits this expression will use the retention periods that we've configured. Regarding these retention periods, we should be able to see detailed statistics for recent data and observe trends when viewing them over longer periods.

As such, we've told Graphite to keep every 10 seconds for 1 day, every minute for a week, every 5 minutes for a month, every 10 minutes for 3 months, and every hour for a year. Feel free to adjust these periods to reflect your preferences. Afterwards, we restart carbon to ensure that it reads the new configuration values we've set.

The next step is to configure the local collectd daemon on the monitoring server to send data to Graphite. Remember, collectd on the monitoring server is also aggregating performance metrics from several other servers. The collectd daemons in `Listen` mode will forward all the data to Graphite, so it makes sense to make our changes there.

We begin by loading the `write_graphite` module. The next step is to configure this module with the settings we want. Many of the default values are actually desirable, so we'll ignore them. Note that we set `Prefix` to `collectd`, because Graphite uses periods as separators for data points. This means that the interface will group all the collectd data under a single heading, as seen here:

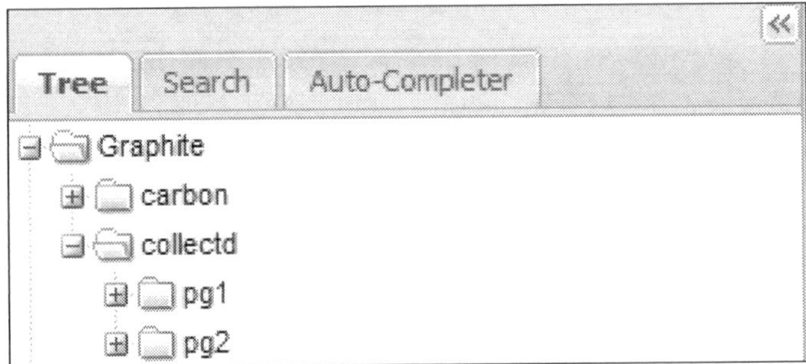

This makes it easier to group data. This also matches the pattern we used when setting the data retention periods. In our preceding example, we have two PostgreSQL servers monitored by collectd, and they're easy to find.

The other notable setting is `SeparateInstances`, which further groups related data. As an example, if data was named `pg2.postgresql-production`, it will now be named `pg2.postgresql.production` instead. By separating the sections with a period, the sections do not get their own header but are grouped together instead. This means we can group environments under the *postgresql* banner, for instance. Otherwise, we would have *postgresql-production*, *postgresql-stage*, *postgresql-dev*, or other separate entries for each system variation.

Finally, we restart the collectd daemon so that it incorporates the `write_graphite` plugin safely. If we wait for a few moments and reload our Graphite web interface, we should see new graph activity. After finding the appropriate node to view, we should be greeted by this:

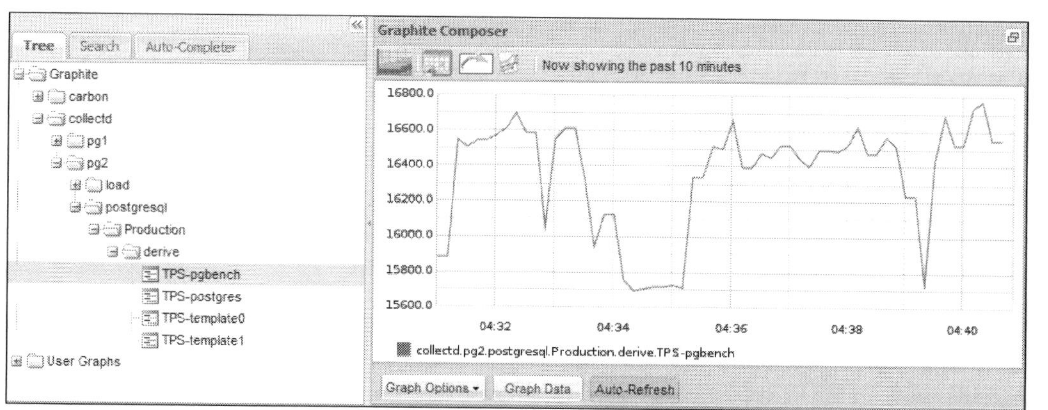

See also

As we've used `write_graphite` from collectd and storage schema settings for Graphite, we've included manuals for both. You may have to search, but these pages should provide more information on the elements covered in this recipe:

- **Configuring Carbon**: `http://graphite.readthedocs.org/en/latest/config-carbon.html`
- **The collectd.conf Manpage**: `http://collectd.org/documentation/manpages/collectd.conf.5.shtml`
- **The write_graphite Plugin**: `https://collectd.org/wiki/index.php/Plugin:Write_Graphite`

Building a graph in Graphite

The Graphite interface introduces several extensive capabilities. In order to use its complete functionality, we must log in. After doing so, we can save graphs, delete saved graphs, load graphs that other users have created and customized, and much more.

This recipe will take you through the interface to create a graph, save it, and load it later. Finally, we can avoid extremely technical discussions for a while!

Getting ready

In this recipe, we will be combining the results of all the previous recipes related to collectd and Graphite. We recommend that you have a functional monitor server configured, as discussed in those recipes.

When we installed and configured Graphite, it should have asked for a username and password for the primary administrative user. This information will be necessary to log in to the interface.

How to do it...

Follow these instructions to build, save, and load a saved graph:

1. Direct a web browser at the monitor server on port 8080.
2. Click on the **Login** link located at the top of the page.
3. Enter the **username** and **password** as requested, and click on **login**.
4. Click on the **Graphite** link on the left pane.
5. Click on the **collectd** link on the left pane.
6. Click on the name of the server you wish to view.
7. Continue by clicking on **postgresql**, **Production**, and then on **derive**.
8. Select the item corresponding to a busy database or default to **TPS-postgres**.
9. Select another item from the **derive** list so that both data points are in the same graph.
10. Click on the save icon shaped like a floppy disk, and name this graph. We suggest that you name it `Production TPS`.
11. Reload the browser window to clear out any selections.
12. Click on **My Graphs** on the left pane.
13. Choose the `Production TPS` graph.

How it works...

Regular guest users can view graphs, but they cannot save views for later. When we installed Graphite, it created a default user, probably named `root`. For now, we can use this for demonstration purposes. The login screen is very terse:

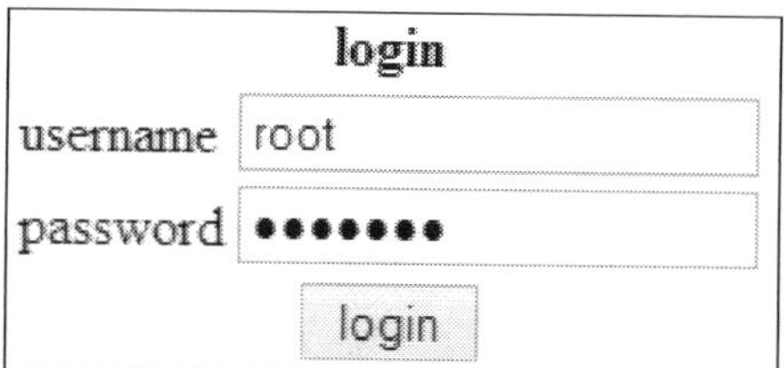

Once we have logged into Graphite, we are free to build a graph. When we click on a link on the left pane, we expand its contents. Every expanded section leads to a list of one or more further sections. As such, we keep clicking on them until we reach items that can be represented on the graph pane. The data we are interested in is being supplied by **collectd**, so we start with it after expanding the **Graphite** section.

We recommended that you select two data series for two reasons. First, it shows that multiple data points can exist in the same graph. Secondly, we believe that saving a graph with only one data point is boring. After the two data points are activated, our interface should look like this:

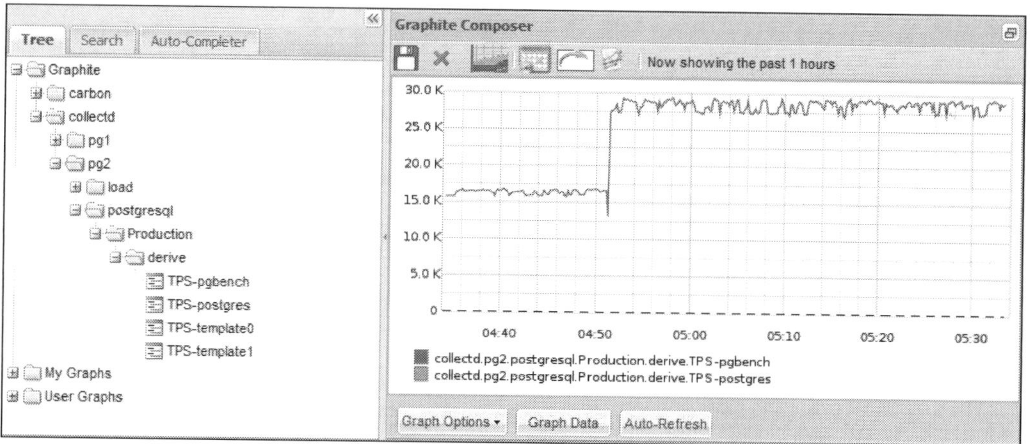

The active line through the graph represents the `pgbench` database in our test system, and it is quite busy. The dashed line at the bottom of the graph is the `postgres` database, which nobody uses, and it is zero for the duration of our view window. Regardless of the contents, we save this graph so that we can load it again later.

After we reload the browser window and expand the **My Graphs** link, we should see the graph that we just saved:

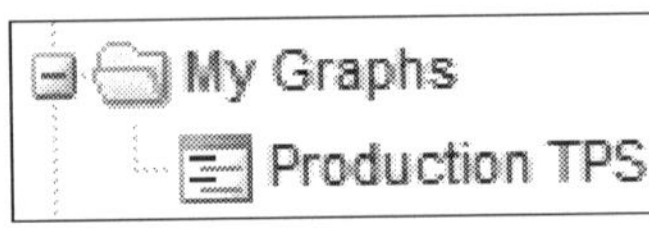

Click on the **Production TPS** chart, and it should load on the right pane automatically.

There's more...

Graphite groups the items that contain a period anywhere in their names. We suggest that you develop a naming scheme to take advantage of this. A good naming scheme should incorporate the environment and a descriptive explanation of the graph's contents. If we used *Trading | Database Write Activity*, our saved graphs would look like this:

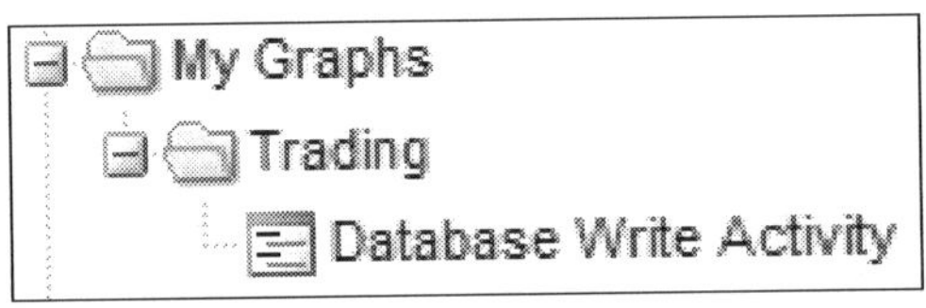

Customizing a Graphite graph

Graphite graphs are very helpful in their default form, even though it simply reflects the data it can access. One of the less obvious features that Graphite offers is data transformation. Graphite has several choices for line and background colors, legend names, and so on. We can calculate moving averages, standard deviations, and logs.

There is a lot of extra functionality available in Graphite, and only exploration will truly unveil much of it. We'll introduce a few basic examples in this recipe.

Getting ready

In this recipe, we will be combining the results of all the previous recipes related to collectd and Graphite. We recommend that you have a functional monitor server configured, as discussed in those recipes.

How to do it...

Follow these instructions to apply several transformations to a simple graph:

1. Direct a web browser at the monitor server on port 8080.
2. Click on the **Graphite** and **collectd** links on the left pane.
3. Click on the name of the server to view.
4. Continue by clicking on **postgresql**, **Production**, and then on **derive**.
5. Select the item corresponding to a busy database or default to **TPS-postgres**.
6. Click on the **Graph Options** button on the graph composer; then, click on **Graph Title**.
7. Enter `Production TPS Graph` as the new graph name.
8. Click on the **Graph Data** button on the graph composer.
9. Click on the only existing data point.
10. Select **Apply Function**, **Calculate**, and then **Moving Average**.
11. Enter `60` as the number of data points.
12. Select **Apply Function**, **Special**, and then **Set Legend Name**.
13. Enter `TPS - Moving Average` as the new legend name.
14. Close the **Graph Data** pane.

How it works...

To begin creating a graph, we first need data to display. The first few steps simply dictate what elements we should select to drill down to an appropriate level where data points are stored. Once we've selected one, it's time to customize the data.

The graph composer has two buttons that directly interest us: **Graph Options** and **Graph Data**. They will look like this:

The **Graph Options** button groups the items that apply to the entire graph. This is the menu we would use to change the graph's title, its line mode, fonts, colors, and so on. For now, we've kept it simple and changed the graph's name.

The **Graph Data** button is the more complicated one of the two. It actually launches a submenu, which looks like this:

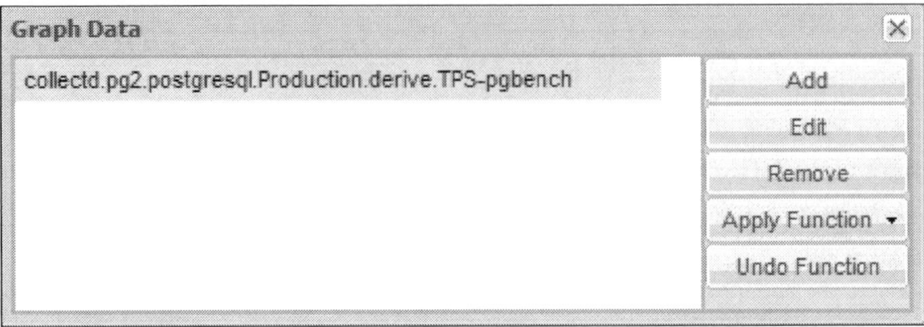

This is where we apply transformations to specific data points or modify the ones that are included in the graph. Of the functions available, we chose to apply a moving average of 60 readings. By default, collectd takes 1 reading every 10 seconds. Thus, 60 readings equates to 10 minutes worth of readings. We now have a 10 minute moving average on our graph instead of the raw data.

However, the full path to the collectd data point is also used as the label in the legend. Even worse, now that we have applied a function to the data, it's included in the label as well. So, our next steps involve changing the label under the **Special** menu to make it more readable. Once we've changed the legend name, our graph should resemble this:

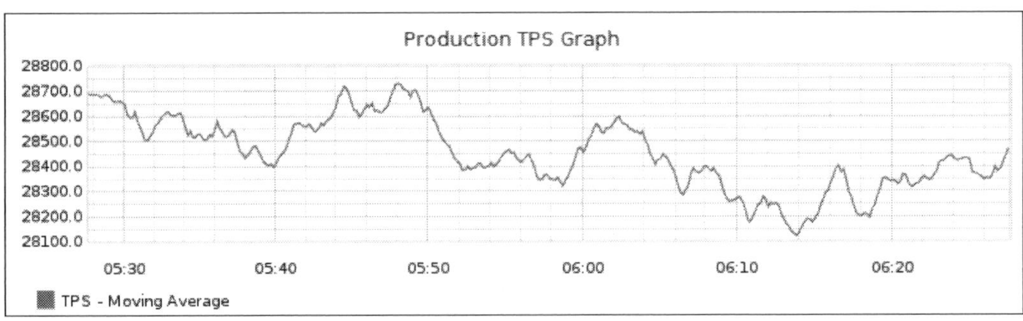

If we were to save this graph, all of the customizations would be saved as well. This allows others to reuse the graphs that we've prepared, whether for system monitor dashboards or presentations.

Creating a Graphite dashboard

Perhaps we saved the best Graphite feature for last. A major concern when monitoring the activity of a highly available PostgreSQL server is that of visibility. So far, we've seen that Graphite makes data visible and offers a lot of customization. However, we still need a solution to view multiple graphs at once.

This at-a-glance usage is invaluable for watching several servers at once or viewing multiple aspects of a single server in depth. Thankfully, Graphite has us covered in this regard and provides a robust dashboard view specifically to view multiple graphs simultaneously.

Let's explore this final exciting feature.

Getting ready

In this recipe, we will be combining the results of all the previous recipes related to collectd and Graphite. We recommend that you have a functional monitor server configured, as discussed in those recipes. We also recommend that you create at least one saved graph that we can load in the dashboard we construct.

How to do it...

Follow these instructions to build, save, and load a monitor dashboard:

1. Direct a web browser at the monitor server on port 8080.
2. Click on the **Dashboard** link located at the top of the page.
3. Click on the icon in the upper-right corner of the window to collapse the search pane.
4. Click on the **Graphs** link on the top menu bar.
5. Continue by selecting **New Graph** and then **From Saved Graph**.
6. Expand the list of saved graphs and navigate to any previously saved graph.
7. Click on the desired graph name, and check **Select**.
8. Repeat as necessary until the dashboard is finished.
9. Click on the **Dashboard** link on the top menu bar.
10. Continue by selecting **Save As**, give the graph a name, and click on **OK** to confirm.
11. Click on OK to confirm new dashboard name.
12. Reload the browser window to clear out any selections.
13. Click on the **Dashboard** link on the top menu bar.
14. Continue by selecting **Finder**, and navigate to the desired dashboard name.
15. Choose **Open** to load the dashboard.

How it works...

The first thing we need to do is enter the dashboard view itself by clicking on the **Dashboard** link in the main menu. Once there, we can load as many graphs as we desire to view at once. The first step is to navigate through the **Graphs** menu as seen here:

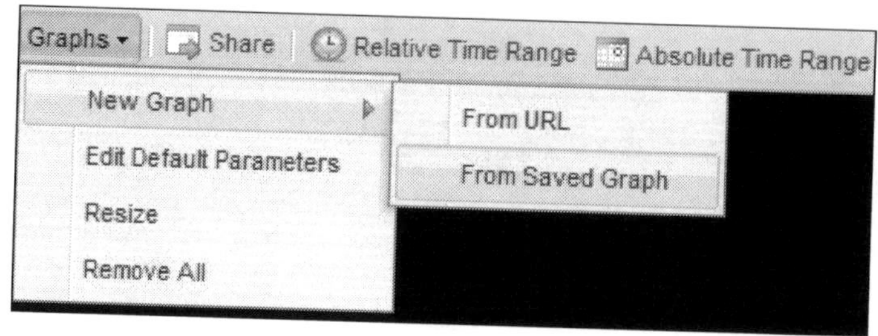

Once we have added one or more graphs using this method, we have created our dashboard. When we installed collectd, we also enabled the system load plugin, which reports how busy the server is. We took the opportunity to create a graph for this and saved it as an example. Your dashboard may look different, but ours has these two saved graphs:

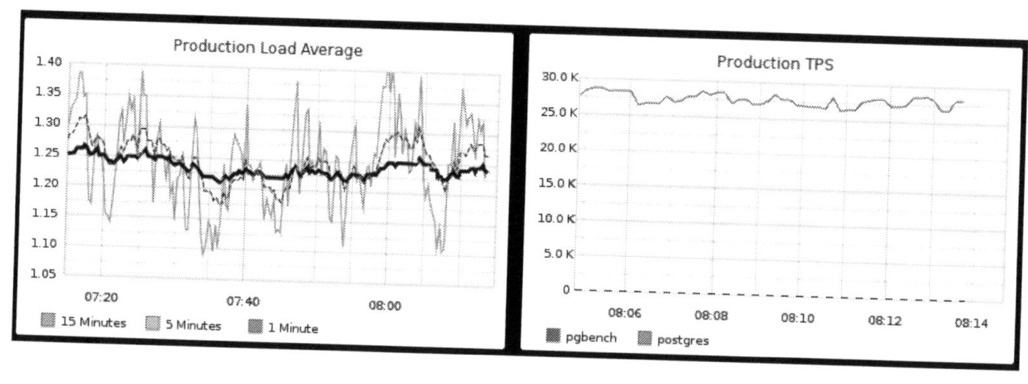

To save this dashboard, we can simply select **Save** or **Save As** in the **Dashboard** menu. Afterwards, this dashboard is available for anyone to use. We can see that for ourselves by locating the dashboard within the **Finder** menu. Here's ours, for reference:

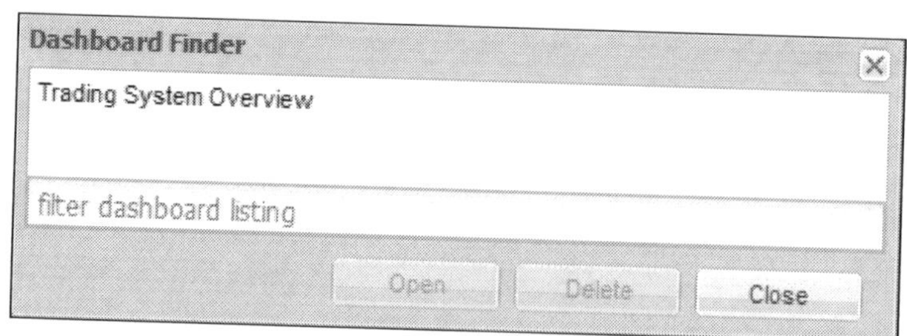

There's more...

A handy technique that the dashboard gives us is the ability to adjust the display range of all the graphs at the same time. If we click on **Relative Time Range** in the top menu, this pop up appears:

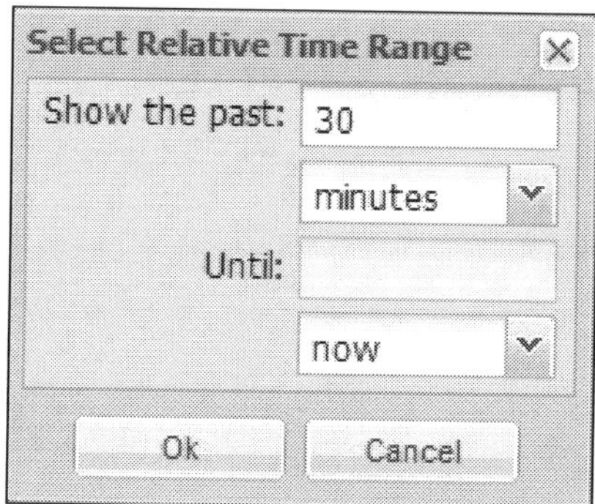

With this, we can observe the past few minutes, hours, days, weeks, or months of data trends for every graph currently being displayed. This functionality is further extended in the **Absolute Time Range** menu, which allows us to choose any date or time range since we installed Graphite.

Explore further to fully leverage the dashboard view!

6
Replication

In this chapter, we will learn several methods to copy entire databases or individual tables. We will cover the following recipes in this chapter:

- Deciding what to copy
- Securing the WAL stream
- Setting up a hot standby
- Upgrading to asynchronous replication
- Bulletproofing with synchronous replication
- Faking replication with pg_receivexlog
- Setting up Slony
- Copying a few tables with Slony
- Setting up Bucardo
- Copying a few tables with Bucardo
- Setting up Londiste
- Copying a few tables with Londiste

Introduction

One element that is absolutely required for any highly available PostgreSQL installation is replication. It does not matter if we have a **SAN** that provides disk redundancy, nor is DRBD or other block-level replication sufficient to protect our investment. Duplicating and backing up data is always a good practice, but when it comes to availability, we need online copies of the database.

Similarly, if other departments need data that resides in our OLTP database, how can we provide it safely? In ideal circumstances, we can supply a copy of the necessary tables. This way, we don't strain the primary database with ad hoc report-based queries. A new DBA might try to accomplish this by building a synchronization library or performing scheduled extracts and copies into a remote database. However, there are easier ways!

PostgreSQL gives us methods to build and maintain a fully online copy of our primary database. Furthermore, there are existing utilities to duplicate tables when we don't need a copy of the whole database. In this chapter, we will utilize PostgreSQL replication as well as third-party table-synchronization tools. Building the best stack requires familiarity with the tools available.

Deciding what to copy

Before copying anything, we need to determine what to copy. In some instances, it might be necessary to copy the entire database for disaster-recovery purposes. At other times, such a copy would waste resources. We need to differentiate between these two scenarios.

Once we've done this, we should decide what to do when we don't want to copy the whole database. We need to know which tables to copy and where to send them. To accomplish this, we will build a very small spreadsheet in this section to keep track of the resources we will need for all of our table and database replicas.

Getting ready

We're going to build a spreadsheet. This spreadsheet will specify the type of replica we want to maintain, as well as where it will reside. Have a spreadsheet program available before starting.

How to do it...

Follow these steps to determine replication resource requirements:

1. Create a spreadsheet with six columns labeled `Source Server`, `Target Server`, `Type`, `DB Name`, `Table`, and `Set`.
2. Under the `Source Server` column, list the role or name of the PostgreSQL server that provides the data.
3. Under the `Target Server` column, list the role or name of the PostgreSQL server that receives the data.
4. Under the `Type` column, select either `Replica` to copy the whole database or `Logical` to copy individual tables.
5. Under the `DB Name` column, enter the name of the database where tables reside on the source server. If you are using `Replica` for `Type`, enter `All` here.

6. Under the `Table` column, enter `All` for every table in the listed database, or enter a single table name. If you are copying multiple individual tables, create a single row for each table.
7. Under the `Set` column, enter a name for the set of tables being copied. Do this only if using `Logical` for the `Type` column.
8. Create at least one row in the spreadsheet for a **Disaster Recovery** (**DR**) copy of every source server in your PostgreSQL clusters.

How it works...

The spreadsheet we're making only requires six columns to fit this recipe. Feel free to include any other relevant information when making your own. In fact, we suggest that you retain this document for reference purposes and revisions.

We begin by listing the name or role of the server where all the data will originate. This `Source Server` column will help us—and everyone else—to keep track of where the original data resides. If a server is listed too often in this column, we may want to reconsider removing some replicas so that we don't overwhelm it.

Next, we need to decide where to send the data. The `Target Server` column lets us define where the tables will reside after being replicated. This allows us to formally dictate how many copies will live in how many locations. There are some limitations based on the type we define for this replica entry.

When listing the type of replication, we have only two options. We can either mirror the entire database as a `Replica`, or single tables in the case of a `Logical` copy. Any target server can only appear once if its value in the `Type` column is `Replica`. Otherwise, a server might receive several `Logical` sources.

Then, we need to list `DB Name` where we can find the table to copy. If we are copying the entire database as a `Replica`, this value will always be `All`. Otherwise, we should list a single database name.

Next, which table will we copy? In the case of a `Replica` type, this value will be `All`. Otherwise, should we copy the entire listed database or an inventory of specific tables? To mirror every table in the database, enter `All` here. Otherwise, use the name of the table (including its schema) that we want to include.

Finally, if we are copying a list of individual tables or a named database, we should name the replica as `Set`. Replication utilities commonly use these set names to address the objects being copied, so we can define any sets we plan to use.

The final step we've listed is to determine where we require at least one copy of the entire database. This replica will be an online copy that we can switch to in the case of server or data center failure. In a truly high availability architecture, this is not optional.

With all of these entries, our spreadsheet might look something like this:

	A	B	C	D	E	F
1	**Source Server**	**Target Server**	**Type**	**DB Name**	**Tables**	**Set**
2	Trading	Trading DR	Replica	All	All	N/A
3	Trading	Trading Ad Hoc	Replica	All	All	N/A
4	Trading	Reporting	Logical	maindb	customer	orders
5	Trading	Reporting	Logical	maindb	order	orders
6	Trading	Reporting	Logical	maindb	product	orders

In this particular example, we have our Disaster Recovery copy of the database and another full replica for departments to query without disturbing the primary system. Then, we copy three tables to the reporting database for our Business Intelligence or Marketing teams to integrate into their customer activity reports.

Securing the WAL stream

The primary mechanism that PostgreSQL uses to provide a data durability guarantee is through its **Write Ahead Log** (**WAL**). All transactional data is written to this location before ever being committed to database files. Once WAL files are no longer necessary for crash recovery, PostgreSQL will either delete or archive them. For the purposes of a highly available server, we recommend that you keep these important files as long as possible. There are several reasons for this; they are as follows:

- Archived WAL files can be used for **Point In Time Recovery** (**PITR**)
- If you are using streaming replication, interrupted streams can be re-established by applying WAL files until the replica has caught up
- WAL files can be reused to service multiple server copies

In order to gain these benefits, we need to enable PostgreSQL WAL archiving and save these files until we no longer need them. This section will address our recommendations for long-term storage of WAL files.

Getting ready

In order to properly archive WAL files, we recommend that you provision a server dedicated to backups or file storage. Depending on the transaction volume, an active PostgreSQL database might produce thousands of these on a daily basis. At 16 MB apiece, this is not an idle concern. For instance, for a 1 TB database, we recommend at least 3 TB of storage space.

In addition, we will be using **rsync** as a daemon on this archive server. To install this on a Debian-based server, execute the following command as a root-level user:

```
sudo apt-get install rsync
```

Red-Hat-based systems will need this command instead:

```
sudo yum install rsync xinetd
```

How to do it...

Our archive server has a 3 TB mount at the /db directory and is named arc_server on our network. The PostgreSQL source server resides at 192.168.56.10. Follow these steps for long-term storage of important WAL files on an archive server:

1. Enable rsync to run as a daemon on the archive server.
2. On Debian-based systems, edit the /etc/default/rsync file and change the RSYNC_ENABLE variable to true.
3. On Red-Hat-based systems, edit the /etc/xinet.d/rsync file and change the disable parameter to no.
4. Create a directory to store archived WAL files as the postgres user with these commands:

   ```
   sudo mkdir /db/pg_archived
   sudo chown postgres:postgres /db/pg_archived
   ```

5. Create a file named /etc/rsyncd.conf and fill it with the following contents:

   ```
   [wal_store]
       path = /db/pg_archived
       comment = DB WAL Archives
       uid = postgres
       gid = postgres
       read only = false
       hosts allow = 192.168.56.10
       hosts deny = *
   ```

6. Start the rsync daemon.
7. Debian-based systems should execute the following command: sudo service rsync start.
8. Red-Hat-based systems can start rsync with this command instead: sudo service xinetd start.
9. Change the archive_mode and archive_command parameters in postgresql.conf to read the following:

   ```
   archive_mode = on
   archive_command = 'rsync -aq %p arc_server::wal_store/%f'
   ```

10. Restart the PostgreSQL server with the following command:

    ```
    pg_ctl -D $PGDATA restart
    ```

How it works...

The rsync utility is normally used to transfer files between two servers. However, we can take advantage of using it as a daemon to avoid connection overhead imposed by using SSH as an rsync protocol. Our first step is to ensure that the service is not disabled in some manner, which would make the rest of this guide moot.

Next, we need a place to store archived WAL files on the archive server. Assuming that we have 3 TB of space in the `/db` directory, we simply claim `/db/pg_archived` as the desired storage location. There should be enough space to use `/db` for backups as well, but we won't discuss that in this recipe.

Next, we create a file named `/etc/rsyncd.conf`, which will configure how rsync operates as a daemon. Here, we name the `/db/pg_archived` directory `wal_store` so that we can address the path by its name when sending files. We give it a human-readable name and ensure that files are owned by the `postgres` user, as this user also controls most of the PostgreSQL-related services.

The next, and possibly the most important step, is to block all hosts but the primary PostgreSQL server from writing to this location. We set `hosts deny` to `*`, which blocks every server. Then, we set `hosts allow` to the primary database server's IP address so that only it has access. If everything goes well, we can start the rsync (or `xinetd` on Red Hat systems) service and we can see that in the following screenshot:

```
$> sudo service rsync start
 * Starting rsync daemon rsync                          [ OK ]
```

Next, we enable `archive_mode` by setting it to `on`. With archive mode enabled, we can specify a command that will execute when PostgreSQL no longer needs a WAL file for crash recovery. In this case, we invoke the `rsync` command with the `-a` parameter to preserve elements such as file ownership, timestamps, and so on.

In addition, we specify the `-q` setting to suppress output, as PostgreSQL only checks the command exit status to determine its success. In the `archive_command` setting, the `%p` value represents the full path to the WAL file, and `%f` resolves to the filename. In this context, we're sending the WAL file to the archive server at the `wal_store` module we defined in `rsyncd.conf`.

Once we restart PostgreSQL, it will start storing all the old WAL files by sending them to the archive server.

In case any `rsync` command fails because the archive server is unreachable, PostgreSQL will keep trying to send it until it is successful. If the archive server is unreachable for too long, we suggest that you change the `archive_command` setting to store files elsewhere. This prevents accidentally overfilling the PostgreSQL server storage.

There's more...

As we will likely want to use the WAL files on other servers, we suggest that you make a list of all the servers that could need WAL files. Then, modify the `rsyncd.conf` file on the archive server and add this section:

```
[wal_fetch]
    path = /db/pg_archived
    comment = DB WAL Archive Retrieval
    uid = postgres
    gid = postgres
    read only = true
    hosts allow = host1, host2, host3
    hosts deny = *
```

Now, we can fetch WAL files from any of the hosts in `hosts allow`. As these are dedicated PostgreSQL replicas, recovery servers, or other defined roles, this makes the archive server a central location for all our WAL needs.

See also

- We suggest that you read more about the `archive_mode` and `archive_command` settings on the PostgreSQL site. We've included a link here: `http://www.postgresql.org/docs/9.3/static/runtime-config-wal.html`
- The `rsyncd.conf` file should also have its own manual page. Read it with this command to learn more about the available settings:

  `man rsyncd.conf`

Setting up a hot standby

It is a very good practice, if not an outright requirement, to have a second online copy of a PostgreSQL server in high availability clusters. Without such an online server, recovery from an outage may require hours of incidence response, backup recovery, and server provisioning. We have everything to gain by having extra online servers.

In addition, the process of setting up a hot standby acts as the basis for creating PostgreSQL streaming replicas. This means that we can reuse this recipe over and over again anytime we need to create PostgreSQL mirrors, provision extra backup copies, set up test instances, and so on.

All of this is made possible by the `pg_basebackup` command.

Getting ready

A hot standby server should have similar, if not exactly the same, specifications as the PostgreSQL server it is subscribed to. Try to accomplish this if possible. Also refer to the previous *Securing the WAL stream* recipe, as we will be consuming WAL files in this recipe.

How to do it...

For this scenario, the server at `192.168.56.10` is the primary PostgreSQL server, and `192.168.56.20` will be the new copy. Once again, `arc_server` will be the location of the archive server with old WAL files. On all PostgreSQL servers, our data directory should be located at `/db/pgdata`.

Follow these steps to build a PostgreSQL hot standby:

1. Ensure that the `pg_hba.conf` file on the primary server contains this line:

   ```
   host    replication    rep_user    192.168.56.20/32    trust
   ```

2. Reload the configuration files on the primary server with the following command as the `postgres` user:

   ```
   pg_ctl -D /db/pgdata reload
   ```

3. Ensure that the `wal_level` and `max_wal_senders` settings in `postgresql.conf` are set as follows on the primary server:

   ```
   wal_level = hot_standby
   max_wal_senders = 5
   ```

4. Create the replication user if it doesn't already exist with this SQL statement:

   ```
   CREATE USER rep_user WITH REPLICATION;
   ```

5. On the new server replica, create the `/db/pgdata` and `/db/pg_archived` directories with these commands as a root-level user:

   ```
   sudo mkdir -p /db/pgdata /db/pg_archived
   sudo chown postgres:postgres /db/*
   sudo chmod 0700 /db/pgdata /db/pg_archived
   ```

6. Create a file named /etc/cron.d/postgres with the following contents in a single line:

```
* * * * * postgres flock /tmp/wal_sync rsync -aq --del
  arc_server::wal_fetch/ /db/pg_archived
```

7. Copy the primary server data with this command on the secondary server as the postgres user:

```
pg_basebackup -D /db/pgdata -h 192.168.56.10 -U rep_user
```

8. Create a file named /db/pgdata/recovery.conf and fill it with the following contents:

```
standby_mode = on
restore_command = 'pg_standby /db/pg_archived %f %p'
```

9. Ensure that the postgresql.conf file on the standby server contains the following setting:

```
hot_standby = on
```

10. Start the PostgreSQL server on the standby server with this command:

```
pg_ctl -D /db/pgdata start
```

How it works...

The first thing we do with this recipe is allow the new PostgreSQL server to retrieve data from the primary server. There are a few ways to do this, but for the sake of demonstration, we created a rule for the server at 192.168.56.20 to connect to the replication pseudo-database. This allows tools such as pg_basebackup to copy database files from the primary database when we initialize the replica. Once we reload the configuration files, rep_user should have sufficient access to copy PostgreSQL data files.

In a related concern, we must ensure that the wal_level setting of the primary server is set to hot_standby and that max_wal_senders is a value greater than 0. Earlier chapters on configuring PostgreSQL have already made this suggestion, but this recipe won't work at all if these parameters are set wrong.

Next, we should make sure that rep_user exists. Earlier chapters contained instructions to create this user, but it doesn't hurt to double-check. Regardless of what user we use to copy data, it must have the replication permission used in the CREATE USER syntax.

Next, the new child server needs the same data directory as its parent. We also want to have a location to synchronize WAL files so that the copy can process them and remain up to date. We set the permissions so that only the `postgres` user can view their contents. We should end up with something like this:

```
drwx------  2 postgres postgres 4096 Feb 22 19:52 pg_archived/
drwx------ 16 postgres postgres 4096 Feb 22 20:15 pgdata/
```

With these two directories in place, it's time to copy WAL files from the archive server. To accomplish this, we create a file in `/etc/cron.d` that will execute an `rsync` command every minute. This `rsync` command will copy WAL files from the archive server to the `/db/pg_archived` directory. The `-a` parameter ensures that it will include file permissions and ownership, and `-q` will suppress non-error messages so it's easier to tell if something went wrong. We have also added the `--del` setting, which will cause `rsync` to delete any files that don't exist on the archive server.

> Why every minute? It prevents the hot standby from falling too far behind, without making use of pure PostgreSQL replication. If you want to use this server as an insurance policy, it might be a good idea to delay it behind the source database by an hour. This way, mistakes will not appear on the standby for an hour, giving us a chance to fix problems before they taint database copies. To sync every hour, change the `* * * * *` portion of the `rsync` command to `0 * * * *`.

As we're launching `rsync` asynchronously, we use `flock` to create a temporary lock file in the `/tmp` directory. This way, if the primary server produced a large burst of WAL files, we won't have two conflicting `rsync` commands trying to copy the files to `/db/pg_archived`.

Once we've established a stream for WAL files, we need to copy the actual database. For this, we use the `pg_basebackup` command. While `pg_basebackup` is, theoretically, a backup utility, it serves a dual purpose. When launched with the `-D` parameter, it copies the server data files from the host indicated by the `-h` parameter and saves them to the indicated directory. Thus, our `pg_basebackup` command copied files from `192.168.56.10` to `/db/pgdata`. This produces a PostgreSQL data directory capable of hosting a running database. We also used the `-U` setting to use the `rep_user` user that we created specifically for replication-related tasks.

Next, we want to start the PostgreSQL hot standby, but first we need to tell it how to recover WAL files. We create a file named `recovery.conf`, and if this file exists, PostgreSQL will enter recovery mode instead of normal operation. In this recovery mode, it expects to process WAL files until there are no more available. However, we set `standby_mode` to `on` in this file, which tells PostgreSQL to wait forever under the assumption that more WAL files will arrive later. This is continuous recovery, and this is what makes a hot standby work.

Another setting that we use in `recovery.conf` is `restore_command`. Here, we use the `pg_standby` utility to regularly consume WAL files in the `/db/pg_archived` directory. We could have simply copied the files with `cp`, but this produces annoying output in our logs that looks like this:

```
cp: cannot stat `/db/pg_archived/00000004000000010000007E': No such file or directory
cp: cannot stat `/db/pg_archived/00000004000000010000007E': No such file or directory
```

These errors do nothing but add useless noise to the logs. We could suppress these errors from `cp`, but if there was an actual error, we would miss it. Using `pg_standby` is just easier.

Before we start the PostgreSQL hot standby, there's one more thing to confirm. Simply having a standby is useful, but having a readable standby is better. By enabling `hot_standby` in the `postgresql.conf` file, we can execute the basic select statements against the standby database.

Once we start the database on the replica, we should have a fully functional hot standby PostgreSQL server.

See also

As this is such a common configuration, the PostgreSQL documents discuss it at great length. We also made extensive use of the `pg_basebackup` and `pg_standby` commands. You can find out more information about these from the following URLs:

- **Hot Standby**: `http://www.postgresql.org/docs/9.3/static/hot-standby.html`
- **pg_basebackup**: `http://www.postgresql.org/docs/9.3/static/app-pgbasebackup.html`
- **pg_standby**: `http://www.postgresql.org/docs/9.3/static/pgstandby.html`

Upgrading to asynchronous replication

Since the release of PostgreSQL 9.0, DBAs have had access to asynchronous streaming replication. Unlike the older hot standby methods used in earlier versions, replica servers can connect to an upstream PostgreSQL server and consume data modifications directly. With low network latency and fast transactions, this means that it is fairly common for streaming replicas to lag behind the master by only a few milliseconds.

In the context of high availability, this means we can scale horizontally by copying the database to multiple servers. Of course, this means that we need to copy the entire database to each server. For small-to medium-sized database instances, this is a relatively minor requirement. This also means that we can produce up-to-date backups, perform ad hoc queries on practically live data, and aggregate information into reports without disrupting our primary database.

This recipe will explain how to set up a streaming asynchronous database replica and explore some of the hidden caveats of doing so.

Getting ready

We will be continuing the work we performed in the *Setting up a hot standby* recipe, so please refer to that recipe to build a working hot standby. We will alter the standby setup to include streaming replication, and better security.

How to do it...

For this scenario, the server at `192.168.56.10` is the primary PostgreSQL server, and `192.168.56.20` will be the asynchronous replica. Follow these steps to build a PostgreSQL asynchronous replica:

1. Give the `rep_user` user a password with this SQL statement:

   ```
   ALTER USER rep_user WITH PASSWORD 'newpass';
   ```

2. On the primary server, modify the `pg_hba.conf` line and remove any references to the `rep_user` user. Then, add this line:

   ```
   host    replication    rep_user    192.168.56.20/32    md5
   ```

3. Reload the configuration files on the primary server with the following command as the `postgres` user:

   ```
   pg_ctl -D /db/pgdata reload
   ```

4. On the replica server, create a file named `.pgpass` in the `postgres` user's home directory with the following contents:

   ```
   192.168.56.10:*:replication:rep_user:newpass
   ```

5. Alter the `.pgpass` file to have the correct permissions with this command:

   ```
   Chmod 600 ~/.pgpass
   ```

6. Modify the `recovery.conf` file on the recovery server to match these lines:

   ```
   standby_mode = on
   primary_conninfo = 'host=192.168.56.10 user=rep_user'
   restore_command = 'cp /db/pg_archived/%f %p 2>/dev/null'
   ```

7. Reload the configuration files on the streaming replica server with the following command as the `postgres` user:

```
pg_ctl -D /db/pgdata reload
```

8. Confirm that the standby is connected by executing this SQL on the primary PostgreSQL server:

```
SELECT client_addr, usename, state
  FROM pg_stat_replication;
```

How it works...

Using `trust` authentication is not generally a recommended practice. It is one thing to copy the database without a password once, but quite another to leave a long-term security hole for all database replicas. This means it is time to ensure that the `rep_user` user has a password. We also need to change `pg_hba.conf` to reflect the fact that we want to use regular `md5` authentication instead of `trust`. Once we reload the configuration files on the primary server, we move on to the streaming replica.

To get into the practice of using `.pgpass` files, we create one on the replica server for the `rep_user` user. The line we created in this file will send our desired password when the sections match; in this case, if we connect to `192.168.56.10` on any port to the `replication` database as the `rep_user` user, authentication will succeed automatically If any of these are different, the PostgreSQL client libraries will not send a password, and the client will receive an error. This is a fairly easy way to automate password submissions securely. PostgreSQL will also ignore this file if the permissions are wrong, so we set the control flags with `chmod` so that only the `postgres` user can access it.

Next, we rewrite the contents of the `recovery.conf` file to include `primary_conninfo`. This line is used to specify the connection information for establishing streaming replication. Since our password is in the `.pgpass` file, we don't need to enter it here. We also removed `pg_standby` in favor of a regular `cp` command with the errors suppressed. Now that our primary method of WAL consumption is directly from another server, we only need WAL files from `/db/pg_archived` as a fail back in case the stream is disrupted.

Why do we use `.pgpass` instead of entering the password in the `recovery.conf` file? It is very common for system automation tools to distribute configuration files to dozens or even hundreds of servers. Using `.pgpass`, we can settle on and redistribute passwords easily. In addition, tools that build `recovery.conf` will not need to know the password for the replication user.

Once we reload the standby server, it should become a streaming replica instead of a regular hot standby. We can confirm this with the SQL statement that checks the `pg_stat_replication` view on the primary server. We should get output similar to this:

```
  client_addr   | usename  |   state
----------------+----------+-----------
 192.168.56.20  | rep_user | streaming
```

There's more...

Though streaming replication has existed since PostgreSQL 9.0, recent changes to 9.3 include two very helpful additional features:

- The `pg_basebackup` tool puts PostgreSQL in backup mode by invoking the `pg_start_backup()` function. As this function writes to the database, it normally can't be used on a streaming server. However, the developers made changes in 9.3 that make it possible to use `pg_basebackup` on standby servers. This can greatly simplify the backup process and reduce overhead on the primary server.
- In the event that we have several streaming replicas, older versions of PostgreSQL required replica servers to connect directly to the primary server. In 9.3 and above versions, PostgreSQL allows streaming replicas to subscribe to other replicas. With this, we can further reduce strain on the primary database server by offloading replication duties to a topology of alternate servers.

See also

There are good resources within the PostgreSQL documentation and Wiki regarding streaming replication. For more information, please visit these URLs:

- **Log-Shipping Standby Servers**: `http://www.postgresql.org/docs/9.3/static/warm-standby.html`
- **Streaming Replication**: `http://wiki.postgresql.org/wiki/Streaming_Replication`
- **Standby Server Settings**: `http://www.postgresql.org/docs/9.3/static/standby-settings.html`
- **The Password File**: `http://www.postgresql.org/docs/9.3/static/libpq-pgpass.html`

Bulletproofing with synchronous replication

Sometimes, in order to provide acceptable data durability, a high availability configuration must utilize synchronous commits. Beginning with PostgreSQL 9.1, database servers can now refuse to commit a transaction until the data is located on at least one alternate server. Unlike asynchronous replication where this is optional, synchronous replicas enforce this requirement to a fault.

Discussions in the PostgreSQL mailing list suggest that there is a long-standing misconception that synchronous replication is similar to RAID-1 operation. In RAID-1, the same exact data exists on two disks (or two disk sets), and if one of the pair fails, it continues to operate in degraded mode until the problem is addressed. This is absolutely not the case with PostgreSQL synchronous replication.

Unlike a RAID-1, PostgreSQL replicas can exist on different servers, on different networks, or even in different countries. PostgreSQL synchronous replication is a guarantee that data is written to at least two servers. Despite the necessary increase in latency to confirm this, the guarantee is upheld at all times.

This recipe is for databases that need this kind of extreme durability.

Getting ready

We will be continuing the work we performed in the *Upgrading to asynchronous replication* recipe, so please refer to that section to build a working asynchronous replica. We will alter the standby setup to include synchronous streaming replication.

How to do it...

For this scenario, the server at `192.168.56.10` is still the primary PostgreSQL server. Follow these steps to change an asynchronous PostgreSQL server into a synchronous replica:

1. Modify the `recovery.conf` file on the recovery server to match these lines:

   ```
   standby_mode = on
   primary_conninfo = 'host=192.168.56.10 user=rep_user
     application_name=node2'
   restore_command = 'cp /db/pg_archived/%f %p 2>/dev/null'
   ```

2. Restart the streaming server with the following command as the `postgres` user:

   ```
   pg_ctl -D /db/pgdata restart
   ```

3. Change the `synchronous_standby_names` setting in the `postgresql.conf` file on the primary server to read the following:

   ```
   synchronous_standby_names = 'node2'
   ```

4. Reload the configuration files on the primary server with the following command as the postgres user:

```
pg_ctl -D /db/pgdata reload
```

5. Confirm that the standby is connected by executing this SQL on the primary PostgreSQL server:

```
SELECT client_addr, state, sync_state, application_name
  FROM pg_stat_replication;
```

How it works...

Promoting an asynchronous standby server to synchronous mode is actually a fairly simple procedure. We begin by modifying the `primary_conninfo` setting in the standby's `recovery.conf` file to include the `application_name` value. PostgreSQL differentiates replicas by their stated application name, so if we change this, we can specifically target that particular replica. Any other synchronous standby nodes should be assigned different names.

Once we restart the PostgreSQL server on the streaming standby, it will reconnect to the primary server with the new `application_name` that we assigned. From this point onward, we can refer to the standby server as `node2`. Thus, when we alter the `synchronous_standby_names` variable in the primary server's `postgresql.conf` file, we use the same name there.

Any time we want to change the `synchronous_standby_names` variable, we merely need to tell PostgreSQL to reload its configuration files. Thus, after we do this, `node2` should now act as a synchronous standby server. Any transaction will only commit if it can write to this server as well as the primary one.

This last point is extremely important. If, for any reason, the synchronous standby becomes unavailable, the primary server will stop writing to the database as well! If you are performing maintenance on the secondary server, we suggest that you set `synchronous_standby_names` to a blank value and reload the PostgreSQL server. This will break the synchronous guarantee until the standby can be reconnected.

Once we have reloaded the primary server's configuration files, we can check the `pg_stat_replication` view again to observe how streaming is currently functioning. After executing the query, we should see something like this:

```
 client_addr   |   state   | sync_state | application_name
---------------+-----------+------------+------------------
 192.168.56.20 | streaming | sync       | node2
```

As we can see in this example, the primary server sees `node2` as a synchronous streaming replica.

There's more...

We really want to confirm if the streaming replication works as advertised. To do this, let's shut down the standby server with this command:

```
pg_ctl -D /db/pgdata stop -m fast
```

Then, try to write to the primary server. This simple SQL statement should wait indefinitely:

```
CREATE TABLE foo ( bar INT );
```

If we then restart the streaming replica using the following command, we should see the transaction complete:

```
pg_ctl -D /db/pgdata start
```

As you might imagine, this can be problematic in true high availability architectures that handle thousands of transactions per second. As such, we don't actually recommend that you use synchronous replication on OLTP servers. As these comprise the bulk of highly available PostgreSQL clusters, opportunities to take advantage of this level of data durability are somewhat slim.

However, synchronous commit is actually somewhat optional. If we want to try the experiment again, we can first issue this SQL statement before trying a basic write query:

```
SET synchronous_commit TO false;
```

This disables synchronous replication temporarily for the current session. Subsequent write queries in this connection should succeed normally as if the remote server was a standard asynchronous copy.

See also

There are good resources within the PostgreSQL documentation and Wiki regarding streaming replication. For more information, please visit these URLs:

- **Log-Shipping Standby Servers**: `http://www.postgresql.org/docs/9.3/static/warm-standby.html`
- **Streaming Replication**: `http://wiki.postgresql.org/wiki/Streaming_Replication`
- **Synchronous Replication**: `https://wiki.postgresql.org/wiki/Synchronous_replication`

Faking replication with pg_receivexlog

Some built-in tools deserve special mention. The `pg_receivexlog` command was introduced with PostgreSQL 9.2. With this new utility, PostgreSQL has the ability to transmit transaction logs to a remote system without the need for a dedicated PostgreSQL server. This also means that we can avoid ad hoc tools such as `rsync` when maintaining an archive server to save old WAL files.

This allows us to set up any server to pull transaction logs directly from the primary PostgreSQL server. For highly available servers, PostgreSQL no longer needs to fork an external command to safeguard transaction logs into an archive location. In addition, we can monitor the state of the transmission through the `pg_stat_replication` system view.

In effect, we remove quite a bit of overhead from our PostgreSQL server and offload it to a less sensitive system. This recipe will provide a quick outline for using this utility.

Getting ready

Before starting with this recipe, ensure that you have a good understanding of how PostgreSQL replication works. To do this, follow the *Upgrading to asynchronous replication* and *Bulletproofing with synchronous replication* recipes.

How to do it...

For this scenario, the server at `192.168.56.10` is still the primary PostgreSQL server, and `192.168.56.100` will be our archive server. Follow these steps to save WAL data remotely:

1. Ensure that the `pg_hba.conf` file on the primary server contains this line:

   ```
   host    replication    rep_user    192.168.56.100/32    md5
   ```

2. Ensure that the `wal_keep_segments` and `archive_mode` settings in `postgresql.conf` are set as follows on the primary server:

   ```
   wal_keep_segments = 1000
   archive_mode = off
   ```

3. Restart the configuration files on the primary server with the following command as the `postgres` user:

   ```
   pg_ctl -D /db/pgdata restart
   ```

4. On the archive server, create the `/db/pg_archived` directory with these commands as a root-level user:

   ```
   sudo mkdir -p /db/pg_archived
   sudo chown postgres:postgres /db/pg_archived
   sudo chmod 0700 /db/pg_archived
   ```

5. Start the `pg_receivexlog` utility on the archive server with the following command:

```
pg_receivexlog -h 192.168.56.10 -U rep_user \
               -D /db/pg_archived -v \
               &> /db/pg_archived/wal_archive.log &
```

How it works...

First, we need to ensure that the archive server at `192.168.56.100` can connect to the primary server to receive the transaction log traffic. Next, unlike other recipes that depend on `archive_mode` to be enabled on the primary server, we want to disable it this time. Instead, we are going to rely on `pg_receivexlog` itself.

One setting that we change might seem a bit odd at first. The `wal_keep_segments` parameter defines how many transaction logs PostgreSQL should keep after it no longer needs them. Normally, it would delete old files or call the archive command to process them if `archive_mode` is `on`. By setting it to `1000`, we are telling it to always have at least 1000 extra files. This helps avoid lost WAL archives if there's a network problem, or we have to restart `pg_receivexlog`.

Is 1000 files too many? At 16 MB each, this accounts for 16 GB of space. Providing this much space should be very easy with modern storage devices. This many files should account for several hours of activity on all but the most active databases. It may actually be prudent to increase the limit further, depending on database activity.

Once these settings are in place, we need to restart PostgreSQL to disable WAL archival. At this point, the primary server will no longer save or transmit old WAL files anywhere. To make up for this, we make sure that the archive server has a location to store these files and that the `postgres` user can write to it. To continue with our examples, we will continue to use the `/db/pg_archived` directory.

Finally, we start the `pg_receivexlog` tool itself. We pass the `-h` parameter to connect to the primary database and use `-U` to enforce the replication user, `rep_user`. The `-D` parameter is required, and we use it to save WAL files to the `/db/pg_archived` directory we created. Then, we enable verbose output with `-v` just so that we are always informed about what `pg_receivexlog` is doing. We direct all output to a file named `wal_archive.log` and consider our work complete. The final `&` character launches the command in the background so that it functions even if we disconnect from the server.

If everything goes well, our /db/pg_archived directory should soon have some WAL files and a log inside it, as shown in the following screenshot:

```
-rw------- 1 postgres postgres 16777216 Feb 25 18:34 000000020000000000000067
-rw------- 1 postgres postgres 16777216 Feb 25 18:34 000000020000000000000068
-rw------- 1 postgres postgres 16777216 Feb 25 18:34 000000020000000000000069
-rw------- 1 postgres postgres 16777216 Feb 25 19:10 00000002000000000000006A.partial
-rw------- 1 postgres postgres       42 Feb 25 17:36 00000002.history
-rw-rw-r-- 1 postgres postgres      609 Feb 25 19:10 wal_archive.log
```

The file that ends in partial is a WAL transfer that is currently in progress.

See also

- The pg_receivexlog utility has more extensive documentation on PostgreSQL's site. Visit this URL to learn more: http://www.postgresql.org/docs/9.3/static/app-pgreceivexlog.html.

Setting up Slony

While there are a few logical asynchronous replication systems for PostgreSQL, **Slony-I** (**Slony** in short) was the first to gain wide adoption. Why would we use Slony when PostgreSQL already has replication? Currently, PostgreSQL replication can only copy the entire installation. Every database, schema, table, and user is copied at the binary level. In effect, streaming replication creates perfect clones of PostgreSQL servers.

Slony is very different. It is designed to copy tables only, capturing changes on a master server and sending them to one or more subscribers. If you want this type of replication, this section will provide a basic installation recipe designed for one master and one subscriber.

Getting ready

In order to install Slony, we will need the source code. At the time of writing this book, the latest version available is 2.2.2. You can obtain a copy of the source at http://slony.info/downloads/2.2/source/.

We only need the primary source package, but feel free to download the documentation as well.

How to do it...

For these instructions, 192.168.56.10 is the master PostgreSQL node, and 192.168.56.30 is our desired subscriber. Follow these instructions to activate Slony on the postgres default database:

1. Extract the source code and change to the resulting directory with these commands:

   ```
   tar -xjf slony1-2.2.2.tar.bz2
   cd slony1-2.2.2
   ```

2. Build and install Slony with these commands as a root-capable user:

   ```
   ./configure --prefix=/usr
   make
   sudo make install
   ```

3. Provide the `rep_user` database user with superuser capabilities by running this SQL statement on both PostgreSQL nodes:

   ```
   ALTER USER rep_user WITH SUPERUSER;
   ```

4. Enter the following line in the `.pgpass` file for the `postgres` user on both nodes:

   ```
   *:*:postgres:rep_user:passwordhere
   ```

5. Ensure that the following line exists within the `pg_hba.conf` file on the master node:

   ```
   host    postgres    rep_user    192.168.56.30/32    md5
   ```

6. Ensure that the following line exists within the `pg_hba.conf` file on the subscriber node:

   ```
   host    postgres    rep_user    192.168.56.10/32    md5
   ```

7. Reload the PostgreSQL service on both nodes with the following command as the `postgres` user:

   ```
   pg_ctl -D /db/pgdata reload
   ```

8. Create a file named `nodes.slonik` in the `/etc/slony` directory of the master node with the following contents:

   ```
   cluster name = replication;
   define master 'dbname=postgres host=192.168.56.10 user=rep_user';
   define sub1 'dbname=postgres host=192.168.56.30 user=rep_user';
   node 1 admin conninfo = @master;
   node 2 admin conninfo = @sub1;
   ```

9. Create a file named `init.slonik` in the `/etc/slony` directory of the master node with the following contents:

   ```
   include </etc/slony/nodes.slonik>;
   init cluster (id=1, comment = 'Master');
   store node (id=2, comment = 'Subscriber', event node=1);
   store path (server = 1, client = 2, conninfo = @master);
   store path (server = 2, client = 1, conninfo = @sub1);
   ```

10. Install Slony on both nodes by executing the following command as the postgres user on the master node:

    ```
    slonik < /etc/slony/init.slonik
    ```

11. Start Slony on the master node with this command as the postgres user:

    ```
    slon replication \
      'dbname=postgres host=192.168.56.10 user=rep_user' \
      &> /var/log/postgresql/slony.log &
    ```

12. Start Slony on the subscriber node with this command as the postgres user:

    ```
    slon replication \
      'dbname=postgres host=192.168.56.30 user=rep_user' \
      &> /var/log/postgresql/slony.log &
    ```

How it works...

The first two steps are common to most Unix-based software. We start by extracting the source code, bootstrapping the build process with configure, and building it with make. We choose to install with a prefix of /usr so that Slony binaries are installed in /usr/bin. This makes executables more easily available.

Once installed, we need to ensure that our rep_user user, which we've used in the past, has PostgreSQL superuser capabilities. Slony performs many tasks that are only available to superusers, so this step is not optional. Then, we modify the postgres user's .pgpass file to allow the rep_user database user to connect from either node. While we're making user changes, we also alter pg_hba.conf on both nodes so that each server can connect to the other. Once we reload the PostgreSQL configuration files, the user setup is complete.

We should note that more advanced installations will probably have a specific user for streaming replicas and a completely separate user for logical replication solutions such as Slony due to the superuser requirement. That wasn't entirely necessary for the purpose of this book, but do consider it when using tools such as Slony.

With our preliminary work complete, we create a basic configuration file in the /etc/slony directory named nodes.slonik. This file describes the name of the cluster as well as each node and its connection parameters. We create this file because it is a preamble commonly used in all Slony-related commands. Why not save some typing effort?

Next, we create init.slonik in the /etc/slony directory. This file actually initializes the Slony cluster. We start by including the nodes.slonik file we created earlier, and then, we initialize node 1 as the master node. After the cluster is created, we store the node for our subscriber. The two store path commands are necessary so that each node knows how to communicate with the other.

We should create two path entries for each subscriber node that we create, as each channel is unidirectional. Slony communicates like this, where each Slony box represents one path:

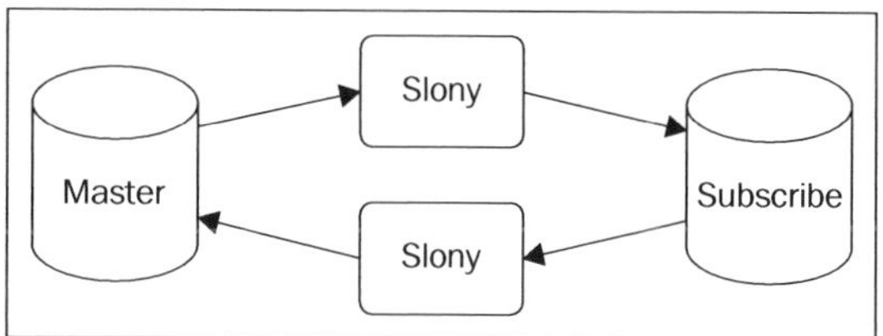

With our configuration files created, we need to install Slony on both nodes. We do this by sending the contents of our `init.slonik` to the `slonik` command. The `slonik` tool has its own language and interprets our configuration files as instructions. For now, these instructions tell it to initialize a cluster named `replication` with one node, one subscriber, and two communication paths.

Now that Slony is installed on both the master and subscriber nodes, we need to start the **slon** utility. This tool does all of the actual work of the Slony software. It copies data to the subscriber, schedules and executes internal events, performs maintenance, and so on. It acts like a multipurpose daemon but does not fork or run in the background by itself. Thus, we send the output to a logfile in `/var/log/postgresql`, and tell it to run in the background by specifying `&` at the end of the command. Once again, we have to specify connection information for these daemons to work properly.

See also

- The Slony documentation is extremely extensive and includes a tutorial similar to this one. It also includes much more in-depth explanations of the process. To gain a deeper understanding of Slony and its use, we recommend this URL: `http://slony.info/documentation/2.2/index.html`

Copying a few tables with Slony

Once Slony has been installed and is running on both nodes, we can actually make use of it and copy tables to a remote database. For high availability PostgreSQL servers, making data available to external systems means long-running and potentially disruptive ad hoc queries run elsewhere. It also means that reporting environments have direct copies of relevant tables and do not need to retrieve this data from our OLTP systems.

While it is possible for OLTP servers to act as OLAP systems as well, these workloads are quite different. For the best performance possible and the least risk of outages, each server should be specialized. So, let's use Slony to do just that.

Getting ready

We will be continuing where we left off in the *Setting up Slony* recipe. Please make sure to have completed that recipe before continuing. As we want tables to test Slony with, we should create some. The `pgbench` utility can do this quickly. Execute this command on the primary PostgreSQL server as the `postgres` user:

```
pgbench -i postgres
```

How to do it...

For this recipe, `192.168.56.30` will remain our subscriber. Follow these instructions to copy the `pgbench` tables and all future changes from `pg1` to `pg2`:

1. Extract the table creation statements from the primary database with the following command as the `postgres` user:

   ```
   pg_dump -s -t 'pgbench*' postgres > /tmp/tables.sql
   ```

2. Create the empty tables on the subscriber node by executing this command as the `postgres` user on the primary node:

   ```
   psql -U rep_user -h 192.168.56.30 -f /tmp/tables.sql postgres
   ```

3. Confirm that the tables exist on the subscriber node by executing the following SQL statement on that system:

   ```
   SELECT schemaname, tablename FROM pg_tables
    WHERE tablename LIKE 'pgbench%';
   ```

4. Create a file named `pgbench_set.slonik` in the `/etc/slony` directory with the following contents:

   ```
   include </etc/slony/nodes.slonik>;
   create set (id=1, origin=1, comment='pgbench Tables');
   set add table (set id=1, origin=1, id=1,
       fully qualified name = 'public.pgbench_accounts');
   set add table (set id=1, origin=1, id=2,
       fully qualified name = 'public.pgbench_branches');
   set add table (set id=1, origin=1, id=3,
       fully qualified name = 'public.pgbench_tellers');
   ```

5. Create a file named `subscribe_pgbench.slonik` in the `/etc/slony` directory with the following contents:

   ```
   include </etc/slony/nodes.slonik>;
   subscribe set (id = 1, provider = 1, receiver = 2,
       forward = no);
   ```

6. Create the pgbench subscription set with this command:

   ```
   slonik < /etc/slony/pgbench_set.slonik
   ```

7. Subscribe our secondary node to the new pgbench set with this command:

   ```
   slonik < /etc/slony/subscribe_pgbench.slonik
   ```

8. Execute the following SQL on the subscriber node to confirm that data is being copied:

   ```
   SELECT count(1) FROM pgbench_accounts;
   ```

How it works...

Before we can copy any data, we need to begin by copying the table structures from the primary node to the subscriber. Slony only copies data and assumes that the source and target tables have the exact same columns. Therefore, we use pg_dump to obtain a schema-only (-s) extract of any table that begins with pgbench (-t 'pgbench*'). Using the -h parameter, we can execute the resulting SQL statement on the subscriber database and create all of the pgbench tables as empty shells.

Before attempting to create the Slony set, we should first confirm that the tables exist on the subscriber. We can check the pg_tables view and should see these records:

```
 schemaname |    tablename
------------+------------------
 public     | pgbench_accounts
 public     | pgbench_branches
 public     | pgbench_history
 public     | pgbench_tellers
(4 rows)
```

Once we've done this, we can continue by creating a slonik script that will create the Slony subscription set itself. Sets can be sent to any node that requests a subscription and only includes tables in that set. This lets us group tables by content if necessary. Observant readers may notice that we didn't add the pgbench_history table to the subscription set. This is because Slony only copies tables with primary keys by default.

> Slony table IDs are assigned manually and must be unique across all sets. We recommend skipping IDs between sets in case tables are added later. An easy rule is to add 100 or 1000 between each set. Thus, if we created another set, its table IDs could start at 100 to provide a sufficient buffer.

Next, we create one more `slonik` script for the subscription command itself. As this is our first set, its `id` is `1`. Though Slony supports chained table replication, we don't need that for our setup, so we disable it by setting `forward` to `no`.

To send table contents to the remote server, we simply need to create the table set on the primary node and subscribe the secondary node to the new set. This is one reason that we created the two `slonik` scripts. Another reason is due to the chance that we might need to rebuild this Slony replication cluster in the future. By having all of these scripts, we can do this in a few quick steps by executing all of the `slonik` scripts.

Provided there were no errors returned by the `slonik` commands, we can confirm that data is being sent to the subscriber with a single SQL query. We should see this:

```
postgres=# SELECT count(1) FROM pgbench_accounts;
 count
--------
 100000
(1 row)
```

Remember that we only extracted and copied the table definitions to the remote server. If we see any rows there, they must have come from Slony.

There's more...

Slony operates by attaching triggers to both the source and target tables. Due to this, creating a Slony set on a very active database can cause locking contention. Why does it need triggers? The triggers on the source system capture *insert*, *update*, and *delete* activities and forwards them to the remote system. On subscriber nodes, the triggers block any insert, update, or delete activity that does not originate from Slony itself.

The triggers also make it possible to switch between which node is the subscriber, and which is the origin without any further table locks. Keep this in mind when copying data via Slony, or the locks could cause query timeouts and customer complaints. Try to schedule new sets and set modifications during maintenance periods or low-usage periods.

See also

- Once again, we recommend that you read the Slony documentation if you plan to use it for logical table replication. The rich syntax and functionality is beyond the scope of this book, but is available at `http://slony.info/documentation/2.2/index.html`.

Setting up Bucardo

Bucardo is another popular logical replication engine that actually seems to have originated earlier than Slony, in 2002. Like Slony, it also uses triggers to perform its synchronization activity, but its syntax is much simpler. Furthermore, it also provides multimaster capabilities; this means that changes made in either the primary or secondary node will appear in both copies of a replicated table.

There is something to be said for tools that encourage simplicity when maintaining a complex high availability architecture. Let's explore Bucardo further.

Getting ready

The latest stable version of Bucardo at the time of writing this book is 4.5.0. Obtain the latest source package from the following URL:

`http://bucardo.org/wiki/Bucardo`

Bucardo is written in Perl, so it requires quite a few Perl-based prerequisites. On Debian-based systems, install them using the following `apt-get` commands:

```
sudo apt-get install libdbix-safe-perl libdbd-pg-perl
sudo apt-get install postgresql-plperl-9.3
```

Red-Hat-based systems require a bit more work. Install the EPEL package for your Red Hat platform from the following URL:

`https://fedoraproject.org/wiki/EPEL`

Then, install these RPMs with the following `yum` command:

```
sudo yum install perl-DBI perl-DBD-Pg perl-DBIx-Safe
```

Next, if it isn't installed already, download and install the PostgreSQL repository by installing the appropriate RPM from this URL:

`http://yum.pgrpms.org/repopackages.php`

Then, install the `plperl` PostgreSQL procedural language with this `yum` command:

```
sudo yum install postgresql93-plperl
```

How to do it...

For these instructions, `192.168.56.10` is the master PostgreSQL node, and `192.168.56.30` is our desired subscriber. Follow these instructions on *both servers* to install Bucardo:

1. Extract the source code and change to the resulting directory with these commands:

   ```
   tar -xzf Bucardo-4.5.0.tar.gz
   cd Bucardo-4.5.0
   ```

2. Build and install Bucardo with these commands as a root-capable user:

   ```
   Perl Makefile.PL
   make
   sudo make install
   ```

3. Next, install Bucardo onto the database by executing the following command as the `postgres` user on both servers:

   ```
   bucardo_ctl install
   ```

Follow these steps only on the *primary server* that will be running the Bucardo service:

1. Create a directory for Bucardo to store `pid` files with these commands as a root-capable user:

   ```
   sudo mkdir /var/run/bucardo
   sudo chown postgres:postgres /var/run/bucardo
   ```

2. Add the `postgres` database from both PostgreSQL servers with these commands as the `postgres` user:

   ```
   bucardo_ctl add db postgres name=pg1 host=192.168.56.10
   bucardo_ctl add db postgres name=pg2 host=192.168.56.30
   ```

3. Finally, start the Bucardo service by executing this command as the `postgres` user:

   ```
   bucardo_ctl start
   ```

How it works...

While Bucardo has a lot of prerequisites, its installation and configuration process is actually much easier. It also provides a proper daemon control utility in `bucardo_ctl`. As proof of this, the usual process of extracting and building the source code is the most time-consuming part. When Bucardo is installed on both servers, we merely have to invoke `bucardo_ctl` with the `install` parameter to finish the process.

When Bucardo is installed, it creates a user named `bucardo` and a database named `bucardo`. The `bucardo` user acts like the `rep_user` user we created for replication, so it must be a PostgreSQL superuser. As such, we need to ensure that we use a superuser for the `User` configuration setting during the installation process. This is why we recommend that you run the `bucardo_ctl` utility as `postgres` when possible. Here's what our installation screen looked like for the second node:

```
Current connection settings:
1. Host:           pg2
2. Port:           5432
3. User:           postgres
4. Database:       postgres
5. PID directory: /var/run/bucardo
Enter a number to change it, P to proceed, or Q to quit: P
```

Once we press *P* and hit *Enter*, Bucardo is installed. This means the only steps that remain involve starting the Bucardo service itself.

To do this, we need to prepare the `/var/run/bucardo` directory so that Bucardo can create files there. As we are going to launch it as the `postgres` user, the `postgres` system user needs to own that directory.

Next, we configure Bucardo itself by adding an internal alias for the `postgres` database on each server. The `bucardo_ctl` command has a lot of operation modes, but for now, all we need to do is add the `postgres` database with a different name for each host. After doing so, we can start Bucardo by calling `bucardo_ctl` with the `start` parameter. If everything goes well, we can call `bucardo_ctl` with the `status` parameter and see that it's running, as shown in the following screenshot:

```
postgres@pg1:~$ bucardo_ctl status
Days back: 3  User: bucardo  Database: bucardo  PID of Bucardo MCP: 10027
No syncs have been created yet.
```

See also

- Bucardo has an easy-to-follow Wiki with instructions on installation and basic configuration. To learn more, please visit their site at `http://bucardo.org/wiki/Bucardo/Installation`.

Copying a few tables with Bucardo

Bucardo provides a very capable control mechanism in `bucardo_ctl`. Unlike Slony, which depends on an arcane programming language to create new replication sets and subscriptions, Bucardo is much more straightforward. As with Slony, we still want to copy data to other servers to avoid overwhelming our primary server.

In this recipe, we will utilize `bucardo_ctl` to create what Bucardo refers to as a **herd**. Bucardo herds contain one or more tables, and they are the basis of its synchronization system.

Let's begin.

Getting ready

We will be continuing where we left off in the *Setting up Bucardo* recipe. Please make sure that you have completed that recipe before continuing. As usual, we will use the `pgbench` utility to create an initial set of tables. Execute this command on the primary PostgreSQL server as the `postgres` user if you haven't already done so:

```
pgbench -i postgres
```

How to do it...

As with all of the previous recipes, `192.168.56.30` will remain our replication subscriber. Execute all commands in this recipe as the `postgres` system user. Follow these steps to copy the sample `pgbench` tables:

1. Extract the table creation statements from the primary node with the following command:

   ```
   pg_dump -s -t 'pgbench*' postgres > /tmp/tables.sql
   ```

2. Create the empty tables on the subscriber node by executing this command on the primary node:

   ```
   psql -U rep_user -h 192.168.56.30 -f /tmp/tables.sql postgres
   ```

3. Add all of the `pgbench` tables to Bucardo with these commands:

   ```
   bucardo_ctl add table pgbench_accounts db=pg1
   bucardo_ctl add table pgbench_branches db=pg1
   bucardo_ctl add table pgbench_tellers db=pg1
   ```

4. Confirm tables are being tracked by executing this command:

   ```
   bucardo_ctl list tables
   ```

5. Create a Bucardo herd by executing this command:

```
bucardo_ctl add herd pgbench pgbench_accounts \
            pgbench_branches pgbench_tellers
```

6. Execute the following command to add a synchronization set to Bucardo:

```
bucardo_ctl add sync pgbench source=pgbench \
            type=pushdelta targetdb=pg2 onetimecopy=1
```

7. Next, execute this command to begin synchronizing these tables:

```
bucardo_ctl activate pgbench
```

8. Finally, execute this command to view the status of Bucardo:

```
bucardo_ctl status
```

How it works...

As with Slony, we need to begin by duplicating table structures to the subscriber. Bucardo only copies data and assumes that the source and target tables have the exact same columns. Therefore, we use `pg_dump` to obtain a schema-only (`-s`) extract of any table that begins with `pgbench` (`-t 'pgbench*'`). Using the `-h` parameter, we can execute the resulting SQL on the subscriber database and create all of the `pgbench` tables as empty shells.

After copying the table definitions, we can use `bucardo_ctl` for all the remaining steps. The first of these include configuring Bucardo to recognize each table we want to replicate. The `add table` parameter to `bucardo_ctl` does this. By adding the `db=pg1` segment, we explicitly state which database owns the table we're adding. In this case, `pg1` is the alias we created for the `192.168.56.10` origin server during the installation of Bucardo.

To prove that Bucardo added these tables to its configuration, we can check with the `list tables` parameter. Output from `bucardo_ctl` should resemble this:

```
postgres@pg1:~$ bucardo_ctl list tables
Table: public.pgbench_accounts  DB: pg1  PK: aid (int4)
Table: public.pgbench_branches  DB: pg1  PK: bid (int4)
Table: public.pgbench_tellers   DB: pg1  PK: tid (int4)
```

Bucardo refers to tables as goats, and a gathering of goats becomes a herd. This is the equivalent of a Slony table set. We can add one with the `bucardo_ctl` command by passing the `add herd` parameter and a list of every table to include in the new herd. This herd will stampede in any direction we specify.

To give directions to our herd, we use `bucardo_ctl` again. This time, we send the `add sync` parameter and quite a few other elements. The `source` parameter tells Bucardo which herd we will be copying, and the `targetdb` parameter specifies which database server the herd should target.

Bucardo has three methods to synchronize data, and we choose one by setting the `type` parameter. We choose `pushdelta` because Bucardo is only sending changes to the tables. Any existing data is completely ignored. These tables are empty on the target, and this is not the behavior we want. So, we also set the `onetimecopy` value to `1`, indicating that it should fill the tables before keeping them updated.

This behavior is much different from how Slony works. If the source and target tables already contain data, Slony will truncate the target and copy all data from the source. If a table has already been synchronized before adding it to a replication set, this redundant copying can be very expensive. Bucardo only copies all data if it is told to do so with the `onetimecopy` parameter, which is a major benefit when running a sensitive high availability cluster.

Having added the set, no data is being copied at this time. Bucardo maintains separate child processes for each replication set so that it can handle multiple synchronization sets simultaneously. We don't have to copy the set simply because we've created it. To do this, the sync must be activated with the `bucardo_ctl activate` command.

After the sync has been activated, we should view Bucardo's status to confirm that it is active and copying our herd properly. The `status` output from `bucardo_ctl` should look like this:

```
postgres@pg1:~$ bucardo_ctl status
Days back: 3  User: bucardo  Database: bucardo  PID of Bucardo MCP: 10027
Name     Type  State PID   Last_good Time  I/U/D        Last_bad Time
=======+=====+=====+=====+=========+=====+===========+========+====
pgbench| P    |idle |11449|41m4s     |1s   |100000/0/0|unknown  |
```

From this output, we can see that Bucardo is running as PID `10027` and that it has copied 100,000 rows within the `pgbench` synchronization set. Furthermore, we can see that the `pgbench` synchronization set process PID is `11449`, indicating that Bucardo is indeed a multiprocess daemon.

See also

- The `bucardo_ctl` command is extremely versatile. You can learn more about how it controls Bucardo replication at `http://bucardo.org/wiki/Bucardo_ctl`.

Setting up Londiste

To complete our suite of popular logical replication tools, we would like to introduce **Londiste**. It is one of the SkyTools PostgreSQL utilities contributed by Skype in 2007. Why another replication system? Due to other capabilities offered by this suite of tools, you may decide to use one or more of them. Knowing how to leverage Londiste can simplify the total software stack and thereby increase server stability and simplicity.

In addition, like Bucardo, its usage is much simpler than Slony due to its suite of command-line tools. Let's continue with the installation of Londiste on two PostgreSQL servers, and perhaps, we might utilize other SkyTools functionality later.

Getting ready

At the time of writing this book, the latest version of Londiste is 3.1.5. Download the latest source package from PGFoundry at `http://pgfoundry.org/projects/skytools`.

Londiste is written in Python and uses the `psycopg2` PostgreSQL database library. Make sure that this is installed before continuing. On Debian-based systems, this command will install `psycopg2` if it isn't already available:

```
sudo apt-get install python-psycopg2
```

Red-Hat-based systems should obtain the latest EPEL package from the following URL:

`https://fedoraproject.org/wiki/EPEL`

Then, install `psycopg2` with the following `yum` command:

```
sudo yum install python-psycopg2
```

How to do it...

As before, `192.168.56.10` is the master PostgreSQL node and `192.168.56.30` is our desired subscriber. All of the steps here should only be performed on the primary PostgreSQL server. Follow these instructions to activate Londiste on the `postgres` default database:

1. Extract the source code and change to the resulting directory with these commands:

   ```
   tar -xzf skytools-3.1.5.tar.gz
   cd skytools-3.1.5
   ```

2. Build and install Londiste with these commands as a root-capable user:

   ```
   ./configure
   make
   sudo make install
   ```

3. Create a file named `primary.ini` in the `/etc/skytools` directory with the following contents:

```
[londiste3]
job_name = primary
db = dbname=postgres host=192.168.56.10
queue_name = replication
logfile = /var/log/postgresql/londiste-%(job_name)s.log
pidfile = /var/run/postgresql/londiste-%(job_name)s.pid
```

4. Create a file named `subscriber.ini` in the `/etc/skytools` directory with the following contents:

```
[londiste3]
job_name = subscriber
db = dbname=postgres host=192.168.56.30
queue_name = replication
logfile = /var/log/postgresql/londiste-%(job_name)s.log
pidfile = /var/run/postgresql/londiste-%(job_name)s.pid
```

5. Create a file named `pgq.ini` in the `/etc/skytools` directory with the following contents:

```
[pgqd]
logfile = /var/log/postgresql/pgqd.log
pidfile = /var/run/postgresql/pgqd.pid
```

From this point on, all steps should be executed within the `/etc/skytools` directory as the `postgres` user. Continue with these instructions:

1. Configure the Londiste primary node by executing this command:

```
londiste3 primary.ini create-root primary \
          "dbname=postgres host=192.168.56.10"
```

2. Configure the Londiste secondary node by executing this command:

```
londiste3 subscriber.ini create-leaf subscriber \
          "dbname=postgres host=192.168.56.30" \
          --provider="dbname=postgres host=192.168.56.10"
```

3. Launch the Londiste background workers with the following commands:

```
londiste3 -d primary.ini worker
londiste3 -d subscriber.ini worker
```

4. Finally, launch the communication queue with this command:

```
pgqd -d pgqd.ini
```

How it works...

Unfortunately, Londiste is not as easy to install as Bucardo. Once we extract and install the source code, we still need to create a few configuration files and launch several background daemons to facilitate data movement.

The first of these configuration files is `primary.ini`. This file should tell Londiste everything it needs to know about connecting to the primary PostgreSQL node where the original data resides. When we launch the worker, it will operate under the `job_name` specified in this file.

Next, Londiste needs to know how to connect to the database it is copying. Here, we specify the `host` of the primary server, and `dbname` should be `postgres`. The `queue_name` is the communication channel Londiste will use to send data to the subscriber, so we choose something that is easy to remember. Finally, we configure a directory for the PID file and logging output. To save time, we reused the same directories that PostgreSQL uses for the PID file and log output by default.

The subscriber also has a configuration file. This time we name it `subscriber.ini`, and only change `host` for the database server and `job_name` of the worker. Otherwise, everything is the same as in `primary.ini`.

The last configuration file we create is `pgqd.ini`. This file provides configuration information to the `pgqd` queue process through which Londiste communicates. Without this configuration file and the accompanying `pgqd` daemon, Londiste will simply not function. This is very different from Slony, which operates entirely through worker processes. Imagine the situation like this diagram:

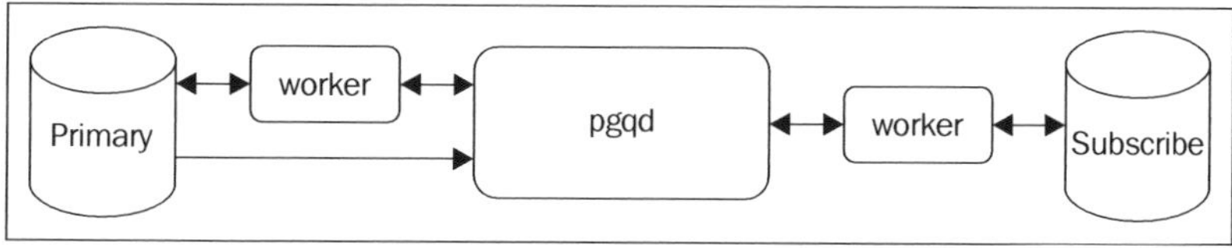

The queue reads from the database where the queue contents are stored, and workers can interact with each database server in any direction. In turn, they can also communicate with the queue. Due to this structure, the queue daemon can be relocated as long as the communication channels are preserved. Some users of Londiste leave the queue on the primary server and run the workers from subscriber nodes. This would be a good architecture to try for high availability, as it leaves fewer services competing for primary server resources.

In any case, the time has come to configure nodes by installing various database-related components. All management of Londiste is performed with the `londiste3` command-line utility. The first required parameter is always the name of a configuration file for the node that should be affected. Thus, we change our location to `/etc/skytools` so that the configuration files exist locally.

We begin by registering the master node. Londiste will do this for us on the primary node when we specify the `create-root` parameter to `londiste3`. This parameter also requires us to name the node, so we use `primary` to keep things clear. Finally, we need a connection string where this database configuration will be stored. Again, for the sake of simplicity, we repeat the connection information for the primary node.

Then, we register the subscriber as a leaf node by calling `londiste3` with `create-leaf`. Once again, we need to specify connection information. This time, it should not be for the primary node, but for the subscriber. Yet, registering the subscriber is not enough; we must also designate the node where the subscriber should be registered. In this case, the primary node is where all node registrations reside, so we repeat the primary node connection string.

Now that the nodes are registered, we can launch the worker processes. This too is done with the `londiste3` utility and should be done for both nodes. The `-d` parameter tells the workers to run in the background as standard Unix daemons, and the `worker` parameter instructs `londiste3` to launch a worker process. Assuming that these workers did not encounter an error, we can see them with a quick execution of `pgrep`:

```
postgres@pg1:/etc/skytools$ pgrep -lf londiste
27781 /usr/bin/python /usr/bin/londiste3 -d primary.ini worker
27785 /usr/bin/python /usr/bin/londiste3 -d subscriber.ini worker
```

The last process we launch is the queue, which ties all of the Londiste pieces together. This time, we rely on the `pgqd` command and use the `-d` parameter again so that it runs as a background daemon.

See also

- The Londiste documentation is primarily located at PGFoundry and isn't quite as organized as what Slony and Bucardo provide. Nevertheless, the `http://skytools.projects.pgfoundry.org/skytools-3.0/doc/howto/londiste3_simple_rep_howto.html` URL contains their explanation of a very basic Londiste setup, which is similar to this recipe.

  Do not refer to the Londiste documents on the PostgreSQL Wiki; they are extremely out of date with the current versions of Londiste.

Copying a few tables with Londiste

Londiste provides a very capable control mechanism in `londiste3`. Unlike Bucardo, we don't need to create a herd or sync, nor do we have to launch the process that handles data for a particular herd. With Londiste, it's all about the tables.

In this recipe, we will utilize `londiste3` to register all of the tables we want to copy and verify that the data is the same on each PostgreSQL server.

Getting ready

We will be continuing where we left off in the *Setting up Londiste* recipe. Please make sure that you have completed that recipe before continuing. Once again, we will use the `pgbench` utility to create an initial set of tables. Execute this command on the primary PostgreSQL server as the `postgres` user if you haven't already done so:

```
pgbench -i postgres
```

How to do it...

Execute all commands in this recipe as the `postgres` system user. Follow these steps to copy the sample `pgbench` tables:

1. Extract the table creation statements from the primary node with the following command:

   ```
   pg_dump -s -t 'pgbench*' postgres > /tmp/tables.sql
   ```

2. Create the empty tables on the subscriber node by executing this command on the primary node:

   ```
   psql -U rep_user -h 192.168.56.30 -f /tmp/tables.sql postgres
   ```

3. Make sure that you are in the `/etc/skytools` directory for the following steps.
4. Register all of the `pgbench` tables with the primary PostgreSQL server with these commands:

   ```
   londiste3 primary.ini add-table pgbench_accounts
   londiste3 primary.ini add-table pgbench_branches
   londiste3 primary.ini add-table pgbench_tellers
   ```

5. Register all of the `pgbench` tables with the subscriber PostgreSQL server with these commands:

   ```
   londiste3 subscriber.ini add-table pgbench_accounts
   londiste3 subscriber.ini add-table pgbench_branches
   londiste3 subscriber.ini add-table pgbench_tellers
   ```

6. Compare data on both nodes with this command:

   ```
   londiste3 subscriber.ini compare
   ```

How it works...

Once again, we need to begin by duplicating table structures to the subscriber. Londiste only copies data and assumes that the source and target tables have the exact same columns. Therefore, we use `pg_dump` to obtain a schema-only (`-s`) extract of any table that begins with `pgbench` (`-t 'pgbench*'`). Using the `-h` parameter, we can execute the resulting SQL on the subscriber database and create all of the `pgbench` tables as empty shells.

Next, we need to be in the `/etc/skytools` directory. This isn't strictly required, but as the configuration file is always the first parameter to `londiste3`, we would need to type the full path to each file every time.

To register each table with the primary server, we specify its configuration file, the `add-table` parameter, and the table we want to register. As with Slony and Bucardo, we need to add the three `pgbench` tables with primary keys. We repeat this process for the subscriber, using its configuration file instead.

Once we have done this, Londiste will begin by checking the table contents on each server and copying any data that is missing on the subscriber. All future modifications will also be copied to the subscriber.

An interesting function that `londiste3` provides is the ability to confirm that data is synchronized by performing checksum comparisons. If we wait a moment for the data to synchronize and execute `londiste3` with the `compare` parameter, we should see these lines for each table:

```
2014-02-26 11:51:51,671 30313 INFO Locking public.pgbench_accounts
2014-02-26 11:51:51,673 30313 INFO Syncing public.pgbench_accounts
2014-02-26 11:51:54,197 30313 INFO Counting public.pgbench_accounts
2014-02-26 11:51:54,377 30313 INFO srcdb: 100000 rows, checksum=39460277388
2014-02-26 11:51:54,610 30313 INFO dstdb: 100000 rows, checksum=39460277388
```

See also

- The `londiste3` utility is very versatile. We highly recommend that you use the `http://skytools.projects.pgfoundry.org/skytools-3.0/doc/londiste3.html` URL to learn more about its capabilities.

7
Replication Management Tools

In this chapter, we will learn where to turn when management of large PostgreSQL clusters becomes a concern. We will cover the following recipes in this chapter:

- Deciding when to use third-party tools
- Installing and configuring Barman
- Backing up a database with Barman
- Restoring a database with Barman
- Installing and configuring OmniPITR
- Managing WAL files with OmniPITR
- Installing and configuring repmgr
- Cloning a database with repmgr
- Swapping active nodes with repmgr
- Installing and configuring walctl
- Cloning a database with walctl
- Managing WAL files with walctl

Introduction

When it comes to maintaining a single PostgreSQL cluster with a single source of WAL files, our job is an easy one. Even a small number of streaming replicas is easily managed manually with PostgreSQL-provided tools. However, what happens when we have a large constellation of PostgreSQL servers, such as this:

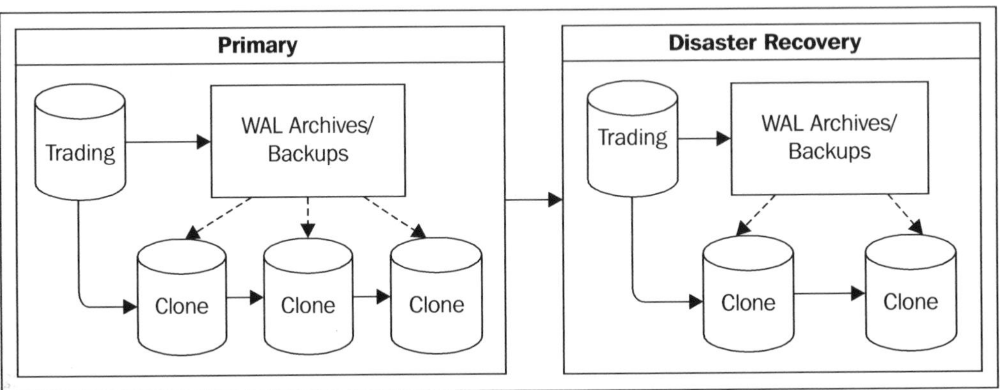

This diagram represents seven PostgreSQL servers for a single source of data. The Trading server sends its WAL data to a secondary system for safekeeping. One replica subscribes directly to the **Trading** database, while two others acquire their data through cascading replication. All clones are attached to the WAL archive in case their respective streams get disconnected.

Further complicating the situation, there's an off-site copy of the entire architecture for disaster recovery. Even though the recovery copy in the alternate data center is reduced in terms of capabilities, it still requires several servers for the client applications to run properly. Worse still, in the event of a failure in the primary data center, we will need to promote the Disaster Recovery systems into full write functionality. How then, do we rebuild the primary architecture and all of its clones when it's time to revert?

There are too many moving parts to reliably handle so many servers. This chapter is dedicated to managing several servers with automated tools, thus removing the risk of human error. When maintaining a high availability cluster, leveraging these tools is essential.

Deciding when to use third-party tools

Not every PostgreSQL cluster is as advanced as the example we used in the introduction, yet some are far larger. How do we decide when a cluster architecture becomes unsafe to manage by hand? How do we integrate backups, WAL archival, and streaming targets without overloading the primary server? Are the included PostgreSQL tools sufficient, or do we need something more advanced?

There are a lot of questions to ask, and thanks to the PostgreSQL community, we have answers for many of them. This recipe will act as a worksheet to asses the interconnections between all of the various necessary servers. Once we've properly summarized the intricacy involved, we can decide if outside assistance is needed.

Getting ready

We will be filling out a very short spreadsheet inventory of our PostgreSQL servers. Be sure to have access to a spreadsheet program before continuing. We also strongly recommend a diagram of all PostgreSQL servers for each segment of your database architecture. Whether we are in the planning or deployment phases, we need to know how servers will be interconnected.

How to do it...

Follow these steps to determine the extent of necessary automated tooling:

1. Create a spreadsheet with the following columns: `Server Name`, `Source`, `Environment`, `Streaming`, `Promotion`, and `Backup`.
2. Create a row for each server indicating its `Server Name` and the `Source` of its data.
3. For each row, set the corresponding attribute column as follows:
    - For `Environment`, use `Production` or `Disaster Recovery` (**DR**)
    - Specify `True` or `False` for `Streaming` if the server is a streaming provider or recipient
    - Mark the `Promotion` column as `True` or `False` if the server can be promoted to be the master copy for the whole constellation of servers
    - Indicate `True` or `False` for `Backup` if the server is used for backups
4. Consider using an external tool if any of these are true:
    - The Disaster Recovery environment has three or more servers
    - Any server has more than two rows in the spreadsheet
    - Three or more servers use streaming replication

How it works...

The idea behind this spreadsheet is that we want to list every connection between every server. This means some servers may be listed multiple times. With this in mind, we start with six columns to track important attributes. This example spreadsheet represents part of our architecture in the introduction:

	A	B	C	D	E	F
1	Server Name	Source	Environment	Streaming	Promotion	Backup
2	trading		Production	TRUE	TRUE	FALSE
3	clone-1	trading	Production	TRUE	FALSE	FALSE
4	wal-archive	trading	Production	FALSE	FALSE	TRUE
5	trading-dr	trading	DR	TRUE	TRUE	TRUE
6	dr-clone-1	trading-dr	DR	TRUE	FALSE	FALSE

As the current production server has no data source, we leave that field blank. Otherwise, each row has important attributes. The `Environment` column, for instance, helps us decide whether or not we need tools to coordinate data movement between data centers or server clusters. If there are too many `Streaming` servers or too many clones are eligible for `Promotion`, rearranging might be excessively difficult.

However, why does `Backup` get its own attribute column? Backup servers deserve special attention due to their importance. Not only might data or WAL backups be sources for new clones, but their role might change based on the current primary server. If this is overly complex, tools might be the best approach to management.

If we consider our rules, they are arbitrary for a reason. Some DBAs may find it easy to handle server rebuilds, and we commend them. However, we believe three or more servers in any major role render a constellation effectively unmanageable. This is true whether it is the DR environment as a whole, any server is used in two or more relationships, or streams are used extensively.

There's more...

Why do we think that *three* is the magic number when evaluating our ability to manage PostgreSQL relationships? The answer is *reorganization*.

If we ever need to utilize the Disaster Recovery environment, the entire primary system must eventually be rebuilt. Likewise, if a streaming replica is promoted, every server that once depended on the primary must switch to its stream instead. These actions take time and must be repeated at least twice as three or more servers are involved. Every time a command is manually invoked, there's a chance for a mistake.

Highly available servers do not have the luxury to withstand accidents. One misapplied stream change might spell the difference between platform errors, a system outage, or normal operation. We can't take that chance. So, we can either write our own tools to prevent these types of problems or take advantage of those that are already available.

Installing and configuring Barman

Though PostgreSQL provides a very capable tool in `pg_basebackup`, it's not really a complete backup management system. **Barman** is a **Backup and Recovery Manager** developed by **2ndQuadrant** to remedy that situation.

Unlike included utilities, Barman can receive WAL archives, produce and restore database backups, list available backups, control backup retention policies, and more. With a single command, we can manage backups of any PostgreSQL server we've configured Barman to recognize. Further, we can accomplish this from the backup server itself and not need to perform any local post-installation tasks on any PostgreSQL servers.

However, before we can get any of these abilities, we must first install and configure Barman. This recipe will walk you through this process as simply as possible.

Getting ready

At the time of writing this book, the most recent version of Barman is 1.3.0. Because of 2ndQuadrant's close interaction with the PostgreSQL community, it is available within the PostgreSQL package repositories. If you are using a Debian or Ubuntu-based system, follow the instructions at this URL to add the PostgreSQL repository to the system that will be running Barman:

`http://wiki.postgresql.org/wiki/Apt`

Otherwise, Red-Hat-based systems should add the PostgreSQL repository by installing the derivative-appropriate RPM located at this URL:

`http://yum.postgresql.org/repopackages.php`

We recommend that you use repositories only, as the repository-provided packages perform tasks other than software installation, such as user creation.

How to do it...

For this procedure, we will need two servers. The backup server will be named `pg-backup`, and our primary PostgreSQL server will be named `pg-primary`. Make sure to have passwords for both the `barman` and `postgres` system users and the `postgres` database user. As usual, our database is located at `/db/pgdata`.

Follow these steps:

1. Install the Barman toolkit as a root-capable user:
   - For Red-Hat-based servers, use the following command: `sudo yum install barman`
   - Debian-based systems should use this command instead: `sudo apt-get install barman`

2. On the `pg-backup` server as the `barman` user, execute the following commands for direct SSH access to `pg-primary` as the `postgres` user:

   ```
   ssh-keygen -t rsa -N ''
   ssh-copy-id postgres@pg-primary
   ```

3. On the `pg-primary` server as the `postgres` user, execute the following commands for direct SSH access to `pg-backup` as the `barman` user:

   ```
   ssh-keygen -t rsa -N ''
   ssh-copy-id barman@pg-backup
   ```

4. Ensure that the following line exists in the `pg_hba.conf` file on `pg-primary`:

   ```
   host    all    postgres    pg-backup    md5
   ```

5. Make sure that the following settings are configured in `postgresql.conf` on `pg-primary`:

   ```
   archive_mode = on
   archive_command = 'rsync -aq %p \
             barman@pg-backup:primary/incoming/%f'
   ```

6. Enter the following line in the `.pgpass` file for the `barman` user on `pg-backup`:

   ```
   *:*:*:postgres:postgres-password
   ```

7. Restart the PostgreSQL service on `pg-primary` with the following command as the `postgres` user:

   ```
   pg_ctl -D /db/pgdata restart
   ```

8. Add the following to the end of `/etc/barman.conf` or `/etc/barman/barman.conf`, depending on which exists:

   ```
   [primary]
   description = "Primary PostgreSQL Server"
   conninfo = "host=pg-primary user=postgres"
   ssh_command = "ssh postgres@pg-primary"
   ```

9. As the `barman` user on `pg-backup`, execute the following command to check the primary server's configuration entry:

   ```
   barman check primary
   ```

How it works...

Our first step is to install Barman itself. As this book focuses on Red-Hat-based and Debian-based Linux systems, this process is very simple. Barman is available in the PostgreSQL repositories for either platform, making the first step the easiest. Unfortunately, we have quite a few more steps to complete.

In order for Barman to work properly, it must be able to retrieve PostgreSQL files from the `pg-primary` server. Similarly, the `postgres` user needs to be able to transmit files to `pg-backup` through `rsync`. To facilitate this, we generate SSH keys on each server with `ssh-keygen`. We set the key type to RSA with the `-t` parameter and set the pass-phrase to a blank value with `-N`. This allows each server to communicate with the other without a password, yet do so securely. The `ssh-copy-id` command sends the public key to the desired server. This is why we need the `barman` and `postgres` system user passwords.

Next, we need to modify `pg_hba.conf` on the `pg-primary` server to allow the `postgres` database user to connect from `pg-backup`. While we're changing PostgreSQL settings, we also need to enable `archive_mode` and set `archive_command` to send archived WAL files to the `pg-backup` server for storage in a directory where Barman expects to find them. Once we restart PostgreSQL with `pg_ctl`, we are finished making changes on the `pg-primary` server.

When we install the Barman packages, they should create a configuration file named `barman.conf` in either the `/etc` or `/etc/barman` directory. In order to manage our `pg-primary` server, we need to add a few new lines to this file. The first is a label for the section so that Barman knows *primary* refers to the `pg-primary` PostgreSQL server. By setting `conninfo`, Barman can use internal Python libraries to perform management functions that require direct database access. And `ssh_command` tells Barman how to access files on the `pg-primary` server as the `postgres` system user.

That's a lot of preliminary work, but if everything goes well, the **barman** command-line tool will be fully functional. We can test this by checking the status of the server that we've configured under the *primary* label. It's important that we use `barman` with the `check primary` parameters, because it doesn't just check the server status—it also creates various directories and tracking files that it uses to manage the PostgreSQL server backups. If everything goes as expected, server status should resemble this output:

```
Server primary:
        ssh: OK
        PostgreSQL: OK
        archive_mode: OK
        archive_command: OK
        directories: OK
        retention policy settings: OK
        compression settings: OK
        minimum redundancy requirements: OK (have 0 backups, expected at least 0)
```

See also

Barman has a very clean and concise website, which includes basic documentation on installation and usage. For further reading, we recommend these URLs:

- **Barman**: `http://www.pgbarman.org/`
- **The Barman documentation**: `http://docs.pgbarman.org/`

Backing up a database with Barman

After Barman is installed, we should be able to leverage any of its capabilities using the **barman** command-line tool. For now, we will focus entirely on creating a backup, verifying that the new backup exists, and examining its contents.

Barman doesn't just produce backups, it also catalogs them extensively. We will use this to our advantage in this recipe to prove that Barman works as advertised.

Getting ready

This recipe depends on Barman being installed on a backup server. Please follow the *Installing and configuring Barman* recipe before continuing.

How to do it...

All steps should be executed as the `barman` system user on the `pg-backup` server that we were using in the previous recipe. Follow these steps to create, verify, and examine a Barman backup:

1. Create the first backup with this command:

   ```
   barman backup primary
   ```

2. Examine the list of backups with this command:

   ```
   barman list-backup primary
   ```

3. View the metadata of the most recent backup with this command:

   ```
   barman show-backup primary latest
   ```

4. View all of the files in the most recent backup with this command:

   ```
   barman list-files primary latest
   ```

How it works...

Creating a backup is extremely easy. To do so, we merely need to invoke the `barman` command with the `backup` parameter and specify *primary* as the label we want to back up. When activated, Barman contacts the `pg-primary` server and tells it to enter backup mode. It then retrieves all database files over SSH and saves them in its backup catalog. We can view the contents of the catalog in several ways.

The first way to examine the catalog is using the `list-backup` parameter. On our test server, we would expect to see output similar to this:

```
barman@pg1:~$ barman list-backup primary
primary 20140302T055627 - Sun Mar  2 05:56:37 2014 - Size: 71.0 MiB - WAL Size: 0 B
```

Backups are listed from least to most recent. The first column is the name of the server that Barman backed up. The second column details the unique ID of the backup and is composed primarily of the time and date the backup started. All further commands need this ID, as it tells Barman which backup we want to view.

Barman provides a few convenient shortcuts to avoid needing the backup IDs. The **latest** keyword, for example, always resolves to the ID of the most recent backup.

We won't show the output of the next two commands because they're very large. However, we can explain what they would display. In the case of the `show-backup` parameter to `barman`, we get to see the metadata of the backup itself. Meta-data may include the start and stop time of the backup, the timeline the server was on, the range of WAL files produced during the backup, and so on.

We can also observe the full contents of the backup. If we invoke `barman` with the `list-files` parameter and pass the ID of the backup we want to view, it sends a list of every file that it has stored. This includes any WAL files necessary to restore this particular backup.

There's more...

We referred to retention policies at the beginning of this recipe. This means that we can configure Barman to only retain a certain number of backups to avoid exhausting disk space. We begin by adding this line to the `barman.conf` file under the `primary` label:

```
retention_policy = RECOVERY WINDOW OF 1 WEEK
```

Then, Barman will delete any backup files or WAL archives not necessary to restore backups less than 1 week in age. To perform this maintenance, execute the following command regularly:

```
barman cron
```

We suggest that you invoke `barman` with the `cron` parameter daily within `cron` itself to automate the process.

See also

- The `barman` command tool has a manual that we can view locally. Use this command to learn more about what it can do:

  ```
  man barman
  ```

- We would also like to recommend the Barman documentation again. It really does a very good job at describing some of the more advanced functionality. The URL for reference is `http://docs.pgbarman.org/`.

Restoring a database with Barman

As you might expect, Barman does not just create backups, it can also restore them. This functionality can be used to restore the current server, but its real power lies in its ability to restore data remotely. With this capability and a little bit of preparation, we can clone a PostgreSQL backup any number of times without straining the primary database server.

In this recipe, we will explore Barman's recovery aptitude and the steps necessary to start a PostgreSQL server cloned by Barman.

Getting ready

This recipe depends on Barman being installed on a backup server and at least one backup registered in the backup catalog. Please follow the *Installing and configuring Barman* and *Backing up a database with Barman* recipes before continuing.

How to do it...

For this procedure, we will need one new server. The backup server will remain `pg-backup`, but we need a target server for the restore. This sever will be named `pg-clone`. Make sure to have the password for the `postgres` system user on this server. As usual, our database will be located at `/db/pgdata`:

1. On the `pg-backup` server as the `barman` user, execute the following command for direct SSH access to `pg-clone` as the `postgres` user:

   ```
   ssh-copy-id postgres@pg-clone
   ```

2. Ensure that the target restore directory is empty on `pg-clone` with this command executed as the `postgres` user:

   ```
   rm -Rf /db/pgdata
   ```

3. Transmit the backup to `pg-clone` by running this command as `barman` on the `pg-backup` server:

```
barman recover --remote-ssh-command "ssh postgres@pg-clone" \
       primary latest /db/pgdata
```

4. As the `postgres` user on `pg-clone`, start the PostgreSQL service with the following command:

```
pg_ctl -D /db/pgdata start
```

How it works...

As with our Barman installation process, we need to ensure that Barman can communicate directly with the PostgreSQL clone system. Once more, we rely on `ssh-copy-id` to transmit the necessary SSH key to the `pg-clone` server.

The next step is to erase any existing PostgreSQL files on the target server. This step should not be necessary on a new server, but it never hurts to double-check. Assuming that the `postgres` user has permission to write to the `/db` directory, we are now ready to recover the backup to the `pg-clone` server.

At this point, we want to invoke the `barman` command with its `recover` operand. Remember, the default recovery system is the local server. As we're executing commands from `pg-backup`, that's not entirely useful to us. Instead, we want to send the data to `pg-clone`. We do this using the `--remote-ssh-command` parameter and by specifying the `ssh` command necessary to reach the `pg-clone` server. This is why we copied Barman's public RSA key to `pg-clone`.

The next parameter to `barman` includes the label of the backup we want to restore, the ID of the specific backup, and the directory where the files should be located. In this case, we are restoring the `primary` database using the `latest` backup and restoring to the `/db/pgdata` directory. We want the output of this command to look like this:

```
Starting remote restore for server primary using backup 20140302T063546
Destination directory: /db/pgdata
Copying the base backup.
Copying required wal segments.
The archive_command was set to 'false' to prevent data losses.

Your PostgreSQL server has been successfully prepared for recovery!

Please review network and archive related settings in the PostgreSQL
configuration file before starting the just recovered instance.
```

If we follow the advice that Barman gives after this step completes, we should give a cursory look at `postgresql.conf` to ensure that the server will run properly on `pg-clone`. Barman also disabled the `archive_command` setting on the newly restored server. As this was a command to send files to `pg-backup`, this is a very good thing! We don't want the new server polluting our WAL archive with invalid files.

The final step is to start the PostgreSQL server on the new `pg-clone` server with `pg_ctl`.

There's more...

Barman does not have a mode to initialize the newly restored server as a streaming replica of the original. To do this, create a file named `recovery.conf` in the `/db/pgdata` directory with the following contents before starting PostgreSQL:

```
standby_mode = 'on'
primary_conninfo = 'host=pg-primary user=postgres'
```

If you've followed the recipes in the previous chapters, you may also consider using the `rep_user` user instead, as we created it specifically for replication purposes.

See also

- The `barman` command tool has a manual we can view locally. Use this command to learn more about what it can do:

  ```
  man barman
  ```

- To get more immediate output of the restore mode's parameters, execute this command:

  ```
  barman recover
  ```

Installing and configuring OmniPITR

Up until now, we've been managing WAL files with tools such as `cp` or `rsync`. Our end goal was to transmit these to a backup server so that the WAL files were safe long term in case we needed them for PITR recovery. As a bonus, the backup server is a central location that can be committed to tape regularly so that our PostgreSQL databases are preserved so long as we retain the tapes.

While this is a valid and functional approach, logging options, debugging, and flexibility are somewhat limited. Regular operating-system tools are not designed specifically to process PostgreSQL WAL files. Though we can use them for that purpose, there are better utilities available. OmniPITR is a powerful toolkit developed by OmniTI to manage PostgreSQL backup, restore, and WAL files.

This recipe will focus on installing OmniPITR so that we can use it later.

Getting ready

At the time of writing this book, the most recent version of OmniPITR is 1.3.2. In order to install it, we would like to introduce the **PostgreSQL Extension Network** (**PGXN**). PGXN is a site that attempts to collect PostgreSQL-related tools and extensions in a single place to simplify usage. PGXN is located at `http://pgxn.org/`.

PGXN provides a command-line tool named **pgxn** to access the PGXN repository, which we can install with Python's `setuptools`. Use this command to install `pgxn`:

```
sudo easy_install pgxnclient
```

How to do it...

For this procedure, we will continue to use two servers. The backup server will still be named `pg-backup`, and our primary PostgreSQL server is still `pg-primary`. Make sure to have the password for the `postgres` system user.

Follow these steps to install OmniPITR on both `pg-backup` and `pg-primary`:

1. Download OmniPITR using the `pgxn` utility with this command:

   ```
   pgxn download omnipitr
   ```

2. Unzip and relocate the OmniPITR files with these commands as a root-capable user:

   ```
   unzip omnipitr-1.3.2.zip
   cd omnipitr-1.3.2
   sudo cp bin/* /usr/local/bin
   sudo cp -R lib/OmniPITR /usr/local/lib
   sudo cp -R doc /usr/local
   ```

3. Check the OmniPITR installation with the following command:

   ```
   sanity-check.sh
   ```

4. As the `postgres` user on `pg-primary`, generate an RSA key pair and transmit it to `pg-backup` with these commands:

   ```
   ssh-keygen -t rsa -N ''
   ssh-copy-id postgres@pg-backup
   ```

5. As the `postgres` user on `pg-backup`, generate an RSA key pair and transmit it to `pg-primary` with these commands:

   ```
   ssh-keygen -t rsa -N ''
   ssh-copy-id postgres@pg-primary
   ```

How it works...

Unlike some other toolkits, OmniPITR is purely a set of command-line utilities. As such, its authors never created a proper installation process. With this in mind, we start by downloading the latest `omnipitr` package from PGXN. Unlike the `omnipitr` package's `install` parameter, the `download` parameter simply retrieves the indicated package and saves it in the local directory.

With the archive saved locally, we begin by extracting its contents and entering the resulting directory. OmniPITR itself is the collection of tools located in the `bin/` directory, so we move those files into `/usr/local/bin` for easy invocation. Due to the way OmniPITR was written, it searches for the `doc/` and `lib/` directories at the same level as the `bin/` directory. This means that the utilities should work if we copy the contents of these directories to `/usr/local` as well.

The `doc/` directory is important for one simple reason: usage. As OmniPITR has no traditional manual pages, the only way to view help for each command is with the `--help` or `--man` parameter. This will only work if we *install* the `doc/` directory where OmniPITR expects to find it.

Next, we should verify that OmniPITR is properly installed and will function as expected. It is distributed with a file named `sanity-check.sh`, which we installed with the other files in the `bin/` directory. If we execute this command, it will examine various resources and produce a report. The report for our test system looked like this:

```
test@pg1:~$ sanity-check.sh
Checking:
- /usr/local/bin
- /usr/local/lib
9 programs, 62 libraries.
Tar version
All checked, and looks ok.
```

Provided the sanity check succeeded, we still need to facilitate communication between `pg-backup` and `pg-primary`. To do that, we generate an RSA key pair on each server as the `postgres` user and send it to the other system. We've performed this task before, so it should come as no surprise now. We do this so that automated tools can transmit files securely.

At this point in the book, it is extremely likely that you already have an SSH key for the `postgres` user on `pg-primary`. If that's the case, you only need to use the `ssh-copy-id` command to ensure that the key is located on `pg-backup`. Don't overwrite the key you already have!

See also

Both OmniPITR's documentation and the software itself are available on PGXN. To view their installation and usage documents, please use the following URLs:

- **OmniPITR—Installation**: `http://pgxn.org/dist/omnipitr/doc/install.html`
- **OmniPITR—how to setup**: `http://pgxn.org/dist/omnipitr/doc/howto.html`

Managing WAL files with OmniPITR

We've stated on several occasions that WAL files are very important. Their role in PostgreSQL crash recovery, backup restoration, and replication gives them a central role in maintaining a high availability cluster. With OmniPITR, we can upgrade communication between servers to ensure that we have logging for every step of a WAL file's movement. This is no small benefit, and we can use it to audit the entire transmission path if we encounter a problem.

Though OmniPITR is a full suite of backup-related tools, we wish to focus on its ability to give us better control of WAL archival and recovery. As a consequence, this recipe will describe usage of the `omnipitr-archive` command.

Getting ready

This recipe depends on OmniPITR being installed on all servers that need to utilize it. Please follow the *Installing and configuring OmniPITR* recipe before continuing.

How to do it...

For this procedure, we will continue to use two servers. The backup server will still be named `pg-backup`, and our primary PostgreSQL server is `pg-primary`. As usual, the PostgreSQL data directory will be located at `/db/pgdata`.

Follow these steps to send WAL files from `pg-primary` to `pg-backup`:

1. On the `pg-backup` server, create a directory writable to the `postgres` user with the following commands as a root-capable user:

   ```
   sudo mkdir /db/pg_archived
   sudo chown postgres:postgres /db/pg_archived
   ```

2. Create a file named omnipitr.conf in the /etc directory on pg-primary with the following contents:

```
--data-dir /db/pgdata
--dst-remote postgres@pg-backup:/db/pg_archived
--log /var/log/postgresql/omnipitr.log
```

3. Modify the postgresql.conf file on pg-primary and ensure that the following parameters are set:

```
archive_mode = on
archive_command = 'omnipitr-archive -- \
                   cfg=/etc/omnipitr.conf %p'
```

4. Restart the PostgreSQL server with the following command as the postgres user:

```
pg_ctl -D /db/pgdata restart
```

5. Examine the contents of the omnipitr.log logfile with this command as the postgres user:

```
tail /var/log/postgresql/omnipitr.log
```

How it works...

We start by ensuring that the postgres user can write to the /db/pg_archived directory on the pg-backup server, which is the location we've set aside to hold WAL files. This is also the only step we perform on the pg-backup server.

One interesting thing to consider about OmniPITR is that it reads configuration files in a similar manner as command-line parameters. With this in mind, and to avoid long and confusing command-lines, we save several in a configuration file for later use.

The first is the path to the PostgreSQL data directory. If this is unset, OmniPITR will assume that the WAL files are local to the data directory in pg_xlog. While this will work, it's better for logging purposes to set this explicitly to /db/pgdata. The second is the remote path to WAL files. As we created the /db/pg_archived directory on pg-backup, we use that same location here. Finally, we'll commit logs to the /var/log/postgresql directory, which should already exist on most Red Hat and Debian-based servers.

Now, we need to ensure PostgreSQL uses OmniPITR to send the files to pg-backup. Once we've confirmed that archive_mode is on, we can set archive_command to invoke omnipitr-archive. Because of our earlier work, we only need to set two parameters. The first is the full path to the configuration file we created, and the second is %p, which represents the full path to the WAL file that PostgreSQL wants to archive. Once PostgreSQL is restarted, it will use OmniPITR to manage its WAL files.

We should note that we only need to fully restart PostgreSQL if `archive_mode` was previously set to `off`. Otherwise, a simple reload will cause PostgreSQL to use the newly defined `archive_command` value.

Unlike Barman, OmniPITR has no command to verify that it's working properly. To do this, we must examine the logfile. If we look at the end of the `omnipitr.log` file in `/var/log/postgresql/` with `tail`, we should see something like this:

```
postgres@pg1:~$ tail -f /var/log/postgresql/omnipitr.log
2014-03-02 09:23:14.909364 -0600 : 1258 : omnipitr-archive : LOG : Segment
 ./pg_xlog/000000040000000100000090 successfully sent to all destinations.
```

There's more...

Perceptive readers may have noticed that we don't present an analogous situation to pull WAL files from the `pg-backup` server to a hot-standby. Unfortunately, while the provided `omnipitr-restore` command will move WAL files to their expected locations and include logging, it can not retrieve these files from a remote server. We are not entirely sure why the authors of OmniPITR would neglect to include this functionality, but it is an issue that we can not overcome.

As such, we do not recommend using OmniPITR to maintain clones or streaming replicas with our suggested architecture. An off-site backup server is invaluable, which means that remote WAL files are an inescapable reality.

This does not imply that OmniPITR is completely unsuited to manage certain elements of larger clusters. If you have time, examine the documentation of each OmniPITR utility and consider how each might be beneficial to your architecture.

See also

- While OmniPITR does not install manuals locally, we can invoke its tools to learn more about them. To see the full capabilities of `omnipitr-archive`, use this command:

  `Omnipitr-archive --help`

- OmniPITR's documentation is also available on PGXN. To view the manual for `omnipitr-archive` there, please visit `http://pgxn.org/dist/omnipitr/doc/omnipitr-archive.html`.

Installing and configuring repmgr

It's time to address the elephant in the room. When managing a wide PostgreSQL cluster, we will often need to rebuild, reassign, and repair nodes that are replicas of our primary server. If we remember our rule-of-threes, three or more nodes make it difficult and error prone to perform any task related to replication.

While Barman and OmniPITR are useful, neither of them is capable of managing a wide network of PostgreSQL replicas. This is why we would like to thank 2ndQuadrant for **repmgr**. With it, we can create new clones and add them to an existing cluster of PostgreSQL servers. We can shut down the existing primary server and promote any node in this network. Further, all of the existing replicas automatically consider the promoted node their new source of streaming updates.

This may not be the first tool to perform this task, but it is one of the best available. We'll tackle the process of installing it in this recipe before moving on to usage scenarios.

Getting ready

At the time of writing this book, the most recent version of repmgr is 2.0. As with Barman, repmgr is available within the PostgreSQL package repositories. If you are using a Debian or Ubuntu-based system, follow the instructions at `http://wiki.postgresql.org/wiki/Apt` to add the PostgreSQL repository to any system that will be running as a repmgr server or client.

Otherwise, Red-Hat-based systems should add the PostgreSQL repository by installing the derivative-appropriate RPM located at `http://yum.postgresql.org/repopackages.php`.

We recommend that you use repositories only, as the repository-provided packages perform tasks other than software installation, such as user creation.

How to do it...

For the purposes of this recipe, we will need two servers. The primary PostgreSQL node will be named `pg-primary`, and the replica will be `pg-clone`. Both servers exist on the `192.168.56.0` subnet. As always, the `/db/pgdata` path will be our default data directory. Be sure to have the password for the `postgres` system user ready.

Follow these steps to install repmgr on both servers:

1. Red-Hat-based systems should use this command as a root-capable user:

   ```
   sudo yum install repmgr
   ```

2. Debian-based systems should use this command instead:

   ```
   sudo apt-get install repmgr postgresql-9.3-repmgr
   ```

3. Optionally, copy the `repmgr` script from the `/init` directory in this chapter to the `/etc/init.d` directory on each server.
4. If the supplied `init` script was copied, execute these commands as a root-capable user:

   ```
   sudo rm -f /etc/init.d/repmgrd
   sudo chmod 755 /etc/init.d/repmgr
   ```

Next, follow these steps on `pg-primary` to set it up as a master node. We'll consider `pg-clone` in the next section:

1. As the `postgres` user, generate an RSA key pair and transmit it to `pg-clone` with these commands:

   ```
   ssh-keygen -t rsa -N ''
   ssh-copy-id postgres@pg-clone
   ```

2. Modify the `postgresql.conf` file and set the following parameters:

   ```
   wal_level = hot_standby
   archive_mode = on
   archive_command = 'exit 0'
   wal_keep_segments = 5000
   hot_standby = on
   ```

3. Modify the `pg_hba.conf` file and add the following lines:

   ```
   host    all            postgres    192.168.56.0/24    trust
   host    replication    postgres    192.168.56.0/24    trust
   ```

4. Restart the PostgreSQL service as the `postgres` user with this command:

   ```
   pg_ctl -D /db/pgdata restart
   ```

5. Execute this command to find the binary path to PostgreSQL tools:

   ```
   pg_config --bindir
   ```

6. Create a file named `/etc/repmgr.conf` with the following contents:

   ```
   cluster=pgnet
   node=1
   node_name=parent
   conninfo='host=pg-primary dbname=postgres'
   pg_bindir=[value from step 5]
   ```

7. Register the master node with the following command as the `postgres` user:

   ```
   repmgr -f /etc/repmgr.conf master register
   ```

8. Start the `repmgrd` daemon with the following command as a root-level user:

```
sudo service repmgr start
```

9. Examine the `repmgr` logfile with `cat`:

```
cat /var/log/repmgr/repmgr.log
```

How it works...

These may seem like a lot of instructions, but they're actually very simple, merely numerous. We start the process by actually installing repmgr on both nodes. Depending on our OS, we do this either with `yum` or `apt-get`. Afterwards, we have a choice. This chapter supplies an initialization script for repmgr that we know is fully LSB compliant and functional. The script bundled with the Debian-based packages didn't daemonize, log, or stop the service. We suggest that you use ours, but it is not required.

Once we've installed repmgr, we want to focus on `pg-primary` as it will be the source of all of our data clones. To facilitate secure communication, our first job is to establish an RSA SSH key pair and transmit it to the clone. For repmgr to work best, every server should be able to interact with every other server in this manner.

Then, we need to modify some PostgreSQL configuration files. We start with the `postgresql.conf` file. Earlier chapters recommend that you set `wal_level` to `hot_standby`, but what about the other settings? We've already used `archive_mode` in this chapter; however, we've set `archive_command` to `exit 0`. In Unix, any command that exits with a status of `0` is assumed to be functioning properly. Thus, PostgreSQL will believe that its archive process always succeeds.

Next, we set `wal_keep_segments` to `5000`. Why such a high value? That's almost 80 GB of extra files! For one, it's required by repmgr, so we have no choice. Yet, it's a small price to pay for easy management of multiple PostgreSQL clones. We enable `hot_standby` for similar reasons; it's ignored on master nodes but ready when the configuration file is copied to a replica.

Next, we add two lines to the `pg_hba.conf` file to allow the `postgres` user to connect to any database, including the `replication` pseudo-database. To follow our example, we allow these connections to originate from anywhere within the `192.168.56.0` subnet.

Though our example uses `trust` authorization, we suggest that real production systems utilize `.pgpass` files and `md5` authentication instead. Unless the PostgreSQL servers can communicate directly on a private firewalled network, this setup allows any user on these servers to clone our database. Further, only use the `postgres` database user when configuring repmgr. There is currently a bug that prevents repmgr from working properly if you are using any other superuser name.

To finish our configuration duties, we create a single file named `repmgr.conf` in the `/etc` directory. We named the repmgr cluster `pgnet`, noted that this is our first node, and named our node `parent` as it is easy to remember. The connection information needs to match our entry in `pg_hba.conf`; thus, we use the `repmgr` user that we added to the database earlier. Finally, we set `pg_bindir` so that repmgr always knows where to find certain PostgreSQL binaries. This setting is supposed to be optional, but we ran into several problems when we tried to omit this entry; just keep it for now.

Now that everything is prepared, we can finally register the primary node and complete the installation process by creating various database objects. These steps are all performed by the `repmgr` command, provided we specify the configuration file with `-f` and use the `master register` parameter. Our output should look something like this:

```
postgres@pg-primary:~$ repmgr -f /etc/repmgr.conf master register
[2014-03-10 20:12:08] [NOTICE] Master node correctly registered for cluster
pgnet with id 1 (conninfo: host=pg-primary dbname=postgres)
```

We're almost done! The repmgr system comes with a daemon that manages communication and controls behavior between other repmgr nodes. If we start this daemon, repmgr will run in the background and await the arrival of new clones. If we examine the log output in `/var/log/repmgr`, we'll see the initial startup messages:

```
[2014-03-13 20:18:03] [INFO] repmgrd Connecting to database 'host=pg-primary dbname=pos
tgres'
[2014-03-13 20:18:03] [INFO] repmgrd Connected to database, checking its state
[2014-03-13 20:18:03] [INFO] repmgrd Checking cluster configuration with schema 'repmgr
_pgnet'
[2014-03-13 20:18:03] [INFO] repmgrd Checking node 1 in cluster 'pgnet'
[2014-03-13 20:18:03] [INFO] Reloading configuration file and updating repmgr tables
[2014-03-13 20:18:03] [INFO] repmgrd Starting continuous primary connection check
```

You will only see this output if you used our supplied initialization script. The repmgr daemon is not overly verbose and would have produced no output at all under normal launch conditions.

See also

- The repmgr system exists mainly as a source repository. Though, like Barman, it is maintained by 2ndQuadrant, its documentation is much more sparse. However, it does provide a very lengthy installation and usage overview at `https://github.com/2ndQuadrant/repmgr`.

Cloning a database with repmgr

As repmgr is a client/server PostgreSQL management suite, we need at least two nodes involved before we're really using it. We can perform the tasks outlined in this recipe as many times as we wish, creating several clones and registering them with repmgr. Of course, this book is for demonstration purposes, so we'll leave the larger clusters to you. With multiple nodes involved, the chances of data loss or system outages decline, which is excellent for our goal of high availability.

This recipe will focus on the process necessary to add a node to an existing repmgr cluster. The *existing cluster* in our case is the one that we established on `pg-primary` in the previous recipe.

Getting ready

This recipe depends on repmgr being installed on both a primary server and the clone that we will use. Please follow the *Installing and configuring repmgr* recipe before continuing.

How to do it...

For the purposes of this recipe, `pg-primary` will remain our master node, and the replica will be `pg-clone`. As always, the `/db/pgdata` path will be our default data directory. Be sure to have the password for the `postgres` system user ready.

All of these commands should be executed from `pg-clone`. Follow these steps to produce a fully functional repmgr replica:

1. As the `postgres` user, generate an RSA key pair and send it to `pg-primary` with these commands:

   ```
   ssh-keygen -t rsa -N ''
   ssh-copy-id postgres@pg-primary
   ```

2. Clone the data on `pg-primary` with the following command as the `postgres` user:

   ```
   repmgr -D /db/pgdata standby clone pg-primary
   ```

3. Start the new clone as the `postgres` user with `pg_ctl`:

   ```
   pg_ctl -D /db/pgdata start
   ```

4. Execute this command to find the binary path to PostgreSQL tools:

   ```
   pg_config --bindir
   ```

5. Create a file named /etc/repmgr.conf and enter the following contents:

```
cluster=pgnet
node=2
node_name=child1
conninfo='host=pg-clone dbname=postgres'
pg_bindir=[value from step 4]
```

6. Register pg-clone with pg-primary as the postgres user:

```
repmgr -f /etc/repmgr.conf standby register
```

7. Start the repmgrd daemon with the following command as a root-level user:

```
sudo service repmgr start
```

8. Connect to the postgres database and view the status of repmgr with this SQL statement:

```
SELECT standby_node, standby_name, replication_lag
  FROM repmgr_pgnet.repl_status;
```

How it works...

Because the replica is based on the primary, much of the preliminary work we performed in the previous recipe is inherited. One thing we can't avoid is creating an SSH key for direct server-to-server communication. Any time we create a new clone, it's a good practice to generate a key with ssh-keygen and copy that key to the current primary server.

> In fact, every server should have the postgres SSH key for every other server. In situations where any server in the cluster can be promoted to be the new primary, this ensures repmgr commands always work as expected. We strongly recommend that you use system automation tools such as Ansible, Chef, or Puppet to manage these keys.

With the SSH key established, we can clone pg-primary with the repmgr command. Because no PostgreSQL instance exists on pg-clone yet, we can't use our configuration file just yet. Instead, we specify -D to define the path to the database. Assuming that there were no errors, the command should produce a lot of extremely verbose output, with this at the end:

```
[2014-03-11 10:36:52] [NOTICE] Finishing backup...
NOTICE:  pg_stop_backup complete, all required WAL segments have been archived
[2014-03-11 10:36:53] [NOTICE] repmgr standby clone complete
[2014-03-11 10:36:53] [NOTICE] HINT: You can now start your postgresql server
[2014-03-11 10:36:53] [NOTICE] for example : pg_ctl -D /db/pgdata start
```

If we follow the advice in the last line and start PostgreSQL with `pg_ctl`, the clone should immediately connect to `pg-primary` and begin replication. We can do this because repmgr knows all of the connection information necessary to establish a streaming replication connection with `pg-primary`. During the cloning process, it automatically created a `recovery.conf` file suitable to start directly in replication mode.

Now, we must configure repmgr to recognize the clone. When we create `/etc/repmgr.conf`, we need to use the same `cluster` name as we used on `pg-primary`. We also tell repmgr that this is node `2`, and it should be named `child1`. The `conninfo` value should always reflect the connection string necessary for repmgr to connect to PostgreSQL on the named node. As we did earlier, we set `pg_bindir` to avoid encountering possible repmgr bugs.

With the configuration file in place, we can register the new clone similarly to the process that we used to register the primary. By calling the `repmgr` command with `-f` and the full path to the configuration file, there are several operations we can invoke. For now, we will settle with `standby register` to tell repmgr that it should track `pg-clone` as part of the `pgnet` cluster.

Once we start the `repmgrd` daemon, all nodes are aware of each other and the current status of each. We can confirm this by checking the `repl_status` view on any node. If we execute the supplied SQL statement, we should see this:

```
 standby_node | standby_name | replication_lag
--------------+--------------+-----------------
            2 | child1       | 0 bytes
(1 row)
```

The `repl_status` view has other useful columns, but for now we can see that the cluster considers `child1` the only standby node, and it's not lagging behind the primary at all.

If you are using Version 2.0 of repmgr, this view will be empty unless the `repmgrd` daemon is launched with the `--monitoring-history` parameter. The authors of repmgr claim that the view is no longer necessary for operation, but we feel more comfortable knowing that we can check the status of the cluster via SQL at any time. As such, the default for our included repmgr initialization script sets this option.

There's more...

There is another way to obtain cluster status. The `repmgr` command can also report how it perceives the cluster from any active node, given the `cluster show` parameter. Here is the entire command:

```
repmgr -f /etc/repmgr.conf cluster show
```

The result of this command as executed on `pg-clone` is as follows:

```
postgres@pg-clone:~$ repmgr -f /etc/repmgr.conf cluster show
Role      | Connection String
* master  | host=pg-primary dbname=postgres
  standby | host=pg-clone dbname=postgres
```

See also

- Though the process that we used differs slightly from the repmgr documentation, it is fully viable. If you would like to see the entire process in greater detail, repmgr documentation is available at `https://github.com/2ndQuadrant/repmgr`.

Swapping active nodes with repmgr

Creating a clone can be surprisingly dangerous. When using a utility such as `rsync`, accidentally transposing the source and target can result in erasing the source PostgreSQL data directory. This is especially true when swapping from one node to another and then reversing the process. It's all too easy to accidentally invoke the wrong script when the source and target are so readily switched.

We've already established how repmgr can ease the process of clone creation, and now it's time to discuss node promotion. There are two questions we will answer in this recipe. How do we swap from one active PostgreSQL node to another? How do we then reactivate the original node without risking our data? The second question is perhaps more important due to the fact that we are at reduced capacity following node deactivation.

Let's explore how to keep our database available through multiple node swaps.

Getting ready

This recipe depends on repmgr being installed on both a primary server and at least one clone. Please follow the *Installing and configuring repmgr* and *Cloning a database with repmgr* recipes before continuing.

How to do it...

For the purposes of this recipe, `pg-primary` will remain our master node, and the replica will be `pg-clone`. As always, the `/db/pgdata` path will be our default data directory.

Follow these steps to promote `pg-clone` to be the new cluster master:

1. Stop the PostgreSQL service on the `pg-primary` node with `pg_ctl`:

   ```
   pg_ctl -D /db/pgdata stop -m fast
   ```

2. As the `postgres` user on `pg-clone`, execute this command to promote it from standby status to primary:

   ```
   repmgr -f /etc/repmgr.conf standby promote
   ```

3. View the status of the cluster with this command as `postgres` on `pg-clone`:

   ```
   repmgr -f /etc/repmgr.conf cluster show
   ```

Follow these steps to rebuild `pg-primary` (while logged into `pg-primary`) to be the new cluster standby:

1. Clone the data on `pg-clone` with the following command as the `postgres` user:

   ```
   repmgr -D /db/pgdata --force standby clone pg-clone
   ```

2. Start the PostgreSQL service as the `postgres` user with `pg_ctl`:

   ```
   pg_ctl -D /db/pgdata start
   ```

3. Start the `repmgrd` daemon with the following command as a root-level user:

   ```
   sudo service repmgr start
   ```

4. View the status of the cluster with this command as `postgres`:

   ```
   repmgr -f /etc/repmgr.conf cluster show
   ```

How it works...

To start the process, we simulate a failure of the `pg-primary` PostgreSQL node. The simplest way to do this is to stop the PostgreSQL service. After the database stops serving requests, repmgr will detect that `pg-primary` is no longer active. If we tried the next step before stopping the existing master node, repmgr would refuse to honor the request. After all, we can't promote a standby when there's already a functional master.

Next, we invoke the `repmgr` tool from `pg-clone` with `standby promote`. This tells repmgr that this node should be the new master. This is necessary because repmgr allows several nodes to act as standby systems, and any could be a candidate for promotion. Following this action, it's a good idea to check the status of the repmgr cluster to ensure that it shows the correct status. We expect `pg-clone` to be the new master, as seen here:

```
postgres@pg-clone:/db/pgdata$ repmgr -f /etc/repmgr.conf cluster show
Role      | Connection String
* master  | host=pg-clone dbname=postgres
  FAILED  | host=pg-primary dbname=postgres
```

We can also see that repmgr has properly detected `pg-primary` as **FAILED**. However, this is not desirable long term. If we ever want to switch back to `pg-primary`, or our architecture works best with two active nodes, we need to restart the old master node as the new standby. Once again, we turn to the `repmgr` command-line utility.

If we log in to `pg-primary` as the `postgres` user, we can actually clone the standby the same way we initially provisioned the data on `pg-clone`. This means that we call `repmgr` once again with the standby clone parameter, except this time, we are cloning `pg-clone` as it is the new data master. There is also another important addition: the `--force` parameter. Without requesting that repmgr overwrite existing data on `pg-primary`, it will refuse. By forcing the operation, repmgr only copies data that is different between `pg-clone` and `pg-primary`.

After the data is copied, PostgreSQL should be ready to start on `pg-primary`, which we do with `pg_ctl` as usual. With PostgreSQL running, we can safely launch the daemon to reintegrate `pg-primary` into the repmgr cluster as a standby node. Once again, we can invoke `repmgr` with `cluster show` to verify this has occurred:

```
postgres@pg-primary:/db/pgdata$ repmgr -f /etc/repmgr.conf cluster show
Role      | Connection String
* master  | host=pg-clone dbname=postgres
  standby | host=pg-primary dbname=postgres
```

We can complete the previous recipe as many times as we wish. If we followed the recipe again, we could revert the cluster to its original layout, with `pg-primary` as the master node and `pg-clone` as the standby.

There's more...

Remember that we mentioned the possibility of multiple nodes acting as standby. As a test, we created another clone using the process described in the *Cloning a database with repmgr* recipe. Then, we followed the recipes in this section and stopped `pg-primary` before promoting `pg-clone`. What do you think we saw while examining the repmgr logfile on the second standby node? This:

```
[2014-03-13 20:27:47] [INFO] finding node list for cluster 'pgnet'
[2014-03-13 20:27:47] [INFO] checking role of cluster node 'host=pg-primary dbname=postgres'
[2014-03-13 20:27:47] [ERROR] Connection to database failed: could not connect to server: Co
nnection refused
        Is the server running on host "pg-primary" (192.168.56.10) and accepting
        TCP/IP connections on port 5432?
[2014-03-13 20:27:47] [INFO] checking role of cluster node 'host=pg-clone dbname=postgres'
[2014-03-13 20:27:47] [ERROR] Connected to node 2, continue monitoring.
```

Notice how the other standby started checking known repmgr cluster nodes to find a new master to follow. Once we promoted `pg-clone`, the second standby had a new target. If this doesn't happen automatically, you may have to bootstrap the process by running this command on any standby that didn't transition properly:

```
repmgr -f /etc/repmgr.conf standby follow
```

See also

- At the time of writing this book, the repmgr documentation has not been fully updated to reflect functionality changes to the 2.0 version. As such, we refer you to it with some trepidation. Regardless, we based our recipes on what we found at `https://github.com/2ndQuadrant/repmgr`.

Installing and configuring walctl

There's something to be said for simplicity. So far, the tools we've discussed in this chapter are larger client-server mechanisms or components of entire toolkits. One of the central tenets of the Unix philosophy is to build tools that do one thing well. In this case, we turn to Peak6 and their **walctl** WAL-management tools.

I created walctl specifically to address shortcomings in existing WAL-related utilities. Primarily of note is the question of architecture. Existing WAL tools follow an architecture diametrically opposed to the end goal of high availability. We often see this:

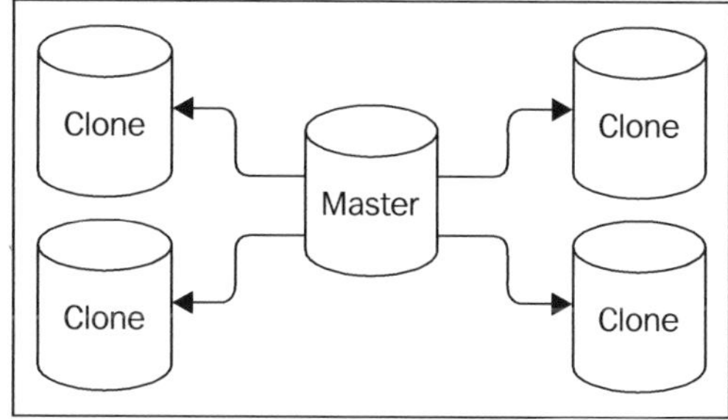

In this kind of model, the master node is tasked with transmitting transaction streams or WAL files to every node in the cluster. This makes it fantastically difficult to change the active master node and potentially overloads the master node itself. The primary write node of any cluster should be focused on fulfilling client requests. The purpose of walctl is to impose a structure like this:

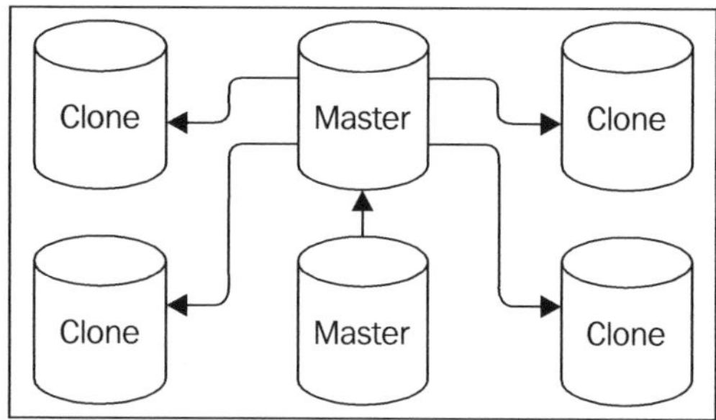

Instead of forcing the master node to supply each standby, the master transmits WAL data to a central archive server. Then, each clone can pull from that location as needed. In this recipe, we will install walctl so that we can take advantage of the structure it advocates.

Getting ready

Currently, walctl is very new. As such, it resides primarily on GitHub. You can download a copy of walctl from `https://github.com/OptionsHouse/walctl`.

We also suggest that you install **rsync**, **openssh**, and PostgreSQL server development libraries. For most PostgreSQL servers, it's very likely these are already installed.

How to do it...

For this procedure, we will need three servers. The archive server should be named `pg-arc`, our primary PostgreSQL server is `pg-primary`, and the new standby will be `pg-clone`. As usual, the PostgreSQL data directory will be located at `/db/pgdata`. For simplicity, the system user on all machines will be `postgres`. Be sure to have the password for this user!

1. As a root-capable user on `pg-primary` and `pg-clone`, run these commands to install walctl:

   ```
   git clone https://github.com/OptionsHouse/walctl
   cd walctl
   sudo make install
   ```

2. As a root-capable user on `pg-arc`, create the WAL storage directory:

   ```
   sudo mkdir -m 0600 /db/wal_archive
   sudo chown postgres:postgres /db/wal_archive
   ```

3. On `pg-primary`, create and export an SSH key to the `pg-arc` and `pg-clone` servers:

   ```
   ssh-keygen -t rsa -N ''
   ssh-copy-id pg-arc
   ssh-copy-id pg-clone
   ```

4. Repeat the previous step on the `pg-clone` server:

   ```
   ssh-keygen -t rsa -N ''
   ssh-copy-id pg-arc
   ssh-copy-id pg-primary
   ```

5. Execute this SQL on `pg-primary` to create a database user for walctl:

   ```
   CREATE USER walctl
     WITH PASSWORD 'test' SUPERUSER REPLICATION;
   ```

6. Modify `pg_hba.conf` on `pg-primary` and add these lines:

   ```
   host    replication    walctl    pg-clone      md5
   host    replication    walctl    pg-primary    md5
   ```

7. On `pg-clone` and `pg-primary`, ensure this line appears in the `.pgpass` file for the `postgres` user:

   ```
   *:*:*:walctl:test
   ```

8. On `pg-clone` and `pg-primary`, create a file named `/etc/walctl.conf` with these contents:

```
PGDATA=/db/pgdata
ARC_HOST=pg-arc
ARC_PATH=/db/wal_archive
```

9. On `pg-primary`, execute this command to set up walctl:

```
walctl_setup master
```

10. If instructed by `walctl_setup`, restart the PostgreSQL server:

```
pg_ctl -D /db/pgdata restart
```

How it works...

Currently, the best source for the walctl files is from GitHub. We suggest that you clone the repository and install the latest version with the included `Makefile`. After doing so, most of the installation steps are actually things that we've already done, such as creating and distributing SSH keys, allowing host connections in `pg_hba.conf`, or adding authentication information to `.pgpass`. It doesn't actually matter how you do this, but the end result must match these requirements:

- Both `pg-primary` and `pg-clone` must be able to communicate via SSH with `pg-arc`
- The `pg-clone` server must be able to connect to `pg-primary` to clone data and potentially stream it as well
- We don't suggest using trust-based authentication, so some higher-security method such as `md5` should be used to authenticate the `walctl` database user

Given the above has been accomplished—either by our instructions or otherwise—we can configure walctl. A minimal configuration requires three settings before walctl will operate normally. To read or write WAL files to their expected locations, `PGDATA` must be set. Then, it needs `ARC_HOST` to send files to the archive server, and `ARC_PATH` so that it knows where to store archived WAL files.

The `walctl_setup` utility has one purpose: prepare PostgreSQL for walctl integration. When called with the `master` parameter as we've done here, it modifies `postgresql.conf` so that WAL files are compatible with archival, and streaming replicas can connect. In addition, it enables archive mode and sets `archive_command` to invoke a walctl utility named `walctl_push`, which sends WAL files to the archive server. While calling `walctl_setup` on our test server, this was the output:

```
Modifying postgresql.conf for WAL management...
 * Checking wal_level:  ok. (hot_standby)
 * Checking max_wal_senders:  changed to 5. (Minimum value)
 * Checking archive_mode:  changed to on.
 * Checking archive_command:  changed to '/usr/bin/walctl_push %p'.
 * Checking hot_standby:  changed to on.
Done modifying config.

Reloading PostgreSQL configuration files... done

NOTICE: Some config values changed require PostgreSQL restart.
        Restart PostgreSQL with this command to enable these:
        /usr/lib/postgresql/9.3/bin/pg_ctl -D /db/pgdata restart
```

Walctl knows which settings can be changed by reloading PostgreSQL configuration files and which require a full service restart. It even tells us how to do it if we don't already know. If that last `NOTICE` doesn't appear in the output, the `pg-primary` server is already archiving WAL files on `pg-arc`. Otherwise, restarting PostgreSQL will initialize the process.

See also

- Currently, all documentation for walctl is located at the GitHub repository at `https://github.com/OptionsHouse/walctl`

  The README file in the source code also contains very similar instructions to what we described in this recipe

Cloning a database with walctl

One of the utilities that walctl includes is a script dedicated to creating a copy of the source database. Why don't we just use `pg_basebackup`? When dealing with large databases common to high availability systems, we want to copy as little data as possible. The `pg_basebackup` utility is a great basic tool, but it always copies every file. The `walctl_clone` program that we use in this recipe relies on `rsync`.

Of course, this raises another question: why not just use `rsync` directly? Due to its extensive capabilities, `rsync` is inherently dangerous. Did you accidentally transpose the source and target destination parameters? If you did so, you've just erased or corrupted your database master. The `walctl_clone` tool wraps `rsync` in such a way that it can only retrieve data from a master node. We can stay safe by limiting its use to clone servers.

In this recipe, we'll introduce and invoke the `walctl_clone` command, which does a few other useful things on our behalf. Not only does it copy the database files, it creates a `recovery.conf` to retrieve WAL files from a remote archive and starts the PostgreSQL server. There isn't much manual work involved. Let's try it out!

Getting ready

This recipe depends on walctl being installed on both a primary server and the clone that we will use. Please follow the *Installing and configuring walctl* recipe before continuing.

How to do it...

For this recipe, we only care about two servers. The primary PostgreSQL server is `pg-primary`, and the new standby will be `pg-clone`. Execute this command as the `postgres` system user on the `pg-clone` server:

```
walctl_clone pg-primary walctl
```

When the command finishes, we should have a fully operational clone of `pg-primary`.

How it works...

It may seem impossible that such a simple command can clone an entire database. Yet, in the previous recipe, we wrote a configuration file, and that's all walctl needs to operate. The `walctl_clone` command only has two parameters: the hostname of the database we are cloning and the name of the database superuser necessary to invoke a backup. Given these settings, `walctl_clone` performs a number of actions on our behalf:

- Puts the master node into backup mode.
- Retrieves all files from the database. If data files already exist in the `PGDATA` directory, it only copies changed files.
- Ends backup mode on the master node.
- Creates a `recovery.conf` file that will continuously retrieve files from `pg-arc` and connect as a streaming standby to `pg-primary`.
- Starts the PostgreSQL server.

We can't think of any other PostgreSQL clone utility that is as easy to use. This is important when maintaining a high availability cluster, because simplicity prevents accidents.

Managing WAL files with walctl

The walctl toolkit provides two extra scripts that a DBA should never have to call manually: `walctl_push` and `walctl_pull`. These are intended purely to facilitate the preferred architecture of walctl. However, we also understand that many PostgreSQL servers exist already, and not every cluster is new.

It's actually very likely that at least one clone exists now that such behavior is directly supported by PostgreSQL 9.1 and above. In this recipe, we'll explore how to convert an existing cluster to use walctl for WAL management instead.

Getting ready

This recipe depends on walctl being installed on a primary server and any existing PostgreSQL clones. Please follow the *Installing and configuring walctl* recipe before continuing.

How to do it...

For this recipe, imagine we have four PostgreSQL servers. The primary PostgreSQL server is `pg-primary`, and we also have three existing replicas named `pg-clone1`, `pg-clone2`, and `pg-clone3`. Execute this command as the `postgres` system user on each of the existing clone systems:

```
walctl_setup clone
```

Once again, this one command does all the work for us.

How it works...

The beauty of `walctl_setup` is that it never needs to communicate with `pg-primary` at all. Everything this tool needs is in the `/etc/walctl.conf` file we created after installing walctl. By calling `walctl_setup` with the `clone` parameter, it performs three basic actions:

- Modifies `archive_command` in `postgresql.conf` to always produce a true value in case we ever need to change it to `walctl_push` later
- Removes any existing `restore_command` in `recovery.conf`
- Sets `restore_command` to `walctl_pull` with necessary parameters

Did you notice that walctl_setup does not touch the primary_conninfo setting in recovery.conf? This means existing streaming standby servers will continue to operate as they always have. The only difference is that they will retrieve WAL files from pg-arc (or whatever ARC_HOST is set to) instead of the previous source.

There's more...

What happens if we ever need to promote a clone to be a fully operational master node? Well, as we have subscribed to a detached design model, it means clones don't need pg-primary to continue replication. All we need to do is alter one clone such that it writes to pg-arc so that other clones will consume the new WAL files. We can do this using walctl_setup on the node we're promoting:

```
walctl_setup master
pg_ctl -D /db/pgdata promote
```

This will make the same modifications on the clone as it did to the master when we installed walctl. Principally, this means it sets archive_command in postgresql.conf to walctl_push to send WAL files to pg-arc.

Now, perhaps it's easier to understand why we're such strong advocates of including an archive server in the WAL-management process.

8
Advanced Stack

In this chapter, we will learn to build and manipulate a fault-tolerant, high-performance foundation for our PostgreSQL clusters. We will cover the following recipes in this chapter:

- Preparing systems for the stack
- Starting with the Linux Volume Manager
- Adding block-level replication
- Incorporating the second LVM layer
- Verifying a DRBD filesystem
- Correcting a DRBD split brain
- Formatting an XFS filesystem
- Tweaking XFS performance
- Maintaining an XFS filesystem
- Using LVM snapshots
- Switching live stack systems
- Detaching a problematic node
- Building and attaching a new node

Introduction

Thus far in this book, we've discussed quite an array of functionality and methodology dedicated to keeping PostgreSQL systems online. By now, we have a burgeoning menagerie of replication utilities, system monitoring tools, connection pooling layers, and even a handful of troubleshooting tips. What could we possibly cover next?

As it turns out, simply installing PostgreSQL on a server can be done too early. Presuming that we have all of the hardware and software we discussed earlier, our servers are still missing the following three things:

- The ability to synchronize data to two servers simultaneously
- The capacity to freeze data to prevent changes for backup purposes
- A durable filesystem designed for multiprocess I/O

There are several solutions for each of these missing elements, yet we've settled on three in particular: DRBD, LVM, and XFS. Let's explore a bit about each of these technologies and why we've chosen them to represent what we've deemed our *Advanced Stack*.

Why DRBD?

DRBD stands for **Distributed Replicated Block Device**. DRBD is meant to operate below the filesystem layer, mirroring the contents of one server's storage to another at the block level. This means the operating system doesn't even know that its data is located on another server as well. Having trouble imagining how it works? We hope the following diagram will help:

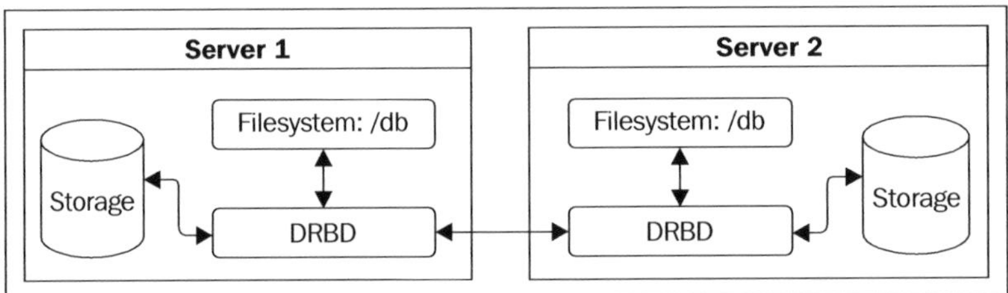

As we can see here, DRBD acts as an abstraction from the disk device that normally hosts our PostgreSQL database. The primary benefit we gain from this situation is that data is always located on at least two servers at all times. If one server crashes and its storage is rendered unusable, we have a backup available.

Why not use streaming replication instead? Even PostgreSQL synchronous streaming replication only guarantees that transactions are written to the standby, not replayed within the actual database. As we've already discussed, streaming replication means that the master node will halt on commit if there isn't at least one replica available at all times. With DRBD, the other server has a copy, which is identical in all aspects. Any block written to one server is always available on the other.

Why LVM?

LVM is the **Linux Volume Manager**. Like DRBD, LVM is another abstraction layer that sits between the filesystem and the underlying disk devices. Why is this necessary? LVM allows us to dynamically manage disk devices as one single continuous piece of storage that we can arbitrarily extend, group, freeze, or reorganize, all while remaining online.

Have you ever wanted to simply add storage to a filesystem without messy symbolic links or a server reboot? What about moving data from one device to another after an upgrade? With LVM, all of this is easy. Using a modern server with hot-swappable disks or a SAN, we never even have to reboot the server to completely reconfigure its disk devices.

Through the entire process of almost any LVM change, PostgreSQL can remain online and serve requests. This is the ultimate in high availability.

Why XFS?

XFS stands for **eXtended File System**. Some may consider this a somewhat controversial selection, given that **ext4** performs perfectly well and is the current default for all of the major Linux distributions. Both XFS and ext4 are journaling filesystems; they provide online growth, LVM freezing, and numerous maintenance and repair tools.

However, XFS still has something that ext4 does not: allocation groups. ext4, like all of its predecessors, has a single file allocation table for the entire formatted device. XFS, on the other hand, can split the allocation table into several segments so that multiple independent CPU processes can write to the disk simultaneously. The end result of this is that large servers with many CPUs and random writes, such as a PostgreSQL database, will perform better on an XFS-formatted device.

> If you are using **Red Hat Enterprise Linux** (**RHEL**) and have a support contract with Red Hat, be wary of using XFS. Red Hat considers XFS enterprise-grade storage and distributes it separately as a paid extension. If this becomes a problem, please feel free to use ext4 and ignore the XFS-related sections of this chapter.

The stack

At the end of this chapter, we will have a software stack that looks like the following:

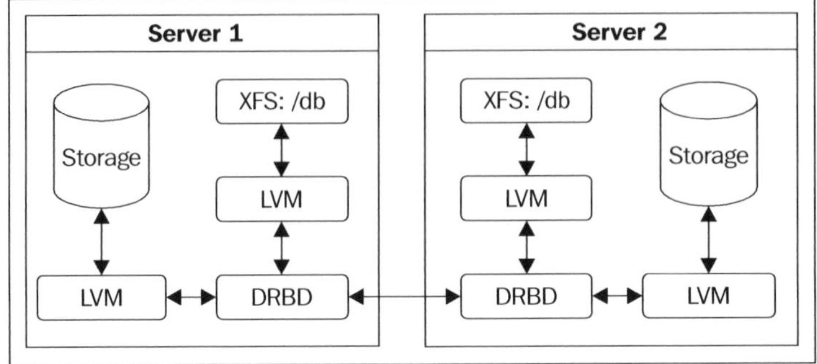

Each of the following layers represents one enhancement necessary for best long-term high availability:

- The first LVM layer (starting at the storage) protects DRBD from inheriting device-specific block sizes and allows for online resizing or migration to new devices
- The DRBD layer replicates data to another server for immediate use
- The second LVM layer provides snapshot capabilities and other potentially useful LVM functionality to the filesystem
- The XFS layer is the last element where data resides and is available for direct manipulation by programs such as PostgreSQL

The recipes we provide in this chapter should make this easier to understand, despite its advanced nature.

These layers in our stack do come at a cost. Since each is an abstraction above the raw storage device, performance will decrease slightly. We believe this tradeoff is worth the security and availability the stack provides. The makers of DRBD provide a good summary of how storage speed is affected at `http://blogs.linbit.com/p/469/843-random-writes-faster/`.

Preparing systems for the stack

Before we can use LVM, DRBD, or XFS on our servers, we must take some preliminary steps. We've never encountered a Linux system that is optimized for this kind of advanced usage directly after installation. In this recipe, we will modify several configuration files and even reboot the server.

We're trying to put each system in a standard state that we'll use for all future database servers. This means that LVM needs to ignore some devices to prevent disrupting DRBD, the initial RAM disks during boot should reflect this same allocation, and device performance shouldn't be lost between abstraction layers. We also need all of the tools that we'll use throughout this chapter.

This recipe will guarantee that these criteria are true, so be prepared!

Getting ready

The only things we should need at this point are the ability to run commands as root and a device dedicated to database storage. However, if you are running a RHEL system (not a derivative such as CentOS or Scientific Linux), you may need to contact Red Hat to obtain necessary licenses and packages to add XFS functionality. Thus, we will approach this recipe under the assumption that packages are available on Debian-based servers and RHEL derivatives.

How to do it...

To keep things simple, we will assume that each server we prepare has a device named `/dev/sdb` for database storage. Follow these steps as `root`:

1. Install the `xfsprogs` package with `apt-get` or `yum`.
2. Install `drbd8-utils` with `apt-get` on Debian-based systems, or `drbd` with `yum` on Red Hat derivatives.
3. In the `devices` section of `/etc/lvm/lvm.conf`, change the `filter` setting to read the following:
   ```
   filter = [ "a|/dev/sd.*|", "a|/dev/drbd.*|", "r|.*|" ]
   ```
4. In the `devices` section of `/etc/lvm/lvm.conf`, change the `write_cache_state` setting to read the following:
   ```
   write_cache_state = 0
   ```
5. Remove the existing LVM cache file with the following command:
   ```
   rm /etc/lvm/cache/.cache
   ```
6. Update the kernel's list of available devices with the following command:
   ```
   update-initramfs -u
   ```

7. Create a file named `/etc/udev/rules.d/20-postgresql.rules` with the following contents:

```
ACTION=="add|change", KERNEL=="sd[a-z]",
  ATTR{queue/read_ahead_kb}="4096"
ACTION=="add|change", KERNEL=="drbd[0-9]",
  ATTR{bdi/read_ahead_kb}="4096"
```

8. Finally, reboot the server using the following command:

```
reboot
```

How it works...

In order for the stack to work properly, we need to get the server ready. For now, this means installing basic toolkits such as `xfsprogs` for XFS maintenance tools and `drbd8-utils` for DRBD administrative scripts. Once this is complete, we move on to preparing LVM.

Since LVM is so highly integrated into the system, we need to perform several steps. The first is to modify the primary `lvm.conf` file so that it only watches certain devices, and while it does so, it never caches the result. Due to the way Linux is designed, there are several different aliases and paths that point to the same device in the `/dev` filesystem. To remove these extra paths, we set a very strict `filter` that only includes `/dev/sd*` devices and `/dev/drbd*` devices.

We avoid caching by setting `write_cache_state` to `0` because the DRBD devices may disappear or reappear based on their statuses. We don't want an invalid cache poisoning the actual device state. Just to make sure there are no stale LVM caches, we remove the existing `/etc/lvm/cache/.cache` so that all readings are current. By invoking `initramfs` with the `-u` parameter, it generates a new device map that will be used when the system boots. This ensures that devices are consistent at all availability levels in case we need emergency access.

Before we venture further, we need to address performance. In Greg Smith's *PostgreSQL 9.0 High Performance, Packt Publishing*, he suggests that we increase the `read_ahead_kb` setting for every block device to `4096` kilobytes or higher. Unfortunately, due to the transient nature of our devices, there is no static method we can use that would survive a device appearing after boot. This is where the **udev** filesystem comes in. It watches as various system devices change state, appear, or reappear. Thanks to this, we can give it parameters to use when new storage devices appear, such as our DRBD or LVM devices.

The two lines we added to `20-postgresql.rules` tell the udev filesystem to set the `read_ahead_kb` value to `4096` any time a new device is added or modified. In our case, we are specifically interested in the `sdb` and `drbd0` devices, but we include all `sd` or `drbd` devices for future expansion purposes if necessary. This ensures that we'll always have a large read buffer for good PostgreSQL performance, no matter how many abstraction layers we place between the device and the database.

The last thing we do is reboot the server. This gives us a fresh slate, with a cleanly generated device map based on the changes we made.

There's more...

The version of DRBD you receive with these instructions may vary considerably depending on the age of your distribution. As DRBD 8.4 is the most recent stable version at the time of writing this book, all recipes assume that this is the installed version. To see if you are using 8.4, execute `drbdadm` with the `-V` parameter, and check the module and tooling versions. If these versions don't match, or are 8.3 or below, please follow the instructions from one of these URLs to upgrade to 8.4:

- For Red Hat systems: `http://www.drbd.org/users-guide/s-build-rpm.html`
- For Debian systems: `http://www.drbd.org/users-guide/s-build-deb.html`

See also

- The DRBD website has a good supplementary installation guide at `http://www.drbd.org/users-guide/s-distro-packages.html`.
- Greg Smith's *PostgreSQL 9.0 High Performance* book is another great resource from Packt Publishing. It is available at `http://www.packtpub.com/postgresql-90-high-performance/book`.

Getting started with the Linux Volume Manager

The **Linux Volume Manager** (**LVM**) is something of an optional master control panel for Linux storage devices. It can combine several devices into one, allows arbitrary storage grouping far more granular than simple partitions, and provides functionality such as data snapshots and reorganization. It's very powerful, and in the right hands, greatly improves potential server uptime.

It is also the first layer above the raw storage device in our stack. We start with LVM instead of DRBD, because DRBD at the device level is extremely messy. What do we gain by insulating DRBD from the raw storage device?

- We can easily add storage to the LVM device group assigned to DRBD
- DRBD can be resized while in an online state
- We can perform storage migrations without taking PostgreSQL offline

None of this is possible unless LVM is the first layer. For a high-availability server, this is extremely desirable. Follow along to see how it works.

Getting ready

At this point, all we need is a single unformatted device to use for database storage. In addition, make sure you've prepared the system as described in the *Preparing systems for the stack* recipe.

How to do it...

For the purposes of this recipe, we will assume that the `/dev/sdb` device has been dedicated to PostgreSQL use. Follow these steps as the `root` user *on two servers* to create the first LVM layer:

1. Create and verify a single LVM partition on the device with these commands:

   ```
   parted /dev/sdb mklabel gpt
   parted /dev/sdb mkpart primary 1 100%
   parted /dev/sdb set 1 lvm on
   parted /dev/sdb print
   ```

2. Register `/dev/sdb` as an LVM physical device with this command:

   ```
   pvcreate /dev/sdb1
   ```

3. Create a single volume group to contain `/dev/sdb1` with this command:

   ```
   vgcreate VG_DRBD /dev/sdb1
   ```

4. Create a single logical volume as `100%` of the outer volume group with this command:

   ```
   lvcreate -n LV_DATA -l 100%VG VG_DRBD
   ```

5. Verify whether the new volume exists and is available with this command:

   ```
   lvdisplay VG_DRBD/LV_DATA | grep LV
   ```

How it works...

Before we can use LVM safely, we should create at least one partition on the raw device. For this, we use `parted`, a more advanced partition editor than `fdisk`. We need `parted` because it can set the partition table type as GPT, which allows filesystems greater than 2 TB. This is what the first invocation of `parted` does, with the `mklabel` parameter set to `gpt`.

To create the partition itself, we call `parted` with the `mkpart` parameter. By using `mkpart`, we also need to specify the type of partition we want, and its starting and ending positions. We keep things simple by starting at the beginning of the device and using `100%` of the available storage.

Finally, we set the LVM flag to true by invoking `parted` with the `set` parameter. The `set` parameter requires a partition number, the flag we want to set, and the value. In our case, we are using the first partition and setting the `lvm` flag to `on`.

It's always a good idea to verify our creations, and `parted` has a `print` setting to output the current partition table for a specified disk device. Here is `/dev/sdb` on our test system:

```
root@pg1:~# parted /dev/sdb print
Model: ATA VBOX HARDDISK (scsi)
Disk /dev/sdb: 4295MB
Sector size (logical/physical): 512B/512B
Partition Table: gpt

Number  Start   End     Size    File system  Name     Flags
 1      1049kB  4294MB  4293MB               primary  lvm
```

As you can see, the test device we've used for this example is very small, at just over 4 GB. However, we can also see that the partition table is `gpt`, and the `lvm` flag is set as expected.

Now we can start with LVM itself. The first step is to use `pvcreate` to *create* a physical LVM device. This allows LVM to manage the device, and only requires us to name `/dev/sdb1` as the device we're adding.

Next, we need a volume group. Volume groups can be comprised of multiple physical volumes and be split into several logical volumes. By calling `vgcreate`, we need to name the group with the first parameter. Every subsequent parameter is a device that should be part of the new group. In our case, we only have the `/dev/sdb1` device, so that becomes our last parameter.

Since the volume group can host several logical volumes, we need to create at least one. Unlike `vgcreate`, the `lvcreate` command does not assume the first parameter is the volume name. Thus, we need to specify the `-n` parameter to name the volume. By using the `-l` parameter, we can specify a percentage of the volume group as the size of our volume. For the base volume, we want to use all available storage space (`100%VG`) since DRBD will be the next layer. The last parameter for `lvcreate` is the name of the volume group we are using for this logical volume.

The last thing we do is verify that the logical volume has the elements we expect. We can do this with the `lvdisplay` command as seen here:

```
root@pg1:~# lvdisplay VG_DRBD/LV_DATA | grep LV
  LV Name                /dev/VG_DRBD/LV_DATA
  LV UUID                P7Zret-DTbI-SJnV-pGXh-aOqw-GCcO-7s12QR
  LV Write Access        read/write
  LV Status              available
  LV Size                4.00 GiB
```

From this, we can see that the new logical volume is `4.00 GiB` in size and is `available` for use. We can also observe that LVM created a new device path at `/dev/VG_DRBD/LV_DATA`. This path will be how we address the storage in the future. It can be formatted, mounted, or treated just like any other Linux storage device.

As we'll discuss in the next recipe, this new `/dev` location can be used as the target device for another resource such as DRBD.

There's more...

We hope you noticed the naming scheme inherent in all of the LVM commands. Commands prefixed with `pv` are meant for physical volume management. Similarly, `vg` is used for volume groups, and `lv` is for logical volumes. This greatly simplifies management of LVM devices.

We used `pvcreate`, `vgcreate`, and `lvcreate` in this recipe. However, it shouldn't surprise you that there are also analogous `pvremove`, `vgremove`, and `lvremove` commands as well. There are also commands to retrieve information about volumes and groups: `pvdisplay`, `vgdisplay`, and `lvdisplay`.

This is one of the reasons we enjoy working with LVM; we rarely have to guess at commands.

See also

- LVM itself is a conceptual architecture. To understand more about how it works, we recommend the **Linux Documentation Project** discussion on the topic at `http://tldp.org/HOWTO/LVM-HOWTO/`.
- In addition, all of the LVM commands have their own `man` page. We highly recommend at least viewing the man page for each utility before using it. For example:

  ```
  man lvextend
  ```

Adding block-level replication

DRBD is the next component of our software stack. Unlike LVM, it requires at least two servers to function normally. One server acts as the data **Primary**, and the other acts as a **Secondary**. These roles can be switched at any time, depending on which server is running PostgreSQL.

For now, we are going to focus on configuring and activating DRBD as part of our stack.

Getting ready

By now, we hope you've followed the recipe in *Getting started with the Linux Volume Manager* on *two servers* with `/dev/sdb` as physically identical storage on each server. While DRBD can operate in standalone mode on a single server, this is actually more advanced usage. The steps in this recipe are best applied the same on both of the servers simultaneously, unless noted otherwise.

How to do it...

For the purposes of this recipe, we will assume that the `/dev/VG_DRBD/LV_DATA` device already exists. The two PostgreSQL nodes for this example are named `pg1` and `pg2` and are located on the `192.168.56.0` subnet. Follow these steps as the `root` user *on each server* to add DRBD:

1. Create a file named `/etc/drbd.d/pg.res` with the following contents:

   ```
   resource pg {
     device minor 0;
     disk /dev/VG_DRBD/LV_DATA;
     meta-disk internal;
     on pg1 {
       address 192.168.56.10:7788;
     }
     on pg2 {
       address 192.168.56.20:7788;
     }
   }
   ```

2. Allocate the DRBD storage with this command:

   ```
   drbdadm create-md pg
   ```

3. Restart the DRBD service:

   ```
   service drbd restart
   ```

4. Use drbdadm on pg1 to invalidate the data on pg2:

   drbdadm invalidate-remote pg

5. View the status of DRBD from any node, using this command:

   cat /proc/drbd

6. Run this command on pg1 to declare it as the primary node:

   drbdadm primary pg

How it works...

We begin by creating a configuration file for DRBD with the least amount of information necessary. In the pg.res file, we define a DRBD resource named pg for our PostgreSQL data. DRBD resource numbers start at zero, so we use the define keyword to set the DRBD minor device number to 0. This means our DRBD device will be named /dev/drbd0.

After setting the device number, we specify which storage volume this DRBD resource should use with the disk keyword. The meta-disk keyword allows us to define a device to store DRBD metadata. To keep things simple, we've used the internal setting so that metadata is stored on the same device as the data we are synchronizing.

The last thing we do in the resource configuration file is define each host involved in replication. The on keyword expects a host name that matches our PostgreSQL nodes, followed by a block of settings. The only setting we actually need is the IP address of the server we name, followed by a port, which DRBD should use for communication and transfer purposes. A common port number is 7788 as in our example, but really, this can be any arbitrary unused value.

Once we have a valid configuration file, we need to initialize the DRBD device. When we invoke drbdadm with the create-md parameter, it allocates metadata for the named DRBD resource. Since pg is the name of our resource, we specify that here as well. We could have also used all, which applies the command to any configured resources. This produces quite a bit of output, but should look like the following near the end:

```
Writing meta data...
initializing activity log
NOT initializing bitmap
New drbd meta data block successfully created.
success
```

With metadata in place, we can start (or restart) the DRBD service. Once we do this, DRBD will attempt to connect both nodes named in our resource definition file. This is why DRBD should be started on both nodes consecutively, or the running node will wait indefinitely for the other to start as well.

At this point, DRBD is connected, but it doesn't know the state of the underlying storage data. Due to this, we must invalidate one of the nodes so DRBD considers the other node up-to-date. When we use `drbdadm` with `invalidate-remote`, we tell DRBD to consider local data valid and all data on any other node in need of replacement. If we examine the contents of `/proc/drbd` at this moment, we should see synchronization taking place:

```
0: cs:SyncSource ro:Secondary/Secondary ds:UpToDate/Inconsistent C r---n-
   ns:61896 nr:0 dw:0 dr:63488 al:0 bm:3 lo:0 pe:1 ua:2 ap:0 ep:1 wo:f oos:4128604
        [>....................] sync'ed:  1.6% (4128604/4190044)K
        finish: 0:02:14 speed: 30,720 (30,720) K/sec
```

The top line of this output actually provides most of the DRBD status information. The section labeled `ro` stands for **roles**, and the slash always separates the current node from the remote node. By default, both DRBD systems report their role as a `Secondary` node. Similarly, `ds` represents **disk states** and tells us the status of data on each node. Based on this, we can see that the current node is `UpToDate`, while the remote is `Inconsistent`. We invalidated the data on `pg2` from `pg1`, so this is exactly what we should expect.

Once synchronization is complete, it is time to declare one of the nodes as the primary resource. For this task, we run `drbdadm` with the `primary` parameter. The only difference we should see is a change in the `ro` reading in `/proc/drbd`. It should reflect `Primary/Secondary` when viewed from `pg1`, and `Secondary/Primary` when viewed from `pg2`. At this point, DRBD is working, and any data we save on one node should automatically exist on the other as well.

See also

- DRBD documentation is extremely detailed. We strongly recommend browsing `http://www.drbd.org/users-guide/drbd-users-guide.html` to truly understand how DRBD works.
- In addition, the `drbdadm` tool that administers almost all DRBD functionality has a `man` page:

  `man drbdadm`

Incorporating the second LVM layer

In this recipe, we are going to create the second of our two LVM abstraction layers. While the first layer provides an elastic base for DRBD, this one will provide most of the LVM functionality that we will actually use on a regular basis.

Tasks such as creating filesystem snapshots or reorganizing data are within the domain of the second layer. This is because we create the filesystem on top of this second LVM definition. We can mount or otherwise manipulate a snapshot like any other filesystem. If we tried to create a snapshot with the first LVM layer, we would still have a snapshot, but it would be of an unreadable DRBD binary blob.

With that in mind, let's add the LVM layer necessary for filesystem manipulation.

Getting ready

Please follow all previous recipes before starting.

How to do it...

Perform these steps *only* on `pg1` as the `root` user:

1. Register `/dev/drbd0` as an LVM physical device, using this command:

   ```
   pvcreate /dev/drbd0
   ```

2. Create a single volume group to contain `/dev/drbd0`, using this command:

   ```
   vgcreate VG_POSTGRES /dev/drbd0
   ```

3. Create a single logical volume as `95%` of the outer volume group, using this command:

   ```
   lvcreate -n LV_DATA -l 95%VG VG_POSTGRES
   ```

4. Verify that the new volume exists and is available, using this command:

   ```
   vgdisplay VG_POSTGRES | grep Size
   ```

How it works...

Do these steps seem familiar? They should! With a few minor exceptions, this is almost the same as the recipe we used in *Getting started with the Linux Volume Manager*. Unlike the other instructions, we don't need to partition the `/dev/drbd0` device and can immediately add it to LVM with `pvcreate`.

Following this, we use `vgcreate` to define a new volume group named `VG_POSTGRES` containing `/dev/drbd0` as its only device. The definition for this volume group actually exists on the `/dev/drbd0` device itself, meaning it is replicated by DRBD to the other node. This is why we only need to execute these commands on `pg1`.

Next, we use `lvcreate` with the `-n` parameter to create a logical volume named `LV_DATA` within the `VG_POSTGRES` group. This time we use the `-l` parameter to set the volume size at `95%VG` instead of `100%VG`. This means `LV_DATA` will contain 95 percent of the total available space within the `VG_POSTGRES` volume group.

Why did we neglect to allocate the remaining 5 percent? Snapshot space. We can use snapshots for backups, risky temporary work, or simply as a placeholder. If you never plan on using filesystem snapshots, feel free to use 100 percent of the VG_POSTGRES group instead.

Instead of verifying the allocation of our logical volume, our last command retrieves some of the information about the volume group. On our testing system, it looks like the following:

```
root@pg1:~# vgdisplay VG_POSTGRES | grep Size
  VG Size               3.99 GiB
  PE Size               4.00 MiB
  Alloc PE / Size       970 / 3.79 GiB
  Free  PE / Size       52 / 208.00 MiB
```

We can see that the volume group is 3.99 GiB in size, that 3.79 GiB is allocated, and that 208.00 MiB is free. Based on this information, we can presume 3.79 GiB is allocated to the LV_DATA volume, leaving us 208 MiB for allocating snapshots. We are glad this is only an example, as 208 MiB is not very much free snapshot space!

There's more...

Is 5 percent too much space to set aside for snapshots, especially in multi-terabyte volumes? Probably! Unfortunately, the only other mechanism available to define volume size is the -L parameter to lvcreate, which only works with absolute measurements. Yet, we know the size of our devices, and we are free to make loose estimates.

For example, imagine we have a 4 TB storage device, and we only want to leave around 50 GB for snapshots instead of 200 GB. This lvcreate command specifies the size of our device in GB:

```
lvcreate -n LV_DATA -L 3950G VG_POSTGRES
```

See also

- As before, we strongly recommend examining the LVM documentation and man pages to fully leverage its capabilities. We leave http://tldp.org/HOWTO/LVM-HOWTO/ to the Linux Documentation Project once again, for posterity.

Verifying a DRBD filesystem

A semi-common maintenance concern regarding synchronized devices is verification. The question we should always ask ourselves in a high-availability scenario is how confident we are that data on both nodes match.

The `drbdadm` utility provides a parameter specifically for addressing this need. However, there are some caveats to consider when using it, which we will explain in this recipe.

Getting ready

Follow the recipes defined in all previous sections before starting here. At the very least, we need a fully-operational DRBD node pair to follow this recipe.

How to do it...

Follow these steps as the `root` user on `pg1`:

1. Add this block of text inside the `resource` section defined in `/etc/drbd.d/pg.res`:

   ```
   net {
     verify-alg md5;
   }
   ```

2. Run this command to make DRBD reread its configuration files:

   ```
   drbdadm adjust pg
   ```

3. Begin verification with this command:

   ```
   drbdadm verify pg
   ```

4. Monitor `/proc/drbd` until verification is complete:

   ```
   watch cat /proc/drbd
   ```

5. Disconnect and reconnect the DRBD resource:

   ```
   drbdadm disconnect pg
   drbdadm connect pg
   ```

How it works...

Our first job is to define what we mean by *verify*. By default, DRBD is somewhat minimal, and it has no default for the algorithm it should use for checksum comparisons. The `verify-alg` setting is a network-oriented value and defines how DRBD should compare data segments. We also know `md5` as a widely-used checksum algorithm. Thus, we set the `verify-alg` in a `net` block within the `resource` definition for `pg`.

Afterwards, we need to reread the configuration files so that the `verify-alg` setting is defined for the verification step. By invoking `drbdadm` with the `adjust` parameter, it will read and apply any valid changes we made to `/etc/drbd.d/pg.res`. When we're ready, we can launch the verification process by calling `drbdadm` with the `verify` parameter. Due to the CPU overhead of `md5`, this will be noticeably slower than a full device synchronization. We can watch its progress by paying attention to `/proc/drbd`:

```
0: cs:VerifyS ro:Primary/Secondary ds:UpToDate/UpToDate C r-----
   ns:4190132 nr:0 dw:88 dr:5315648 al:1 bm:256 lo:0 pe:96 ua:179 ap:0 ep:1 wo:f oos:0
       [====>...............] verified: 26.8% (3068412/4190044)K
       finish: 0:01:58 speed: 25,912 (14,952) want: 28,600 K/sec
```

We can see that our example verification is `26.8%` complete, with an estimated completion time of almost 2 minutes. The estimate is produced based on network speed, `md5` speed, and the amount of remaining data. These details can fluctuate frequently, as writes to the DRBD device slow down the verification process.

The last step is to disconnect, then reconnect the `pg` resource from the DRBD network. During verification, DRBD marks blocks that have unmatched `md5` checksums, but does not resend them until a new connection is established. We can't speculate about the reason for this step, but it is required to correct errors.

> The last step is only required if any block failed verification. Errors (bad blocks) will be located in the kernel log according to DRBD documentation. We recommend checking for `drbd0` messages in `/var/log/syslog`, `/var/log/messages`, and `/var/log/kern.log`, depending on your distribution.

See also

- The DRBD documentation explains online verification in more detail than we do. Please refer to `http://www.drbd.org/users-guide/s-use-online-verify.html` for a full discussion of the process.

Correcting a DRBD split brain

One looming danger when running any replication system is that of node status conflicts. This happens when more than one node has been primary, and we want to reestablish the previous mirror state. This can happen in many ways, but a common scenario can occur if the existing primary node experiences a sudden failure and the remaining secondary node is promoted to primary status.

In the case where we repair the old primary node, we can't simply reattach it to the DRBD network and expect successful synchronization. In cases where the last status for each node is that of a primary, DRBD will not resolve this conflict automatically. It is our job to manually choose the best primary node from our available choices, and reattach the other node.

In this recipe, we'll explore the steps necessary to reattach a malfunctioning node to an existing DRBD architecture. We can't have a highly available PostgreSQL cluster with only one functional node.

Getting ready

Since we're working with DRBD and need a fully established mirror, please follow steps in all the recipes up to *Adding block-level replication* before continuing. In addition, we need to simulate a split brain. A very easy way to do this is to put both nodes in primary state while disconnected from each other.

Assuming that we have nodes `pg1` and `pg2`, where `pg1` is the current primary node, follow these instructions as the `root` user to cause a split brain:

1. On both nodes, disconnect from DRBD with this command:

   ```
   drbdadm disconnect pg
   ```

2. On `pg2`, execute this command to force it into primary status:

   ```
   drbdadm primary --force pg
   ```

If we were to use `drbdadm` to attempt and connect the nodes now, we would see the following message in the system logs:

```
Split-Brain detected but unresolved, dropping connection!
```

How to do it...

Follow these instructions as the `root` user to repair a split-brain scenario:

1. First, decide which node should be the new primary. This should be relatively easy, since some event likely precipitated the node mismatch. For the remainder of this recipe, we will assume `pg2` should be the new primary node.
2. Prepare each server by assuring that each is disconnected from the other:

   ```
   drbdadm disconnect pg
   ```

3. Disable the `VG_POSTGRES` volume with `vgchange` on `pg1`:

   ```
   vgchange -a n VG_POSTGRES
   ```

4. Use `drbdadm` to downgrade `pg1` to `secondary` status:

   ```
   drbdadm secondary pg
   ```

5. Execute this command on `pg1` to connect while discarding metadata:

   ```
   drbdadm connect --discard-my-data pg
   ```

6. Execute this command on `pg2` to connect to DRBD:

   ```
   drbdadm connect pg
   ```

How it works...

The first step is clearly the most critical. We need to determine which node has the most recent valid data. In almost all cases, there should be sufficient logs to make this determination. However, in some network disruption scenarios coupled with automated failover solutions, this may not be obvious. Unfortunately, resolving this step is too varied to adequately express in a simple guide.

If you are unsure of how to continue following an extremely complicated failure scenario, we strongly recommend contacting Linbit, which maintains the DRBD software. Their support information is available at this URL: `http://www.linbit.com/en/products-and-services/drbd-support`

For our example, we manually promoted the `pg2` node, so it should be the new primary. With that in mind, there are many states DRBD could have right now, and we want one in particular: `StandAlone`. By disconnecting both nodes, we don't have to worry about aborted or premature connection attempts disrupting our progress. We want both nodes to report `StandAlone` in `/proc/drbd` as the connection state (`cs`), as shown in this screenshot:

```
0: cs:StandAlone ro:Primary/Unknown ds:UpToDate/DUnknown   r-----
   ns:0 nr:0 dw:4190132 dr:8380700 al:0 bm:256 lo:0 pe:0 ua:0 ap:0 ep:1 wo:f oos:0
```

Our next step is actually related to LVM. If DRBD is primary on a node, the second LVM layer is probably active as well. Since LVM uses the underlying DRBD device, we can't demote this node to secondary status until we use `vgchange` to set the active (`-a`) state of `VG_POSTGRES` to no (`n`).

Given that there are no other elements connected to `/dev/drbd0`, we can set its status to `secondary` with `drbdadm`. While in secondary state, we can attempt to connect to the DRBD network with `drbdadm connect`. Since both nodes were primary at one point, each was maintaining a different map of modified blocks; these maps will not match. If this happens, DRBD will refuse to connect to the network, and it will revert to the `StandAlone` status.

To prevent that, we add `--discard-my-data` to the `connect` operation. This option acknowledges the situation, and it tells the secondary node to ignore its own change map in favor of what the primary node may contain. If the secondary node is too out-of-date for the update map, DRBD will simply resynchronize all data on the device.

Of course, none of this will happen until we invoke `drbdadm connect` from the new primary node. We do this last because we can always change our minds and abort the process. If we did this before connecting the secondary node, previously existing storage maps have already been discarded, and resynchronization is already taking place.

See also

- DRBD addresses this exact scenario in their documentation. We recommend reading through `http://www.drbd.org/users-guide/s-resolve-split-brain.html` for a different perspective on the operation.

Formatting an XFS filesystem

The next and last part of our stack is the filesystem layer. This is where the PostgreSQL data will reside, so we need to ensure it's allocated properly. Unlike the underlying LVM layers, the filesystem is not so easily modified.

In this recipe, we will discuss some common formatting options and why we recommend them in addition to necessary commands.

Getting ready

Since this is the last layer in our complete stack, we strongly suggest following all the recipes up to *Incorporating the second LVM layer* before starting here.

How to do it...

Assuming `pg1` is our current primary node, follow these steps there as the `root` user:

1. Activate the second LVM volume with this command:

   ```
   lvchange -a y VG_POSTGRES/LV_DATA
   ```

2. Count the number of CPUs on the primary node.
3. Multiply the CPU count by four.
4. If the total in the previous step is less than 256, use 256.
5. Use this command to find the Linux kernel version:

   ```
   uname -r
   ```

6. For kernel versions `3.0` and above, format the XFS filesystem with this command, setting `agcount` to the value derived in the preceding steps:

   ```
   mkfs.xfs -d agcount=256 /dev/VG_POSTGRES/LV_DATA
   ```

7. For kernels below `3.0`, format with this command:

```
mkfs.xfs -d agcount=256 -l size=128m -l lazy-count=1 \
         -i attr=2 /dev/VG_POSTGRES/LV_DATA
```

How it works...

We begin by activating (`-a y`) the `VG_POSTGRES/LV_DATA` volume with `lvchange`. This is like `vgchange`, but only affects the named volume, instead of every volume in the named group. We used this command merely to demonstrate that either command will work for our stack, especially since there is only one volume to activate.

The next three steps involve a simple calculation, but it deserves some explanation. The main feature we want to exploit here is the count of allocation groups. Each allocation group can be addressed independently when making filesystem modifications. Presumably, this enhances performance in several different categories since it reduces allocation table contention.

To reach our desired number, we start with the total CPU count in our primary server. This is the maximum number of concurrent processes that can touch the filesystem simultaneously. However, we live in a world where upgrades are frequent and CPU core counts are only increasing. Thus, we suggest multiplying the current CPU count by four, because we only get one chance to create the XFS layer once it contains data. We want to keep time-consuming data migrations to a minimum if possible.

With this calculated allocation group count in hand, we can begin formatting. The `mkfs.xfs` utility supplied by `xfsprogs` will perform this step for us. The command we used contained several parameters, separated into data (`-d`), log (`-l`), and inode (`-i`) settings. Here is a quick summary of what these options do:

- The `agcount` setting defines how many allocation groups XFS should create. Our example uses `256`, but you may have more.
- We set the log `size` to `128m` for a 128 MB journal. Journaling filesystems are not new, but we need a sufficient size to track many concurrent changes on active databases. On kernels at and above `3.0`, this value is calculated based on the device size, so we don't need to set it.
- By setting `lazy-count` to `1`, we get the full power of our `agcount` setting. Though there are several allocation groups, there is still a master superblock that tracks some universal counters. By enabling this, XFS uses other techniques to maintain these values, avoiding sequential superblock access. On kernels `3.0` and higher, this is set to `1` by default.
- The `attr` inode setting configures an internal mechanism to store inline attributes. This is more of an implementation detail, but Version `2` is more efficient. On kernels above `2.6.16`, this is set to `2` by default.

While this is a lot to digest, it should be clear by now that newer kernels make it much easier to use XFS. Instead of all these other options, we merely need to set `agcount` and format the filesystem. If everything works as expected, we should see this output from the `mkfs.xfs` command:

```
meta-data=/dev/VG_POSTGRES/LV_DATA isize=256    agcount=256, agsize=124160 blks
         =                       sectsz=512   attr=2, projid32bit=0
data     =                       bsize=4096   blocks=993280, imaxpct=25
         =                       sunit=0      swidth=0 blks
naming   =version 2              bsize=4096   ascii-ci=0
log      =internal log           bsize=4096   blocks=32768, version=2
         =                       sectsz=512   sunit=0 blks, lazy-count=1
realtime =none                   extsz=4096   blocks=0, rtextents=0
```

From this, we can see that our `agcount` is indeed set to `256`, `lazy-count` is set to `1`, and `attr` is set to `2`.

See also

- A definitive source of current XFS documentation is oddly difficult to find. Instead, we recommend you examine the `mkfs.xfs` manual provided by `man` for more information:

  `man mkfs.xfs`

Tweaking XFS performance

When it comes to performance optimization on XFS filesystems, allocation groups are only the beginning. To maintain a high-availability PostgreSQL server, we want to get the most out of XFS. For us, this means using specific mount options.

Thankfully, unlike formatting, mount options can be changed frequently and require very little downtime. Though it isn't essential that we apply these values immediately, the options discussed in this recipe are our recommendation for this stack.

Getting ready

In order to mount an XFS filesystem, we need one to exist. Please follow the recipe contained in *Formatting an XFS Filesystem* before continuing.

How to do it...

Assuming `pg1` is our current primary node, follow these steps as the `root` user:

1. Use this command to find the Linux kernel version:

   ```
   uname -r
   ```

2. For kernel versions `3.0` and above, mount the filesystem with this command:

   ```
   mount -t xfs -o noatime,nodiratime \
         -o logbsize=256k,allocsize=1m \
         /dev/VG_POSTGRES/LV_DATA /db
   ```

3. For kernels below `3.0`, mount with this command:

   ```
   mount -t xfs -o noatime,nodiratime \
         -o logbufs=8,logbsize=256k,attr2 \
         -o allocsize=1m /dev/VG_POSTGRES/LV_DATA /db
   ```

4. Execute this command to confirm a successful mount:

   ```
   df /dev/mapper/VG_POSTGRES-LV_DATA
   ```

How it works...

Our first step is to find our current kernel version as this will dictate which settings are default to our desired values. Then, we continue with the `mount` command and specify `-t` to set the filesystem type to `xfs`. The last two parameters are to the `mount` command, define the device we are mounting and which directory it should be attached to. In this case, we use our `/dev/VG_POSTGRES/LV_DATA` device and the `/db` directory that we've discussed throughout the book.

All of the parameters prefixed with `-o` are options that `mount` should apply during the mounting process. These options define how certain aspects of the filesystem behave. Here is a quick overview of the options we selected, and what they mean:

- We use `noatime` to prevent file metadata from reflecting the last time the file was accessed. In a PostgreSQL database, storage files are likely constantly being accessed and modified, so tracking this information is a waste of time and incurs unnecessary writes.
- We use `nodiratime` for a similar reason regarding directory access times.
- By ensuring `logbufs` is set to `8`, we get the maximum amount of available buffers for the filesystem data journal. On kernels `3.0` and above, this is set to `8` by default.
- The maximum value for `logbsize` is `256k`. This is a very small amount of memory, and it ensures good performance for file deletion operations.

- The `attr2` option reflects the `attr=2` value that we set when formatting XFS, and it produces more efficient inode tables. On kernels `3.0` and above, this is enabled by default.
- The `allocsize` setting is extremely important. It defines the amount of space associated with each newly created file. It's meant to prevent excessive file fragmentation by preallocating larger amounts than requested. By setting this to `1m`, these allocations are limited to 1 MB in size.

In `3.0` kernels and above, XFS implemented a dynamic allocation calculation that will often use values above 256 MB *per file*. Due to aggressive kernel caching, these larger allocations may not be released for hours or even days, causing a mismatch between used and free space in the filesystem. This can result in 0 percent free space, even if the usage percentage is very low. Never forget this setting in newer kernels.

A successful mount will return no output, so we need to confirm that the space is available some other way. The `df` command will report the amount of used and free space on a device, and we can pass it the `-h` parameter to make the output human readable. On our test system, this is what we see:

```
root@pg1:~# df /dev/mapper/VG_POSTGRES-LV_DATA
Filesystem                        Size  Used Avail Use% Mounted on
/dev/mapper/VG_POSTGRES-LV_DATA  3.8G   33M  3.8G   1% /db
```

There's more...

There is one final important mount option that we have not yet discussed: `nobarrier`. Write barriers insert a flush operation between a filesystem write and disk sync to prevent inadvertent data reordering. Some storage devices contain a battery-backed disk cache such as high-end RAID solutions, SANs, and some solid state disks with on-board capacitors. This kind of hardware can survive sudden power loss and does not require explicit barrier-imposed data flushing.

Without this excessive data flushing, write performance can improve noticeably. To use this setting, merely include `nobarrier` in the list of mount options. For example:

```
mount -t xfs -o noatime,nodiratime,logbsize=256k \
      -o allocsize=1m,nobarrier /dev/VG_POSTGRES/LV_DATA /db
```

See also

- The XFS FAQ contains a lot of information related to performance and tweaking XFS in general. This is available at `http://xfs.org/index.php/XFS_FAQ`.
- Otherwise, the `mount` manual provided by `man` has a section specifically pertaining to XFS mount options:

  ```
  man mount
  ```

Maintaining an XFS filesystem

Conventional wisdom regarding Linux filesystems suggests that file defragmentation is not a necessary task. While this is true in general, file fragmentation isn't something we should allow to spiral out of control. PostgreSQL storage files are limited to 1 GB in size, yet we configured XFS to preallocate no more than 1 MB at a time.

This introduces the potential for data fragmentation on OLTP systems or any database cluster where several tables experience high turnover. To prevent this from adversely affecting sequential scans, and to promote good filesystem health in general, we need to track and potentially correct overly fragmented files.

XFS provides two tools suited to this activity. The first is `xfs_db`, which provides information about an XFS filesystem. The second is `xfs_fsr`, which allows us to defragment XFS while it is still mounted and active. This recipe will cover the basic usage of these tools to keep our high availability server performing well.

Getting ready

For this recipe, we want a formatted and active XFS filesystem. Follow the recipe in *Formatting an XFS filesystem* before continuing. It may also be a good idea to set up a dummy database where you mounted XFS. This way, you can run a `pgbench` test to create a lot of database write activity so that there is a small amount of data fragmentation. This is not required to follow along with this recipe.

How to do it...

Assuming `pg1` is our current primary node and `/dev/VG_POSTGRES/LV_DATA` is the device we formatted with XFS, follow these steps there as the `root` user:

1. Examine the current fragmentation status with this command:

   ```
   xfs_db -f -c frag /dev/VG_POSTGRES/LV_DATA
   ```

2. Defragment the filesystem with `xfs_fsr`:

   ```
   xfs_fsr -t 600 /dev/VG_POSTGRES/LV_DATA
   ```

3. View real-time fragmentation status afterwards:

   xfs_db -f -c frag -r /dev/VG_POSTGRES/LV_DATA

How it works...

We begin with the `xfs_db` utility to view the current fragmentation status of the filesystem. The `-c` parameter lets us specify a command that `xfs_db` should invoke. In this case, we want it to check the fragmentation status, so we set `-c` to `frag`. We set the `-f` parameter as it allows us to use `xfs_db` on a mounted filesystem.

Fragmentation status is calculated by counting the number of non-contiguous extents on all files and comparing that number to the total amount of files. To prepare for this, we continuously invoked `pgbench` to cause a high amount of fragmentation. Here is the fragmentation on our system:

```
root@pg1:~# sudo xfs_db -f -c frag /dev/mapper/VG_POSTGRES-LV_DATA
actual 1302, ideal 920, fragmentation factor 41.52%
```

As you can see, our filesystem is `41.52%` fragmented. To correct this, we need to use `xfs_fsr` to reorganize any fragmented files. To do this, we only need to call `xfs_fsr` with either the device path or the path where the device is mounted. For the sake of consistency, we choose the former.

We can also limit the amount of time XFS spends fixing fragmentation with the `-t` parameter, which sets the run time in seconds. We chose `600` seconds for an even 10 minutes, but larger systems might require an hour or longer. By setting the `-t` parameter, we can run `xfs_fsr` regularly as a maintenance item, so fragmentation is regularly kept in check.

XFS defragmentation proceeds on a file-by-file basis. Thus, if the `xfs_fsr` command is canceled, or does not defragment every file before it exceeds our time limit, no progress is lost.

If we examine the filesystem again with `xfs_db`, our fragmentation should be significantly reduced. Let's consider the following screenshot:

```
root@pg1:~# sudo xfs_db -f -c frag -r /dev/mapper/VG_POSTGRES-LV_DATA
actual 928, ideal 922, fragmentation factor 0.65%
```

Now our fragmentation is down to `0.65%`, which is well within tolerances for good sequential access performance. However, you might have noticed that we added an `-r` setting just after the `-c frag` declaration.

Remember when we said XFS maintained an internal database? Due to caching and update intervals, parts of the XFS database are not always accurate. The `-r` option to the `-c frag` command tells XFS that we want real-time information about the filesystem, and not what is currently stored in the tracking database.

There's more...

While we use the `xfs_db` command to obtain file fragmentation information, it can actually do much more. XFS maintains a small internal database which `xfs_db` can view or manipulate. Unfortunately, modifying XFS metadata can render the filesystem corrupt or otherwise unusable. We highly recommend never using `xfs_db` for anything but checking fragmentation statuses.

Only experts should ever use `xfs_db` command parameters other than `frag`.

See also

- Both the `xfs_db` and `xfs_fsr` commands have fairly extensive manual pages. We recommend using these to learn more about the other functionalities these tools provide:

  man xfs_db

  man xfs_fsr

Using LVM snapshots

One of the reasons we created a second layer of LVM on top of DRBD was to provide filesystem snapshot capabilities. When we create a snapshot, all files on a particular volume will appear static on that snapshot until one of the following two things happens:

- We destroy the snapshot
- The amount of changes on the source volume is larger than the space we reserved for the snapshot

This is the primary reason we left 5 percent space unused within our PostgreSQL volume group. If we create a snapshot, up to 5 percent of the database can change before we have to remove it. For larger storage devices, this should give us a lot of time to perform emergency restores, create byte-stable backups, or any other operation that requires consistent data.

In this recipe, we'll learn how to properly allocate, use, and remove an LVM snapshot.

Getting ready

For this recipe, we want a formatted and active XFS filesystem. Please follow the recipe in *Formatting an XFS filesystem* before continuing.

How to do it...

For this, we will assume `pg1` is our current primary node and `VG_POSTGRES/LV_DATA` is the principal data volume. Follow these steps as the `root` user to create and use an LVM snapshot:

1. Create the snapshot with `lvcreate`:

   ```
   lvcreate -l 100%FREE -s -n snap VG_POSTGRES/LV_DATA
   ```

2. Create a directory on which to mount the snapshot using this command:

   ```
   mkdir /mnt/db_snap
   ```

3. Mount the snapshot as a regular XFS filesystem using this command:

   ```
   mount -t xfs -o nouuid /dev/VG_POSTGRES/snap /mnt/db_snap
   ```

4. Enter the snapshot `pgdata` directory using this command:

   ```
   cd /mnt/db_snap/pgdata
   ```

5. Examine snapshot information with `lvdisplay`:

   ```
   lvdisplay VG_POSTGRES/snap | grep snap
   ```

Follow these steps as the `root` user to unmount and remove an LVM snapshot:

1. Unmount the snapshot with this command:

   ```
   umount /mnt/db_snap
   ```

2. Destroy the snapshot with `lvremove`:

   ```
   lvremove VG_POSTGRES/snap
   ```

How it works...

We can use the same `lvcreate` utility that helped us provision the PostgreSQL volume. We start the command with the `-l` parameter set to `100%FREE` to use any unallocated space in the `VG_POSTGRES` volume group. While we can specify sizes in MB or GB with the `-L` setting, we really only need to do this if we plan on creating multiple snapshots.

The `-s` parameter makes this volume a snapshot, which causes LVM to base its contents on those of another volume. Thus, we specify `VG_POSTGRES/LV_DATA` as the origin volume group and volume we want to use for the snapshot. We also use the `-n` parameter to set the name of the new volume to `snap`, making our intentions more obvious.

With the volume created, we simply need to mount it to access the contents. A quick `mkdir` later, we have a location in `/mnt/db_snap`, where we can find the files after mounting.

The `mount` command itself contains the basic parts. We set the type to `xfs` with `-t`, while the last two parameters dictate the device and the location where it should be mounted. Since we are using an XFS filesystem, we also need to provide the `nouuid` mount option. By default, XFS will not allow the same filesystem to be mounted more than once. The `nouuid` option skips this check, allowing us to mount the snapshot.

At this point, the files in the `/mnt/db_snap/pgdata` directory will be the same as those in `/db/pgdata`. The primary difference between the two lies in the fact that `/db/pgdata` is our live database instance, and it has continued changing. The files at `/mnt/db_snap/pgdata` are frozen in time from when the `lvcreate` command was completed. If we view the snapshot volume with `lvdisplay`, we can see this in action:

```
root@pg1:~# lvdisplay VG_POSTGRES/snap | grep snap
  LV Name                /dev/VG_POSTGRES/snap
  LV snapshot status     active destination for /dev/VG_POSTGRES/LV_DATA
  Allocated to snapshot  8.27%
```

Notice that LVM tells us that this is a snapshot volume and what the source volume is. We can also see that `8.27%` of the snapshot space is used. This means that files have changed on the source volume, and the snapshot responded by storing the original blocks locally. When all of its space is consumed, the snapshot will be marked as invalid by LVM. Periodic checks with `lvdisplay` are important to determine the validity of the files we are using that reside on a snapshot.

When we are finished with the snapshot, it's good practice to destroy it. We start the process by unmounting the snapshot volume from `/mnt/db_snap`. Afterwards, we can use `lvremove` for the first time to destroy the snapshot volume. The `lvremove` command only requires the name of the volume we want to destroy, and it will confirm our intent before doing so. Once a volume is removed, there's no way to restore it.

> Be careful with keeping snapshots around too long or creating them during business hours. Depending on the underlying device, performance can suffer significantly due to the extra writes necessary to maintain the snapshot.

See also

- **The Linux Documentation Project** has a very simple usage example of snapshot usage. Feel free to browse the example at `http://www.tldp.org/HOWTO/LVM-HOWTO/snapshots_backup.html`.

Switching live stack systems

At this point, we have our data located simultaneously on two servers. The second system can fulfill many possible roles. It can replace the current node in case of hardware failure, or allow us to perform server maintenance or upgrades with very little downtime.

Regardless of our intent, properly utilizing the second system is the key to a highly available database server. In this recipe, we'll discuss the proper method for activating the second server in a two-node pair so that we can make changes to one or both nodes.

Getting ready

By now, we need the full stack and probably a fully active database server as well. Follow all the recipes up to *Tweaking XFS performance* before starting here.

How to do it...

For this recipe, we will need two PostgreSQL servers, `pg1` and `pg2`, where `pg1` is the currently active node. Follow these steps as the `root` user on the system indicated to move an active PostgreSQL service from one node to another:

1. Stop the PostgreSQL service with `pg_ctl` on `pg1`:

   ```
   pg_ctl -D /db/pgdata stop -m fast
   ```

2. Unmount the `/db/pgdata` filesystem on `pg1`:

   ```
   umount /db/pgdata
   ```

3. Mark the `VG_POSTGRES` group as inactive using `vgchange` on `pg1`:

   ```
   vgchange -a n VG_POSTGRES
   ```

4. Demote DRBD status to secondary with `drbdadm` on `pg1`:

   ```
   drbdadm secondary pg
   ```

5. Promote DRBD status to primary with `drbdadm` on `pg2`:

   ```
   drbdadm primary pg
   ```

6. Mark the `VG_POSTGRES` group as active using `vgchange` on `pg2`:

   ```
   vgchange -a y VG_POSTGRES
   ```

7. Mount the `/db/pgdata` filesystem on `pg2`:

   ```
   mount -t xfs -o noatime,nodiratime \
         -o logbsize=256k,allocsize=1m \
         /dev/VG_POSTGRES/LV_DATA /db
   ```

8. Start PostgreSQL on pg2:

   pg_ctl -D /db/pgdata start

How it works...

There is actually very little in this recipe that we have not done in this chapter. What we have actually done here is formalized the steps necessary to tear down and build up an active stack. We start the process by stopping the PostgreSQL service with pg_ctl, as we clearly can't move the data while it's still in use.

Next, we use umount to decouple the /dev/VG_POSTGRES/LV_DATA device from the /db directory. With no locks on the storage volume, we can use vgchange with the -a parameter set to n to deactivate any volume in the VG_POSTGRES group. Since the VG_POSTGRES group actually resides on the DRBD device, it can only be active on one node at a time.

Once the volumes are no longer active, we can set the DRBD status to secondary with drbdadm. After we perform this step, the /dev/VG_POSTGRES directory and any corresponding device will actually disappear. This is because a DRBD device in secondary status is only active within DRBD. Here is what DRBD shows us in /proc/drbd regarding the situation:

```
0: cs:Connected ro:Secondary/Secondary ds:UpToDate/UpToDate C r-----
    ns:9400 nr:2540420 dw:2549908 dr:12578590 al:8 bm:462 lo:0 pe:0 ua:0 ap:0 ep:1 wo:f oos:0
```

DRBD sees the device as Secondary on both nodes; currently, neither node can access our PostgreSQL data. From this point, we merely reverse the process to reactivate all of these resources on pg2 instead.

We begin reactivating PostgreSQL by promoting the storage to primary status with drbdadm on the pg2 node. This causes the requisite VG_POSTGRES volume group to appear on pg2, making it a candidate for activation with vgchange.

Now we simply reuse the mount command that we discussed in the *Tweaking XFS performance* recipe on the pg2 node, making the data available to us once again. If we start PostgreSQL with the pg_ctl control script, our database will begin running as if it were still on the pg1 node. PostgreSQL does not know anything has changed.

There's more...

Since data can switch nodes arbitrarily as demonstrated here, upgrades and maintenance to server hardware are much easier. What can we do with the *extra* node? We can reboot it, apply firmware or kernel updates, apply security patches, or even update the database software to a bug-fix release.

Following any required or suggested changes to the secondary node, we merely promote it to run PostgreSQL in place of the current server. Then, we can repeat modifications on the other node. With this, we can limit outages to a matter of seconds while still providing high uptime guarantees, all without skipping system maintenance.

In fact, this process is so standardized that we will be exploring it in great detail in the next chapter. Once this tear-down and build-up procedure is automated, maintaining or replacing servers is even easier.

Detaching a problematic node

There's one last thing we need to cover before ending this chapter. If a server is causing problems, there's a good chance that the infrastructure department will want to reclaim, rebuild, or replace it. Simply stopping the broken server is a possible solution, but there is a safer way to decouple DRBD from another system.

In this recipe, we'll quickly cover partially dismantling a running DRBD system without disrupting the active server.

Getting ready

By now, we need the full stack and probably a fully active database server as well. Follow all the recipes up to *Tweaking XFS performance* before starting here.

How to do it...

For this recipe, we will need two PostgreSQL servers: `pg1` and `pg2`, where `pg1` is the currently active node. Follow these steps as the `root` user on the system indicated to permanently remove `pg2` from the DRBD cluster:

1. Execute this command on both `pg1` and `pg2` to disconnect DRBD:

   ```
   drbdadm disconnect pg
   ```

2. Invalidate the data on the remote node with `drbdadm` on `pg1`:

   ```
   drbdadm invalidate-remote pg
   ```

3. Invalidate the data on the current node with `drbdadm` on `pg2`:

   ```
   drbdadm invalidate pg
   ```

How it works...

This recipe is one of the easiest in our list, but it is equally important. We begin by using `drbdadm` to `disconnect` each node from the communication link DRBD uses to copy data between servers.

Then we use drbdadm again to doubly invalidate the data on the bad node. First, we use the invalidate-remote parameter on pg1 to ensure it sees pg2 as unusable. Then we use the invalidate parameter on pg2, so it sees its own data as incorrect.

At this point, we can release pg2 to its fate, no matter what that might be.

There's more...

Some might claim that any data invalidation is excessive. DRBD has its own safeguards to protect against inadvertent data copies. While true, server pools are not always cleaned up properly. Invalidating the data on pg2 does more than protect pg1 from being adversely affected if or when pg2 reconnects. We've effectively ensured pg2 cannot contribute data to any other DRBD cluster as a primary node.

However, we can go even further. We can actually physically destroy all traces of DRBD data on the decommissioned node. These commands on pg2 will do the work for us:

```
drbdadm down pg
drbdadm wipe-md pg
dd if=/dev/zero of=/dev/VG_DRBD/LV_DATA bs=1024 count=1024
```

The first drbdadm command stops the DRBD device itself. The second erases its metadata. Why do we need the third, then?

The dd utility is absurdly dangerous because it can write arbitrary blocks to any device on a server with almost no restrictions. We set the input file (if) to /dev/zero, and the output file (of) to /dev/VG_DRBD/LV_DATA, which we know as the device DRBD was using. Then we set the block size (bs) to 1024, and write a count of 1024 blocks to the device. Basically, we just overwrite the first megabyte of data on the DRBD device with zeroes.

We did this because metadata can be extracted from other nodes and reapplied. Theoretically, this means pg2 can be salvaged with enough expertise. By corrupting the data on the device itself, this is no longer possible. Furthermore, if we use drbdadm with create-md later, there's no existing data to interfere with the new metadata.

See also

- Linbit, the maker of DRBD, has very extensive documentation on system troubleshooting. Refer to http://www.drbd.org/users-guide/ch-troubleshooting.html for more information.

9

Cluster Control

In this chapter, we will learn how to automate cluster management and ensure high availability. We will cover the following recipes in this chapter:

- Installing the components
- Configuring Corosync
- Preparing startup services
- Starting with base options
- Adding DRBD to cluster management
- Adding LVM to cluster management
- Adding XFS to cluster management
- Adding PostgreSQL to cluster management
- Adding a virtual IP to hide the cluster
- Adding an e-mail alert
- Grouping associated resources
- Combining and ordering related actions
- Performing a managed resource migration
- Using an outage to test migration

Introduction

Almost everything that we've discussed so far has lead directly to this chapter. By now, we have multiple servers, redundant alternates, backup, synchronization, and much more. If we combine all of these techniques, management becomes more difficult with each component we add.

In the previous chapter, we covered all of the elements for a robust and elastic storage structure. Even then, we noted the arduous nature of moving a running server from one node to another. Typing commands safely takes time, as does conferring with a checklist and verifying commands before running them in a production environment. We would never recommend anything less.

Finally, we will learn how to configure the two linked nodes to manage themselves. It's not entirely foolproof, yet the process we are about to undergo is robust and implemented safely by many enterprises. Instead of a dozen commands to move an active PostgreSQL instance to another server, we will need only one. Further, the software can detect several failure scenarios and relocate PostgreSQL on our behalf if something goes wrong.

The safest cluster in a high-availability architecture is one that requires the least amount of manual intervention. To that end, this chapter will cover **Corosync** and **Pacemaker** and the steps to manage dual-node servers with this software. By the end of this chapter, we should have something similar to this diagram:

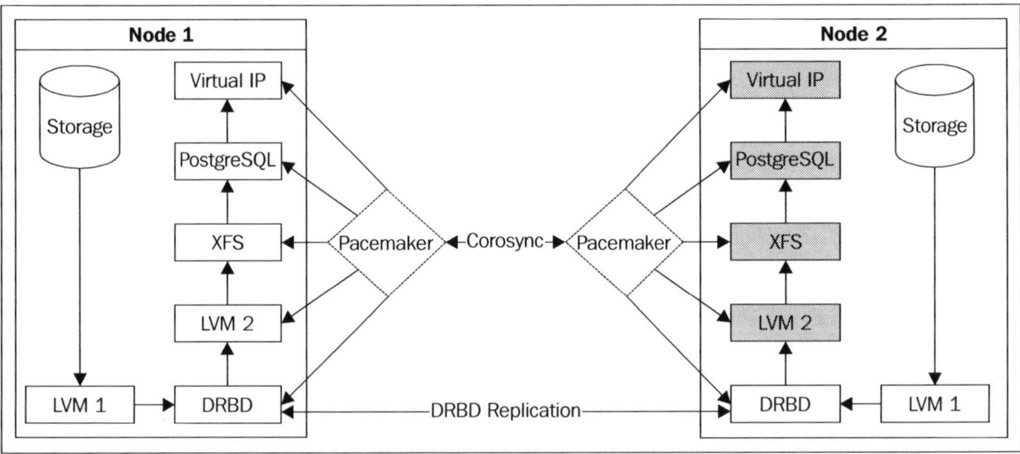

Here, all of the grayed-out components are installed on both nodes, but they are unavailable on **node 2**. Yet, we could use Pacemaker to reverse the graph so that **node 2** is the active server instead of **node 1**. That is a lot of changes to make manually.

Before we begin...

Before we spend any more time on this chapter, we should ask ourselves a question: is automation necessary? It's certainly nice to have, but is it required? Will we benefit from the admittedly esoteric incantations needed to install and configure these tools?

The answer is not always so straightforward. While exceedingly powerful, Pacemaker is infamously difficult to use and even a little overzealous in applying its rules. An improperly built Pacemaker cluster might produce a database that moves to another node at the slightest provocation. Worse, Pacemaker enforces its current status and will actively thwart management attempts it didn't personally invoke.

We won't lie; the learning curve is immense and should extend far longer than what this chapter teaches. If this is too much for now, skip this chapter with our best regards.

Otherwise, we want you to know that this chapter is only the beginning. We will guide you through the creation of a functional Pacemaker-managed system, but we strongly recommend experimenting frequently on a pair of virtual servers. This gives you a safe area to make mistakes, break Pacemaker in all kinds of interesting ways, and learn more about the material we present here.

None of this content is easy, but we promise it's worth the time to absorb. We will introduce this material slowly to help aid in the process.

Installing the components

The two main components to the software we use in this chapter are Corosync and Pacemaker. Each of these is comprised of or depends on several other elements and prerequisites. For now, we'll simply refer to the entire suite as Pacemaker, as it comprises the bulk of how we will control the failover system.

This recipe should be relatively short, as we will only discuss installation of Corosync and Pacemaker, not their configuration.

Getting ready

Red-Hat-based systems such as Fedora, CentOS, and Scientific Linux will already have Pacemaker in their repositories. Debian and its derivatives such as Ubuntu also include Pacemaker as an optional install from standard repositories. **Red Hat Enterprise Linux** (**RHEL**) itself, however, only offers the software as a paid add-on, available at `http://www.redhat.com/products/enterprise-linux-add-ons/high-availability/`.

Whatever choice you make, it shouldn't be necessary to compile Pacemaker from source on most Linux distributions.

How to do it...

Follow these quick steps to install Pacemaker and Corosync on all PostgreSQL server pairs running a Debian-based distribution:

1. Install the main packages and all dependencies with this command as a root-capable user:

   ```
   sudo apt-get install corosync pacemaker
   ```

2. Disable the cluster software from starting on system boot:

   ```
   sudo update-rc.d corosync disable
   ```

For those running a Red-Hat-based operating system, follow these steps to install and prepare Pacemaker:

1. Install the main packages and all dependencies with this command as a root-capable user:

   ```
   sudo yum install corosync pacemaker
   ```

2. Disable the cluster software from starting on system boot:

   ```
   sudo chkconfig corosync off
   ```

How it works...

Each of these short recipes consists of two steps:

1. Install Corosync and Pacemaker.
2. Disable Corosync on server boot.

While the first step makes sense, why do we need the second? When running a highly available cluster, caution is a beneficial attribute. A server may reboot for any number of reasons, and many of those include crashes that require further investigation.

Were Pacemaker to start immediately following a server reboot, we could potentially lose valuable diagnostic information. More importantly, a rebooted server should be considered in an unknown or potentially damaged state until it is examined by an experienced system administrator. We don't want a misbehaving server as part of our critical infrastructure.

Corosync is the communication layer between each Pacemaker node. It also launches the Pacemaker management system. This means that we can prevent all node management simply by disabling it.

There's more...

If you believe we are being too wary, simply skip the second step in our recipe. However, it's important to remember that services are easy to start on Linux servers. This command, for instance, will start Corosync normally:

```
sudo service corosync start
```

If the server was rebooted as the result of maintenance, the preceding command will return the system to normal operation. Otherwise, a few cursory checks through server logs may determine that the cause of the system crash does not adversely affect PostgreSQL data. If so, once again, it is easy to start Corosync and re-establish the dual-node cluster.

What we have done here is a very rudimentary form of **STONITH**, which means to **Shoot The Other Node In The Head**. Dedicated STONITH hardware may power a server off completely or remove it from the network, making it inaccessible through anything other than console emulation or direct access. Truly high-availability systems cannot afford to introduce unknown entities into a carefully crafted and manicured architecture. To do so invites undefined behavior across the spectrum of database services that could lead to outages or data loss.

If we want to claim that our data is important and our uptime is essential, we need to adopt a similar stance toward crashed or damaged servers. We haven't gone so far as to completely disable the server in this recipe; we only prevent it from rejoining a functioning Pacemaker pair. In a true STONITH-enabled organization, our measures would be much more drastic.

See also

- The `clusterlabs.org` website is a repository of all things related to pacemaker. It has several relevant tutorials, examples, and copious documentation. If you had trouble installing with our recipe, try an alternative listed at `http://clusterlabs.org/wiki/Install`.

Configuring Corosync

Once Corosync and Pacemaker are installed, we only need to modify a single configuration file to activate them. As we've mentioned earlier and shown in the introduction diagram, Corosync is the conduit that Pacemaker uses for communication. Corosync also binds itself to services that rely on its channels, so it will also launch Pacemaker on our behalf.

This recipe will explain how to create a simple configuration for Corosync that will establish a secure Pacemaker cluster.

Getting ready

We have already installed everything we need, but if we are running a Debian-based system such as Ubuntu or Mint, we have one more step. Before Corosync will work properly, we need to enable its startup script. Open the `/etc/default/corosync` file and make sure it contains this line:

```
START=yes
```

Without it, Corosync won't run even if we start it manually. We removed it from system boot time, but that doesn't mean we never want it to run at all!

How to do it...

For this recipe, we have two PostgreSQL nodes: `pg1` and `pg2`, which are assigned IP addresses in the `192.168.56.0` subnet. Follow these steps as a root-capable user:

1. On `pg1`, run this command to generate an authorization key file:

   ```
   corosync-keygen
   ```

2. Open another connection to `pg1` and perform several activities until `corosync-keygen` completes.
3. Copy the resulting `/etc/corosync/authkey` file to `pg2`. Make sure it is copied to `/etc/corosync/authkey` as well.
4. Modify the `bindnetaddr` line in the `/etc/corosync/corosync.conf` file on both `pg1` and `pg2` so that it contains the following value:

   ```
   bindnetaddr: 192.168.56.0
   ```

5. Modify the `secauth` line in the `/etc/corosync/corosync.conf` file on both `pg1` and `pg2` so that it contains the following value:

   ```
   secauth: on
   ```

6. Start Corosync on both `pg1` and `pg2` with this command:

   ```
   sudo service corosync start
   ```

7. Show the status of Pacemaker with the `crm` utility on `pg1`:

   ```
   sudo crm status
   ```

How it works...

The first step involves securing our Corosync communication channel. The `corosync-keygen` utility will generate a 1024-bit key that helps Pacemaker nodes identify each other, but to do so, it involves a lot of random input.

We can generate entropy by making the server perform tasks. If the server is otherwise idle, running commands, testing SQL, or simply waiting, it will eventually exit and save a file named `authkey` in the `/etc/corosync` configuration directory. As we want this file to be the same on all nodes, we also copy it from `pg1` to `pg2`.

Next, we only need to change two lines in the existing configuration files to suit our needs. First, we need to tell Corosync which network interface it should bind to with `bindnetaddr`. In our case, both servers are on the `192.168.56.0` network, so we can use that value. This address will likely be different on your system, but it's easily obtained.

> If you don't know how network subnets work, find the IP address of your server and simply replace the last number with a zero. This skips a lot of calculating, and works in our case. So, if the address is `10.2.8.14`, use `10.2.8.0`.

Then, we change `secauth` to `on` to enable secure and encrypted communication between nodes. When this is done on both nodes, we can start Corosync with the service command, and our work is done.

To verify that the Pacemaker cluster exists, we can use the `crm` command. What is `crm`? It stands for **Cluster Resource Manager** and will be the command we use for all Pacemaker interactions from now on. The status parameter displays the current state of the cluster, and for our test systems, it looks like this:

```
============
Last updated: Wed Apr  2 01:51:52 2014
Last change: Wed Apr  2 01:34:22 2014 via crmd on pg1
Stack: openais
Current DC: pg1 - partition with quorum
Version: 1.1.6-9971ebba4494012a93c03b40a2c58ec0eb60f50c
2 Nodes configured, 2 expected votes
0 Resources configured.
============

Online: [ pg1 pg2 ]
```

As we can see, Pacemaker can communicate with both nodes, so it lists them as `Online`. The rest of the information presented here regarding `quorum` and `votes` can be ignored for now, but we'll cover it soon enough.

See also

- As mentioned earlier, the `clusterlabs.org` site should be considered the ultimate resource regarding Corosync and Pacemaker. To learn more about the process we used here, proceed to `http://clusterlabs.org/wiki/Initial_Configuration`.
- Otherwise, the `corosync.conf` file actually has its own extensive manual page available via the `man` utility. It's extremely useful to create more advanced clusters. Use the following command:

  ```
  man corosync.conf
  ```

Preparing startup services

A common interpretation of a functional server is one that runs on its own recognizance. After being rebooted, it starts all necessary services and does its job as configured. It might be hard to believe, but we want to fight that inclination for two important reasons:

- Pacemaker is a state machine
- Pacemaker needs total control of any service it manages

Pacemaker wants to start services itself so it knows that the current status is the one it created. It will perform tests to obtain this information, but for things like DRBD, this isn't always reliable. It's generally safer to start from scratch. Beyond this, if a service that isn't supposed to be running starts, Pacemaker will only have to stop it anyway.

In this recipe, we'll quickly cover which services to disable on each of our PostgreSQL nodes.

Getting ready

As we're continuing to configure Corosync and Pacemaker, make sure you've followed all the previous recipes.

How to do it...

For this recipe, we will use the same two PostgreSQL nodes: `pg1` and `pg2`. We will also continue to assume that our PostgreSQL data is located at `/db/pgdata`.

On Red-Hat-based systems, follow these steps on both servers as a root-capable user:

1. Prevent the PostgreSQL service from starting automatically with this command:

   ```
   sudo chkconfig postgresql off
   ```

2. Do the same for the DRBD service with this command:

   sudo chkconfig drbd off

3. Create a file named `/etc/sysconfig/postgresql` with the following line:

   ```
   PGDATA=/db/pgdata
   ```

On Debian-based systems, follow these steps on both servers as a root-capable user:

1. Prevent the PostgreSQL service from starting automatically with this command:

   sudo update-rc.d postgresql disable

2. Do the same for the DRBD service with this command:

   sudo update-rc.d drbd disable

3. Create a file named `/etc/default/postgresql` with the following line:

   ```
   PGDATA=/db/pgdata
   ```

No matter what Linux system you are using, install the `/init/postgresql` script from this book into the `/etc/init.d` directory.

How it works...

Both of these short recipes perform the same task. The first step is to remove PostgreSQL from the list of services that start at system boot time. The next does the same to DRBD. These are the only two services that are controlled via system startup scripts, so our work here is very short indeed. Then, we create a file and provide a value for `PGDATA` so that the `/etc/init.d/postgresql` startup script can find our PostgreSQL data.

Our final, and perhaps the most important step, is to replace any provided PostgreSQL initialization script with one that is fully compatible with Pacemaker. Pacemaker is extremely dependent on the expected Linux Standard Base exit codes. At least in the case of Debian and Ubuntu, the provided initialization script does not return the proper exit code because it expects to manage multiple PostgreSQL instances per server.

Without the correct exit value, Pacemaker will interpret the service as up, down, or unknown and will make improper management decisions. This is excessively dangerous when trying to run a highly available PostgreSQL installation. The script provided by this book has been tested with Pacemaker, and we know it works as intended.

There's more...

If you have another test server with PostgreSQL installed and running, try some of these tests to confirm it works as described:

1. Start PostgreSQL and confirm the exit status is `0` for success with this command:

   ```
   sudo service postgresql start
   echo $?
   ```

2. Stop PostgreSQL and confirm the exit status is `0` for success with this command:

   ```
   sudo service postgresql stop
   echo $?
   ```

3. Finally, check the status of PostgreSQL and confirm the exit value is `3`, indicating the service isn't running with this command:

   ```
   sudo service postgresql status
   echo $?
   ```

The `$?` variable holds the exit status of the previous command. It's an easy way to visualize what is normally an invisible piece of information. Any script that does not return these three exit codes for these specific conditions cannot be used with Pacemaker.

See also

- The Linux Standard Base specification for initialization scripts is fully documented. We recommend that you read `http://refspecs.linuxbase.org/LSB_3.1.1/LSB-Core-generic/LSB-Core-generic/iniscrptact.html` to see why we used a script not supplied by the distribution.

Starting with base options

Pacemaker, as a cluster resource manager, has some defaults that we are interested in changing. As Pacemaker is so powerful, it makes several assumptions about the composition of cluster resources and nodes it controls. One of which is that there are several nodes, and not just two.

This works well for large cooperative networks of web servers or independent services which can operate in a transient manner. However, we have two nodes that are very much dependent on shared storage that can only be used by one node at a time. So, in this recipe, we are going to perform three tasks:

- Disable STONITH because we don't currently have STONITH-enabled hardware
- Disable cluster quorum because two systems cannot produce a meaningful vote
- Enable resource stickiness to prevent disruptive automated node swaps

Getting ready

As we're continuing to configure Corosync and Pacemaker, make sure you've followed all previous recipes.

How to do it...

For this recipe, we will use the same two PostgreSQL nodes: `pg1` and `pg2`. Perform the following steps on either server as the `root` user:

1. Disable STONITH with this `crm` command:

   ```
   crm configure property stonith-enabled=false
   ```

2. Ignore quorum voting with this `crm` command:

   ```
   crm configure property no-quorum-policy=ignore
   ```

3. Increase the default resource stickiness with this `crm` command:

   ```
   crm configure property default-resource-stickiness=100
   ```

4. Finally, view the current state of the cluster configuration with this command:

   ```
   crm configure show
   ```

How it works...

This recipe differs from those in the previous sections in that we can execute these steps from any server. Commands issued by the `crm` utility are sent to the cluster itself, so any node will transmit them successfully, and Pacemaker will act accordingly. In the case of our configuration changes, the only action that Pacemaker takes is to alter its stored settings.

The first thing we do is disable STONITH by calling `crm` with the `configure property` parameter for `stonith-enabled`. While STONITH is an amusing acronym, there are actual devices on the market that fill this role. These devices can isolate a node from a network in several ways, and Pacemaker is designed to interact with them by default. As we don't have one right now, it's best to tell Pacemaker that it shouldn't expect such functionality.

Our next step includes shutting down our fledgling democracy by disabling quorum verification. We only have two nodes, and votes comprised of only two voters are entirely meaningless because they will always result in a tie. Without an odd number of nodes, no quorum (agreement) can be reached. This time, we `configure property` for `no-quorum-policy` and set it to `ignore`. This essentially means that the nodes will continue to vote, but we don't care unless they can reach a quorum. As two servers can't reach a quorum, resources will run where we tell them to run, and they have no say in the matter.

The last setting we change with `configure property` is `default-resource-stickiness`. As we mentioned earlier, Pacemaker is really built for transient services that act as independent agents. If an HTTP daemon moves from one node to another, nobody really cares or notices. If PostgreSQL acted in a similar manner, there would be several broken applications and irritated users.

By changing this setting to 100, we give every resource a default weight, so it sticks to whichever server it started on. Unless there's a crash or forced migration, it will stay there indefinitely.

Our last step is to view our handiwork by issuing `crm` with `configure show`. Pacemaker stores its configuration as XML, and while this is somewhat human readable, it's hardly concise. On our test cluster, it produces this output:

```
root@pg1:/etc/init.d# crm configure show
node pg1
node pg2
property $id="cib-bootstrap-options" \
        dc-version="1.1.6-9971ebba4494012a93c03b40a2c58ec0eb60f50c" \
        cluster-infrastructure="openais" \
        expected-quorum-votes="2" \
        stonith-enabled="false" \
        no-quorum-policy="ignore" \
        default-resource-stickiness="100"
```

As we can see, both `pg1` and `pg2` are each labeled as a `node`. In addition, `stonith-enabled`, `no-quorum-policy`, and `default-resource-stickiness` are all set as we described in the recipe.

We're well on our way to building a Pacemaker cluster.

There's more...

The `crm` command is actually a fully functional pseudo-shell. If executed without parameters, it presents a prompt and waits for valid `crm` commands. These commands include `help` for every level chosen. For example, to see what options are available when putting a `node` into `standby`, we can type this input while in a `crm` shell:

```
node help standby
```

Then, we can use what we learned previously and put the node into standby state until it is rebooted and Corosync is started again. Like this:

```
node standby pg1 reboot
```

This is extremely helpful as Pacemaker has a lot of commands, and it's easy to forget the proper syntax.

See also

- The `crm` shell has undergone a lot of changes in the last few years, including splitting from the Pacemaker project itself. As such, its documentation is somewhat fragmented. The new `crm` shell maintainers have information that is mostly compatible with versions packaged with Debian and Red-Hat-based systems at `http://crmsh.github.io/crm.1.2.6.html`.

  However, it might be easier to simply explore the `help` for each command as we described earlier.

Adding DRBD to cluster management

DRBD is actually one of the most difficult resources to manage with Pacemaker. Unlike a regular service that is started or stopped depending on where it is active, DRBD is always active. The only thing that changes between two nodes running DRBD is the `Primary` or `Secondary` state ascribed to each.

Due to this complication, DRBD is not one resource, but two:

- A DRBD resource to manage starting and stopping DRBD
- A master/slave resource to control which node acts as the `Primary`

In this recipe, we'll allocate both of these resources so that Pacemaker can manage DRBD properly.

Getting ready

As we're continuing to configure Pacemaker, make sure you've followed all previous recipes.

How to do it...

In the previous chapter, we created a DRBD resource named pg. With this in mind, follow these steps as the root user to add DRBD to Pacemaker:

1. Create a basic Pacemaker primitive for DRBD with this command:

```
crm configure primitive drbd_pg ocf:linbit:drbd \
    params drbd_resource="pg" \
    op monitor interval="15" role="Master" \
    op monitor interval="20" role="Slave" \
    op start interval="0" timeout="240" \
    op stop interval="0" timeout="120"
```

2. Create a master/slave resource with this command:

```
crm configure ms ms_drbd_pg drbd_pg \
    meta master-max="1" master-node-max="1" \
    clone-max="2" clone-node-max="1" notify="true"
```

3. Clean up any errors that might have accumulated with crm:

```
crm resource cleanup drbd_pg
```

4. Display the status of our new resources with crm:

```
crm resource status
```

How it works...

Most of the resources we create in subsequent sections are called primitives. These should be considered the base resource element that Pacemaker controls, as they have a one-to-one relationship with each service. The first of these we create is for our DRBD service.

When creating new configuration entries with crm, we declare them with configure primitive, and then we must supply a name. To keep things simple, we named this resource drbd_pg. After the name, we must supply a resource agent to actually manage this service. Pacemaker is shipped with several, but we are specifically interested in the ocf:linbit:drbd agent, as it was written by the makers of DRBD themselves.

Next, we can configure the resource agent by specifying params, followed by the options it recognizes, labeled with op. Among these options, we define a monitor interval for the master server and one for the slave that isn't quite as frequent. Then, finally, we override the start timeout and stop timeout so that they match the minimum values expected by Pacemaker. It will complain if we use values lower than this, but feel free to increase them.

Next, we create the master/slave resource that controls how Pacemaker views the `drbd_pg` resource. Instead of adding and configuring a primitive, this time we `configure` a `ms` (**master slave resource**) and name it `ms_drbd_pg`. After naming our `ms` resource, we designate `drbd_pg` as the primitive to treat as a master or slave service. All of the entries after the `meta` designation are somewhat confusing and arbitrary, so we hope these pointers help:

- By setting `master-max` to `1`, we tell Pacemaker that only one node in the cluster can ever be promoted to master for this service.
- Similarly, setting `master-node-max` to `1` limits Pacemaker to a single copy of this resource per server.
- The `clone-max` setting actually describes the amount of active copies for this resource, which is `2` in our case.
- Oddly enough, the `clone-node-max` setting means basically the same thing as `master-node-max`. We set this to `1` as well to safeguard the DRBD resource from potential Pacemaker bugs or future changes in default settings.
- Finally, the `notify` setting effectively transmits master/slave notices to all nodes so that Pacemaker knows the new status of the shared resource everywhere it is running.

What do we mean by a resource *copy*? Internally, Pacemaker stores resources as defined roles. If a single resource has two roles, it actually exists as two items within Pacemaker. In Pacemaker lingo, these are referred to as **clones**. The `crm` system hides these details from us, but they're still very real and difficult to manage.

The values we chose for all of the `meta` options are actually Pacemaker defaults. We could have omitted them, but a high-availability system cannot remain safe while it is at the mercy of malleable defaults. We set these in stone now to prevent Pacemaker upgrades from potentially causing problems in the future.

When adding new resources, sometimes Pacemaker enters an undefined state and lists errors that aren't actually valid. We can clear these out using the `resource cleanup` parameter to target the `drbd_pg` primitive. It's always a good idea to keep Pacemaker status clean to avoid possible conflicts later.

Our final job is to view the status of all configured resources by calling `crm` with `resource status`. Our test system showed this output:

```
root@pg1:~# crm resource status
 Master/Slave Set: ms_drbd_pg [drbd_pg]
     Masters: [ pg1 ]
     Slaves: [ pg2 ]
```

Even though we created two primitive resources, we only see one entry: `ms_drbd_pg`. Note, however, that it represents the `drbd_pg` resource. We can also see the `Masters` and `Slaves` for this `Set`, though there should never be more than one of each with the configuration we used.

There's more...

In Pacemaker, resource agents can be viewed separately with the `crm` program, and many are available. To get a list of all the LSB resource agents (scripts in `/etc/init.d`) Pacemaker can see, use this command:

```
crm ra list lsb
```

For a list of Pacemaker-specific agents, use this command:

```
crm ra list ocf
```

By itself, this information isn't entirely helpful. Knowing that the agents exist does not tell us what parameters they have. To see this, we need to view the `meta` information for the agent. We used the `ocf:linbit:drbd` agent in this recipe, and we can view its usage information with this command:

```
crm ra meta ocf:linbit:drbd
```

If this is not convenient enough, we can actually use the `man` command for most agents as well. If we know the class, provider, and name of an agent, we can view its Unix manual. For example, to see the manual for the `ocf:heartbeat:nginx` agent, we could use this command:

```
man ocf_heartbeat_nginx
```

See also

- Some of this information is also available within the DRBD documentation at `http://www.drbd.org/users-guide/s-pacemaker-crm-drbd-backed-service.html`.

Adding LVM to cluster management

To avoid potential conflicts, we will continue to add resources to Pacemaker in the same order as if we were starting them manually. After DRBD comes our second LVM layer. The primary purpose of Pacemaker in this instance is to activate or deactivate the `VG_POSTGRES` volume group that we created in the previous chapter.

This is necessary because DRBD can not demote a primary resource to secondary status as long as there are any open locks. Any LVM volume group that contains active volumes can cause these kind of locks. Also, we cannot utilize a volume group that has no active volumes when DRBD is promoted on the second node.

This recipe will explain the steps necessary to manage our `VG_POSTGRES/LV_DATA` data volume with Pacemaker.

Getting ready

As we're continuing to configure Pacemaker, make sure you've followed all the previous recipes.

Debian-derivative systems such as Ubuntu need to beware! To avoid potential issues, immediately delete the `/lib/udev/rules.d/85-lvm2.rules` file if it exists. It automatically mounts LVM devices when they appear; these devices can interfere with Pacemaker LVM management.

How to do it...

Perform these steps on any Pacemaker node as the `root` user:

1. Add an LVM `primitive` to Pacemaker with `crm`:

```
crm configure primitive pg_lvm ocf:heartbeat:LVM \
    params volgrpname="VG_POSTGRES" \
    op start interval="0" timeout="30" \
    op stop interval="0" timeout="30"
```

2. Clean up any errors that might have accumulated with `crm`:

```
crm resource cleanup pg_lvm
```

3. Display the status of our new LVM resource with `crm`:

```
crm resource status
```

How it works...

As with the previous recipe, we begin by adding a `primitive` to Pacemaker. For the sake of consistency and simplicity, we name this resource `pg_lvm`. In order to manage LVM, we also need to specify the `ocf:heartbeat:LVM` resource agent.

Remember, to see the list of parameters for a resource agent, use the `ra meta` command to the `crm` shell. For the LVM agent, this invocation would display usage information:

```
crm ra meta ocf:heartbeat:LVM
```

The only parameter (`params`) that concerns us regarding the LVM resource agent is `volgrpname`, which we set to `VG_POSTGRES`. The other options we set are more advisory minimum values, which reflect the number of seconds we should wait before considering an operation as failed.

In our case, we wait 30 seconds before declaring a start or stop ping a failed action. If Pacemaker is unable to start LVM, it will attempt to do so on other available nodes. In the event where Pacemaker can't stop LVM, it will report an error and perform no further actions until the error is cleared or corrected.

Speaking of clearing errors, it's a good practice to perform a `resource cleanup` after adding a new resource to Pacemaker. While not strictly required, this keeps the status output clean and ensures that Pacemaker will add the next resource as expected. Sometimes, Pacemaker will refuse to perform further actions if the error list contains any entries.

As we will do with all recipes in this chapter, our last action is to view the status of the resources to prove that the new addition is listed. Our test server shows that it is:

```
root@pg1:~# crm resource status
 Master/Slave Set: ms_drbd_pg [drbd_pg]
     Masters: [ pg1 ]
     Slaves: [ pg2 ]
 pg_lvm (ocf::heartbeat:LVM) Started
```

Now, in addition to the `ms_drbd_pg` resource that represents `drbd_pg`, we can see the new `pg_lvm` resource. Pacemaker also checked the status of LVM and displays it as `Started`.

There's more...

If you're tired of always checking the status of Pacemaker manually, there is a tool we can use instead. Much like `top`, which displays the current list of running processes, the `crm_mon` command monitors the status of a Pacemaker cluster and prints the same output as `crm status`. For our cluster in its current state, it looks like this:

```
Last updated: Fri Apr 11 22:12:15 2014
Last change: Fri Apr 11 21:35:33 2014 via cibadmin on pg1
Stack: openais
Current DC: pg1 - partition with quorum
Version: 1.1.6-9971ebba4494012a93c03b40a2c58ec0eb60f50c
2 Nodes configured, 2 expected votes
3 Resources configured.

Online: [ pg1 pg2 ]

 Master/Slave Set: ms_drbd_pg [drbd_pg]
     Masters: [ pg1 ]
     Slaves: [ pg2 ]
pg_lvm  (ocf::heartbeat:LVM):   Started pg1
```

This will refresh regularly and makes it easy to watch live transition states as Pacemaker performs actions related to cluster management. Feel free to keep this running in another terminal window for the sake of convenience.

Adding XFS to cluster management

Next in our list of resources to manage with Pacemaker is the filesystem. As with LVM and DRBD, Pacemaker needs the ability to start and stop the resource arbitrarily to clear locks or enable activation. In addition, filesystems are somewhat more complex than LVM simply due to the amount of necessary parameters required to use them.

In order for Pacemaker to manage a filesystem, we need to tell it about the device it's mounting, which directory the mount should target, the type of filesystem, and any extra options we want to use. While DRBD and LVM encode metadata within reserved storage areas on the device, filesystem mounts require explicit parameters.

This recipe will explain the steps necessary to manage our XFS filesystem with Pacemaker.

Getting ready

As we're continuing to configure Pacemaker, make sure you've followed all the previous recipes.

How to do it...

Perform these steps on any Pacemaker node as the `root` user:

1. Export our list of XFS mount options to avoid long lines by executing these commands:

   ```
   OPS=noatime,nodiratime,logbufs=8,logbsize=256k
   OPS=$OPS,attr2,allocsize=1m
   ```

2. Add an XFS `primitive` to Pacemaker with `crm`:

   ```
   crm configure primitive pg_fs ocf:heartbeat:Filesystem \
       params device="/dev/VG_POSTGRES/LV_DATA" \
              directory="/db" \
              fstype="xfs" \
              options="$OPS" \
       op start interval="0" timeout="60" \
       op stop interval="0" timeout="120"
   ```

3. Clean up any errors that might have accumulated with `crm`:

   ```
   crm resource cleanup pg_fs
   ```

4. Display the status of our new XFS resource with `crm`:

   ```
   crm resource status
   ```

How it works...

Due to the limited format of this book, we wanted to avoid excessive line wrapping in the commands we present. Thus, the first step simply saves all of the XFS mount options from the previous chapter in a variable named `OPS` that we can reuse when adding the Pacemaker `primitive`.

Regarding the `primitive` itself, we continue our preferred naming scheme and label it `pg_fs` (for the PostgreSQL filesystem). As usual, we need a resource agent to facilitate Pacemaker management, and the `ocf:heartbeat:Filesystem` agent fills that role nicely.

> As with all agents, to see the list of parameters for a resource agent, use the `ra meta` command to the `crm` shell. For the `Filesystem` agent, this invocation would display usage information:
>
> ```
> crm ra meta ocf:heartbeat:Filesystem
> ```
>
> We highly recommend that you use this command in each recipe, if only to verify the parameters act as we claim they do.

This time, the list of parameters (`params`) we set for the resource agent is somewhat longer than what we used for LVM. Here's a short explanation of each:

- The `device` parameter tells Pacemaker which device it should try to mount. From the previous chapter, this is `/dev/VG_POSTGRES/LV_DATA`.
- The `directory` specifies where the device should be mounted. Following the example set by our previous chapter, this is the `/db` directory.
- By setting `fstype`, we explicitly tell Pacemaker we are attempting to mount an `xfs` filesystem. Modern mount commands can often determine the filesystem automatically, but we advocate a more cautious approach.
- Finally, we set the mount `options`. Our list of options was very long, so we stored it in the `$OPS` variable, which we used here.

The other options (`op`) we set are more advisory minimum values, which reflect the number of seconds we should wait before considering an operation as failed. The timeouts to start and stop a filesystem are somewhat longer than an LVM device, because filesystems can have direct users. A filesystem user includes any terminals currently located in a mounted directory, automated tasks using it as a file target, or files held open by a running process—any one of these can prevent a filesystem from being unmounted.

As usual, we perform a `resource cleanup` on the `pg_fs` device to clear out any invalid errors. Afterwards, we can view the clean `resource status` with `crm`, which looks like this on our test system:

```
root@pg1:~# crm resource status
 Master/Slave Set: ms_drbd_pg [drbd_pg]
     Masters: [ pg1 ]
     Slaves: [ pg2 ]
 pg_lvm (ocf::heartbeat:LVM) Started
 pg_fs  (ocf::heartbeat:Filesystem) Started
```

As expected, we can see that `pg_fs` has joined our growing list of Pacemaker resources.

Adding PostgreSQL to cluster management

By now, we've fulfilled a fairly long series of prerequisites simply to add PostgreSQL to the list of services managed by Pacemaker. We're over half way through the chapter and are just now getting to the parts relevant to a PostgreSQL DBA. If you're new to DBA work, this might come as quite a shock, but it comes with the territory.

Once we add this resource, Pacemaker will be capable of starting and stopping everything necessary to run a PostgreSQL server. We'll still need to add several more elements to control factors such as start order and associated services, but we've reached a critical juncture. We are very close to having a highly available PostgreSQL cluster.

In this recipe, we'll discuss the steps required to add PostgreSQL itself to Pacemaker control.

Getting ready

As we're continuing to configure Pacemaker, make sure you've followed all the previous recipes.

How to do it...

Perform these steps on any Pacemaker node as the `root` user:

1. Add a PostgreSQL `primitive` to Pacemaker with `crm`:

   ```
   crm configure primitive pg_lsb lsb:postgresql \
       op monitor interval="30" timeout="60" \
       op start interval="0" timeout="60" \
       op stop interval="0" timeout="60"
   ```

2. Clean up any errors that might have accumulated with `crm`:

   ```
   crm resource cleanup pg_lsb
   ```

3. Display the status of our new PostgreSQL resource with `crm`:

   ```
   crm resource status
   ```

How it works...

The next `primitive` that we add to Pacemaker will need to call the script we saved as `/etc/init.d/postgresql`. Scripts in this location are known as Linux Standard Base scripts, and Pacemaker knows to find LSB items in the `/etc/init.d` directory. Thus, when we call crm with the call crm with the `configure primitive` parameters, we name the new primitive `pg_lsb` to remain consistent and use the `lsb:postgresql` resource agent. In reality, the `lsb:postgresql` agent is merely an alias for our script.

One of the consequences of this is that our resource agent is not fully integrated into Pacemaker and has no configurable parameters. The only things we can change are the generic options (`op`) such as monitor intervals and start or stop timeouts. For this agent, we've set all of the timeouts to 1 minute, but you may need to adjust these based on your PostgreSQL usage.

We set the monitor interval to `30` seconds and the timeout to `60` seconds for one reason: system overload. If a checkpoint causes enough write activity, PostgreSQL may fail to respond, though it is still running. If this happens frequently, we strongly recommend that you look into the problem and correct it.

However, with Pacemaker, the problem is compounded. If a monitor action fails, Pacemaker assumes that the service is dead, and it will try to restart it. If that fails, it will move everything over to the alternate node. This can cause an outage seemingly at random, which is not good in a high-availability environment.

Following this, we continue our usual steps of clearing out any invalid errors and viewing the Pacemaker cluster status. On our test system, the status shows this output:

```
root@pg1:~# crm resource status
 Master/Slave Set: ms_drbd_pg [drbd_pg]
     Masters: [ pg1 ]
     Slaves: [ pg2 ]
 pg_lvm (ocf::heartbeat:LVM) Started
 pg_fs  (ocf::heartbeat:Filesystem) Started
 pg_lsb (lsb:postgresql) Started
```

As expected, we can see that `pg_lsb` is `Started`.

Until we add a few more rules, Pacemaker isn't very smart. On our test system, Pacemaker repeatedly attempted to start PostgreSQL on the `pg2` node, even though it was already running on `pg1`. Of course, this failed, and it eventually checked `pg1` to reach the preceding output. We were not kidding when we said Pacemaker considers resources transitory until told otherwise! Be wary of this behavior in the next few recipes.

There's more...

Though we provided our own PostgreSQL control script, the `resource-agents` repository package installed with Pacemaker contains a resource agent specifically designed for PostgreSQL. However, its usage is far more complicated. It can also monitor PostgreSQL by querying it, instead of simply using a process ID test. If you want to use this agent instead, follow these steps as `root`:

1. Set the path of `pg_ctl` with this command:

   ```
   CTL=$(pg_config --bindir)/pg_ctl
   ```

2. Add the `pgsql` resource agent as a `primary` with this command:

   ```
   crm configure primitive pg_agent ocf:heartbeat:pgsql \
       params pgctl="$CTL" \
              pgdata="/db/pgdata" \
       op monitor interval="30" timeout="60" \
       op start interval="0" timeout="60" \
       op stop interval="0" timeout="60"
   ```

In order to get the full benefit of this resource agent, you'll also want to set the `monitor_user` and `monitor_password` agent parameters. To see the full list of parameters for this agent, use this `crm` command:

```
crm ra meta ocf:heartbeat:pgsql
```

Alternatively, view the `man` page:

```
man ocf_heartbeat_pgsql
```

Adding a virtual IP to hide the cluster

We discussed virtual IP addresses earlier; now, it's time to leverage them properly. A virtual IP is not a service in the traditional sense, but it does provide functionality that we need in a highly-available configuration. In cases where we also have control over DNS resolution, we can even assign a name to the virtual IP address to insulate applications from future changes.

For now, this recipe will limit itself to outlining the steps required to add a transitory IP address to Pacemaker.

Getting ready

As we're continuing to configure Pacemaker, make sure you've followed all the previous recipes.

How to do it...

We will assume that the `192.168.56.30` IP address exists as a predefined target for our PostgreSQL cluster. Users and applications will connect to it instead of the actual addresses of `pg1` or `pg2`.

Perform these steps on any Pacemaker node as the `root` user:

1. Add an IP address `primitive` to Pacemaker with `crm`:

   ```
   crm configure primitive pg_vip ocf:heartbeat:IPaddr2 \
       params ip="192.168.56.30" \
              iflabel="pgvip" \
       op monitor interval="5"
   ```

2. Try to view the IP allocation on `pg1` and `pg2`:

   ```
   ifconfig | grep -A3 :pgvip
   ```

3. Clean up any errors that might have accumulated with `crm`:

   ```
   crm resource cleanup pg_vip
   ```

4. Display the status of our new IP address with `crm`:

   ```
   crm resource status
   ```

How it works...

This call to `crm` with `configure primitive` allows us to associate an arbitrary IP address with our Pacemaker cluster. Once again, we follow the simple naming scheme and label our resource `pg_vip`. As we always require a resource agent, we need one that is designed to handle network interfaces. There are actually two that fit this role: `IPaddr` and `IPaddr2`. Though we can use either, the `IPaddr2` agent is designed specifically for Linux hosts, so we might as well use it for maximum compatibility.

The minimum parameters (`params`) we need for this resource agent include the IP address (`ip`) and a label for network management (`iflabel`). We chose to set these to the IP address that we set aside earlier (`192.168.56.30`). We also chose a descriptive label to associate with the interface (`pgvip`). Due to the nature of IP addresses, it's a good idea to check the interface on both machines to see that it is properly listed. Our test system looks like this:

```
root@pg1:~# ifconfig | grep -A3 :pgvip
eth1:pgvip Link encap:Ethernet  HWaddr 08:00:27:11:bf:39
          inet addr:192.168.56.30  Bcast:192.168.56.255  Mask:255.255.255.0
          UP BROADCAST RUNNING MULTICAST  MTU:1500  Metric:1
```

As our test system has a second interface representing the `192.168.56.255` mask, `pgvip` was attached to `eth1` instead of the usual `eth0`. We check both `pg1` and `pg2` because Pacemaker still starts resources independently, and the new IP address might be on either node. We'll be resolving this soon, so don't worry if the IP address is allocated to the wrong node.

As usual, we run a `resource cleanup` and then display the `resource status` of the cluster. No matter where `pgvip` is running, we should see output similar to this:

```
root@pg1:~# crm resource status
 Master/Slave Set: ms_drbd_pg [drbd_pg]
     Masters: [ pg1 ]
     Slaves: [ pg2 ]
 pg_lvm (ocf::heartbeat:LVM) Started
 pg_fs  (ocf::heartbeat:Filesystem) Started
 pg_lsb (lsb:postgresql) Started
 pg_vip (ocf::heartbeat:IPaddr2) Started
```

As expected, the `pg_vip` Pacemaker resource is `Started` and part of our growing list of resources.

Adding an e-mail alert

The last thing we are going to add should be considered a requirement when building a high-availability PostgreSQL cluster. Any time the status of Pacemaker changes, we can have it transmit an e-mail alerting us to the activity. Not only is this possible with Pacemaker, it's relatively easy to set up.

This recipe will outline the steps necessary to add an e-mail alert to Pacemaker.

Getting ready

As we're continuing to configure Pacemaker, make sure you've followed all the previous recipes.

How to do it...

Perform these steps on any Pacemaker node as the `root` user:

1. Add a PostgreSQL `primitive` to Pacemaker with `crm`:

```
crm configure primitive pg_mail ocf:heartbeat:MailTo \
    params email="dbas@mycompany.com" \
           subject="Pacemaker\ cluster\ status\ changed:\ "
```

2. Clean up any errors that might have accumulated with `crm`:

```
crm resource cleanup pg_mail
```

3. Display the status of our new e-mail alert with `crm`:

```
crm resource status
```

How it works...

To add an e-mail alert, we need to `configure` another `primitive` with `crm`. We name this resource `pg_mail` so that it fits in with the other services that we've configured so far. As always, we need a resource agent for Pacemaker to invoke when necessary, and the `ocf:heartbeat:MailTo` agent works well for our use case.

The `MailTo` agent is not a regular resource, as it does not represent any actual system service. It's more of a defined action that Pacemaker should invoke while managing *other* cluster resources. This means it's essentially useless until we associate it with another Pacemaker `primitive`.

The `MailTo` agent also has two parameters (`params`) we are interested in setting. We begin by setting `email` to an e-mail address for a recipient tasked with monitoring the PostgreSQL cluster. In most cases, this is either a single DBA or the entire team. In any case, we strongly suggest that you transmit these alerts to anyone associated with the PostgreSQL database, in case one or more members of the team are unavailable.

> If you don't already have one, speak with the infrastructure team or whoever is in charge of setting up e-mail lists at your company. Using a generic address that reaches everyone in the team, Pacemaker won't need to be changed whenever you hire or fire a DBA.

The next setting that concerns us is the `subject` of the message. If we don't set this, Pacemaker uses a suitable default, but it's good to have more control over the messages in case we want to set up e-mail rules or filters. Use any message you like, but there are a couple of important notes:

- Spaces must be escaped by a backslash (\). Otherwise, Pacemaker will print out a lot of errors and refuse to add the `primitive`.
- The subject is more of a prefix. Pacemaker will add more detail to the subject and body of the e-mail when the message is sent.

With that said, we are now ready to clean up and view our list of resources. Let's see the output of `resource status` on our test system:

```
root@pg1:~# crm resource status
 Master/Slave Set: ms_drbd_pg [drbd_pg]
     Masters: [ pg1 ]
     Slaves: [ pg2 ]
 pg_lvm (ocf::heartbeat:LVM) Started
 pg_fs  (ocf::heartbeat:Filesystem) Started
 pg_lsb (lsb:postgresql) Started
 pg_vip (ocf::heartbeat:IPaddr2) Started
 pg_mail         (ocf::heartbeat:MailTo) Started
```

We can see from this output that `pg_mail` is listed as `Started`, even though it doesn't do anything by itself. We'll be fixing this soon enough.

Grouping associated resources

Defining all of the critical resources within Pacemaker is a good start. However, Pacemaker is not concerned with keeping related services operating together. It is designed to facilitate service management for any series of resources over a large array of servers. This is a recurring theme in this chapter, and one we have to overcome to fully leverage Pacemaker's abilities.

One way we can do this is by creating a **group** of related resources. When we do this, the group represents every member as a whole and must run on one server or another. This prevents the problems we had in the previous recipes, such as the possibility of new resources being started on the wrong node.

We'll create a group in this recipe and discuss other important caveats.

Getting ready

As we're continuing to configure Pacemaker, make sure you've followed all the previous recipes.

How to do it...

Perform these steps on any Pacemaker node as the `root` user:

1. Add a `group` to Pacemaker with `crm`:

   ```
   crm configure group PGServer pg_lvm pg_fs pg_lsb pg_vip
   ```

2. Display the status of our new group with `crm`:

   ```
   crm resource status
   ```

How it works...

For the first time in this chapter, we are not configuring a `primitive`, but a `group`. Unlike primitives, which describe each resource we want to manage, a group tells pacemaker *how*. In this case, any resource listed in the group has a few new attributes:

- Resources must reside on the same node
- Resources must be started in the specified order
- Resources must be stopped by reversing the specified order

We named the group `PGServer`, and now we can address every member as a cohesive unit using that name. The resource order mirrors the order in which we defined the primitives, which is the logical order necessary to start (and stop) a PostgreSQL server.

When `PGServer` is started, Pacemaker will activate LVM, followed by XFS, then PostgreSQL, and finally, it will add our virtual IP address. We didn't add the e-mail alert, because there's no logical place for it within the group. If we list it in the beginning, we'll only get an alert if everything is shut down. We can't place it at the end, or we won't see changes in DRBD.

DRBD has a related complication: it's only a single entry but represents two states. We can't target specific states in the grouping, so we must omit it from the group. However, there is a solution to associate the mail and DRBD resources with our new group; we'll cover this in the next recipe.

Until then, we can view the group with our usual `resource status`. Here's what we have on our test system:

```
root@pg1:~# crm resource status
 Master/Slave Set: ms_drbd_pg [drbd_pg]
     Masters: [ pg1 ]
     Slaves: [ pg2 ]
 pg_mail        (ocf::heartbeat:MailTo) Started
 Resource Group: PGServer
     pg_lvm     (ocf::heartbeat:LVM) Started
     pg_fs      (ocf::heartbeat:Filesystem) Started
     pg_lsb     (lsb:postgresql) Started
     pg_vip     (ocf::heartbeat:IPaddr2) Started
```

Now, we see a new `Resource Group` named `PGServer`. We can also see that all of the items within the group are indented, making the association more obvious.

Combining and ordering related actions

There are two final pieces of the puzzle that will produce a fully functional Pacemaker cluster. At this point, we have three independent base-level entries in Pacemaker: DRBD, the `PGServer` group, and the e-mail alert. They are independent because Pacemaker may start or stop them on any server in the list of active nodes.

We can fix this by defining a **colocation** between related resources. When we create a colocation, we are effectively stating that wherever this service goes, this other service should follow. Of course, this by itself is not sufficient. We also need to declare the expected **order** necessary for the services to start.

In this recipe, we'll finish our Pacemaker setup by creating necessary colocation entries, and define a service start order.

Getting ready

As we're continuing to configure Pacemaker, make sure that you've followed all the previous recipes.

How to do it...

Perform these steps on any Pacemaker node as the `root` user:

1. Add a `colocation` for DRBD to Pacemaker with `crm`:

```
crm configure colocation col_pg_drbd \
    inf: PGServer ms_drbd_pg:Master
```

2. Add a `colocation` for the e-mail alert with `crm`:

```
crm configure colocation col_pg_mail \
    inf: pg_mail PGServer
```

3. Add a resource `order` to Pacemaker with `crm`:

```
crm configure order ord_pg \
    inf: ms_drbd_pg:promote PGServer:start
```

4. Display the status of our new group with `crm`:

```
crm resource status
```

How it works...

As with all of our changes to Pacemaker, we `configure` the item we're adding. For this first step, we are adding a `colocation` named `col_pg_drbd` to represent the dependency between the `PGServer` group and the `ms_drbd_pg` master/slave resource. To do this, we need three elements. They are as follows:

- **The strength of the relationship, as expressed as a score**: We used `inf:` to represent infinity, meaning that these two items should always be associated
- **The name of the resource we are trying to colocate**: We use the group name `PGServer`, as we want all Pacemaker resources to follow it to the same node
- **The name of a resource this entry should be colocated with, and is dependent upon**: By setting this to `ms_drbd_pg:Master`, we are telling Pacemaker that the `PGServer` group must be on the same server where DRBD is the master node, wherever that might be

We then repeat this process with the e-mail alert. This time, we name the colocation `col_pg_mail` to express it as a colocation of the `pg_mail` resource. The score remains at `inf:` for infinity, and we made one final and very important change. When defining a colocation, the order is extremely important. In fact, all colocation entries should be read as: resource a *depends on* resource b.

With the e-mail alert colocation, we now have what amounts to a dependency chain. The e-mail alert depends on the state of the PGServer group, and the PGServer group depends on the DRBD master server. Yet, colocations are rules, so Pacemaker is still free to execute these resources independently of each other, as long as the final result matches the defined state we dictated.

As colocations have no inherent order, we need to impose one. We create one final configure entry by defining an order named ord_pg. Once again, we need to provide a score, and once again, we use inf: for infinity; the order of services is very important to us. When we define the order of our resources, we can also dictate an action that Pacemaker should take, as separated by a colon.

The order we defined tells Pacemaker that it should promote the ms_drbd_pg resource before it is allowed to start the PGServer group. Why didn't we add the e-mail alert to our order definition? Because its order doesn't matter. By being a colocation, it is associated with the PGServer group, but since it has no imposed order, any change to the group or to DRBD will trigger an e-mail alert.

One crm command we haven't used until now is configure show. Colocation and order definitions don't alter the outward appearance of resource status, so we needed another way to prove Pacemaker incorporated our changes. This is what we see on our test system:

```
root@pg2:~# crm configure show | egrep 'colocation|order'
colocation col_pg_drbd inf: PGServer ms_drbd_pg:Master
colocation col_pg_mail inf: pg_mail PGServer
order ord_pg inf: ms_drbd_pg:promote PGServer:start
```

Notice that we ran this command on the pg2 server, and we were still shown the current Pacemaker configuration. Pacemaker also takes it upon itself to remove all of our formatting for these particular entries. If we were to remove the egrep statement, we'd see the entire Pacemaker configuration for our cluster, containing all of the additions we've made in this chapter.

Performing a managed resource migration

Now that we have a working Pacemaker cluster-management system, we should put it to use. There are a lot of scenarios where we might need to manually change the active PostgreSQL node. Doing this with Pacemaker is much easier than the process we outlined in the previous chapter. That was a long process composed of several manual steps, each of which we would want to confirm in a perfect world.

With Pacemaker, we can change the active system by issuing a single command from any node in the cluster. There are some safeguards we'll also need to discuss and possibly a caveat or two to consider, but this will be our first use of Pacemaker as a piece of functional software. We've done a lot of work setting everything up!

Let's make Pacemaker do some work on our behalf for a change.

Getting ready

In order to migrate resources from one node to another, we need a fully functional Pacemaker cluster that manages all of our software layers. Make sure you've followed all the previous recipes before continuing.

How to do it...

This recipe will assume `pg1` is currently the active node, and we want to move PostgreSQL to `pg2`. Perform these steps on either Pacemaker node as the `root` user:

1. Initiate the migration with `crm`:

   ```
   crm resource migrate PGServer pg2
   ```

2. Remove the continued forced migration with this command:

   ```
   crm resource unmigrate PGServer
   ```

3. Use `crm` to display the currently active node:

   ```
   crm resource status PGServer
   ```

How it works...

The process is as simple as we claimed. We can launch a migration by specifying `resource migrate` as our primary `crm` arguments. There are only two remaining parameters for us to set: the resource we want to migrate and the target location. The `PGServer` group represents PostgreSQL and all of its prerequisite storage elements, so that is our third parameter.

The last parameter is the target node, and as `pg2` is the only other node in this Pacemaker configuration, it's an easy choice. What happens during a migration? The following is a screenshot of `crm_mon` during a migration:

```
Online: [ pg1 pg2 ]

 Master/Slave Set: ms_drbd_pg [drbd_pg]
     Masters: [ pg1 ]
     Slaves: [ pg2 ]
 Resource Group: PGServer
     pg_lvm     (ocf::heartbeat:LVM):    Started pg1
     pg_fs      (ocf::heartbeat:Filesystem):    Started pg1
     pg_lsb     (lsb:postgresql):        Stopped
     pg_vip     (ocf::heartbeat:IPaddr2):       Stopped
pg_mail (ocf::heartbeat:MailTo):         Started pg2
```

As you can see, Pacemaker is doing just as we claimed in the previous section and is shutting down `PGServer` resources in reverse order. It has already stopped `pg_vip` and `pg_lsb` and will shortly proceed to the rest of the services. In fact, here is a full ordered list of what Pacemaker does during a migration with our configuration:

1. Create a rule with an infinite score that the `PGServer` group should be running on `pg2`.
2. Stop the `pg_mail` alert on `pg1`, causing an e-mail alert.
3. Start the `pg_mail` resource on `pg2`.
4. Stop the `pg_vip` resource on `pg1`.
5. Stop the `pg_lsb` resource on `pg1`.
6. Stop the `pg_fs` resource on `pg1`.
7. Stop the `pg_lvm` resource on `pg1`.
8. Demote `ms_drbd_pg` to `Secondary` on `pg1`.
9. Promote `ms_drbd_pg` to `Primary` on `pg2`.
10. Start the `pg_lvm` resource on `pg2`.
11. Start the `pg_fs` resource on `pg2`.
12. Start the `pg_lsb` resource on `pg2`.
13. Start the `pg_vip` resource on `pg2`.

We hope you can see the obvious linear progression Pacemaker is following, mirrors the process we used when we performed these tasks manually. After the migration is over, we call `unmigrate` to remove the infinite score that Pacemaker added. This way, `PGServer` can remain on `pg1` again in the future.

Our final step is to examine the `resource status` of the `PGServer` group itself. If we did our job right, we should see this output:

```
resource PGServer is running on: pg2
```

Pacemaker reports that `PGServer` is running on `pg2`, just as we asked.

There's more...

When we call `crm resource migrate`, Pacemaker merely' but makes a simple configuration change. As the `PGServer` resource is running on `pg1` and we set stickiness to `100`, any score higher than that will override the current (and preferred) node.

When we ask for a migration, Pacemaker sets the node score for `pg2` at the highest value possible. The next time the resource target evaluation system runs, it sees that the score has changed and starts reorganizing the cluster to match. It's actually quite elegant. Unfortunately, it means that we need to remove the score, or we could be in trouble later.

When we `unmigrate` the `PGServer` group, Pacemaker removes the infinite score assigned to `pg2`, leaving it with the regular score of `100`. This is enough to keep `PGServer` attached to `pg2`, but nothing more. This is important because the score is absolute.

Imagine if the rule was still in place and Pacemaker vastly preferred `pg2` over `pg1`. In the event `pg2` crashes, Pacemaker will dutifully move PostgreSQL over to `pg1`. This is exactly what we want. However, what happens after we fix `pg2` and reattach it to Pacemaker? That's right; the infinite score means Pacemaker will move it to `pg2` immediately. Oh no!

> We can't overstate how important this is. Never invoke a resource migration without using `unmigrate` as the second step. Failure to do so can result in unplanned outages, which is not something we want in a highly-available PostgreSQL cluster.

Using an outage to test migration

While planned migrations are always preferred, sometimes, hardware failures or server instability will introduce an aspect of surprise. If we had not used Pacemaker, a server crash would be a catastrophic event. Even if we had followed every chapter in this book this far and had Nagios and e-mail alerts galore, a DBA would need to be available to activate the alternate node.

If an outage occurred at night when everyone was sleeping, we would be faced with a worst case scenario. Necessary personnel might not hear the alert for several minutes, and more time is lost on triage and activation steps. Such an outage could extend from a few minutes to over an hour. So much for our high availability!

Yet, at this point, we don't know if Pacemaker would negate the above scenario. While we've tested how Pacemaker handles an expected and safe migration, what happens when a node disappears entirely? Will Pacemaker cover us in the event there is an outage when nobody is immediately available?

In this recipe, we'll attempt to answer all of those questions and test Pacemaker with a server reboot.

Getting ready

For this final recipe, we need a complete and tested Pacemaker stack before causing an automated migration. Make sure you've followed all the previous recipes prior to attempting this.

How to do it...

This recipe will assume pg1 is currently the active node and pg2 is acting as the standby. Perform these steps on the Pacemaker node indicated as the root user:

1. Start crm_mon on pg2.
2. Kill the corosync service on pg1:

   ```
   pkill -9 corosync
   ```

3. Reboot pg1 with this command:

   ```
   reboot
   ```

4. Watch Pacemaker start PostgreSQL on pg2.

How it works...

We've made use of crm_mon before. It's an easy way to view the current status of all Pacemaker cluster resources. By starting this on pg2, we can watch what happens when pg1 shuts down. Unfortunately, simple reboots are too safe. The server will call the Pacemaker shutdown script, which will cause it to migrate to pg2 like it did in the previous recipe.

By calling pkill with the -9 argument on the corosync service, Pacemaker can no longer interfere. The Linux kernel will end the corosync process, negating any safeguards that Pacemaker might try to impose when pg1 reboots. Once we reboot pg1, we should return to pg2 in order to watch the output of crm_mon.

The final result should look something like this:

```
Online: [ pg2 ]
OFFLINE: [ pg1 ]

 Master/Slave Set: ms_drbd_pg [drbd_pg]
     Masters: [ pg2 ]
     Stopped: [ drbd_pg:0 ]
 Resource Group: PGServer
     pg_lvm      (ocf::heartbeat:LVM):    Started pg2
     pg_fs       (ocf::heartbeat:Filesystem):    Started pg2
     pg_lsb      (lsb:postgresql):        Started pg2
     pg_vip      (ocf::heartbeat:IPaddr2):       Started pg2
pg_mail  (ocf::heartbeat:MailTo):        Started pg2
```

Note that pg1 shows up as OFFLINE, and pg2 is the only server in the Online list.

There's more...

There's one final way to force a migration, and it's one we actually suggest for almost all cases. One of the arguments we can pass to `crm node` is the desired state of the node. Instead of killing the `corosync` service and rebooting `pg1`, we could run this command:

```
crm node standby pg1
```

This tells Pacemaker that `pg1` should no longer be considered a valid target for resources. Again, this causes Pacemaker to migrate `PGServer` and any dependencies over to `pg2`. No matter what the state of Pacemaker is, `pg1` will always be listed as `Standby` in the cluster by `crm status`.

This is an easy way to perform maintenance that might require multiple reboots or other potentially disruptive changes. To bring `pg1` online once again, we would use this command:

```
crm node online pg1
```

The effect on Pacemaker is the same as a `migrate` followed by an `unmigrate`. The `pg1` node is simply added to the list of possible target nodes, and the cluster remains on `pg2`. The primary difference is that we've removed any chance of `pg1` interfering with `pg2`. A standby Pacemaker node cannot participate in the cluster, and we can see at a glance that it's undergoing maintenance until we change it back to `online` status.

10
Data Distribution

In this chapter, we will learn how clever data management can increase uptime even further. We will cover the following recipes in this chapter:

- Identifying horizontal candidates
- Setting up a foreign PostgreSQL server
- Mapping a remote user
- Creating a foreign table
- Using a foreign table in a query
- Optimizing foreign table access
- Transforming foreign tables into local tables
- Creating a scalable nextval replacement
- Building a sharding API
- Talking to the right shard
- Moving a shard to another server

Introduction

Every business has the goal of being successful. The consequence of having a successful business when there's a database involved is increasingly high volume. This volume can be composed of query activity, data accumulation, or both. A PostgreSQL database that is not prepared for vast amounts of data or transaction load will slowly falter until the platform suffers.

Customers notice bad performance just as readily as outages. If our database is struggling to service queries, we have three options:

- Spend time optimizing the platform to reduce database interaction
- Buy a more capable database server
- Store data on several PostgreSQL servers

Indeed, we should probably always implement step one in any case. Yet, there is a limit to candidates for optimization. If the platform is using an ORM, making query changes can be difficult. Frontend caching can prevent a vast amount of database accesses, but we need to consider cold caches, refreshes, and write volume. Writes must touch the database regardless of the cache state, so we need a solution independent of optimization.

We can also buy a newer, bigger, and better server. We can add CPUs, memory, and storage to a single expensive server until we saturate its available slots and ports. If we've maximized the most expandable server currently manufactured, we have a problem if the database volume continues to increase. What can we do?

A good platform architect will see this potential disaster before it strikes. We must make the assumption that our business and software will be successful beyond our wildest dreams, and act accordingly. If we were Facebook, Instagram, or Skype, we would recognize the necessity of using multiple database servers early, enabling horizontal growth. It just so happens that PostgreSQL has a rich interface for database federation that we can leverage.

That will be the focus of this chapter. A highly available PostgreSQL cluster isn't only online and responding now, it does so in the future as well. Whether we accomplish horizontal distribution through assigned regions, associated groups, or at random, we need the infrastructure in place to facilitate this type of access. We will use PostgreSQL features to split up our data and ensure that the platform can run for years to come for the millions of users that will follow.

The features we will discuss in this chapter rely on the PostgreSQL foreign data wrapper, which wasn't introduced until **PostgreSQL 9.3**. We strongly recommend that you upgrade any old PostgreSQL clusters to 9.3 when possible if you foresee a future need for widely distributed data. You will not be able to implement many of the ideas discussed here until then.

Identifying horizontal candidates

Before we can really decide how to spread our data across several database servers, we need to find appropriate candidates. To do this, we should start at the database level for databases that are extremely active. What qualifies as extremely active? Databases that fit any of these criteria are a good start:

- The database experiences more than 10 million transactions per day
- The database handles more than 100 million queries per day
- The database writes more than 100 million tuples per day

Once we've chosen a database for horizontal scalability, we need to look at its tables and decide which should be distributed. Tables that make good choices are those that fit one or more of the following criteria:

- Tables that contain more than 10 million rows
- Tables that experience more than 1 million writes per day
- Tables that are larger than 10 GB

This recipe will discuss easy ways to find prospective tables for further study.

Getting ready

This recipe uses an existing database for concrete numbers. If you do not have one of these, create it with `pgbench` using the following commands as the `postgres` user:

```
createdb pgbench
pgbench -i -s 200 pgbench
```

The `-i` flag initializes a new series of benchmark tables, and the `-s` flag specifies the scale of the data. We started with a scale of `200`, so our largest table has 20 million rows and is about 3 GB in size. Feel free to use a higher scale for demonstrative purposes.

We will also be using the `pg_stat_statements` extension that we discussed in the *Checking the pg_stat_statements view* recipe from *Chapter 4, Troubleshooting*. Make sure it's installed in every database with the following SQL statement:

```
CREATE EXTENSION pg_stat_statements;
```

How to do it...

As the `postgres` user on a suitable PostgreSQL cluster, follow these steps to find horizontal scalability candidates:

1. Execute the following query while connected to any database:

```
SELECT * FROM (
SELECT d.datname AS database_name,
       d.xact_commit + d.xact_rollback AS transactions,
       d.tup_inserted + d.tup_updated +
                        d.tup_deleted AS writes,
       (SELECT sum(calls)
```

```
           FROM pg_stat_statements s
          WHERE s.dbid = d.datid) AS queries
    FROM pg_stat_database d
    LEFT JOIN pg_stat_statements s ON (s.dbid = d.datid)
   WHERE d.datname NOT IN ('template0', 'template1',
                           'postgres')
   ) db
   WHERE db.transactions > 10000000
      OR db.writes > 100000000
      OR db.queries > 100000000;
```

2. Create the following view in the candidate database with this SQL statement:

```
CREATE OR REPLACE VIEW v_shard_candidates AS
SELECT c.oid::regclass::text AS table_name,
       c.reltuples::NUMERIC AS num_rows,
       pg_total_relation_size(c.oid) / 1048576 AS size_mb,
       t.n_tup_ins + t.n_tup_upd + t.n_tup_del AS writes
  FROM pg_class c
  JOIN pg_namespace n ON (n.oid = c.relnamespace)
  JOIN pg_stat_user_tables t ON (t.relid = c.oid)
 WHERE n.nspname NOT IN ('pg_catalog',
                         'information_schema')
   AND c.relkind = 'r'
   AND (c.reltuples > 10000000
          OR
        t.n_tup_ins + t.n_tup_upd + t.n_tup_del > 1000000
          OR
        pg_total_relation_size(c.oid) / 1048576 > 10240);
```

3. Use this query to check the view to match tables:

```
SELECT *
  FROM v_shard_candidates
 ORDER BY size_mb DESC;
```

How it works...

The first step checks the `pg_stat_database` system view. This provides various global statistics about all databases in the PostgreSQL database cluster. This is a very easy way to obtain a list of extremely active databases that we can break into smaller pieces. The query gives us all three numbers we want regarding database statistics.

Our example database isn't quite busy enough, so we omitted the entire `WHERE` clause to show the `pgbench` database statistics:

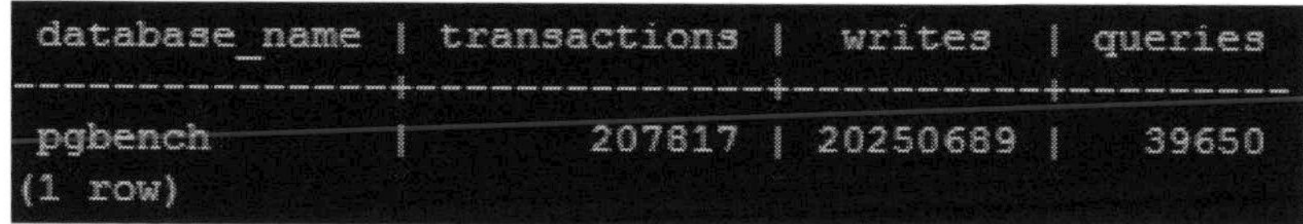

```
database_name | transactions |  writes  | queries
--------------+--------------+----------+---------
pgbench       |       207817 | 20250689 |   39650
(1 row)
```

To get specific table measurements, we need to connect to any databases named by the database activity query. Then, we create a view that will always provide a list of tables that match our three criteria. This will probably be used much more often than the database query, so it's handy to have it defined at all times.

> If you create the view in the `template1` database, all future databases created within this cluster will automatically have the view defined.

The view itself isn't too complicated but deserves some explanation. The `pg_total_relation_size` function provides the size of the table, including all indexes and TOAST data. This is important because the full impact of a table is much more than the data it contains. The `pg_total_relation_size` function returns results in bytes, so we transform it to megabytes so that it's more useful to us.

We restrict `relkind` to `r` because this restricts matches to relations, which is how PostgreSQL identifies tables. The last thing we do is apply our three conditions for candidate tables such that any criterion is enough for the table to appear in our list. The last query simply invokes the view and orders the results nicely for us.

Our `pgbench` database contained a single matching table, as seen here:

```
    table_name     | num_rows | size_mb |  writes
-------------------+----------+---------+----------
 pgbench_accounts  | 20000000 |    2997 | 20062016
(1 row)
```

We can see that the `pgbench_accounts` table contains `20,000,000` rows and is `2997` MB in size.

There's more...

Growth rates are also important. We recommend that you create a scheduled task that checks these results at the end of every day and either e-mails them to you or saves them into a table for further examination. After statistics are checked and logged, call these two functions to reset them to zero:

```
SELECT pg_stat_statements_reset();
SELECT pg_stat_reset();
```

Any tables that are growing quickly are even more critical to identify early.

See also

We used quite a few system views in this recipe. Please use the following URLs to PostgreSQL documentation that provides further depth regarding statistic tables and system catalogs:

- **The Statistics Collector**: `http://www.postgresql.org/docs/9.3/static/monitoring-stats.html`
- **pg_stat_statements**: `http://www.postgresql.org/docs/9.3/static/pgstatstatements.html`
- **pg_class**: `http://www.postgresql.org/docs/9.3/static/catalog-pg-class.html`

Setting up a foreign PostgreSQL server

The first requirement of data federation is the ability to connect to remote databases. With this capability, we can read or write to a remote PostgreSQL database table as if it were local. By doing so, certain query elements can be offloaded to the other server. We can also access metadata that is stored in some central location that acts as a shared resource for all database servers.

This recipe will describe how to create a foreign PostgreSQL server and will be the basis for several of the upcoming segments.

Getting ready

Before we can use the PostgreSQL foreign data wrapper functionality, we need to add the `postgres_fdw` extension to the database that will use it. Execute this SQL statement as the `postgres` user in the database that will be contacting foreign servers (`pgbench`, for example):

```
CREATE EXTENSION postgres_fdw;
```

How to do it...

For this recipe, we have two servers: pg-primary as our main data source and pg-report as a reporting server. As with the previous recipe, we will use pgbench as our sample database. Follow these steps to create a connection from pg-report to pg-primary within pgbench.

1. Connect to pgbench on the pg-report PostgreSQL server as the postgres user.
2. Execute the following SQL statement:

```
CREATE SERVER primary_db
    FOREIGN DATA WRAPPER postgres_fdw
    OPTIONS (host 'pg-primary', dbname 'pgbench');
```

3. Execute this SQL statement to check for the foreign server entry:

```
SELECT srvname, srvoptions
  FROM pg_foreign_server;
```

How it works...

We start by connecting to the database where we will be accessing remote data. As our test database is pgbench, this is where the foreign server will reside.

The server creation itself consists of a server name, a foreign data wrapper, and options to the foreign data wrapper. For the server name, we used primary_db to keep things simple, but anything relatively descriptive is a good choice.

The CREATE SERVER statement can use several available foreign data wrappers, but to contact a PostgreSQL server, we need postgres_fdw. This data wrapper will accept many standard PostgreSQL connection parameters, including host, dbname, port, and so on.

We only used the dbname and host settings because we don't want to force this server connection to always use any specific user or password combination. This allows us to map one or more local users to users on the remote database. When new connections are created to the foreign server, each user will access the remote data as themselves. This is a much more secure usage pattern.

Finally, we check the pg_foreign_server view to make sure PostgreSQL registered it with the options we specified. Once this is verified, we can move on to the next step. Here is our test server's output:

```
pgbench=# SELECT srvname, srvoptions
pgbench-#   FROM pg_foreign_server;
  srvname   |             srvoptions
------------+-------------------------------------
 primary_db | {host=pg-primary,dbname=pgbench}
(1 row)
```

There's more...

Foreign data servers have a couple more pieces of functionality that we should discuss.

Altering foreign servers

Assume for a moment that we need the definition of the `primary_db` foreign server to change. For instance, what if we integrated pgBouncer to reduce user contention and we need to use a nondefault port of `5433`? Here's how we would add the `port` option:

```
ALTER SERVER primary_db OPTIONS (ADD port '5433');
```

If we need to change this again later, we would use this syntax instead:

```
ALTER SERVER primary_db OPTIONS (SET port '5444');
```

We must admit that this difference in syntax is something of an oddity. To PostgreSQL, `SET` only modifies the settings that were specified when we called `CREATE SERVER`. We must use `ADD` to override a default, even though `SET` could have been overloaded to perform both actions. This merely means `ADD` might fail with an error, noting that the option isn't found. If this happens, simply use `SET` instead.

Dropping foreign servers

If we no longer want a foreign server, we can drop it along with all dependent objects. This use case is probably the only one that will work, unless we simply never referenced the foreign server at all. Use this SQL statement as a database superuser:

```
DROP SERVER primary_db CASCADE;
```

See also

The PostgreSQL foreign data wrapper has quite a bit of documentation available. The `CREATE SERVER` statement has its own entry as well. Please refer to these URLs for more information:

- **postgres_fdw**: `http://www.postgresql.org/docs/9.3/static/postgres-fdw.html`
- **CREATE SERVER**: `http://www.postgresql.org/docs/9.3/static/sql-createserver.html`
- **pg_foreign_server**: `http://www.postgresql.org/docs/9.3/static/catalog-pg-foreign-server.html`

Mapping a remote user

Database users and the permissions they are granted may vary between PostgreSQL clusters. This is especially true if we do not directly administer the remote server. The role of user mappings is to overcome this obstacle by linking a local database user with a remote database user.

User mappings must be created for any local user that is going to utilize the remote server. Furthermore, these mappings are only valid for the remote server for which they're defined. In situations where all or most local users will be accessing remote data, this can be somewhat inconvenient. This is, however, a small price to pay for the security inherent in such a design.

In this recipe, we will create a user mapping to access our remote server.

Getting ready

As we will be using a foreign server in this recipe, please follow the *Setting up a foreign PostgreSQL server* recipe before proceeding.

How to do it...

For this recipe, we will continue to use two servers: `pg-primary` as our main data source and `pg-report` as a reporting server. We will keep `pgbench` as our sample database. Follow these steps to create and map a user from `pg-report` to `pg-primary` within `pgbench`:

1. Execute this SQL statement on both PostgreSQL servers as the `postgres` user:

```
CREATE USER bench_user WITH PASSWORD 'testing';
```

2. Connect to `pgbench` on the `pg-report` PostgreSQL server as the `postgres` user.
3. Execute the following SQL statement to create the mapping:

```
CREATE USER MAPPING FOR bench_user
    SERVER primary_db
    OPTIONS (user 'bench_user', password 'testing');
```

4. Execute this SQL statement to check for the foreign server entry:

```
SELECT u.rolname AS user_name,
       s.srvname AS server_name,
       um.umoptions AS map_options
  FROM pg_user_mapping um
  JOIN pg_authid u ON (u.oid = um.umuser)
  JOIN pg_foreign_server s ON (s.oid = um.umserver);
```

How it works...

The first thing we need is a user we know exists on both servers. While we can link a local user with any remote user, this is easiest when they have the same name. This prevents confusion or connection problems in the future. If we are linking to a remote server we don't administer, this may not be possible. For now, however, we have control over both systems, so we can create the `bench_user` safely with a simple password for testing purposes.

Next, we create the user mapping itself. As with the server, we need to fill in three sections: a local user name, the server to use, and options for the mapping. We just created `bench_user`, so this will be our local user to associate with the mapping. Next, we specify the `primary_db` server that we created in the previous recipe. Finally, we set the options for the mapping, which consists of the name of the remote user and their password.

The `password` option is required for non-superusers. This is not noted in the documentation for foreign servers, user mappings, or foreign tables. The PostgreSQL developers included it as a security precaution to prevent mapped users from accessing unauthorized entries in `.pgpass` files or other automated password entry systems.

As a last step, we want to verify that PostgreSQL is storing the user mapping with the options we specified. It's always good to visualize database changes when possible, if only to put our minds at ease. The query we use gets its data from `pg_user_mapping`, though we do perform a couple of joins to transform meaningless IDs into useful information. Here's how it looks on our test server:

```
 user_name  | server_name |              map_options
------------+-------------+---------------------------------------
 bench_user | primary_db  | {user=bench_user,password=testing}
(1 row)
```

As we can see, the `bench_user` is properly associated with the `primary_db` server and shows the correct remote `user` mapping name and associated `password`.

There's more...

As we said in the introduction, every user must have a mapping if they are to access the remote data. This is rather onerous to do manually, so we can use PostgreSQL anonymous blocks to make things easier. This SQL statement, for instance, will map all local users under the assumption that the remote system has the same users:

```
DO $$
DECLARE
  user_name VARCHAR;
```

```
BEGIN
  FOR user_name IN
      SELECT usename FROM pg_user
  LOOP
    EXECUTE
      'CREATE USER MAPPING FOR ' || user_name || '
      SERVER primary_db
      OPTIONS (user ' || quote_literal(user_name) || ')';
  END LOOP;
END;
$$ LANGUAGE plpgsql;
```

Feel free to modify the `SELECT` we used to only target certain groups of users. This isn't the only way PostgreSQL anonymous blocks make maintenance easier. Learn more about them here:

`http://www.postgresql.org/docs/9.3/static/sql-do.html`

Keep in mind that you will need to either use a non-password authentication system in `pg_hba.conf` on the remote server or simply use `trust` authentication. By not specifying passwords, PostgreSQL will refuse to check any local password source, making authentication impossible otherwise.

See also

The `CREATE USER MAPPING` statement has good documentation in the PostgreSQL manual, as does the `pg_user_mapping` view. Please refer to these URLs for more information:

- **CREATE USER MAPPING**: `http://www.postgresql.org/docs/9.3/static/sql-createusermapping.html`
- **pg_user_mapping**: `http://www.postgresql.org/docs/9.3/static/catalog-pg-user-mapping.html`

Creating a foreign table

The last step in initializing foreign data access is the creation of the foreign table itself. While doing so, we are limited to specifying column names, types, default values, and whether or not each column is nullable. This table skeleton helps the PostgreSQL query planner interact with the remote data as efficiently as possible.

In this recipe, we will create a foreign table and make it ready for use by our mapped user.

Getting ready

As we will be using a foreign server and a user mapping in this recipe, please follow all the previous recipes before proceeding.

How to do it...

For this recipe, we will perform all actions on the `pg-report` PostgreSQL server in the `pgbench` database. Follow these steps to create a table in `pg-report`, which refers to a table on `pg-primary` within `pgbench`:

1. Create a user mapping for the `postgres` user with this SQL statement:

   ```
   CREATE USER MAPPING FOR postgres
       SERVER primary_db
       OPTIONS (user 'postgres');
   ```

2. Drop the existing `pgbench_accounts` table with this SQL statement:

   ```
   DROP TABLE pgbench_accounts;
   ```

3. Execute the following SQL statement to create the foreign table:

   ```
   CREATE FOREIGN TABLE pgbench_accounts
   (
       aid         INTEGER NOT NULL,
       bid         INTEGER,
       abalance    INTEGER,
       filler      CHAR(84)
   )
   SERVER primary_db
   OPTIONS (table_name 'pgbench_accounts');
   ```

4. Analyze `pgbench_accounts` to create local statistics:

   ```
   ANALYZE pgbench_accounts;
   ```

5. Grant `bench_user` access to `pgbench_accounts` with this SQL statement on both `pg-primary` and `pg-report`:

   ```
   GRANT ALL ON pgbench_accounts TO bench_user;
   ```

6. Describe the contents of the `pgbench_accounts` table with `psql`:

   ```
   psql pgbench -c '\d pgbench_accounts'
   ```

How it works...

In the first step, we create a user mapping for the `postgres` user. This is primarily a security step; remote tables should be as locked down as possible under the assumption that their contents are untrusted or otherwise sensitive. This allows us to create the foreign table as the `postgres` database superuser, preventing any unauthorized use of the remote server.

Next, we drop the local copy of the `pgbench_accounts` table on the `pg-report` server. This is both the largest table created by `pgbench` and the table we identified as a potential candidate for remote access of some kind. We drop it because we are going to replace it with a foreign table that refers to the same table on `pg-primary`.

To create the foreign table itself, we can look at the table definition of `pgbench_accounts` and ignore things such as primary keys, indexes, and other types of constraint. By issuing a `CREATE FOREIGN TABLE` statement instead of `CREATE TABLE`, PostgreSQL looks for some additional table specification settings. As with user mappings, we set the `SERVER` to `primary_db`. For `OPTIONS`, we simply need to name the remote table that this foreign table represents: `pgbench_accounts`.

The next step is not strictly necessary but one we strongly recommend. PostgreSQL knows very little about the contents of the remote database or the table we've just created. The PostgreSQL query planner makes much better decisions when it is fully informed of table contents. By running `ANALYZE` on `pgbench_accounts`, PostgreSQL fetches enough data to perform statistical analysis and stores that information in `pg_stats` for query-planning purposes.

Then, the `bench_user` user mapping we created needs specific access granted before it can use the new table. If we simply granted access locally, the remote `bench_user` would still not be able to use the table, so we would receive an error by doing so. Any grants for foreign tables must be equivalent on both servers involved.

Finally, we use `psql` to examine the foreign table structure. This is what PostgreSQL sees when a foreign table is used in a query. Our test server provided this output:

```
postgres@pg2:~$ psql pgbench -c '\d pgbench_accounts'
      Foreign table "public.pgbench_accounts"
  Column  |      Type      | Modifiers | FDW Options
----------+----------------+-----------+-------------
 aid      | integer        | not null  |
 bid      | integer        |           |
 abalance | integer        |           |
 filler   | character(84)  |           |
Server: primary_db
FDW Options: (table_name 'pgbench_accounts')
```

PostgreSQL makes it fairly clear that this is a `Foreign table`. The `FDW Options` column lists any column options that we might have attached, though it's empty in our case. We can see that this table resides on the `primary_db` server and that it corresponds to the `pgbench_accounts` table on that system. All of this allows us to see that this isn't a regular table; it also allows us to see where its data is actually stored.

There's more...

PostgreSQL enforces foreign table statements everywhere. For instance, let's try to drop this table using a regular `DROP TABLE` statement:

```
DROP TABLE pgbench_accounts;
```

The server would quickly respond with this output:

```
pgbench=# DROP TABLE pgbench_accounts;
ERROR:  "pgbench_accounts" is not a table
HINT:  Use DROP FOREIGN TABLE to remove a foreign table.
```

Similarly, if we checked the `relkind` column in the `pg_class` catalog table, its type would be listed as `f` for foreign table instead of `r` for relation. PostgreSQL saves several hints and other bread crumbs so that there is never any question as to the nature of foreign tables. Doing so prevents bugs and can even produce better performance, as remote access is taken into consideration before it selects the most efficient query plan. The more you use foreign tables, the more of these reminders you'll encounter.

See also

- If you'd like to learn more about foreign table creation syntax and possible caveats, please visit the PostgreSQL documentation at `http://www.postgresql.org/docs/9.3/static/sql-createforeigntable.html`

Using a foreign table in a query

Foreign tables exist as empty shells on the local database, lending merely their structure for query-planning and data-fetching purposes. The foreign data wrapper transforms data requests to something the remote server can understand and presents it in a way PostgreSQL will recognize.

As we're using the `postgres_fdw` wrapper, the situation is simplified. A PostgreSQL server should have less trouble communicating with another PostgreSQL server than an Oracle server, for instance. Though this means less transformation, there are still limitations to what functionality a foreign table might provide compared to a local table.

In this recipe, we'll use a foreign table in a few scenarios and examine how it performs in each. We'll also explore some of the common caveats involved in foreign table access.

Getting ready

As we will be using the `pgbench_accounts` foreign table in this recipe, please follow all the previous recipes before proceeding.

How to do it...

All queries in this recipe should be performed by the `bench_user` mapped user in the `pgbench` database on the `pg-report` PostgreSQL server. Follow these steps:

1. Execute the following simple query to view a remote query plan:

```
EXPLAIN VERBOSE
SELECT aid, bid, abalance
  FROM pgbench_accounts
 WHERE aid BETWEEN 500000 AND 500004;
```

2. Execute this SQL statement to examine how PostgreSQL handles remote aggregates:

```
EXPLAIN VERBOSE
SELECT sum(abalance)
  FROM pgbench_accounts
 WHERE aid BETWEEN 500000 AND 500004;
```

3. Execute this SQL statement to see a query plan involving a `JOIN`:

```
EXPLAIN VERBOSE
SELECT a2.aid, a2.bid, a2.abalance
  FROM pgbench_accounts a1
  JOIN pgbench_accounts a2 USING (aid)
 WHERE a1.aid BETWEEN 500000 AND 500004
```

How it works...

The first query is very simple. We only fetch the five inclusive records from `500,000` to `500,004`. We chose these values because they are so far into the table that scanning to find them would be very slow. This encourages the remote system to use the index on the `aid` column, and we can easily tell if it does not.

As we used EXPLAIN VERBOSE, PostgreSQL reports the query it would have performed on the remote server as well. This is how the full explain looks on our test server:

```
Foreign Scan on public.pgbench_accounts
        (cost=100.00..628902.08 rows=4 width=12)
  Output: aid, bid, abalance
  Remote SQL: SELECT aid, bid, abalance
                FROM public.pgbench_accounts
               WHERE ((aid >= 500000)) AND ((aid <= 500004))
```

PostgreSQL tries to send WHERE clauses to the remote server when possible. We can see from the Remote SQL lines that aside from some inconsequential transformations, it sent the entire query to the remote server unaltered.

In the next query, we made a very minor change that should have caused the remote server to aggregate the abalance column as a sum and send it back to us. However, the current foreign data wrapper API included with PostgreSQL 9.3 cannot handle aggregates of any kind. Again, let's see the actual output on our test system:

```
Aggregate  (cost=628902.09..628902.10 rows=1 width=4)
  Output: sum(abalance)
  ->  Foreign Scan on public.pgbench_accounts
            (cost=100.00..628902.08 rows=4 width=4)
        Output: aid, bid, abalance, filler
        Remote SQL: SELECT abalance
                      FROM public.pgbench_accounts
                     WHERE ((aid >= 500000)) AND ((aid <= 500004))
```

What happened here? The Remote SQL that PostgreSQL sent to the remote server includes no sum aggregate at all. This means that PostgreSQL fetches all five rows before producing a sum for us. This is probably OK for such a small amount of data, but consider the overhead involved if we had wanted a sum of a million rows.

All of these rows must be fetched from storage, sent over the network, received, and then summarized into an aggregate locally. The situation becomes even more dire when we try to join two foreign tables. We only have the pgbench_accounts table, so we joined it with itself. The query still only asks for five rows, and both of its inputs are on the remote server, so we might expect the remote server to perform the join.

This expectation would be wrong. To illustrate, here's the `EXPLAIN` output for the last query on our test server:

```
Hash Join  (cost=629002.13..1632804.17 rows=4 width=12)
  Output: a2.aid, a2.bid, a2.abalance
  Hash Cond: (a2.aid = a1.aid)
  ->  Foreign Scan on public.pgbench_accounts a2
            (cost=100.00..928902.00 rows=20000000 width=12)
        Output: a2.aid, a2.bid, a2.abalance, a2.filler
        Remote SQL: SELECT aid, bid, abalance
                      FROM public.pgbench_accounts
  ->  Hash  (cost=628902.08..628902.08 rows=4 width=4)
        Output: a1.aid
        ->  Foreign Scan on public.pgbench_accounts a1
                  (cost=100.00..628902.08 rows=4 width=4)
              Output: a1.aid
              Remote SQL: SELECT aid
                            FROM public.pgbench_accounts
                           WHERE ((aid >= 500000)) AND ((aid <= 500004))
```

Don't worry too much about most of this output. Simply direct your attention to both of the `Remote SQL` sections. First, observe that there are two of these sections. This means our single query was transformed into two remote queries. Next, notice that one of the queries has no `WHERE` clause and is fetching all 200 million of the rows in `pgbench_accounts`.

The foreign data wrapper is literal in its interpretation of our `WHERE` clause. We supplied one `WHERE` clause for the first instance of `pgbench_accounts`, and in normal circumstances, this would be enough. Unfortunately, search conditions are not transitive when foreign tables are concerned. One of the queries returns five rows as we expected, while the other must process 200 million rows to find the matching `aid` values for those five rows.

Foreign tables are very powerful, but they must be used judiciously. Failing to observe the previous lessons will result in the same scenarios, or worse.

There's more...

There's actually a very simple reason PostgreSQL is failing our expectations in the last two of our query examples. The answer lies in the structure of foreign tables themselves. When we defined the `pgbench_accounts` table, we specified four column names. PostgreSQL expects to see one or more of those column names within the `SELECT` clause in every interaction with the foreign table.

The second query example changes the `SELECT` clause to read `sum(abalance)`. While the `abalance` column is part of our foreign table definition, `sum` is not. A functional transformation of any kind renders the column mappings moot, and PostgreSQL must apply them *after* data is retrieved from the remote server.

The third query example performs badly for a different reason. If we ignore the problem with the nontransitive `WHERE` clause, there's still another issue. We could add another `WHERE` clause for the second instance of `pgbench_accounts` in that query, but as the `EXPLAIN` output shows, we would still be executing two queries on the remote server instead of one.

This is due to how PostgreSQL currently handles foreign data. If we imagine the `postgres_fdw` wrapper as a worker carrying a large box, every box requires a new worker. In this scenario, every foreign table is a box, and every box is separate. Each time PostgreSQL encounters a foreign table, it dispatches a worker with his box and waits for the results. As `JOIN` is a distinctly separate action, we get two workers and two boxes.

This may change in the future, but for now, this means that the remote server cannot combine requests for foreign tables.

Optimizing foreign table access

If you read the end of the previous recipe, you might assume we don't recommend that you use foreign tables at all. However, we would like to reassure you that foreign tables are not all doom and gloom. To prove it, we're going to use a disarmingly simple technique to optimize them: views.

It's true that PostgreSQL foreign data wrappers cannot combine queries for multiple tables on the same server. Provided we have access to the remote server, we can rectify this situation by creating a view to encapsulate the core of the query we want to perform. We can do this because PostgreSQL only knows the name of remote objects, not their composition. We can take advantage of this and use views to force remote joins.

In this recipe, we will describe how to use a remote view in place of a foreign table.

Getting ready

As we will be using the `pgbench_accounts` foreign table in this recipe, please follow all the previous recipes before proceeding.

How to do it...

For this recipe, we will continue to use the `pg-primary` and `pg-report` database servers. All queries should be performed by the `postgres` user in the `pgbench` database. Follow these steps to enforce better remote `JOIN` performance:

1. Create a view for the basis of the join on `pg-primary`:

```
CREATE VIEW v_pgbench_accounts_self_join AS
SELECT a1.aid, a2.bid, a2.abalance
  FROM pgbench_accounts a1
  JOIN pgbench_accounts a2 USING (aid);
```

2. Grant access to `bench_user` on the new view on `pg-primary`:

```
GRANT SELECT ON v_pgbench_accounts_self_join
   TO bench_user;
```

3. Create a foreign table that references the view on `pg-report`:

```
CREATE FOREIGN TABLE pgbench_accounts_self
(
    aid         INTEGER NOT NULL,
    bid         INTEGER,
    abalance    INTEGER
)
SERVER primary_db
OPTIONS (table_name 'v_pgbench_accounts_self_join');
```

4. Grant access to `bench_user` on the foreign table on `pg-report`:

```
GRANT SELECT ON pgbench_accounts_self
   TO bench_user;
```

5. Examine the new query plan on pg-report with this SQL statement:

```
EXPLAIN VERBOSE
SELECT aid, bid, abalance
  FROM pgbench_accounts_self
 WHERE aid BETWEEN 500000 AND 500005;
```

How it works...

For the first step, we create a view named `v_pgbench_accounts_self_join` on `pg-primary` that uses the same columns and the same self-join we attempted in the previous recipe. Then, we grant access to `bench_user` so that the view is usable on the `pg-report` server.

Next, we create a foreign table just as we did in the *Creating a foreign table* recipe, but this time, we name the local foreign table `pgbench_accounts_self` even though the view has a much different name. This should illustrate that names do not have to necessarily match and that PostgreSQL doesn't care whether the remote object is a table or a view. Once again, we grant access to the foreign table to the mapped `bench_user` user and consider our work complete.

Before we consider this operation a success, let's examine a verbose EXPLAIN that uses the foreign table. Here's the output from our test system:

```
Foreign Scan on public.pgbench_accounts_self
        (cost=100.00..300100.08 rows=4 width=12)
  Output: aid, bid, abalance
  Remote SQL: SELECT aid, bid, abalance
                FROM public.v_pgbench_accounts_self_join
               WHERE ((aid >= 500000)) AND ((aid <= 500004))
```

This is much better! Now, we can see that the WHERE clause is being sent to restrict output from the v_pgbench_accounts_self_join view. As this view is evaluated on the pg-primary server, the join happens there as well. We have successfully combined two foreign tables into one.

There's more...

As powerful as this technique might be, its utility is limited by the fact that we're using views to circumvent normal table access methods. This means our foreign table now has the same limitations as views. Unless the view is very simple—which would defeat the purpose of using a view like this—we cannot perform any of the following actions:

- We cannot insert into a foreign table view
- We cannot update records in a foreign table view
- We cannot delete from a foreign table view

However, there is one thing we can do with a foreign table view that we can't do with a local view. As foreign tables can be analyzed to gather statistics, we can analyze foreign table views as well. This produces local statistics that may include correlations that PostgreSQL would normally not find.

In the current state of the PostgreSQL foreign data architecture, this might not mean much. Yet, as techniques and the underlying code improve, what is now merely an interesting fluke might become an advanced optimization approach. Only time will tell.

Transforming foreign tables into local tables

Remote tables provide an easy and convenient way to access remote data in a PostgreSQL database. This is good for highly available systems, as a properly compartmentalized system invites segmented maintenance. Yet, remote data comes with a rather drastic cost regarding data fetching and handling overhead.

With the release of PostgreSQL 9.3 comes internal support of **materialized views**. Traditionally, materialized views merely instantiate a view into a physical structure to avoid expensive or complicated query plans and result sets. They also make it possible to index or optimize a view in ways not normally possible. Now, imagine what we can do with such a structure when utilizing foreign tables.

In this recipe, we will explore how materialized views can drastically increase local data access capability within a PostgreSQL database.

Getting ready

As we will be using the `pgbench_accounts` foreign table in this recipe, please follow all recipes up to *Creating a foreign table* before proceeding.

How to do it...

For this recipe, we will focus on the `pg-report` database server. All queries should be performed by the `postgres` user in the `pgbench` database. Follow these steps to create and use a materialized view:

1. Rename the `pgbench_accounts` foreign table with this SQL statement:

```
ALTER FOREIGN TABLE pgbench_accounts
      RENAME TO remote_accounts;
```

2. Use this SQL statement to create a materialized view:

```
CREATE MATERIALIZED VIEW pgbench_accounts AS
SELECT *
  FROM remote_accounts
 WHERE bid = 5
  WITH DATA;
```

3. Add an index to `pgbench_accounts` to make it usable:

```
CREATE INDEX idx_pgbench_accounts_aid
    ON pgbench_accounts (aid);
```

4. Execute this SQL statement to produce a simple query plan:

```
EXPLAIN ANALYZE
 SELECT *
   FROM pgbench_accounts
  WHERE aid BETWEEN 400001 AND 400050;
```

How it works...

When it comes to this recipe, we begin by moving the existing `pgbench_accounts` table out of the way. The intent in this case is to prove that we can treat a materialized view similar to a local table. To do this, we want to create it with the same name the foreign table currently uses. Thus, `pgbench_accounts` becomes `remote_accounts` and better illustrates its relationship with the foreign server as a bonus.

Next, we create the actual materialized view. We could define all of the columns manually, but in this case, we want it to simply mirror the remote table. Think of this as object-oriented programming; we have a class named `pgbench_remote`, and we will instantiate it as `pgbench_accounts`.

Notice, however, that we added a `WHERE` clause to restrict the results to rows where `bid` is `5`. For our particular set of test data, this represents only 100,000 rows of the total 20 million. We did this to illustrate that we could have a central repository of data and maintain only a small subset on each local server for better scalability purposes. By finishing the statement with `WITH DATA`, PostgreSQL executes the query and stores the result in our new materialized view. If we had omitted this, the view would be empty and unusable.

At this point, we created an index on the `aid` column. This reflects the primary key that exists on the remote table, and it means any local queries that expect it will perform normally. To prove this, our final step is to perform a basic query that retrieves 50 rows from the table and examines the path that PostgreSQL used to execute our request.

Our test system produced this output:

```
Index Scan using idx_pgbench_accounts_aid on pgbench_accounts
     (cost=0.29..11.19 rows=49 width=97)
     (actual time=0.005..0.009 rows=50 loops=1)
  Index Cond: ((aid >= 400001) AND (aid <= 400050))
Total runtime: 0.024 ms
```

We can see a few important things from this `EXPLAIN` output. First, our results are being supplied by the `idx_pgbench_accounts_aid index` we created. The query run time is reported as `0.024 ms`, which is less than 1/40th of a millisecond. This is the performance we would expect from an indexed retrieval with such a small amount of rows.

There's more...

There are a few unfortunate aspects of materialized views that we must consider:

- The contents are completely static
- They cannot be the target of `INSERT`, `UPDATE`, or `DELETE` statements
- Refreshing their contents may be slow

By static, we mean that the rows stored in the materialized view are the result of the `SELECT` statement we used to define it. It would be a great way to bootstrap a reporting table of some kind, but then, we see the next item in our list: no modifications. A natural consequence of this is that we can't build manual maintenance procedures designed to *top off* the contents. This means we must refresh the contents of the materialized view all at once with this statement:

```
REFRESH MATERIALIZED VIEW pgbench_accounts;
```

If the query that builds the output is slow and we have several materialized views like it, maintenance times could increase dramatically. Some contributed materialized view architectures do not have this limitation, and it's entirely possible future versions of PostgreSQL will also improve this aspect. For now though, we'll want to limit our materialized view definitions to queries that are very well optimized.

Refreshing a materialized view requires an exclusive lock, because its entire contents are replaced during the refresh. Be wary of queries or batch jobs that depend on these views, as they may be temporarily blocked until the refresh is complete.

See also

The PostgreSQL documentation does a pretty good job of explaining materialized views. Please refer to these resources to learn more:

- **CREATE MATERIALIZED VIEW**: `http://www.postgresql.org/docs/9.3/static/sql-creatematerializedview.html`
- **REFRESH MATERIALIZED VIEW**: `http://www.postgresql.org/docs/9.3/static/sql-refreshmaterializedview.html`

You can also build your own materialized view library. The techniques described at `http://tech.jonathangardner.net/wiki/PostgreSQL/Materialized_Views` worked well for several users before the feature was included in PostgreSQL 9.3.

Creating a scalable nextval replacement

Now that we have all of the tools to communicate between disparate servers, we can start building a very rudimentary API to generate ID values that are distinct across a pool of database servers. By doing so, database-level function calls are available to the application and encourage data distribution, otherwise known as application-level sharding. This, in turn, increases our scalability and availability, as it will take far more than a single database outage to truly derail the application.

A company that did this early in the development cycle of their platform is **Instagram**. In fact, they're very open about the process they used, as described in this blog post:

`http://instagram-engineering.tumblr.com/post/10853187575/sharding-ids-at-instagram`

The idea they implemented may seem complicated but is actually deceptively simple. Here's a basic breakdown of what they were trying to create:

- The system should accommodate several thousand logical shards
- Generated `SERIAL` IDs should be unique across all logical shards
- The ID generator should remain viable for several decades at minimum
- The ID generator must handle extremely high insert traffic

For us to accomplish these goals in the same manner as Instagram, we can utilize a standard 64-bit `BIGINT` column type separated into three sections:

- Bits 1-42 represent the number of milliseconds since an arbitrary epoch. This is viable for roughly 140 years.
- Bits 43-53 represent the logical shard number, for up to 2048 shards.
- Bits 54-64 are used for the actual generated ID, for up to 2048 ID values.

This may not seem like much, but this means that we can generate 2048 IDs per 2048 shards per millisecond for almost 140 years. Taken to its extreme, this is over 4 billion IDs per second. It's possible there are systems that have higher insert volumes than this, but we can't think of any.

In this recipe, we'll build such a function using PostgreSQL's `plpgsql` language and explain how each part works.

Getting ready

We will actually be starting from scratch in this recipe and will no longer use the `pgbench` tables. Instead, we want to start with new shell tables designed specifically for sharding. Execute these SQL statements as the `postgres` user on an empty database to get ready:

```
CREATE SCHEMA myapp;
CREATE TABLE myapp.msg_log (
  id        SERIAL  PRIMARY KEY,
  message   TEXT    NOT NULL
);
```

We will be using this schema and table for the rest of this chapter.

How to do it...

Execute the following SQL statements as the `postgres` user to create a function that can generate IDs as we described:

1. Create the schema to hold shard-related functionality:

   ```
   CREATE SCHEMA shard;
   ```

2. Create a sequence to act as an ID generator:

   ```
   CREATE SEQUENCE shard.table_id_seq;
   ```

3. Create the function that will generate IDs:

   ```
   CREATE OR REPLACE FUNCTION shard.next_unique_id(
     shard_id INT
   )
   RETURNS BIGINT AS
   $BODY$
   DECLARE
     epoch    DATE := '2014-01-01';
     epoch_ms BIGINT;
     now_ms   BIGINT;
     next_id  BIGINT;
   BEGIN
     epoch_ms := floor(
       extract(EPOCH FROM epoch) * 1000
     );
     now_ms := floor(
       extract(EPOCH FROM clock_timestamp()) * 1000
     );
     next_id := (now_ms - epoch_ms) << 22
           | (shard_id << 11)
           | (nextval('shard.table_id_seq') % 2048);
     RETURN next_id;
   END;
   $BODY$ LANGUAGE plpgsql;
   ```

4. Execute the following query to generate an ID and view its contents:

   ```
   SELECT (newval & 2047) AS id_value,
          (newval >> 11) & 2047 AS shard_id,
          (newval >> 22) / 1000 / 3600 / 24 AS days
     FROM (SELECT shard.next_unique_id(15)
              AS newval) nv
   ```

How it works...

Our first two steps aren't all that interesting; we merely create the shard schema and a sequence named table_id_seq for the IDs needed for value increments. Our design saves on implementation complexity using the same sequence for every table within a shard, but this is not a requirement.

The bulk of the work is defined in the next_unique_id function we create. We start the function with the epoch variable, set to the beginning of 2014. This is an arbitrary starting date and could have been any date in the past. The important thing to remember is that this value is used as a baseline for how long the IDs will remain unique.

Next, we have this section of code:

```
epoch_ms = floor(
  extract(EPOCH FROM epoch) * 1000
);
```

The extract PostgreSQL function will obtain the date in any format we want. By passing EPOCH, we get the date as the number of seconds since January 1, 1970, with a decimal representing the number of milliseconds as well. If we multiply this by 1000, we're left with the number of milliseconds since the beginning of 1970 to our chosen epoch of 2014-01-01.

We repeat this process for now_ms, but this time, we use the clock_timestamp function instead of a static date. The clock_timestamp function always returns a timestamp obtained from the execution time of the function call. This is important because functions such as now will return the start time of the surrounding transaction. If we used now, we could theoretically experience ID collisions after using more than 2048 IDs.

In this block of code, we calculate the ID we return as a fully unique value:

```
next_id = (now_ms - epoch_ms) << 22
     | (shard_id << 11)
     | (nextval('shard.table_id_seq') % 2048);
```

Remember what we said about using the full size of a 64-bit integer. We begin with the time elapsed since our epoch and shift that value to the left by 22 bits. This left shift makes room for the shard ID and the generated ID, both of which should be between 0 and 2047.

After shifting our time delta, we shift the shard ID by 11 bits to make room for the generated ID and append it to the cumulative ID. Again, 2048 values are represented by 11 bits, so these modifications are nondestructive. The shard ID is unharmed but packed into 43-53 bytes of next_id.

Finally, we append an ID obtained from the sequence that we created at the beginning, modded by 2048 to ensure we don't overflow the 11 bits we're using for this portion. In the end, we are left with an encoded ID with all of the attributes that we discussed at the beginning of this recipe.

If we call our new function once or twice, we should see it generate ID values. However, to prove it's doing what we claim, we need to reverse the encoding process to see what the ID actually contains. On our test system, one call of `next_unique_id` produces this output:

```
pgbench=# SELECT (newval & 2047) AS id_value,
pgbench-#        (newval >> 11) & 2047 AS shard_id,
pgbench-#        (newval >> 22) / 1000 / 3600 / 24 AS days
pgbench-#   FROM (SELECT shard.next_unique_id(15)
pgbench(#           AS newval) nv;
 id_value | shard_id | days
----------+----------+------
       43 |       15 |  115
```

We called the function and passed it `15` as the shard number to use, and after decoding the ID, we can see that it's unchanged. If we called this function several times in a row, we would see the `id_value` increment as well. We discarded a lot of information in our rush to decode the number of days since our `epoch` date, so we only see that `115` days have elapsed. In reality, that portion of the ID represents days, hours, minutes, seconds, and milliseconds since the beginning of 2014.

There's more...

If we wanted to use our new ID generator in a table, we could do it very simply. Assuming we already have our `myapp.msg_log` table, we could create a new table based on it with this SQL statement:

```
CREATE SCHEMA myapp1;
CREATE TABLE myapp1.msg_log (
    LIKE myapp.msg_log INCLUDING INDEXES
);

ALTER TABLE myapp1.msg_log
ALTER id TYPE BIGINT,
ALTER id SET DEFAULT shard.next_unique_id(1);
```

This structure would correspond with shard number `1`. All we need to do is modify the `id` column so that it can store our 64-bit integer and then set the default value to invoke our `next_unique_id` function. By doing so, we can create up to 2048 schemas holding tables like this, and every generated ID will be unique across all of them.

Building a sharding API

When building a horizontally scalable system, we need a database library that facilitates its use. Without this, ad hoc tables can derail the whole process by producing a heterogeneous environment incompatible with a horizontal architecture. We need consistency if we also want reliability.

In the previous recipe, we discussed the necessary components of a function that can generate unique IDs across thousands of logical shards. This will form the core of our API as it ensures that ID collisions are avoided within our application. However, what about the rest? How do we manage each shard? How do we add tables to the application? How can we automate as much management as possible to encourage adhering to the API?

This recipe will attempt to answer these questions and many more by having you create the necessary functions to manage a shard-driven system.

Getting ready

This recipe depends on the work we performed in the *Creating a scalable nextval replacement* recipe. Please review that part of this chapter before continuing.

How to do it...

Follow these steps to build a complete database-sharding API:

1. Learn one of the PostgreSQL procedural languages.
2. Create a table to track shard-configuration settings.
3. Write one or more functions to manage shard-configuration settings.
4. Create a table to track shard tables and source schemas.
5. Write a `next_unique_id` equivalent function.
6. Write one or more functions to control which tables are managed.
7. Write one or more functions to build or alter each shard's structure based on the tables it contains.
8. Create a table to track logical to physical shard mappings.
9. Write one or more functions to manage logical to physical shard mappings.
10. Write one or more functions to grant sufficient permissions to users tasked with using all of the above functions.

How it works...

Before we discuss these steps, we readily admit there is a lot of work involved here, and most of it is beyond the scope of this book. However, this is the minimum list of components necessary for a functional shard API. Fortunately, we only have to build this once!

The first step is to learn one of the procedural languages that PostgreSQL provides for database interaction. The core PostgreSQL server comes with PL/pgSQL, PL/Tcl, PL/Perl, or PL/Python as possible choices, though there are many more such as Java, Ruby, or even PHP. Each of these has different performance characteristics and varying levels of difficulty, so choose whichever you are most comfortable with or whichever produces the best results. We used the pgSQL language for our `next_unique_id` function, but this doesn't mean you must follow our lead.

Next, we need a table and associated functions to manage shard-configuration settings. Perhaps this means a table named `shard_config` and two functions named `get_shard_config` and `set_shard_config`. We use functions so that we can protect the boundaries of our 64-bit integer or to prevent changes to settings that would adversely affect the cluster of shards. Like any API, we should never trust user input.

Now, we need a table and associated functions to manage the architecture of our shards. For instance, the table of API-managed tables might be called `shard_table`. Then, we might create `register_base_table` to add tables to shard management and `unregister_base_table` to remove them.

Then, we might add `create_next_shard` to increment the active shard counter and create an empty schema based on this new value. We might also want `create_id_function` to generate an optimized shard-specific ID generation function whenever a new shard is added. We'll probably need `init_shard_tables` to create table copies of all the base tables we've registered, which will also modify each copy to use our unique ID function.

Beyond managing the actual structure of the shards, we also need to control who can invoke all of these specialty functions, especially since there's so many of them. So, it would be a good idea to create `add_shard_admin` and `drop_shard_admin` to handle necessary grants for shard administrators.

Do we need more? Possibly. This core of functions provides the minimal structure necessary to create and maintain a working sharded database, but few systems exist with only minimal implementations.

There's more...

As we said earlier, building a fully functional API as we discussed here is beyond the scope of this book. However, we have written a reference implementation named Shard Manager, available on GitHub:

`https://github.com/OptionsHouse/shard_manager`

Shard Manager creates all of the configuration tables and functions that we discussed in this recipe, along with a couple extras. Further, it operates as a PostgreSQL extension. For example, to create a schema named `shard` to store the API and configuration tables, we would use these SQL statements:

```
CREATE SCHEMA shard;
CREATE EXTENSION shard_manager WITH SCHEMA shard;
```

Documentation is currently somewhat sparse, but there is enough to install and use the provided functions, as well as some basic usage examples. Feel free to contribute if you come up with fixes or enhancements!

See also

As we suggested that you learn one of the PostgreSQL procedural languages, here is a list of links to several popular choices:

- **PL/pgSQL**: `http://www.postgresql.org/docs/9.3/static/plpgsql.html`
- **PL/Perl**: `http://www.postgresql.org/docs/9.3/static/plperl.html`
- **PL/Python**: `http://www.postgresql.org/docs/9.3/static/plpython.html`
- **PL/Java**: `https://github.com/tada/pljava/wiki`
- **PL/PHP**: `https://github.com/commandprompt/PL-php`
- **PL/Ruby**: `https://github.com/knu/postgresql-plruby`

Talking to the right shard

In this chapter, we have chosen to represent database shards as PostgreSQL schema names. So, if our basic schema is named `myapp`, shard 1 would be `myapp1`, shard 15 would be `myapp15`, and so on. This is what we call the **logical shard** name.

Beyond this, shards should be independent of each other such that they can be relocated to another PostgreSQL server arbitrarily. However, if shards can be moved at will, how do we find them? Much like LVM has a physical drive, logical shards have a corresponding **physical shard**. The physical shard is the server where the logical shard currently resides. Think of it like this diagram:

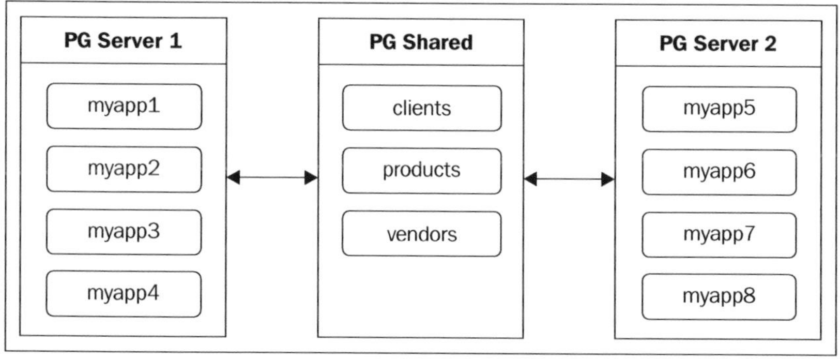

Elements such as `clients`, `products`, and `vendors` are shared resources that all PostgreSQL shard servers can use. This is where our foreign tables would be beneficial. The logical shards (schemas) `myapp1` through `myapp4` all reside on `PG Server 1`, and `myapp5` through `myapp8` live on `PG Server 2`. In this architecture, we have eight logical shards distributed to two physical servers.

In this recipe, we will explore various techniques to preserve and decode the logical to physical mapping necessary to interact with the correct data.

Getting ready

This recipe depends on the work we performed in the *Creating a scalable nextval replacement* recipe. Please review that part of this chapter before continuing.

How to do it...

All SQL statements in this recipe should be executed by the `postgres` database user. Follow these steps to build a table to map logical shards to their physical locations:

1. Execute this SQL statement to create the shard-mapping table:

```
CREATE TABLE shard.shard_map
(
  map_id         SERIAL   PRIMARY KEY,
  shard_id       INT      NOT NULL,
  source_schema  VARCHAR  NOT NULL,
  shard_schema   VARCHAR  NOT NULL,
  server_name    VARCHAR  NOT NULL,
  UNIQUE (shard_id, source_schema)
);
```

2. Create a shard and register it with the shard map with this SQL:

```
CREATE SCHEMA myapp1;
INSERT INTO shard.shard_map
  (shard_id, source_schema, shard_schema, server_name)
VALUES (1, 'myapp', 'myapp1', 'pg-primary');
```

3. Repeat the previous step to create a second shard:

```
CREATE SCHEMA myapp2;
INSERT INTO shard.shard_map
  (shard_id, source_schema, shard_schema, server_name)
VALUES (2, 'myapp', 'myapp2', 'pg-primary');
```

4. View the current status of our shard mappings:

```
SELECT * FROM shard.shard_map;
```

How it works...

If you wish, you can view this as another primer on preparing a shard-management API. Our first step towards this goal is to create a table to store the logical to physical location mappings necessary to locate a specific shard. At minimum, this table needs to track the shard ID (`shard_id`), the skeleton schema the shard is based on (`source_schema`), the shard name itself (`shard_schema`), and the server where the shard resides (`server_name`).

> Some readers may wonder where the `shard_map` table should reside. There's a reason we introduced the shared PostgreSQL server in the introduction to this recipe. Metadata should be stored on that central server. A combination of foreign tables and materialized views will ensure that all servers have immediate access to its contents if necessary.

Next, we should create and save the location of two new shards for illustrative purposes. For our shard names, we chose to simply append the shard name to the source schema name. In addition, we created both shards on the `pg-primary` server we used in various chapters of this book. This kind of naming scheme makes it simple to locate and interact with any particular shard in our cluster.

The final step is to visualize the data we stored regarding our logical to physical mapping. On our test server, the mappings are as follows:

```
pgbench=# SELECT * FROM shard.shard_map;
 map_id | shard_id | source_schema | shard_schema | server_name
--------+----------+---------------+--------------+------------
      1 |        1 | myapp         | myapp1       | pg-primary
      2 |        2 | myapp         | myapp2       | pg-primary
(2 rows)
```

Notice that the `shard_map` table is designed in such a way that we can create mappings for any number of schemas. Any schema can have all 2048 shards, and we can find the physical location for any of them based on this table.

There's more...

While the mapping is an important step, we still need two things to really make use of the mapping. Let's see what they are.

Create a cache

In modern applications, it is becoming increasingly common to inject a secondary cache layer between the application and database. This layer stores commonly retrieved data in memory for immediate use. This layer might be composed of memcached or a NoSQL database such as CouchDB, MongoDB, or Redis.

Once such a layer exists, it's important that the `shard_map` table is one of the first tables copied there. It has very few rows, and storing it in memory removes the relatively expensive round-trip to the database. With this mapping in memory, the application will always know which physical server it should be connected to as long as it also knows which shard it is using.

Choose an application data to logical shard mapping

How does an application know which shard it should use in any particular situation? This answer requires one more modifications to the table structure our application uses. Our last decision involves adding a `shard_id` column to one table. This table can be anything but should be some central value that all data can eventually be traced to.

A good choice for this is a `customer` table. In an order system, all interaction is eventually driven by customer activity. If we assign a customer a specific shard ID, all of their order data will be stored in that shard. As the application likely has the customer row information available at all times, it should also know the associated shard and, hence, which server to store that data.

As a consequence, customer data should also be stored in the shared PostgreSQL instance that other shard servers can see. Customer data is relatively sparse compared to high volumes of order, image, or other types of activity a customer can generate. If the customer table is too large to cache directly, we could create a `customer_shard` table in the shared database instead.

Moving a shard to another server

The final important aspect of database sharding that we are going to explore in this chapter is reorganization. The purpose of allocating a large number of logical shards is to prepare for future expansion needs. If we started with 2048 shards, all of which are currently mapped to a single server, we will eventually want to move some of them elsewhere.

The easiest way to do this is to leverage PostgreSQL replication. Essentially, we will create a streaming replica for the server we want to split and drop the schemas we don't need on each server. Consider a database with two shards. Our end goal is to produce something like this:

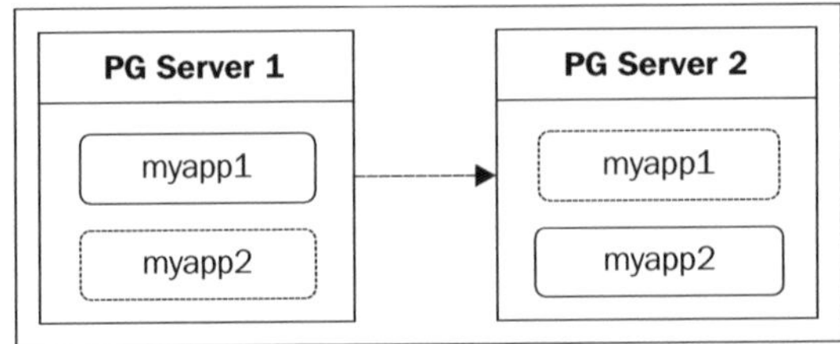

On each server, we simply drop the schema indicated by the dashed box. This way, we still have two shards, and only the location of `myapp2` has changed; its data remains unharmed.

This recipe will cover the process described here, making it easy to move shards to a new physical location.

Getting ready

This recipe depends on the work we performed in the *Creating a scalable nextval replacement* and *Talking to the right shard* recipes. Please review these recipes before continuing.

How to do it...

In addition to our usual `pg-primary` PostgreSQL server, we will also be using `pg-primary2` for this recipe. Database data will remain in the `/db/pgdata` directory. A server named `pg-shared` will play the role of our shared database as well. Follow these steps as the `postgres` system user and `postgres` database user where indicated:

1. Use `pg_basebackup` on `pg-primary2` to clone the data from `pg-primary`:

   ```
   pg_basebackup -h pg-primary -D /db/pgdata
   ```

2. Create a file named `recovery.conf` in `/db/pgdata` on `pg-primary2` with these contents:

   ```
   standby_mode = 'on'
   primary_conninfo = 'host=pg-primary user=postgres'
   ```

3. Start PostgreSQL on `pg-primary2`:

   ```
   pg_ctl -D /db/pgdata start
   ```

4. When ready to split the shards, promote `pg-primary2` to master status:

   ```
   pg_ctl -D /db/pgdata promote
   ```

5. Execute this SQL statement on `pg-shared` to change the shard mapping:

```
UPDATE shard.shard_map
   SET server_name = 'pg-primary2'
 WHERE shard_schema = 'myapp2';
```

6. Refresh any cached copies of the `shard_map` table.
7. Drop the `myapp2` schema on `pg-primary`:

```
DROP SCHEMA myapp2;
```

8. Drop the `myapp1` schema on `pg-primary2`:

```
DROP SCHEMA myapp1;
```

How it works...

We've already discussed the process to create streaming replicas several times through this book, so we've elected to use a shortened version here. Our primary goal here is to create a full database clone of `pg-primary` on `pg-primary2`. This clone should continue to receive data from `pg-primary` until we are ready to split up our application data. When database activity is low or we can temporarily disable write activity to the `myapp2` schema, we can promote `pg-primary2` so that it acts as a writable server.

Once `pg-primary2` is writable, we execute an `UPDATE` statement on the `shard_map` table in `pg-shared`. Then, we either refresh or invalidate cached copies of that table so that they are rebuilt. From this point on, all new requests to interact with data stored in the `myapp2` shard will be directed to the `pg-primary2` server.

With the `myapp2` shard's physical location changed and caches updated, it should be safe to drop the unneeded schemas on each PostgreSQL server. The `pg-primary` server is only in charge of the `myapp1` shard now, so we can drop `myapp2`. Similarly, the `pg-primary2` server is only handling the `myapp2`, so we can drop `myapp1`.

If our data was evenly distributed, each PostgreSQL server should now be half the size of what `pg-primary` originally was. Furthermore, database load, IOPS and TPS requirements, and other metrics are also scaled down. By doubling our server count, we've cut our hardware needs in half and have thereby increased our query response times and availability.

There's more...

Though our example used only two schema shards, this process scales well to any number of preallocated shards. It's surprisingly easy to relocate schemas using the method described here, and there's no reason we must limit ourselves to splitting one server into only two. The only real limitation is that we can't effectively recombine servers once they've been split this way.

There is, however, one important caveat we must explain. This type of database sharding works best when the application is designed to accommodate it. In fact, it's even better to create all of the logical shards upfront, before data is inserted into *any* shard. Why is this?

Consider an existing schema with existing data. Foreign keys, customers, and customer activity has been accumulating for years. Redistributing this data into all of the necessary tables of our shard schemas will be extremely difficult and will likely be an entirely manual migration process.

This same problem exists if we only start our application with a small number of shards instead of allocating the maximum from the beginning. If we only have four out of 2048 active shards and they're already on four physical servers, we will need to create new shards and manually distribute the data once again.

However, we can also start with all 2048 shards at the beginning. From the very start, customers are assigned to shards, and data is inserted to the proper shard. Even if all shards start on one server, we can expand using the method described in this recipe. If we want to immediately grow to four servers, we merely create three clones and evenly distribute the shards to each system.

It's important to advocate and impose this architecture early in systems that are likely to require high transactional volume. Otherwise, the path to horizontal scalability and the availability associated with it will be a long and hard one.

Index

Symbols

A

B

D

E

F

L

M

N

O

P

T

Thank you for buying
PostgreSQL 9 High Availability Cookbook

About Packt Publishing

Packt, pronounced 'packed', published its first book "*Mastering phpMyAdmin for Effective MySQL Management*" in April 2004 and subsequently continued to specialize in publishing highly focused books on specific technologies and solutions.

Our books and publications share the experiences of your fellow IT professionals in adapting and customizing today's systems, applications, and frameworks. Our solution based books give you the knowledge and power to customize the software and technologies you're using to get the job done. Packt books are more specific and less general than the IT books you have seen in the past. Our unique business model allows us to bring you more focused information, giving you more of what you need to know, and less of what you don't.

Packt is a modern, yet unique publishing company, which focuses on producing quality, cutting-edge books for communities of developers, administrators, and newbies alike. For more information, please visit our website: `www.packtpub.com`.

About Packt Open Source

In 2010, Packt launched two new brands, Packt Open Source and Packt Enterprise, in order to continue its focus on specialization. This book is part of the Packt Open Source brand, home to books published on software built around Open Source licenses, and offering information to anybody from advanced developers to budding web designers. The Open Source brand also runs Packt's Open Source Royalty Scheme, by which Packt gives a royalty to each Open Source project about whose software a book is sold.

Writing for Packt

We welcome all inquiries from people who are interested in authoring. Book proposals should be sent to `author@packtpub.com`. If your book idea is still at an early stage and you would like to discuss it first before writing a formal book proposal, contact us; one of our commissioning editors will get in touch with you.

We're not just looking for published authors; if you have strong technical skills but no writing experience, our experienced editors can help you develop a writing career, or simply get some additional reward for your expertise.

[PACKT] open source
community experience distilled
PUBLISHING

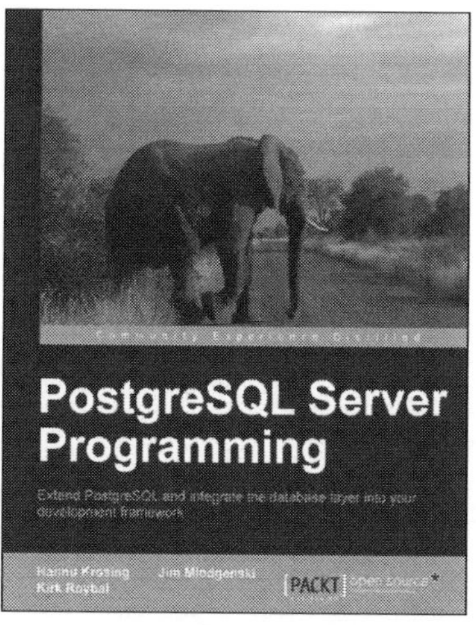

PostgreSQL Server Programming

ISBN: 978-1-84951-698-3 Paperback: 264 pages

Extend PostgreSQL and integrate the database layer into your development framework

1. Understand the extension framework of PostgreSQL, and leverage it in ways that you haven't even invented yet.
2. Write functions, create your own data types, all in your favourite programming language.
3. Step-by-step tutorial with plenty of tips and tricks to kick-start server programming.

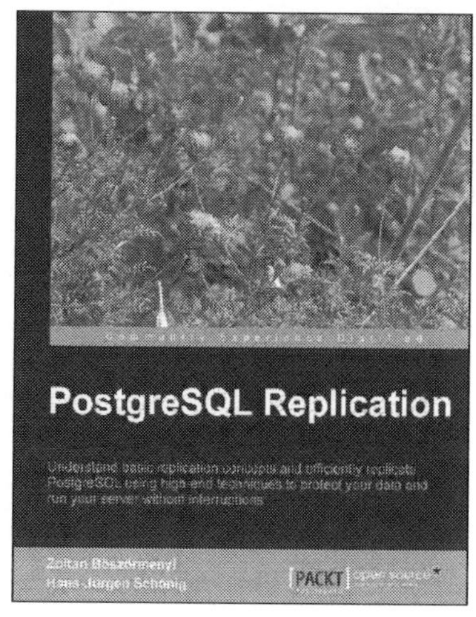

PostgreSQL Replication

ISBN: 978-1-84951-672-3 Paperback: 250 pages

Understand basic replication concepts and efficiently replicate PostgreSQL using high-end techniques to protect your data and run your server without interruptions

1. Explains the new replication features introduced in PostgreSQL 9.
2. Contains easy to understand explanations and lots of screenshots that simplify an advanced topic like replication.
3. Teaches PostgreSQL administrators how to maintain consistency between redundant resources and to improve reliability, fault-tolerance, and accessibility.

Please check **www.PacktPub.com** for information on our titles

25065494R00223

Made in the USA
San Bernardino, CA
16 October 2015